The cost of labor and materials is rising constantly. People are turning to do-it-yourself projects as a means of completing additions and renovations to their houses. If you are a homeowner, a garage significantly increases the value of your property. You will also appreciate the additional storage space that your new garage will provide. This book will enable you to make a new garage a reality if you follow the instructions carefully. Should you ever decide to sell your home, a carefully planned and constructed garage will add considerably to your home's resale value.

Build Your Own Garage Manual is a unique guide that concentrates on the process of building rather than designing the garage. Certainly all of the elements of design and proper plan detailing are considered, but this is foremost a book that graphically demonstrates the latest in garage construction techniques. Each step of the construction process is illustrated in detail. Several design alternatives are presented for your consideration.

Every effort has been made at the time of publication to ensure the accuracy of the information contained herein. However, the reader should check for his or her own assurance and must be responsible for design, selection and use of suppliers, materials and actual construction. Happy garage building!

CREATIVE
HOMEOWNER®
CreativeHomeowner.com

Note: Artist drawings and photos shown in this publication may vary slightly from the actual working drawings. Some photos are shown in mirror reverse. Please refer to the floor plan for accurate layout. Be sure to familiarize yourself with manufacturer's instructions for tools, equipment, and materials before beginning a project. Although all possible measures have been taken to ensure the accuracy of the material presented, neither the author nor the publisher is liable in case of misinterpretation of directions, misapplication, or typographical error.

Garage plans and plan content provided by Design America, Inc.

Printed in Singapore

Current Printing (last digit)
10 9 8 7 6 5 4 3 2 1

Build Your Own Garage Manual, Fifth Edition
ISBN 978-1-58011-789-0

Creative Homeowner®, *www.creativehomeowner.com*, is an imprint of New Design Originals Corporation and distributed exclusively in North America by Fox Chapel Publishing Company, Inc., 800-457-9112, 1970 Broad Street, East Petersburg, PA 17520, and in the United Kingdom by Grantham Book Services, Trent Road, Grantham, Lincolnshire, NG31 7XQ.

Table of Contents

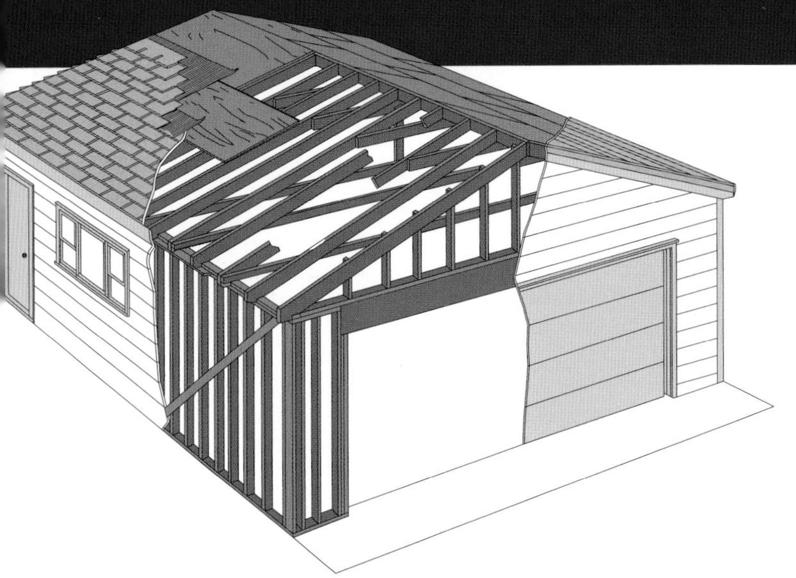

2-Car Garage with Loft and Dormers

2 1/2-Car Reverse Gable with Storage

2-Car Gable

3-Car Reverse Gable

Build Your Own Garage?

The answer is yes! By doing the planning and all or part of the work yourself, you can have the garage you might not otherwise be able to afford. By supplying the labor and buying materials yourself, construction costs can be significantly reduced.

Framing out a garage is not difficult. Standardized materials and construction techniques make it relatively easy if you take the time to plan and work carefully. All of the techniques and tips you'll need are in this book. Read it carefully from cover to cover before beginning. It will help you determine the work you can handle alone, and where a little expert help might be needed to do the job right.

You can also learn many construction basics by studying existing garages. Ask your neighbors if you can take a few minutes to review their garages before you begin building your own.

The first step is determining what you want your garage to do. Store your car or cars? Provide a workshop area or additional storage space? If you have two cars, consider a two-and-one-half car design. But before planning too big, remember that your lot must have sufficient space for the garage site and proper setbacks from adjacent properties, sideyards, and driveways. Local building codes often set guidelines in these areas, so check with your local municipality for any restrictions that apply to your situation.

Planning Driveway and Parking Areas

In addition to the structure itself, you'll also want to plan your new driveway, off-street parking, or turnaround area. The illustrations on this page are designed to give you an idea of the basic space requirements. You may need to alter them to fit your lot, but remember that adequate driveway and parking areas will add greatly to your garage's convenience.

In most cases, short approaches to two-car garages are double-width. For longer driveways, use a single-width driveway that gradually widens to the double-door opening. Driveways should be wider at curves because the back wheels make a track with a smaller radius than do the front wheels.

Construction methods for concrete driveways, walks, and parking areas are similar to those covered under slab foundations later in this guide. Local ordinances can apply to these items, so consult with your local building department for specifications covering required concrete thickness, grade and slope preparations, set backs from boundaries, and so on. In general, concrete thickness is 4" to 5". The driveways must be crowned or sloped at 2% to provide drainage. The slope of any uphill grade should not exceed 14%, and any change in a grade should be as gradual as possible.

You have a lot of options in deciding what kind of garage to build. This book contains designs to help you make that decision, but remember that local zoning and building codes in most municipalities will have some affect on your final choice. There might be lot-size requirements, minimum setback regulations, height restrictions, and certain building materials that must not be used. To save yourself time and future headaches, take a day or so to learn what you cannot do and what you might be required to do. In most localities, for example, at least a building permit will be required. The best place to start is at the local building and zoning code offices.

Take time to consider your possible future needs. Will a two-car garage do, or do you expect that you will need to store two cars and/or possibly a boat someday? Will you use the garage as a workshop? Is storage space in the house running short? Also, consider how it will look in its proposed site. Choose a style and size that will complement its environment. Last, but certainly not least, remember your budget. Build for your needs, not your desires.

Figure 4A - Garage with Side Parking

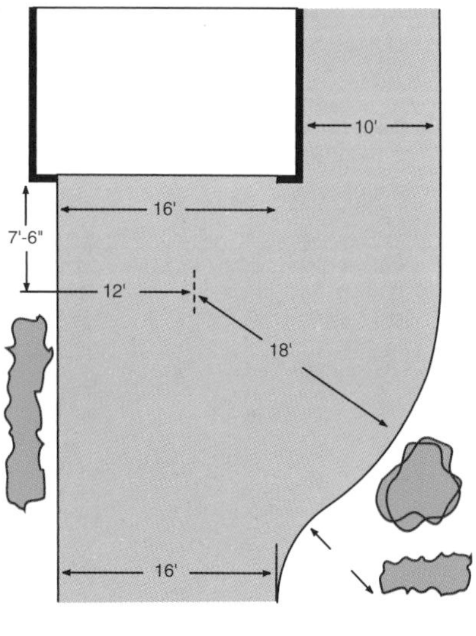

Figure 4B - Garage, Parking, Turnaround

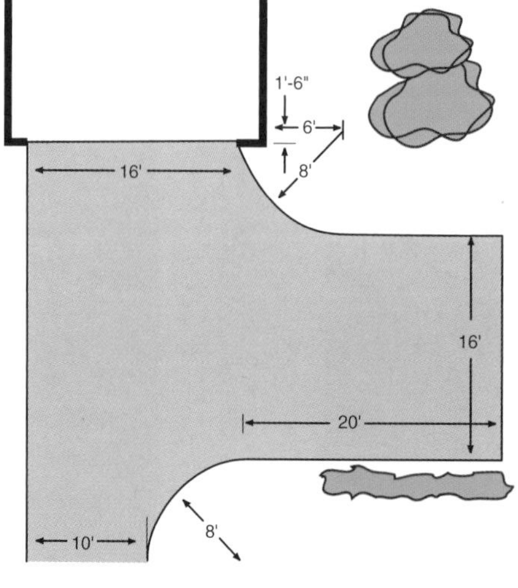

Figure 4C - Driveway Parking Area

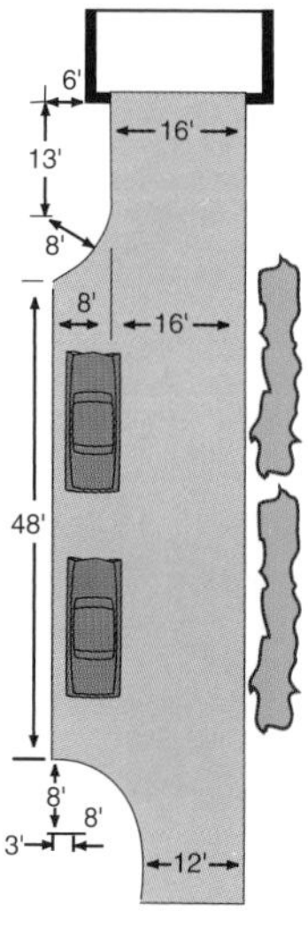

Garage Sizes

Figure 5 - Different Garage Types and Sizes

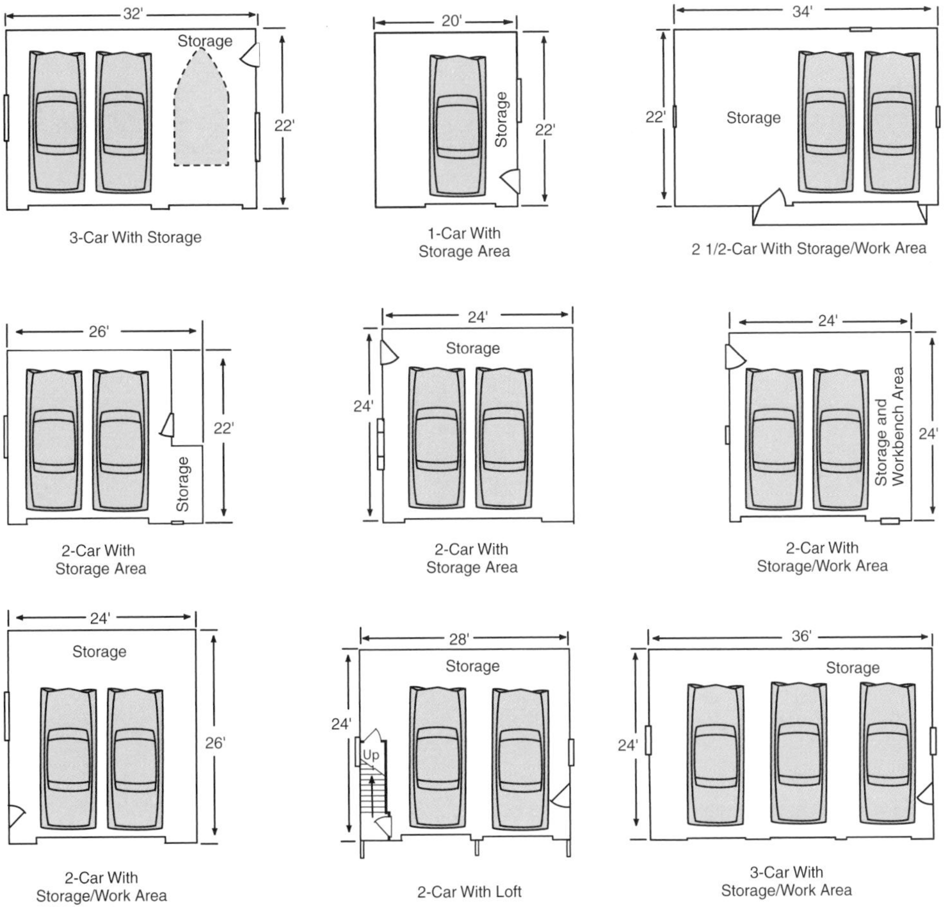

32'
Storage
22'
3-Car With Storage
20'
Storage
22'
1-Car With Storage Area
34'
22'
Storage
2 1/2-Car With Storage/Work Area
26'
22'
Storage
2-Car With Storage Area
24'
Storage
24'
2-Car With Storage Area
24'
Storage and Workbench Area
24'
2-Car With Storage/Work Area
24'
Storage
26'
2-Car With Storage/Work Area
28'
Storage
24'
Up
2-Car With Loft
36'
Storage
24'
3-Car With Storage/Work Area

Anatomy of a Garage

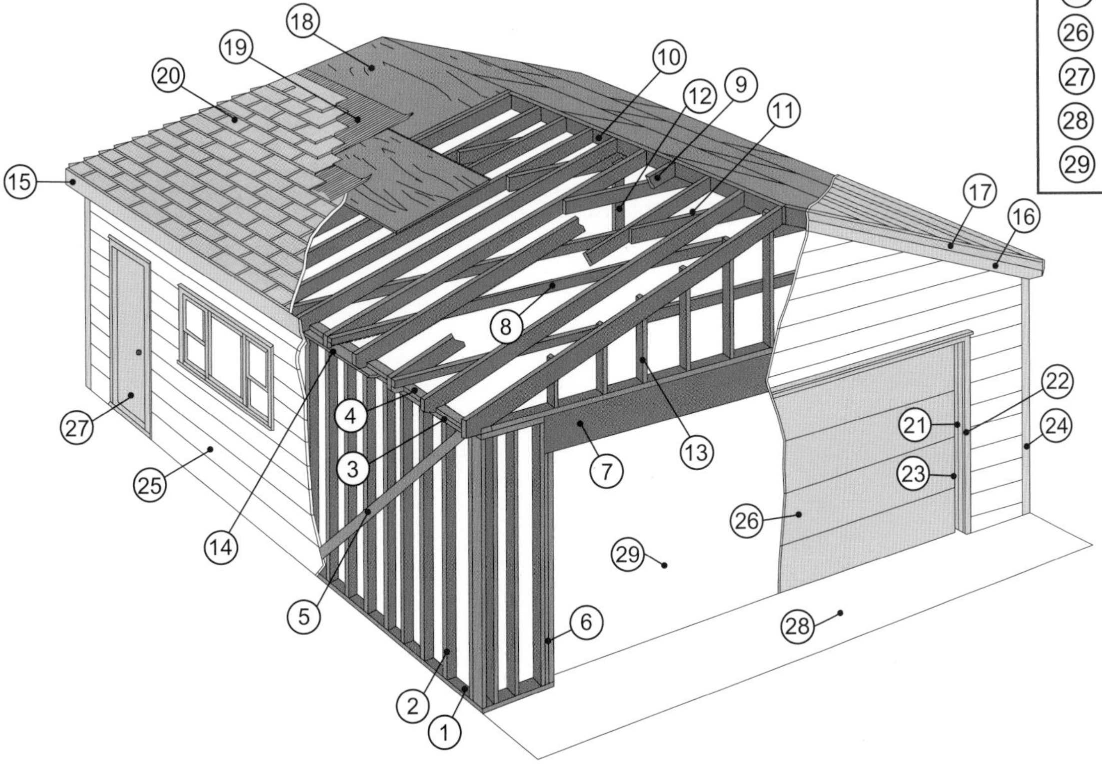

1. **Treated Bottom Plate**
2. **Studs**
3. **Top Plate**
4. **Tie Plate**
5. **Corner Bracing**
6. **Cripple Studs**
7. **Garage Door Header**
8. **Rafter Ties**
9. **Rafters**
10. **Ridge Board**
11. **Collar Ties**
12. **Hangers**
13. **Gable Studs**
14. **Soffit**
15. **Fascia**
16. **Fascia (Rake)**
17. **Gable Shingle Mold**
18. **Roof Sheathing**
19. **Roofing Felt**
20. **Shingles**
21. **Doorjamb**
22. **Trim**
23. **Door Stop**
24. **Corner Boards**
25. **Siding**
26. **Sectional Garage Door**
27. **Service Door**
28. **Concrete Apron**
29. **Concrete Floor Slab**

Establishing Lot Boundaries by the Lot Survey

Before you can begin construction of the garage foundation, the precise boundaries of the building site must be verified by means of a lot survey conducted by a professional surveyor. Lots are normally recorded on maps kept on file by the local building or zoning authorities. By studying these maps and records, the lot surveyor will determine and stake out the precise boundaries of your property. By measuring from the proper reference points, the surveyor will establish the front two corners of the lot. These reference points can be the street curb, the center of the road bordering the lot, or special markers placed in the sidewalk. Once the front corners are marked out, a transit level is most often used to establish the two rear corners of the lot.

Once the lot boundaries are set, you can set up lines showing the exact location of the building, taking into account any setback guidelines set by local building codes. The information required to layout the foundation can be found on the garage blueprints. It is also helpful to design a plot plan showing the location and dimensions of the planned garage, driveway, and sidewalks.

Figure 6A - Measuring Foundation Lines

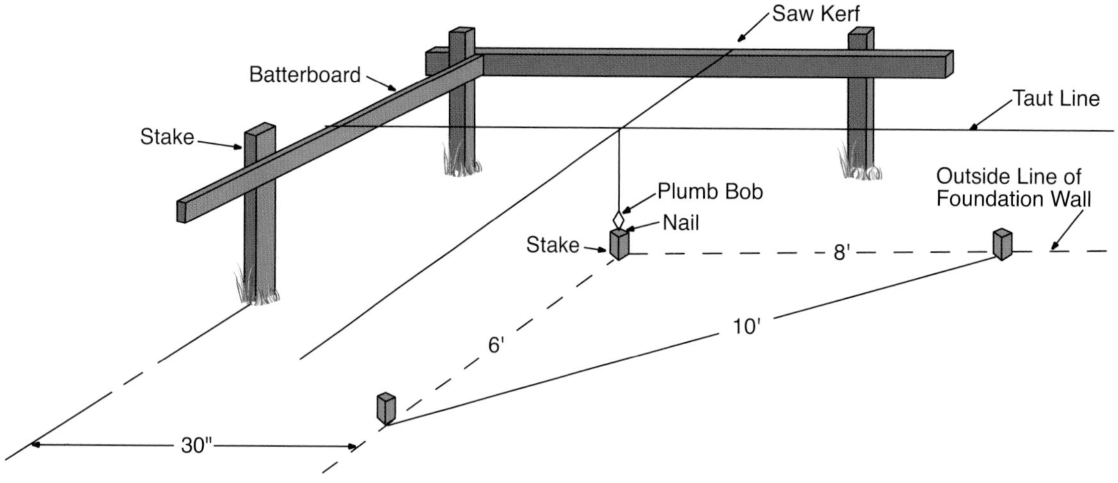

Layout of the Garage Site

Accurately locating the four corners of the building will in turn establish boundaries for the foundation. The site is laid out using batterboards set back from the corners of the planned building in an L-shaped arrangement. Setting them back from the actual building site allows you to maintain an accurate reference point as you dig footings and construct the foundation.

Batterboards are made of pointed stakes connected with 4' lengths of 1x4 lumber. Each batterboard should form an accurate right angle when checked with a framing square. Batterboard tops must be level with each other all the way around. Check for this with a mason's line level.

Figure 6B - Layout of Garage Site

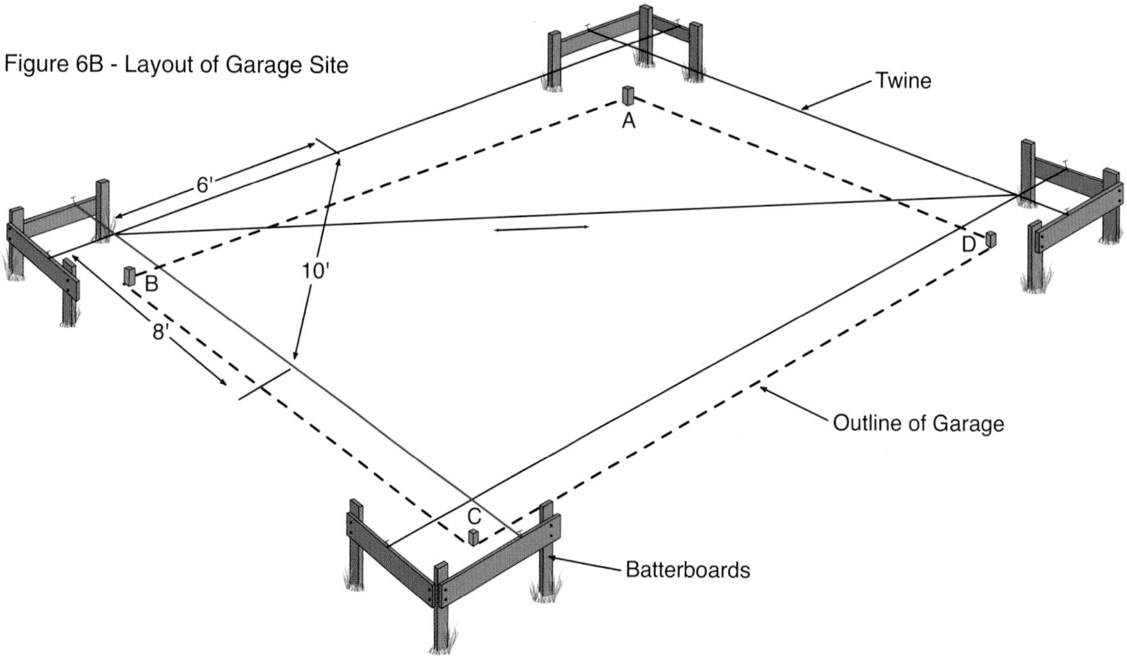

To Set Up Batterboards

1. Accurately locate one corner of the building and drive stake A at that point (see Figure 6B).
2. Measure out along the long side of the building to the next corner. Drive in stake B at this point. Drive a small nail into the stakes and connect with tightly drawn twine.
3. Measure out the approximate positions of corners C and D and drive stakes at these points. Use a framing square to form an approximate right angle at these corners. Run twine from stakes B to C, C to D, and D to A.
4. You will now erect batterboards and adjust stake locations to form a true square or rectangular layout. Erect batterboards so that each corner stake is lined up directly on the diagonal from the opposite corner as illustrated. Use the line level to check that all batterboards are level with each other.
5. Stretch mason's twine between the batterboards so it is aligned directly over stakes A and B. When perfectly aligned, make a saw kerf or cut in the batterboards to make a permanent reference point and tack the twine.
6. Stretch twine over stakes B and C. It must form a perfect right angle with twine A-B. Check for a right angle using the 6/8/10 method. Measure 6' out along twine A-B and 8' along twine B-C. Mark these points with pins. The diagonal between these two pins should measure 10'. Adjust the position of twine B-C until it does and then notch the batterboard at stake C and fasten off line B-C.
7. Using the 6/8/10 method lay out twine C-D and D-A. At each corner carefully measure from the point where the twine lines cross each other to set building dimensions. Drop a plumb line at this intersecting point and set stakes in exact positions.
8. Check the final layout by measuring the diagonals on the layout. They must be equal in length. If they are not, recheck your measurement and make proper adjustments.

Preparing Your Garage Foundation

Inverted T-Shape Forms

The type of foundation you use will depend on your local climate and local building codes. In warmer climates you might only need a simple slab foundation such as those discussed on pages 11 and 12. In colder areas, where the foundation must reach below the frost line, several different designs can be used. The most common is the inverted T-foundation, also known as floating slab foundation (shown below). Whichever type you require, be certain to build a substantial and level foundation. It can save you plenty of problems later in the construction sequence, such as when you frame and level the walls.

Placing concrete footings and foundations is hard work and can be tricky for the inexperienced. So this is one stage in the construction you might want to rely on professionals or friends with experience in working with concrete. Forms must be strongly constructed of sturdy lumber or use premanufactured forms that can be rented. To keep a large job manageable, divide the areas up into convenient sections that you and your crew can pour and finish in one day's time.

The spread footing of an inverted T-foundation provides good bearing on all soil types. Low T-foundations often have the footing and wall poured at the same time. These monolithic pourings eliminate the cold joint between footer and wall and prevents moisture at this joint.

For high T-foundations, the footer and walls are poured separately. Immediately after the concrete footer has been placed, pieces of 2x4 lumber, called key strips, are often pressed into the concrete. Centered on the footing, these strips form the keyways in the footing as it hardens. These keyway grooves help secure the foundation wall to the footing.

As you can see from the illustrations below, several different methods can be used to tie the bottom or sole plate of the wall framing to the foundation wall. Special ties can be embedded in the wet concrete once it begins to set, but the most common method uses anchor bolts.

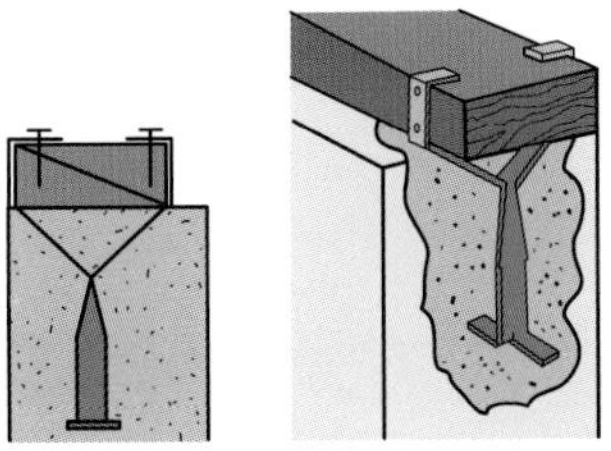

Figure 7A - Special T-Lock Anchors

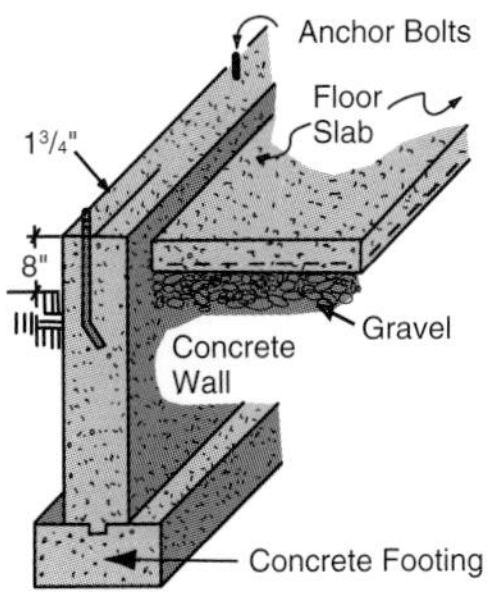

Figure 7B - Foundation Section

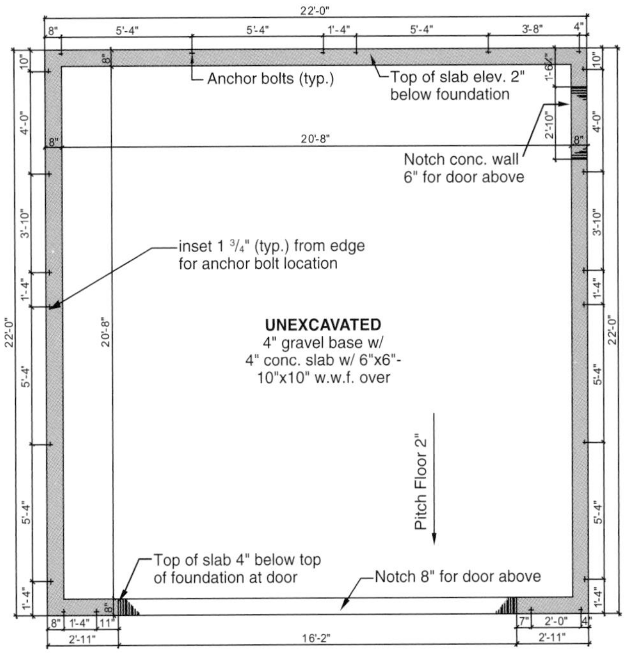

Figure 7C - Floating Slab Foundation Plan

How to Pour a Concrete Footing

Forms for Footings

Typically footings are twice the width of the wall they tie into, but local building codes can vary from this rule of thumb. When the soil is firm and uniform, use an earth form for the footing by simply digging a trench to the required width and depth. When the soil is too soft to hold its form, wood forms for footings and foundation walls will be needed. Several designs are illustrated on the following pages. Concrete is very dense, so build and reinforce the forms strongly. Remember, if you plan to construct a masonry wall on the footing, its top surface must be as level as possible. See page 13 for estimating materials and concrete amounts.

1. **Lay out** the footings using twine and batterboards as a guide for the trench. Use twine as a guide for your forms once the trench is dug.
2. **Level** the bottom of the trench and tap it firm. On sloping ground, use a stepped trench. The trench bottom must be below the frost line.
3. **Build** the forms using the batterboards as a guide for positioning. Support reinforcing steel using brick or stone. Suspend the keyway strip from cleats as shown.
4. **Coat** the forms lightly with release agent. Pour the concrete into the forms, working out air pockets with a flat shovel. Work the concrete into all corners and along edges of the form.
5. **Level** the concrete with the top of the form using a straight length of short lumber as a screed. Work back and forth in a short sawing motion. Knock down high spots and fill all voids. Remove the keyway strip as soon as the concrete will hold its shape.
6. **Cover** it with burlap or plastic sheeting to retain moisture, and lightly spray the concrete with water once or twice daily to keep the surface wet during curing. In hot weather climates cure the concrete for four days.

Figure 8A - Footing Cross Section

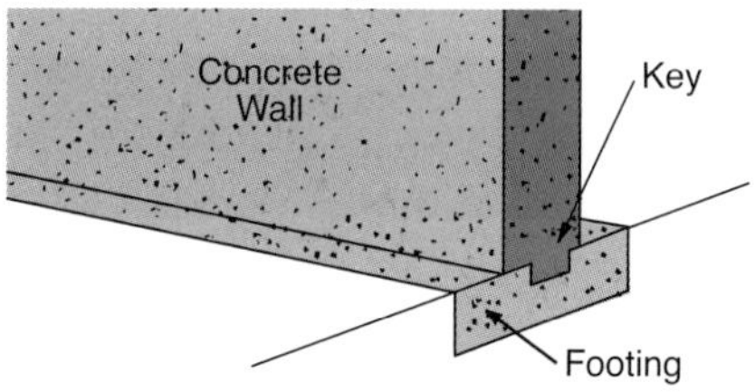

Figure 8B - Laying Out the Footings

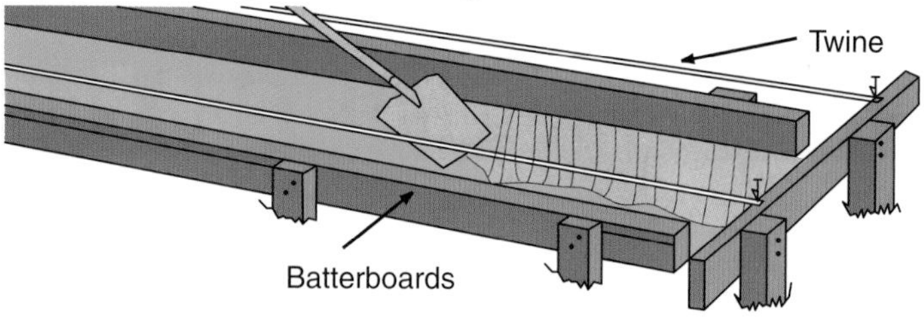

Figure 8C - Leveling

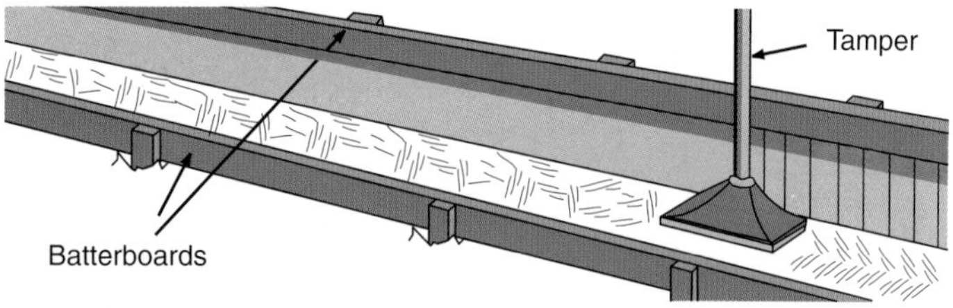

Figure 8D - Building

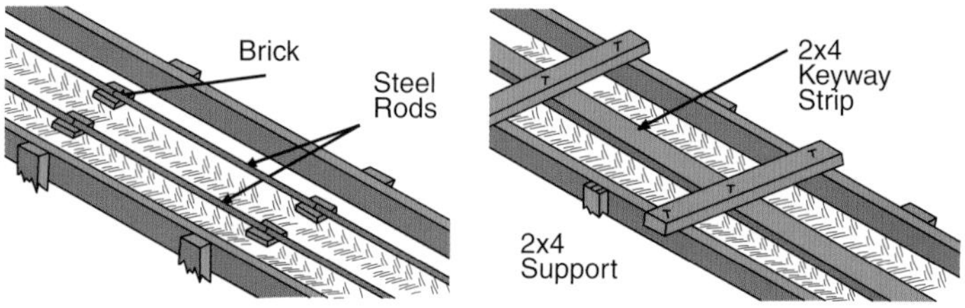

Figure 8E - Coating

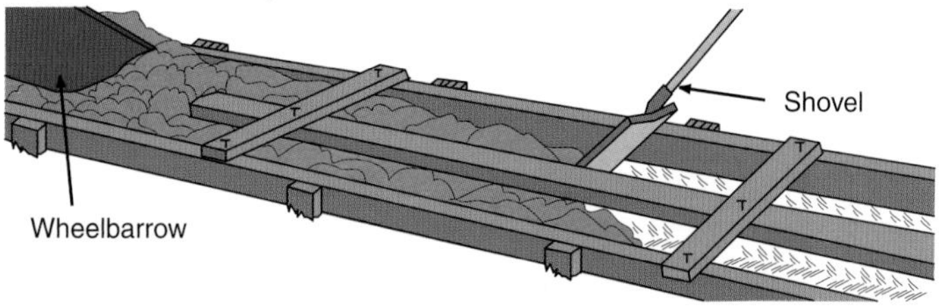

Figure 8F - Leveling

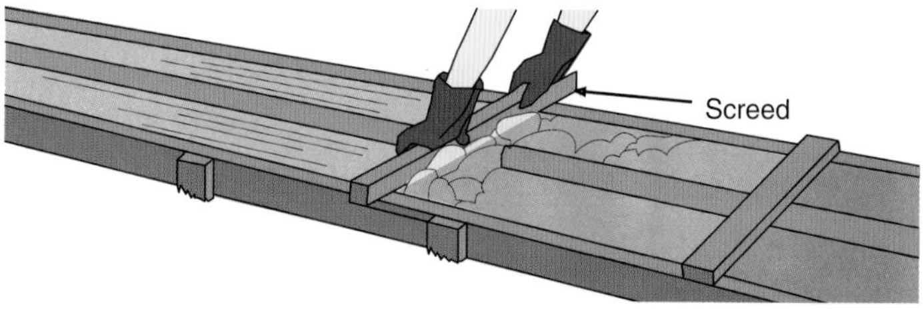

Formwork for Foundation Walls

Once you understand the principles of formwork for concrete walls, you should be able to handle the framework for your garage's foundation wall. Most importantly, the form must be strong enough to withstand the pressure of the wet concrete and the rough treatment it will receive during the pour.

Foundation wall forms are constructed of plywood sheathing, 2x4 lumber framing and studs, wooden spacers, and wire ties. Sheathing forms the mold. The frame and studs support the sheathing. Spacers maintain wall thickness, support the form, and resist pressure exerted by the concrete. Ties hold the form sides together (see Figure 9A).

You may want to explore the option of renting concrete forms, if available in your area. This may save you time and labor preparing wood forms. Wall lengths and heights should be considered when determining which choice you make.

Formwork for Foundation Walls (continued)

Building Forms

Build long forms in sections. The individual sections should be slightly taller than the planned finished foundation wall and no more than 8' in length.

With the lumber laying flat on the ground, construct a frame of 2x4s on edge. Next, nail 2x4 studs into this frame, spacing studs on 16" centers, closer if the wall is particularly thick and will be poured all at one time.

The studded frame is now ready for the sheathing, either 1/2" or 5/8" thick plywood. Lay the sections down, sheathing sides face to face so you can drill holes for the wire ties. Drill 1/8" holes for the wire ties adjacent to the studs as shown. Plan on using plenty of ties to hold the forms together.

Spacers and ties are used to assemble the sections and maintain the proper spacing between them. Spacers are made of 1x2 or 2x4 lumber cut to the same length as the finished wall thickness. Plan to put in spacers every 2' both vertically and horizontally. Wire ties should be made of heavy gauge (8 or 9 gauge) iron wire. Cut the ties long enough to encircle opposing studs on either side of the forms, plus enough excess to comfortably twist the ends together.

Tilt the two sections upright, face to face, and spaced at the wall thickness. Tack the sections together with several crosspieces to make working easier. Thread the 8 to 9 gauge wire ties through the form and around the studs, twisting the wire ends together. Place a 1x2 or 2x4 spacer near the tie.

Place a stick between the wires inside the form and twist the wire tight as illustrated. Do this for all spacers and ties. Tie pull wires on all spacers you will not be able to reach when the pour begins. You must remove all spacers as the pour proceeds (see Figure 9B).

Place the assembled form in position on the footer. Assemble additional sections, butting sections together and nailing through adjacent framing members to create the finished continuous wall form. The running length of the forms should be slightly longer than the planned wall length so that you can cleat in stop boards at the end of the forms.

A properly constructed form is self-supporting, but it must be plumbed and tied in place with braces so it will stay in position during the pour. Nail the bottom of the form to stakes driven firmly in the ground. This will prevent lifting. Prevent lateral movement by installing 2x4 angle braces (see Figure 9C).

Prior to making the pour, coat the forms with concrete release agent to make it easier to remove the form. See page 13 for the tools you'll need to place the concrete, plus tips on estimating the amount of concrete needed.

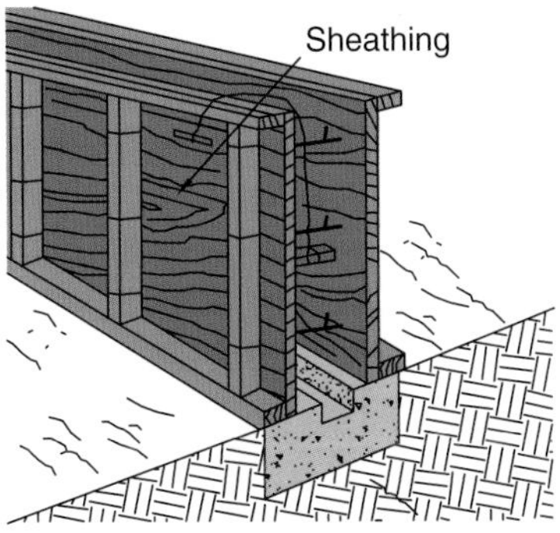

Figure 9A - Plywood Sheathing

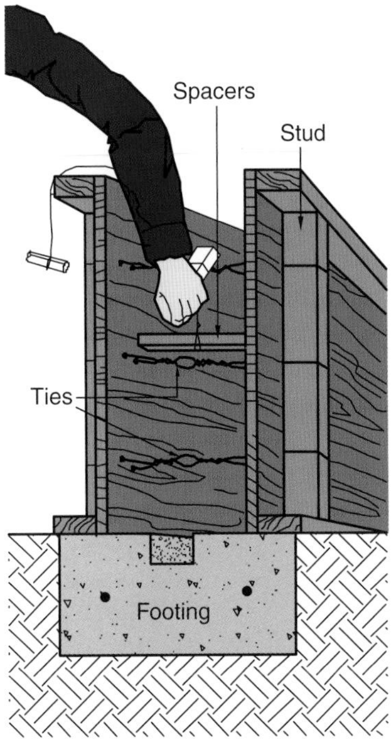

Figure 9B - Using Spacers and Ties

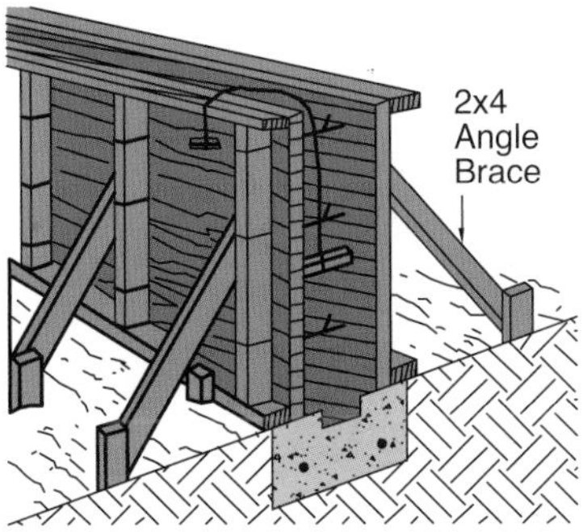

Figure 9C - Using Angle Braces

Casting a Concrete Wall

After the foundation footing has been placed and properly cured, and you've set the wall forms in place, aligned, plumbed, and secured them, then you're ready to make the wall pour. The steps involved in this process include: mounting the forms, pouring and tamping the concrete, striking, floating, and troweling the top edge smooth to accept the bottom plate, and installing the anchor bolts or special anchor ties.

1. **Mount** the forms on the cured footing, centering them over the keyway. See above for more details on securing the forms in place. Snap chalk lines along the inside of the forms to show the desired height of the foundation wall if not level with the top of the form.
2. **Pour** the concrete into the forms, working in 6- to 8-inch layers. Do not stop the work once you begin, or "cold

Figure 9D - Mounting

Figure 9E - Pouring

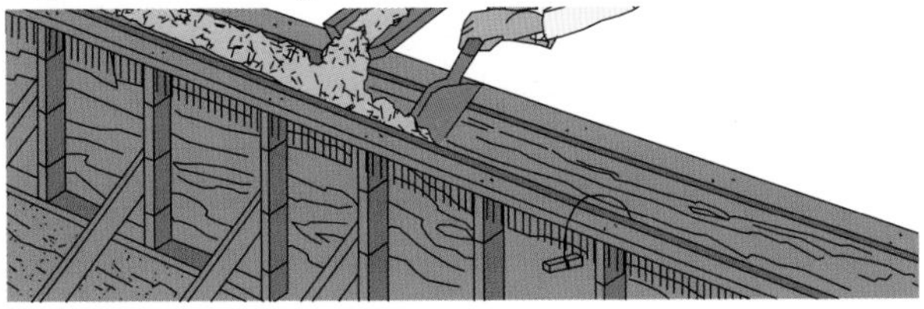

joints" between layers will result and cause cracks in the foundation wall. Work the concrete well up against the sides of the form. Tapping the side of the forms with a hammer will help settle the concrete and avoid air pockets. Pull out the spacers as you proceed.

3. **Strike** the concrete level with the top of the form or your chalk line using a board as a screed as you did with the footing. For a smoother surface, work the top surface with a wooden or steel trowel.
4. **Insert** the anchor bolts at the proper spacing as soon as the concrete is firm enough to support them if you are going to use anchor bolts or anchor ties to secure the framing sill to the foundation. Cure the concrete for four days as you did the footing. Remove the forms after curing.

Figure 10A - Striking

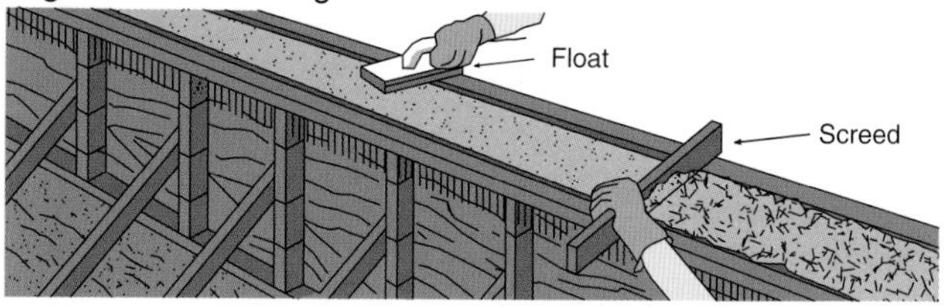
Float
Screed

Figure 10B - Inserting Anchor Bolts

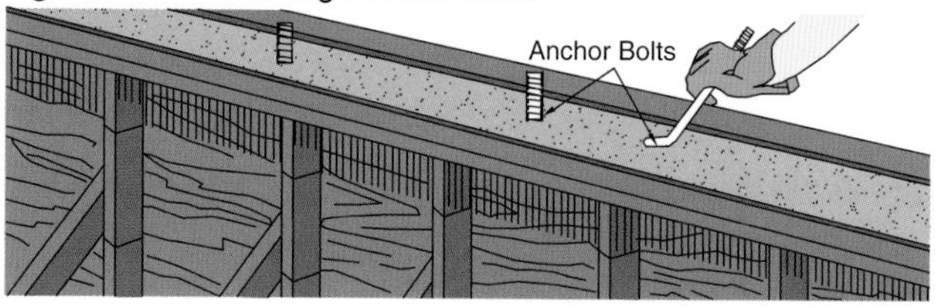
Anchor Bolts

Building Concrete Block Foundation Walls

Concrete block can also be used to construct the foundation wall on the footing. The running bond shown in these illustrations is most commonly used. It allows the block cores to line up, making steel reinforcing and grouting easy.

Use the same type of mortar that is used in bricklaying, but mix it a little on the stiff side to make buttering the block a little easier. The mortar will also be less likely to squeeze out of the joints. Also do not wet the block before beginning work as you would do with brick.

In regions where hurricane and high winds are a factor, special reinforcing may be required. Check with your local building official or building department.

1. Start the lead in a corner, laying a bed of mortar 2" thick for three or four blocks. Lay the corner block carefully and press it down to an accurate 3/8" thick mortar joint. Butter the ends of the next blocks and place each 3/8" from the previous block. Use a level to align, level, and plumb the lead.
2. Continue laying block to complete the lead. Check for squareness at the corner. Use a mason's line to maintain a straight line as you work. All mortar joints are 3/8" wide.
3. Begin leads at each corner and work to the middle. Lay blocks between the leads. To fit the closure block, spread mortar on all edges of the opening and butter the ends of the closure block. Set it carefully in place and check alignment, levelness, and plumbness.
4. With one course remaining, cover the cores with metal screening; this will be used to cap the wall. Fill the cores in the top course with mortar.
5. You can now sink anchor bolts or ties into the mortar filled top course. This will tie down the sill plate on which the garage framing will rest.

Figure 10C - Concrete Blocks

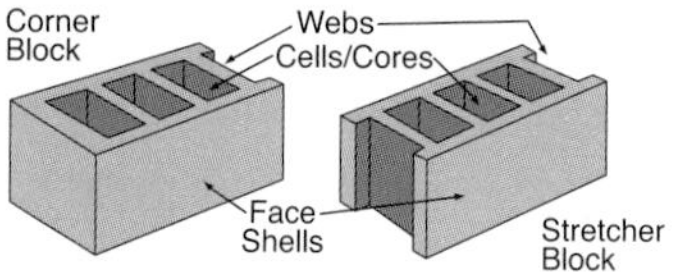
Corner Block
Webs
Cells/Cores
Face Shells
Stretcher Block

Figure 10D - Starting the Lead

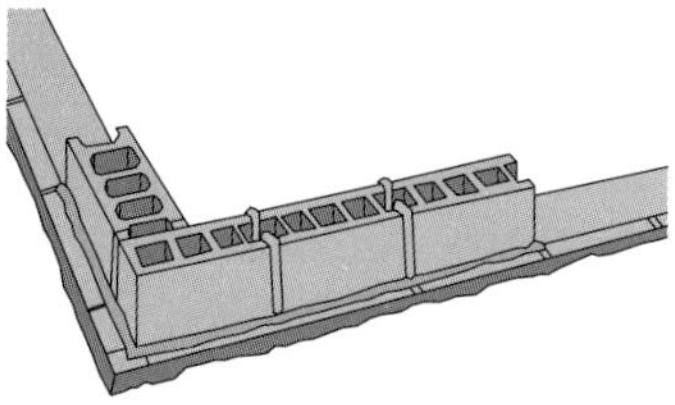

Figure 10E - Laying Blocks Using Mason's Line

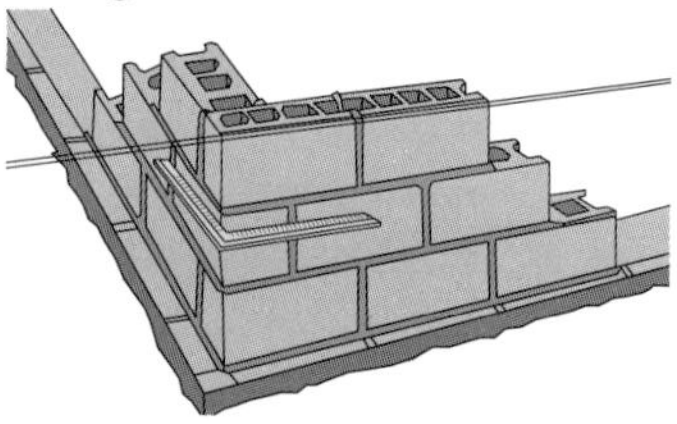

Figure 10F - Fitting Closure Block

Figure 10G - Fill Cores with Mortar

Figure 10H - Add Anchor Bolts and Bottom Plate

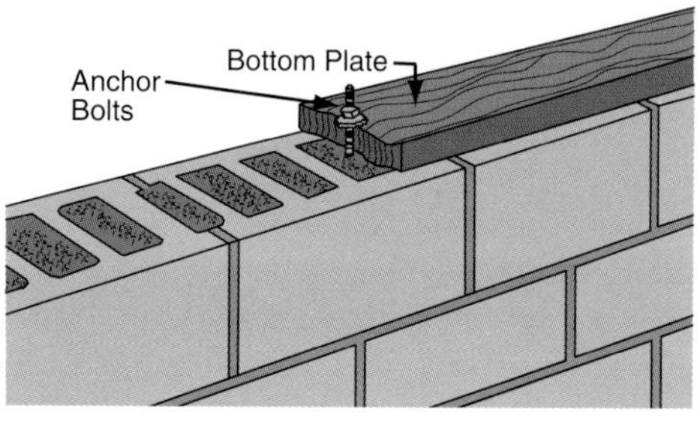
Bottom Plate
Anchor Bolts

Pouring a T-Shaped Foundation Concrete Floor

Placing a concrete floor inside a T-foundation is similar to placing a slab foundation as described on pages 9 and 10. Rather than using forms, the foundation walls are the outside boundaries of the floor. Be sure the area inside the foundation boundaries is properly backfilled, leveled, and prepared with a gravel base and reinforcing mesh set on stones to raise it slightly off of the gravel.

Pouring a large slab is hard work so be sure you have two or three helpers, one or two wheelbarrows and shovels, plus all of the concrete finishing tools you'll need (see page 13).

The height of the foundation walls makes screeding over the entire length of the slab impossible, so stake a number of temporary screeding guides inside the foundation. These will help you level the concrete to the correct thickness, usually 4". Once the initial screeding is complete, the guides are pulled out and these voids filled with concrete. You can also use a wide wooden darby to level the concrete.

As the work progresses, watch the concrete carefully. In hot or windy weather, the first sections might be setting up too fast while you are still pouring the remaining sections. If this is the case, some members of your crew will have to begin finishing work a little sooner than planned. Never add water to the concrete to keep it workable until you are ready to finish the concrete.

After each section has been screeded, use a wooden bull float or darby to smooth it. Once the initial smoothing has been completed, wait for the concrete to lose its initial shine before beginning final troweling. For a smooth finish use a wooden float (see Figure 11B). A really slick finish requires a steel trowel. For large slabs, use a rented power trowel.

Figure 11A - Anatomy of T-Shaped Foundation with Concrete Slab Floor

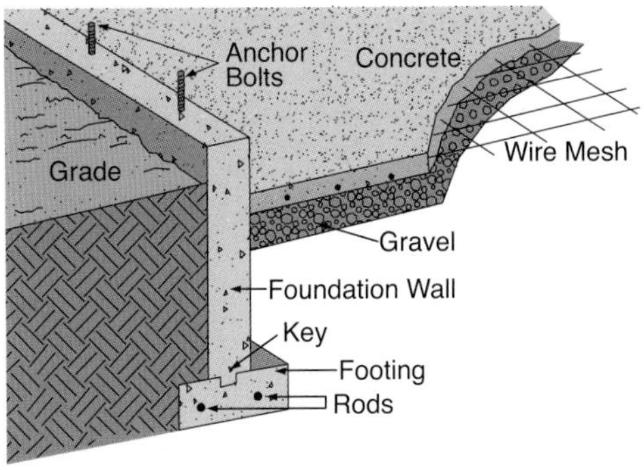

Anchor Bolts
Concrete
Wire Mesh
Grade
Gravel
Foundation Wall
Key
Footing
Rods

Figure 11B - Bull floating levels ridges and fills voids left after striking. It is used for large areas.

Bull Float

Foundation Details for Turned-Down Monolithic Slabs

If you live in an area where frost upheaval is not a problem, a basic slab foundation can be used for your garage (see Figure 11C). Again, check the local building requirements in your area, and follow their specifications. Here's a checklist of common code requirements:

- ❑ A slab thickness of 4" with the top of the slab set a minimum of 8" above the surrounding soil.
- ❑ A footing ditch dug around the perimeter of the slab – 6" wide at the base of the trench and 12" deep or deeper, depending on frost or grade conditions. Footings must contain a layer of reinforcing steel rod 3" up from the base of the footing trench.
- ❑ You'll need a gravel base under the slab 3" to 4" thick. A layer of 6" square welded wire mesh must be placed in the slab. Raise this wire mesh 2" off of the gravel by using stones, brick halves, or broken concrete to support it.
- ❑ Anchor bolts or ties need to be embedded in the footing to accept the mudsill for framing the garage. Use 10" long anchors embedded 7" deep in concrete, but no more than 6' on center, and not more than 12" away from each end (with a minimum of 2 anchors per mudsill). Do not place anchors in doorways.

Figure 11C - Slab Foundation Plan

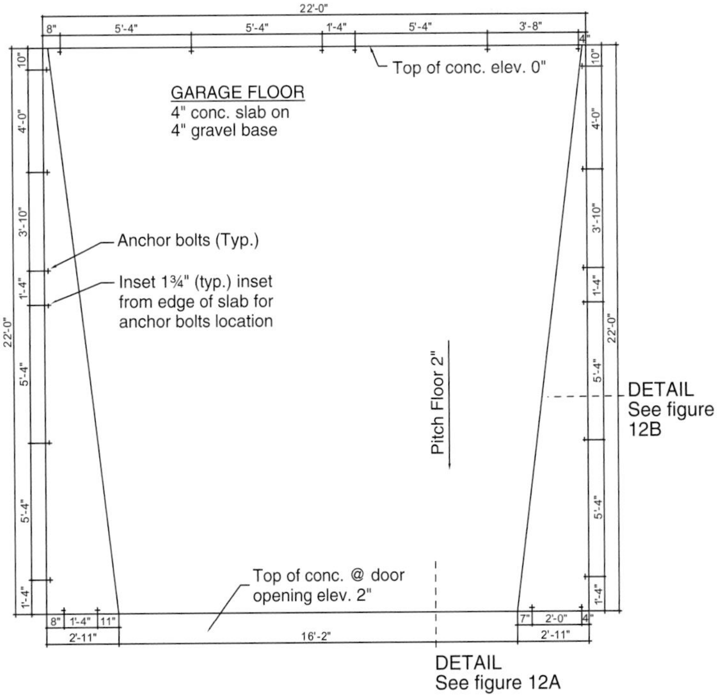

22'-0"
8"
5'-4"
5'-4"
1'-4"
5'-4"
3'-8"
Top of conc. elev. 0"
GARAGE FLOOR
4" conc. slab on
4" gravel base
10"
4'-0"
3'-10"
1'-4"
22'-0"
5'-4"
5'-4"
1'-4"
Anchor bolts (Typ.)
Inset 1¾" (typ.) inset from edge of slab for anchor bolts location
Pitch Floor 2"
DETAIL
See figure
12B
Top of conc. @ door opening elev. 2"
8"
1'-4"
11"
2'-11"
16'-2"
7"
2'-0"
4"
2'-11"
DETAIL
See figure 12A

Foundation Details for Turned-Down Monolithic Slabs

Slab Forms

Level the site. Small depressions can be filled with gravel and concrete. Use 2x8 lumber for the forms and brace it securely. Begin laying out the forms at the highest point of the site and work to the lowest. The top of the forms should be perfectly level. In some cases, you might prefer a slope of 1/4" per 1'-0" toward the overhead garage door location to help with drainage. Double-check dimensions and squareness by measuring the diagonals across the forms. Once forms are square and level, install bracing stakes every 3' or so on the outside face of the forms. Be sure to use sufficient bracing driven well into firm ground. The inside dimensions of the forms will be the finished outside dimension of the slab, exclusive of any apron.

This apron can be poured as part of the slab or added later. If it is part of the slab, bevel apron form boards so the apron slopes to a point level or slightly above the driveway surface (see Figure 12A).

Once the forms are in place, dig the required footing trench at the inside form perimeters and place the required reinforcing steel in the trench. Lay the gravel base and wire mesh according to code requirements, and wet the gravel before the pour (See page 13 for the tools needed and estimating your concrete needs).

Have the local building inspector check the forms prior to the pour date. If electrical service is desired, place the electrical conduit in proper location prior to the pour.

Figure 12A - Apron Formwork

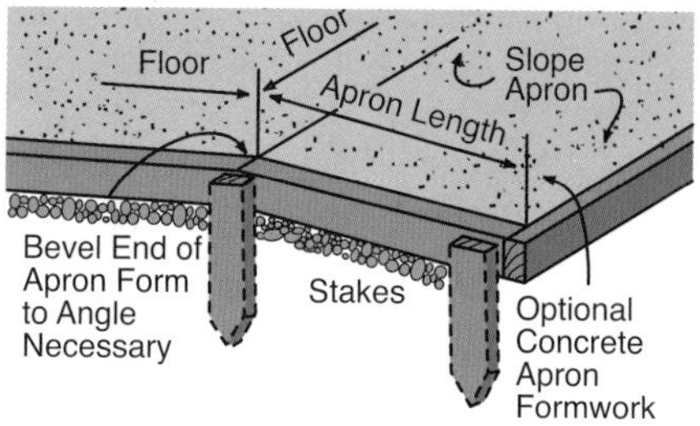

Figure 12B - Turned-Down Slab (Monolithic)

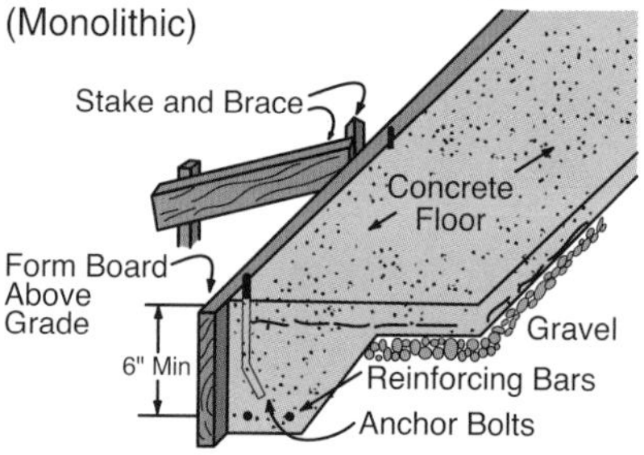

Pouring the Concrete Slab

Placing

Have adequate help, wheelbarrows, and tools ready when the concrete truck arrives. Start by pouring in the area farthest away from the truck, using wheelbarrows to move the concrete. Begin by filling the footing trench. For larger areas, break the work into smaller sections by installing temporary screeding guides. When one section is poured, move to the next section while helpers screed off the first section (Figure 12D). Tap on the outside of the form boards to help settle the concrete. Be sure all voids are filled. Pay special attention along the perimeters of the form boards. Remove the temporary screed guides while filling in these voids.

Finishing

Once the concrete has lost its initial shine, begin finishing it with a bull float. Larger floats have a handle like a broom. If you are using smaller hand floats, use toe and knee boards placed on the concrete so you can kneel on the concrete without leaving much of an impression. Move the float in long sweeping motions (Figure 12E).

Anchor bolts should be placed after the concrete has been screeded and bull floated. Place the bolts 1-3/4" away from the edge of the slab. Double-check spacing of bolts and alignment (Figure 12F).

For a coarser finish, bull floating is all that is required. For a slicker, smoother finish, use a steel trowel to go over the work once bull floating is complete. Use a light touch so you don't gouge the concrete surface. Before the concrete hardens completely, take a trowel and cut between the edge of the concrete and the form.

Curing

Once all finishing is completed, mist down the slab with water, and cover it with a layer of plastic or burlap. Keep the surface moist for four days as the concrete cures.

Figure 12C - Steel reinforcing rods and wire mesh are laid into place over gravel and optional plastic vapor barrier.

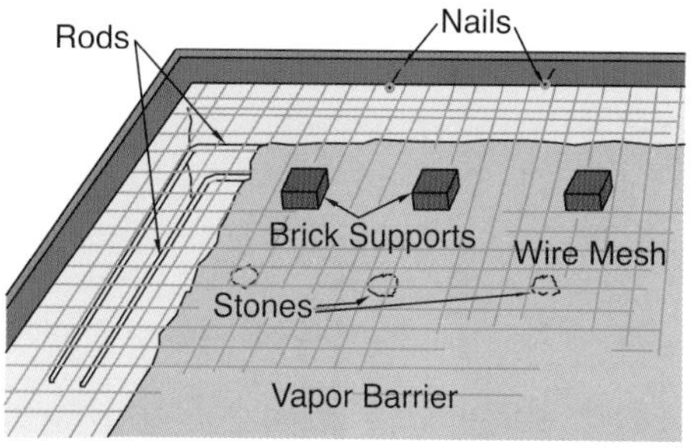

Figure 12D - Workers level concrete slab with a strike board.

Figure 12E - Smooth concrete surface with a bull float.

Figure 12F - Add anchor bolts.

Some of the Tools Needed

Mason's Trowel
Hammer
Kneeler and Pads
Tamper
Wheelbarrow
Hand Sledge
Striker
Carpenter's Square
Bull Float
Shovel
Broom
Mason's Level
Hand Darby
Edger
Steel Trowel
Groover
Wood Float
Chalk Line
Tape Measure
Twine

Calculating Concrete Volume

Concrete is measured in cubic yards. To calculate cubic yards, multiply thickness (in inches) x width (in feet) x length (in feet) and divide by 12. This gives cubic feet. Divide this number by 27 to determine cubic yards. Figure measurements carefully. While you do not want to order more than your needs, being short can cause major problems.

Estimating Cubic Yards of Concrete

Cubic Yards of Concrete

Area in sq. ft. (width x length)	Thickness (inches) 4	5
10	0.12	0.15
25	0.31	0.39
50	0.62	0.77
100	1.23	1.54
200	2.47	3.09
300	3.70	4.63

For Slab*

To find the amount of concrete required for a 4" thick driveway 20 ft. wide by 20 ft. long, for example, first figure the number of square feet by multiplying:

20 ft. x 20 ft. = 400 sq. ft.

Then add the appropriate amounts from the table:

300 sq. ft. = 3.70 cu. yd.
+100 sq. ft. = 1.23 cu. yd.
400 sq. ft. = 4.93 cu. yd.

With a perfect subgrade and no losses from spillage, 5 cu. yd. might be enough. But for insurance against contingencies, the order should be increased to 5-1/2 cu. yd. It is always better to have some concrete left over than run short.

*Does not allow for losses due to uneven subgrade, spillage, etc.
Add 5-10 percent for such contingencies. Does not allow for turn-down areas.

Choosing Lumber for Framing

Nearly all types of general construction are done using softwoods, such as Douglas Fir or Southern Pine. As a rule softwoods are less expensive, easier to work with, and more readily available than hardwoods, which are normally reserved for fine finishing work.

Lumber Sizes

In general, construction softwood lengths run from 8' to 22' in 2' increments. ***Dimension lumber***, graded primarily for strength, is used in structural framing. These pieces range from 2" to 4" thick and are at least 2" wide. ***Beams*** and ***stringers*** are structural lumber pieces 5" thick or more, having a width at least 2" greater than the thickness. ***Posts*** and ***timbers*** are heavy construction members that are 5" x 5" or larger with a width not exceeding a thickness of more than 2".

The actual final dimensions of lumber are slightly smaller than the nominal dimensions. The chart to the right lists nominal and actual width and thickness for common structural lumber.

Estimate a list of materials from the plans, listing the quantity, size, and length of the pieces you'll need. Prices will be by the linear foot or by the board foot for larger orders. Linear feet considers only the length of the piece, for example, twenty 2x4s, 10' long or 200 linear feet of 2x4. However, board feet pricing considers total volume, for example, a 2x4 that is 10' long would be (2 x 4 x 10) divided by 12 = 6.66 or 6-2/3 board feet.

Select lumber that is seasoned or dried. Green lumber can cause problems as it shrinks. Dimension lumber is usually stamped **MC-15** (15% moisture content) or **S-DRY** (19% moisture content or less).

When you can, select vertical grain lumber and be on the lookout for the common lumber defects (see Figure 14A).

Standard Dimensions of Surfaced Lumber

Nominal Size	Surfaced (Actual) Size
1 x 2	3/4" x 1-1/2"
1 x 3	3/4" x 2-1/2"
1 x 4	3/4" x 3-1/2"
1 x 6	3/4" x 5-1/2"
1 x 8	3/4" x 7-1/4"
1 x 10	3/4" x 9-1/4"
1 x 12	3/4" x 11-1/4"
2 x 3	1-1/2" x 2-1/2"
2 x 4	1-1/2" x 3-1/2"
2 x 6	1-1/2" x 5-1/2"
2 x 8	1-1/2" x 7-1/4"
2 x 10	1-1/2" x 9-1/4"
2 x 12	1-1/2" x 11-1/4"
4 x 4	3-1/2" x 3-1/2"
4 x 10	3-1/2" x 9-1/4"
6 x 8	5-1/2" x 7-1/2"

Figure 14A - Lumber Defects

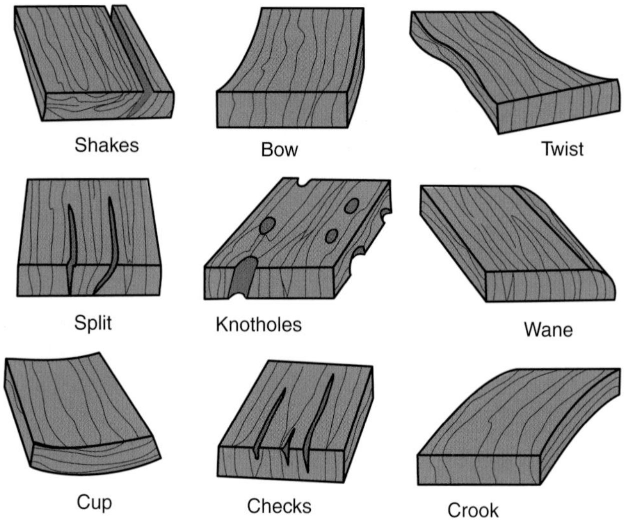
Shakes
Bow
Twist
Split
Knotholes
Wane
Cup
Checks
Crook

Figure 14B - Engineered Lumber

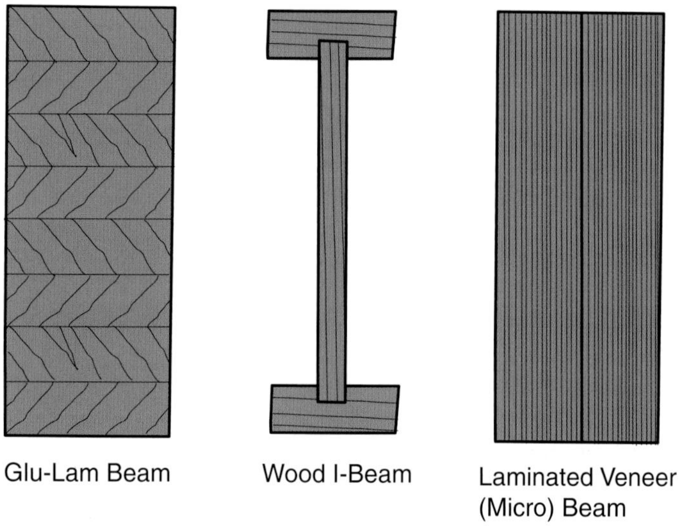
Glu-Lam Beam
Wood I-Beam
Laminated Veneer
(Micro) Beam

Engineered Lumber

Due to recent developments in timber cutting practices and the reduced availability of certain sizes of framing lumber, engineered lumber manufactured from plywood, wood chips, and special glue resins offers an attractive alternative to dimensional lumber used for joists, beams, headers, and rafters. Unlike sawn dimensional lumber, engineered lumber is a manufactured product that will not warp and shrink over time.

Engineered lumber is manufactured to meet stringent criteria for strength, uniformity, and reliability. Glu-Lam beams offer great strength over spans. Wood I-Beams provide a lightweight alternative to conventional joists or rafters. Some typical laminated veneer lumber products are above.

Nails and Fasteners for Framing and Finishing

Nails are the most common fastener used in framing and construction. Nail lengths are indicated by the term ***penny***, noted by a small letter d. In most cases, nails increase in diameter as they increase in length. Most framing for heavier construction is done with common nails. The extra thick shank of common nails has greater strength than most other types. A wide thick head spreads the load and resists pull-through. The larger head also makes a good target for a hammer.

Box nails are similar in shape and use to common nails, but they have a slimmer shank that is less likely to split wood. Finishing nails are used in work where you do not want the nail head to show such as in trim and fascia work. Casing nails, similar to finishing nails but with a thicker shank and angular head, are used for heavier work such as adding casings around windows and doors.

Spiraled shanks rotate slightly for better holding power as you drive the nail in wood. Annular-ring nails also provide extra holding power, especially in softer woods.

Discuss your project with your local home improvement store, or building supply dealer to determine the best nail and fastener selections for the project.

Screws create neat, strong joints for finished work, such as door and window treatments. Heavy-duty lag screws are also used in some types of heavier framing and construction.

Table of Common Nails

Size	Length	Gauge	# per lb.
2d	1"	15	840
3d	1 1/4"	14	540
4d	1 1/2"	12 1/2	290
5d	1 3/4"	12 1/2	250
6d	2"	11 1/2	160
7d	2 1/4"	11 1/2	150
8d	2 1/2"	10 1/4	100
9d	2 3/4"	10 1/4	90
10d	3"	9	65
12d	3 1/4"	9	60
16d	3 1/2"	8	45
20d	4"	6	30
30d	4 1/2"	5	20
40d	5"	4	16
50d	5 1/2"	3	12
60d	6"	2	10

The Table of Common Nails and the Finishing Nail Selection Chart show the approximate number of nails you get in a pound. You'll need more pounds of larger sizes to do a job. For outside jobs, get galvanized or cadmium-plated nails. Aluminum nails are a bit expensive unless you are doing a smaller project.

Finishing Nail Selection Chart

Size	Length	Gauge	# per lb.
2d	1"	16	1000
3d	1 1/4"	15 1/2	870
4d	1 1/4"	15	600
6d	2"	13	310
8d	2 1/2"	12 1/2	190
10d	3"	11 1/2	120

Screw Selection Chart

Size	Length	Gauge	# per lb.
0	1/4-3/8	9	1/2-3
1	1/4-1/2	10	1/2-3 1/2
2	1/4-3/4	11	5/8-3 1/2
3	1/4-1	12	5/8-4
4	1/4-1 1/2	14	3/4-5
5	3/8-1 1/2	16	1-5
6	3/8-2 1/2	18	1 1/4-5
7	3/8-2 1/2	20	1 1/2-5
8	3/8-3	24	3-5

The Screw Selection Chart shows sizes and the lengths in which they're available. The larger sizes come in longer lengths. Most jobs call for sizes 6-12 in 1/2 to 3 inch lengths. Check size and length before you buy.

Figure 15A - Different Types of Fasteners

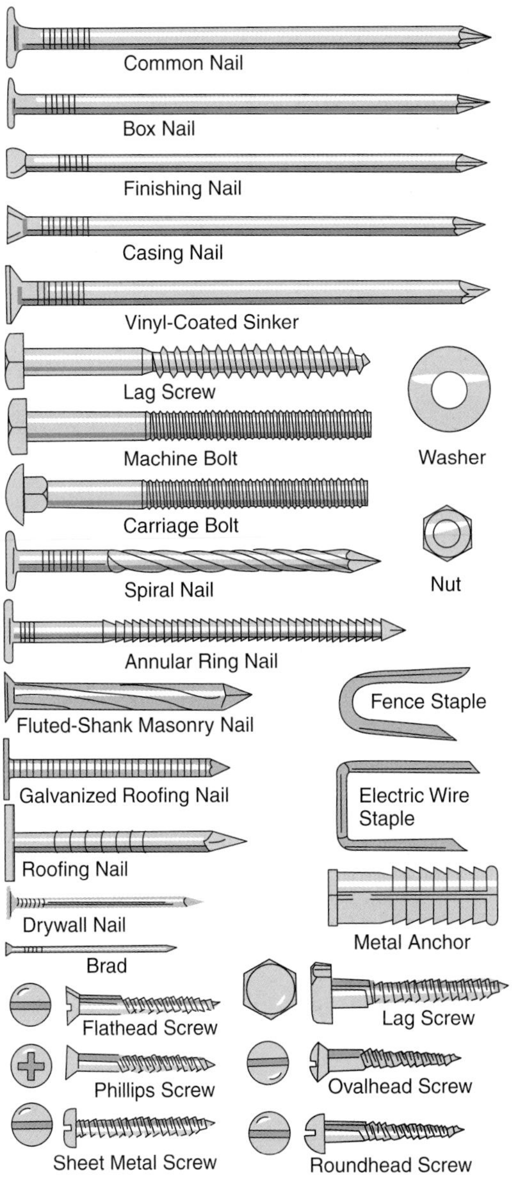

Selecting Your Doors

Exterior doors are commonly 1-3/4" thick, not less than 80" high, and 32" to 36" wide. Exterior doors should be solid-core wood or insulated metal construction. Solid core means the space between the front and back surfaces is filled with either wood or particle board. A solid door offers more security and is less subject to warping that can be caused by humidity and differences in temperature between the indoors and outdoors.

Figure 15B - Door Types

Decide on the quantity and sizes of doors along with which way the door swings before framing begins. Be sure all framing openings for doors (and windows) are correctly dimensioned and squared. The door manufacturer provides dimensioning information, so be sure to obtain this data from your building supply dealer.

Selecting Your Windows

Most garage designs incorporate one or more windows to admit light and provide a view to the outdoors. Fixed window designs do not open but provide excellent protection against air infiltration. Operable windows include awning, double hung, casement and slider designs as shown. Casement windows usually open outward and provide excellent ventilation. Single- and double-hung windows, as their names imply, have one or two sashes that open. They provide slightly less ventilation when compared to casement designs. Awning windows are hinged at the top or bottom and open either in or out. They provide excellent airflow and are easy to clean from the exterior.

There are several different types of materials used in window manufacturing. Wood windows do require some maintenance, while aluminum or vinyl require little or no maintenance.

Selection is more or less a matter of personal taste, but there might be some local code restrictions. Know the exact frame-out dimensions or rough opening sizes for the windows you selected before wall framing begins.

Figure 16 - Window Types

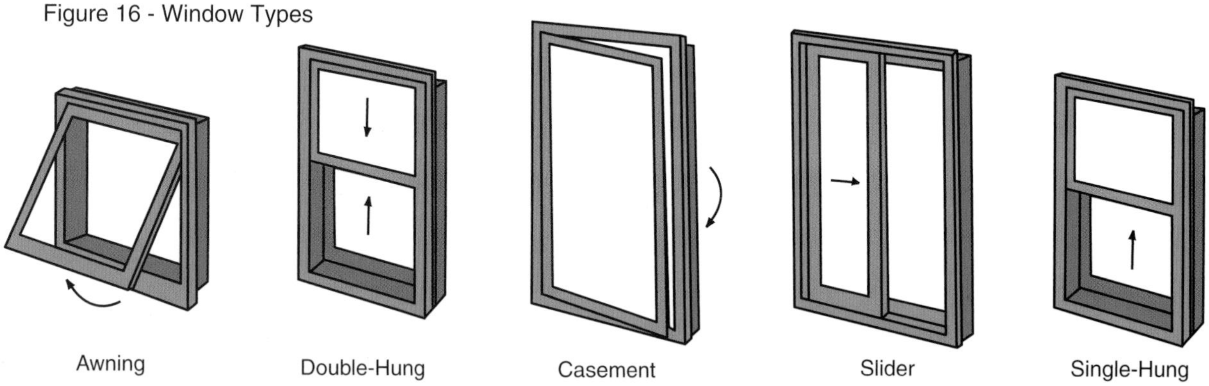

Typical Garage Wall and Roof Framing Plan

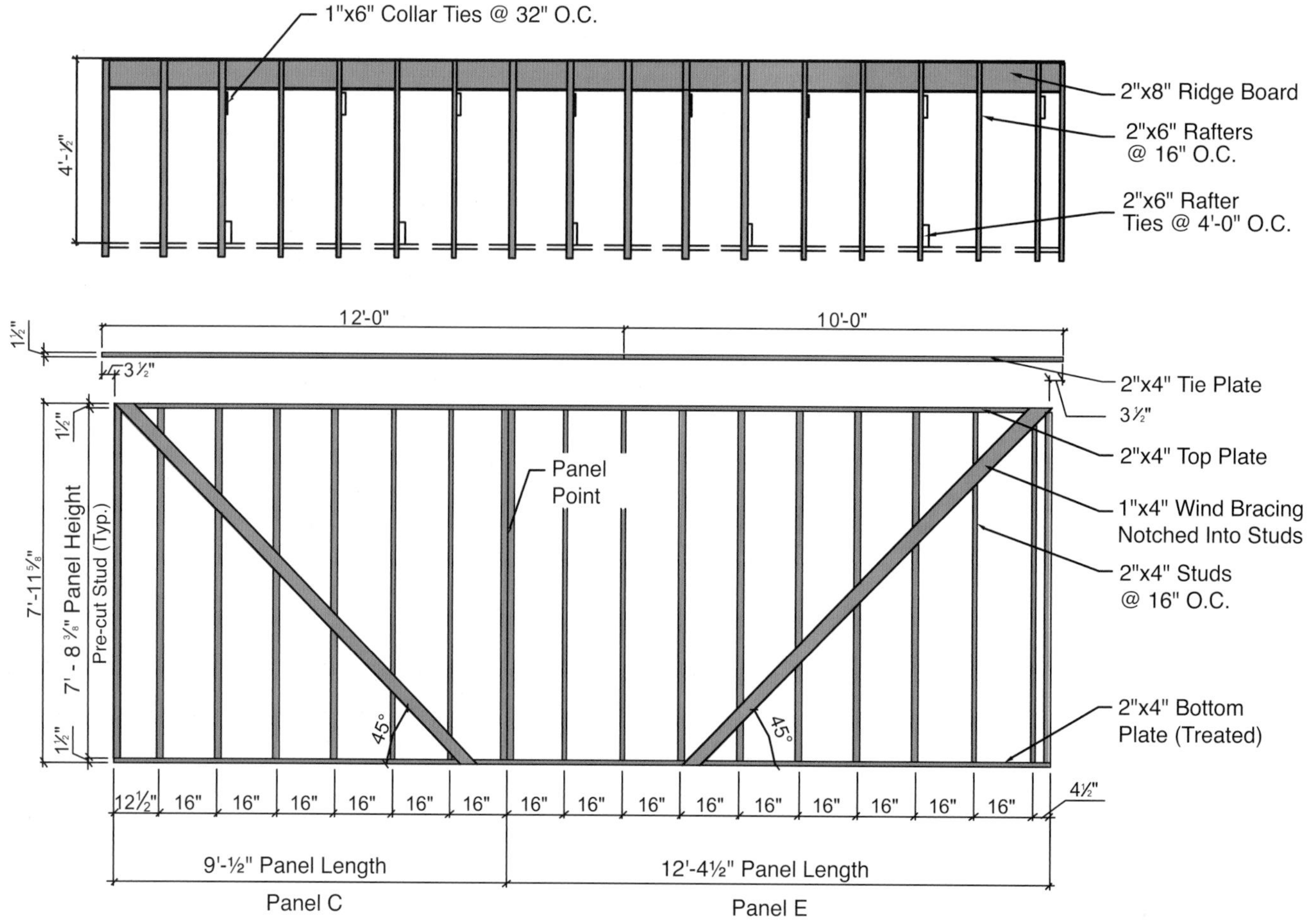

Typical Garage Floor Panel (Wall Panel System)

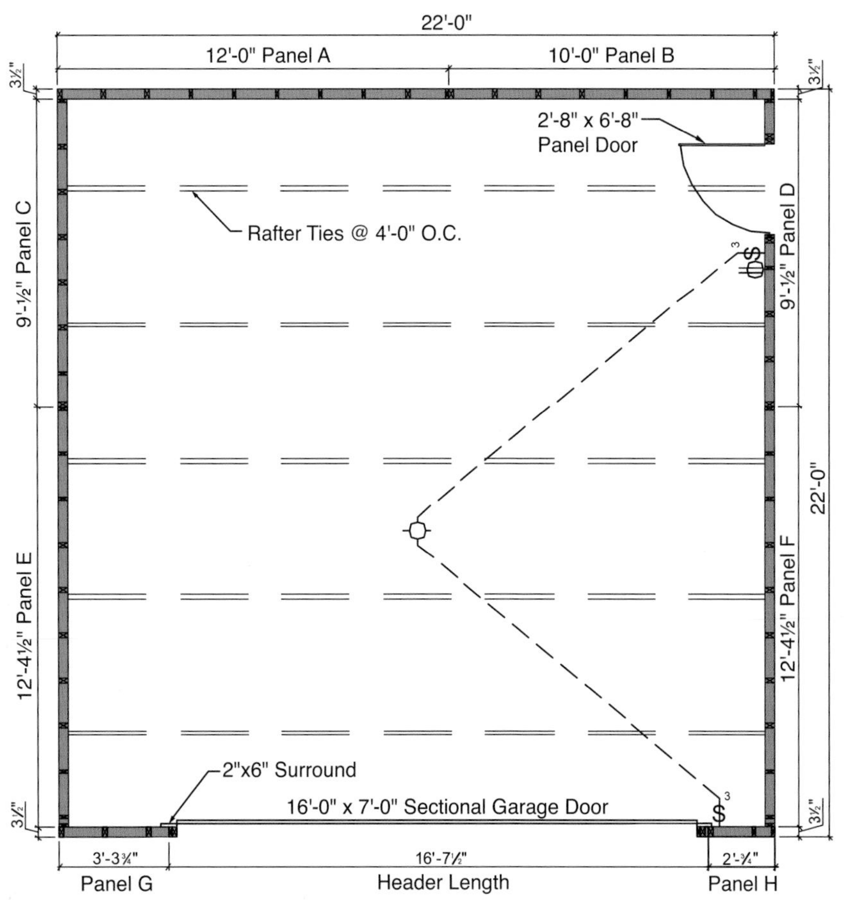

22'-0"
12'-0" Panel A
10'-0" Panel B
3½"
2'-8" x 6'-8" Panel Door
Rafter Ties @ 4'-0" O.C.
9'-½" Panel C
9'-½" Panel D
22'-0"
12'-4½" Panel E
12'-4½" Panel F
2"x6" Surround
16'-0" x 7'-0" Sectional Garage Door
3'-3¾"
Panel G
16'-7½"
Header Length
2'-¾"
Panel H

Garage Wall Framing

The basic wall framing outlined on the following pages can be used for whatever roof system you choose. It is recommended you work from a professionally drawn set of plans, like the garage plans that are available on pages 47-141. Review the blueprints to determine the materials you will need and to make any special alterations to the basic framing, such as rough opening dimensions for doors and windows. You should also determine if the siding you plan to install will require three studs at the corners for nailing and if sheathing is necessary.

Wall framing includes a bottom or sole plate, evenly spaced wall studs, and a top plate. A tie plate is added to the top plate once the walls are raised. Extra studding and headers are needed at door and window openings.

In most cases, walls are built of 2x4 studs and plates with studs spaced on 16" centers. Also, 2x6 studs can be used with a stud spacing of 24". Bottom plates should be treated lumber to resist rot.

Some vehicles require 8' high garage doors versus a standard 7' high door. You should consider what types of vehicles will use your new garage. If 8' doors are required, you will need to substitute 9' studs instead of 8' studs.

Set Bottom Plate

The bottom plate rests on the foundation walls, flush with the outside edge of each wall. Snap chalk lines to set the plate's inner edge and check for squareness by measuring the diagonals. If anchor bolts were used, position the bottom plates against the anchor bolts and mark off the hole locations. When using standard 1/2" diameter anchor bolts, drill 3/4" holes at these locations. Temporarily install bottom plates over the anchor bolts to check positioning.

Figure 17 - Setting Bottom Plates

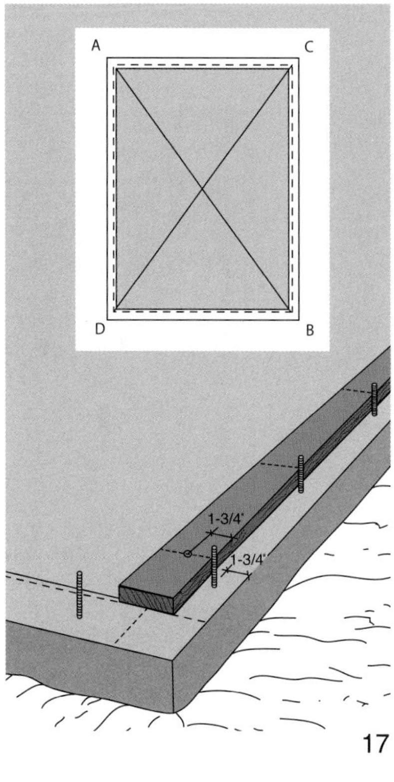

A
C
D
B
1-3/4"
1-3/4"

Constructing the Basic Wall Frame

To begin, cut both the top and bottom plates to length. In most cases, you will need more than one piece of lumber for each plate. So locate the joints at stud centers and offset joints between top and bottom plates by at least 4'.

Lay the top plate against the bottom plate on the slab as illustrated below. Beginning at one end, measure in 15-1/4" and draw a line across both plates. Measure out farther along the plates an additional distance of 1-1/2" from this line, and draw a second line. The first interior stud will be placed between these lines.

From these lines, advance 16" at a time, drawing new lines, until you reach the far end of the plates. Each set of lines will outline the placement of a stud, with all studs evenly spaced at 16" on center. If you are using studs on 24" centers, the first measurement in from the edge would be 23-1/4".

Figure 18A - Measuring Bottom Plates

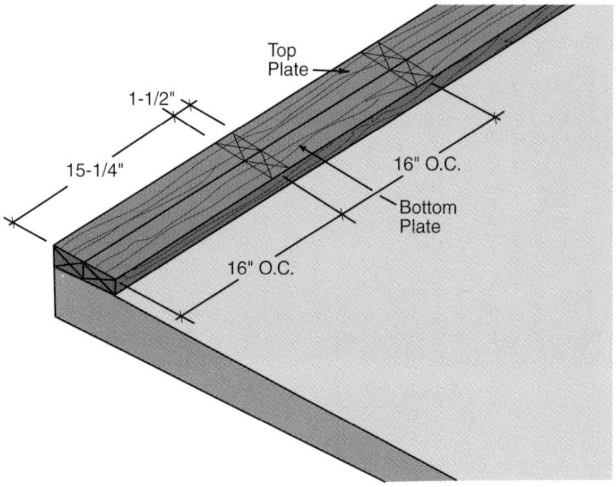

Assembling the Pieces

Unless you are using precut studs, the next step is to measure and cut the wall studs to exact length. Position the plates apart on the slab and turn them on edge with stud marking toward the center. Place the studs between the lines and nail them through each plate with two 16d common nails.

Framing Corners

Where walls meet, you might need extra studs to handle the corner tie to the adjacent wall. These extra studs should be added to the ends of the longer two of the four walls. The exact positioning of these extra corner studs is shown on pages 19 and 20.

Figure 18B - Assembling the Walls

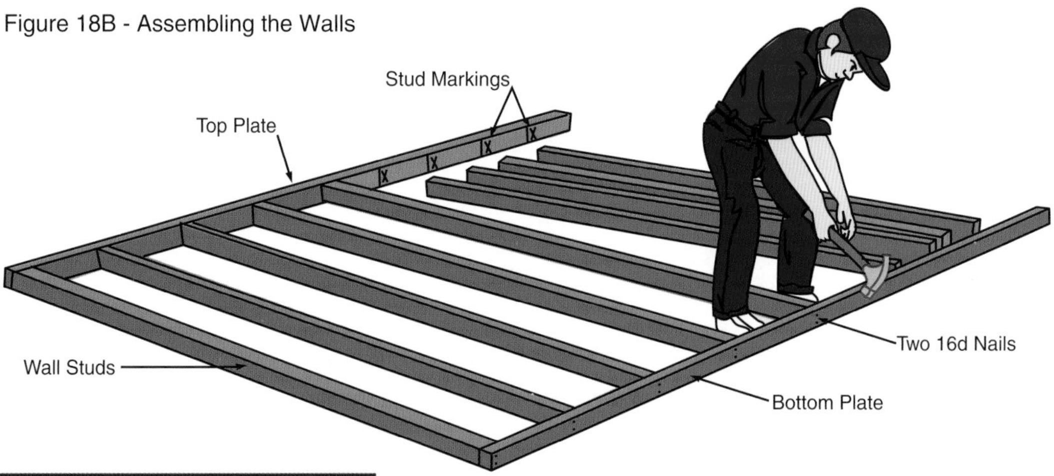

Door and Window Framing

At door and window openings there is no stud support, so a header is required. Door and window headers can be constructed either from 4x dimensional lumber, veneer laminate lumber also known as engineered lumber, or two lengths of 2x material on edge with a 1/2" piece of plywood sandwiched between them. When you are constructing a built-up header from doubled-up 2x material, the plywood makes the header the same 3-1/2" width as the studs.

Headers are always installed on edge as shown in Figure 18C. Consult the chart to the right to determine the header size required for a given span.

Header Size (4x or built-up 2x)	Maximum Span (feet)
4 x 4	4
4 x 6	6
4 x 8	8
4 x 10	10
4 x 12	12

The spaces above door openings and above and below windows are framed with cripple studs spaced 16" on center. Study the illustrations in Figure 19A to become familiar with the king and trimmer stud locations used in framing doors and windows.

The rough framed door should be 1-1/2" higher than the usual 80" actual door height and 2-1/2" wider than the door to account for door jamb material. When the 1-1/2" bottom plate is cut from the opening, this adds the needed 1-1/2" in extra height.

In addition to cripple studs, king studs, and trimmer studs, window framing also uses a rough sill to support the window. Headers should be set at the same time as the door headers. Two cripple studs may be required on each side for openings greater than 8'-0". Consult the manufacturer's instructions for a suggested roughout opening to accommodate a given window.

Header Assembly

Nail two pieces of 2xs and plywood to the length between king studs with 16d nails spaced 16" apart along both top and bottom edges as shown in Figure 18C.

Figure 18C - Header Assembly

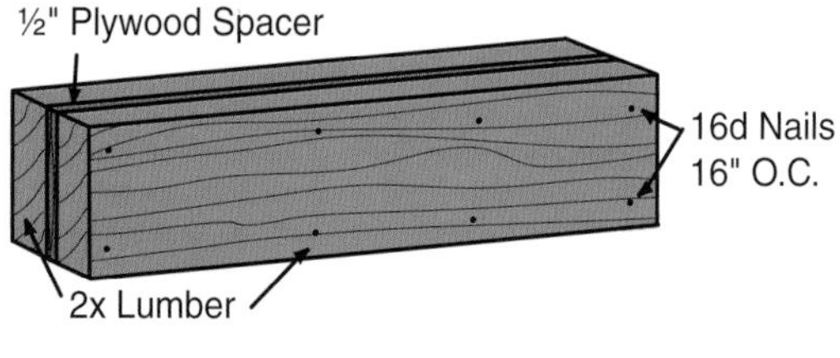

Door and Window Framing (continued)

Figure 19A - Framing Illustrations

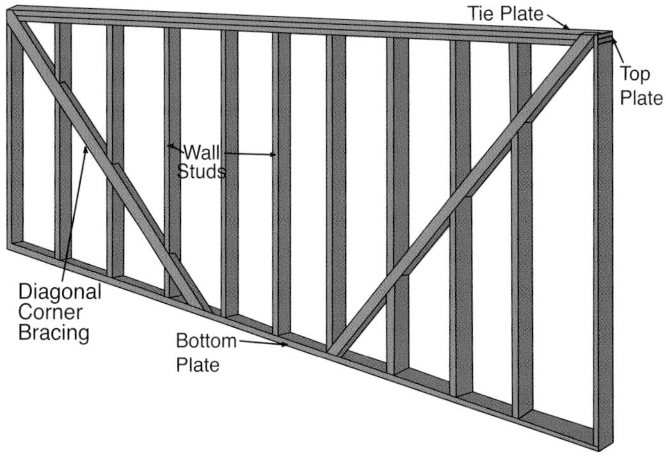

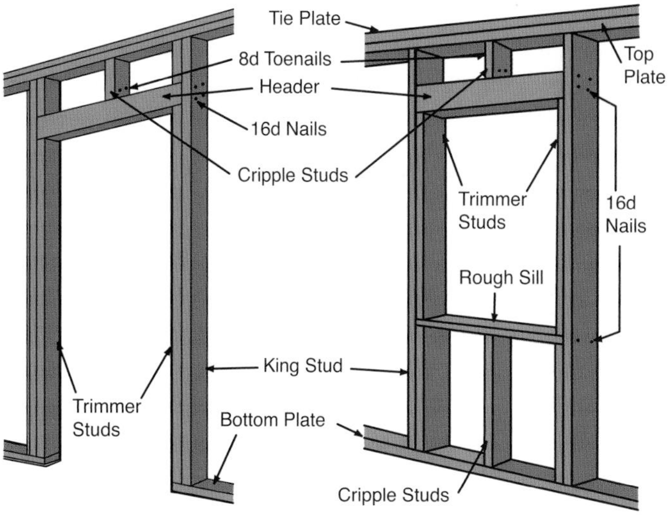

Diagonal Bracing

Structures with plywood siding normally do not require bracing, but all others do. The three most commonly used types of bracing are wooden "let-in" bracing made of 1x4 stock, metal strap bracing, and plywood sheathing at corners.

Let-In Bracing

This type of wooden bracing runs from the top outside corners of the wall to the bottom center of the wall. It forms a V-shaped configuration as shown on Figure 19A. These braces are set into notched studs and are prepared while the wall frame is still lying on the slab.

Lay the 1x4 on the frame with one end at a top corner and the other end as far out on the bottom plate as possible without running into any door or window opening. Mark the underside of the brace where it overhangs the top and bottom plates to determine the angle at which the plates cross. Also mark both sides of the studs and plates at each point the brace crosses them. Notch the studs at these locations by making repeated cuts with your circular saw. Use a hammer and wood chisel to knock out any stubborn chips. Trim the ends of the 1x4 and put the brace in place. Hold it in place with a single nail until the wall is raised and plumbed. Then nail the brace with 8d nails wherever it crosses a plate or stud.

Metal Strap Bracing

Commonly available in 10' to 12' lengths, this type of bracing is nailed to the outside of the studded walls after they are raised, square, and plumb. Metal bracing is thin enough not to obstruct the exterior wall sheathing. The straps have predrilled holes every 2" sized to accept an 8d nail. Strap bracing must always be installed in crossed pairs, similar to a large X design (see Figure 19C).

Plywood Corner Bracing

If wall sheathing is used, you may substitute 48" wide structural plywood sheathing at corners for wood let-ins or metal bracing. See nailing schedule on page 20 for proper nailing conditions when using wood sheathing.

Figure 19C - Alternate Metal Strap

Figure 19B - Steps for Wood Bracing

Step 1. Mark bracing locations.

Step 2. Notch out studs.

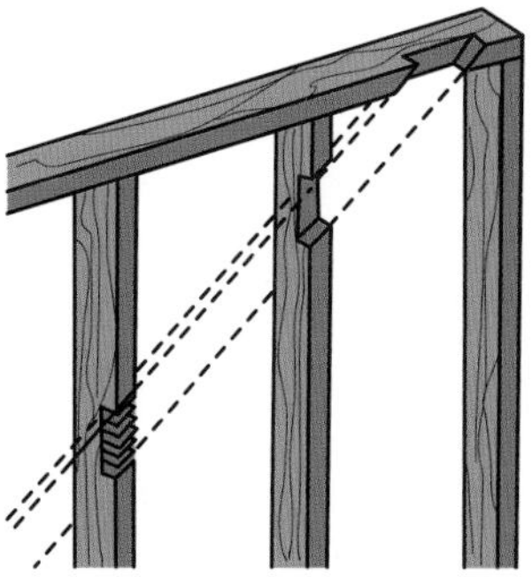

Step 3. Nail bracing into stud locations.

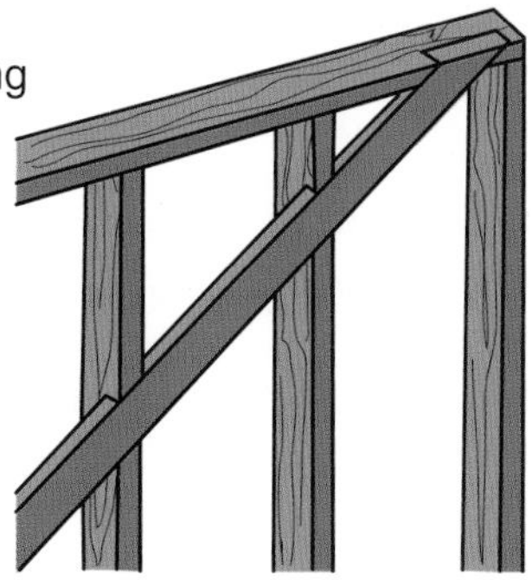

Raising the Walls

Most walls can be raised by hand if enough help is available on the job site. It is advisable to have one person for every 10' of wall for the lifting operation.

The order in which walls are framed and raised can vary from job to job, but in general, the longer exterior walls are framed first. The shorter exterior walls are then raised and the corners are nailed together.

Once the first wall is framed out, there are only a few short steps until it is up and standing. If you are raising a wall on a slab, slide the wall along the slab until the bottom plate lies near the anchor bolt at the floor's edge. If you are raising a wall on a wood floor, you might want to tack some scrap lumber along the floor rim joists to prevent the wall from slipping over the edge. To raise the wall, have your workers grip it at the top plate in unison and work their hands beneath the plate. Now everyone walks down the wall until it is in the upright position. On a slab you need to slip the bottom plate in place over the anchor bolts as you tilt the wall up.

To brace the wall, tack 2x4 braces to the wall studs, one at each end and one in the middle if the wall is particularly long. Tie these braces into stakes driven firmly into the ground or tack them to the wood floor rim joists if appropriate. Secure the wall by using washers and nuts if you have anchor bolts, or tack the bottom plate to the wood floor. Do not securely nail the bottom plate to the floor until you are certain that the walls are in proper alignment.

To check alignment, use a carpenter's level to check the wall for plumb along both end studs on adjacent faces. If the wall is out of plumb, loosen that brace, align the wall, and secure the brace again. If an end stud is warped, bridge the warp with a straight board. When both ends are plumb, adjust the middle.

Figure 20 - To raise the wall, have your workers grip it at the top plate in unison and work their hands beneath the plate. Now everyone walks down the wall until it is in the upright position. To check alignment, use a carpenter's level.

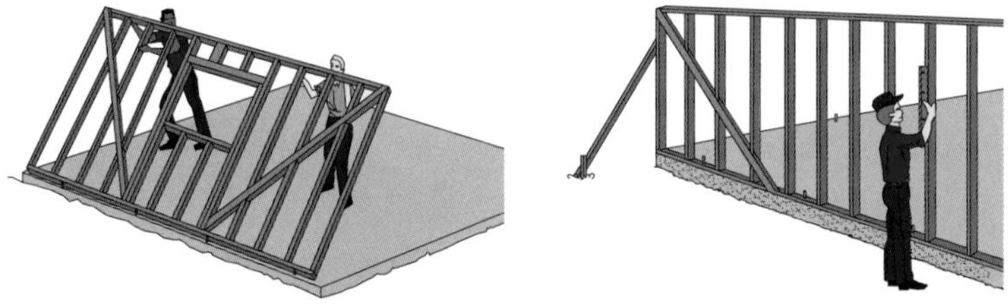

Nailing Schedule for Structural Members

Description of Building Materials	Number & Type of Fastener	Spacing of Fasteners
Top or sole plate to stud, end nail	2-16d	-
Stud to sole plate, toenail	4-8d or 3-16d	-
Doubled studs, face nail	16d	24" O.C.
Doubled top plates, face nail	16d	16" O.C.
Top plates, taps and intersections face nail	2-16d	-
Continued header, two pieces	16d	16" O.C. along each edge
Ceiling joists to plate, toenail	2-16d	-
Continuous header to stud, toenail	4-8d	-
Ceiling joist, taps over partitions, face nail	3-16d	-
Ceiling joist to parallel rafters, face nail	3-16d	-
Rafter to plate, toe nail	2-16d	-
1" brace to each stud and plate, face nail	2-8d	-
Built-up corner studs	16d	30" O.C.
Built-up girder and beams	16d	32" O.C. at top & bottom & staggered 2-20d at ends & at each splice
Roof rafters to ridge, valley or hip rafters, toenail	4-16d	-
Face nail	3-16d	-
Collar ties to rafters, face nail	3-8d	-

Description of Building Materials	Description of Fasteners	Spacing of Fasteners
Roof and wall sheathing to frame		
1/2 inch to 5/16 inch roof & wall sheathing to frame	6d	6" edges 12" intermediate supports
Other wall sheathing		
1/2 inch fiberboard sheathing	1 1/2" galvanized roofing nail 6d common nail	3" edges 6" intermediate supports

Leveling and Corner Details

Once raised, the wall should also be checked for levelness. If needed, it can be shimmed level using tapered cedar shingles driven between the foundation and the bottom plate. Once the wall is plumb and level, tighten the anchor nuts to their final tightness, or on wooden floors nail two 16d common nails between each stud. Do not nail the bottom plate in a door opening since this section must be cut out for the door.

At corners, nail through the end walls into the stud using 16d common nails staggered every 12". When the walls are up, you can add the 2x4 tie plates to the top plates on each wall. These tie plates lap over onto adjacent walls to interlock the walls and give added strength to the structure.

Leveling and Corner Details (continued)

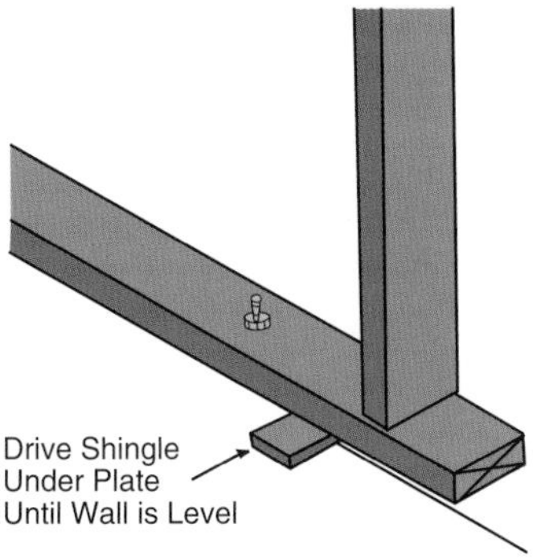
Drive Shingle
Under Plate
Until Wall is Level

Figure 21A - Corner Detail

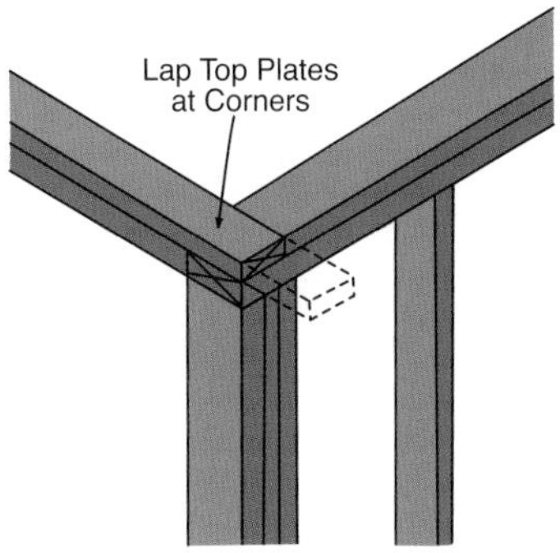
Lap Top Plates
at Corners

Figure 21B - Leveling Wall

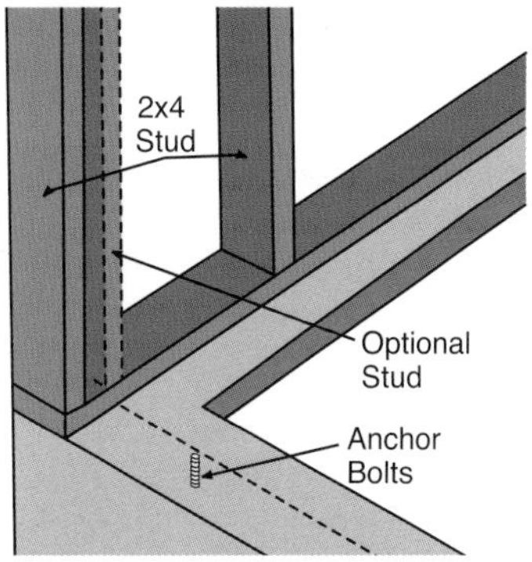
2x4
Stud
Optional
Stud
Anchor
Bolts

Figure 21C - Corner Detail Top Plates

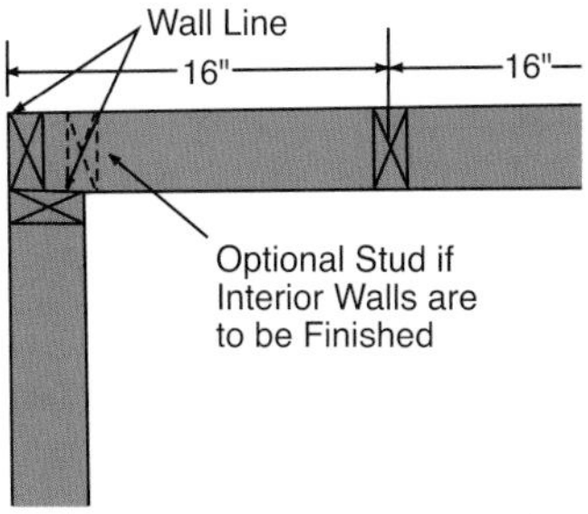
Wall Line
16"
16"
Optional Stud if
Interior Walls are
to be Finished

Figure 21D - Corner Detail

Framing with Metal Fasteners

When undertaking a large-scale construction project, such as the building of your garage, you may find it easier to use a variety of metal fasteners and supports to tie beams together, hang joists, support posts, or tie rafters. These metal fasteners come in different sizes to accommodate all sizes of structural lumber, and most home improvement stores carry a large selection. In some areas, the use of metal fasteners is optional, but in other regions where hurricanes and high wind factors are a problem, special connectors may be required to meet your local building codes. While metal framing connectors will add some additional expense to your project, they will save you time and create a more durable garage.

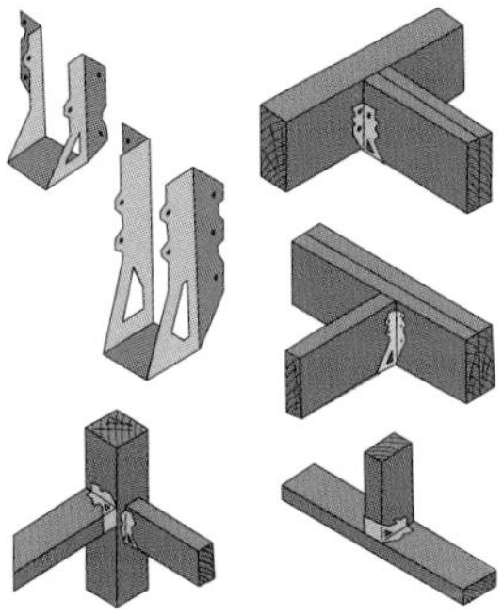

Figure 21E - Joist Hangers

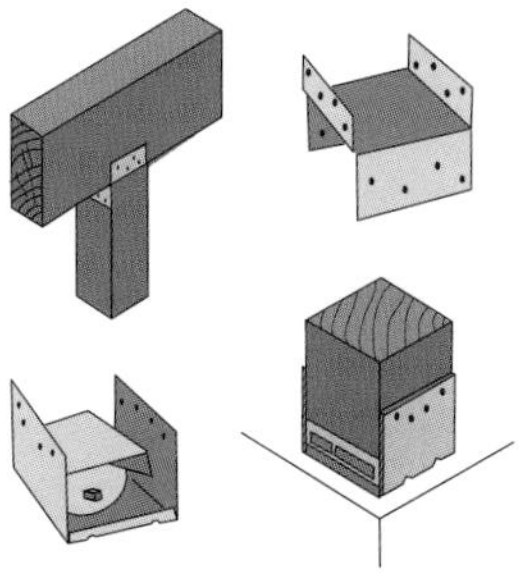

Figure 21F - Post Anchors

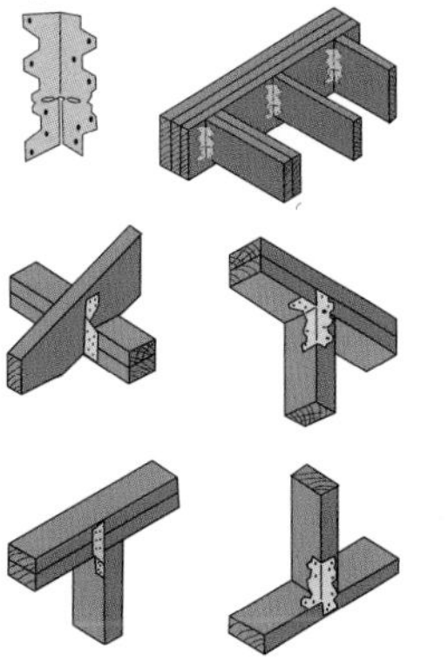

Figure 21G - Framing Anchors

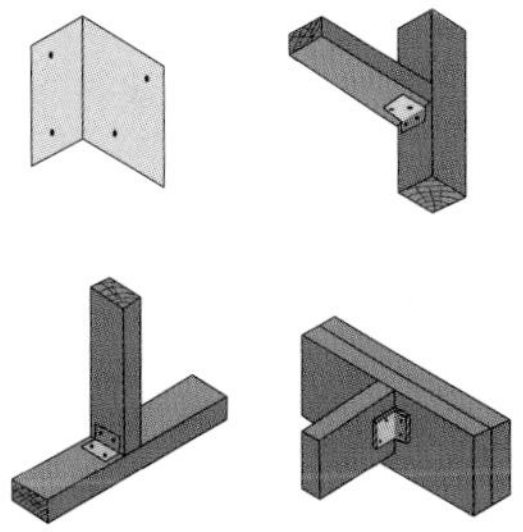

Figure 21H - Framing Angles

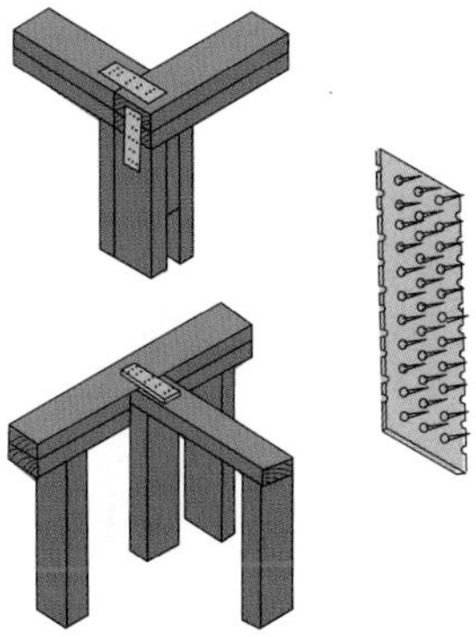

Figure 21I - Nail-On Plates

Roof Framing

There are two major types of roof framing. One type is the use of pre-engineered roof trusses, which is less time consuming than conventional rafters or stick framing. Check with your local lumberyard for availability in your area. Generally rafters are 2x6s or 2x8s, depending on span, spacing, load and roof slope, and are installed on 16-inch or 24-inch centers. Check with your local building office for help with these variables. At the peak, rafter boards butt against a central ridge board. The ridge board is generally made up of 2x lumber and is one size wider than the rafter lumber. For example, use 2x8 ridge board if the rafters are 2x6s, 2x10 ridge board with 2x8s, and so on. Slope, or pitch, is referred to in terms of **unit rise** in **unit run**. **Unit run** is fixed at 12 inches. **Unit rise** is the slope over those 12". A rise of 4" over 12" is a slope of 4" in 12".

Cutting the Rafters

A **common rafter** has three cuts: the **plumb cut** to form the angle where the rafter meets the ridge board, the **bird's mouth notch** to fit the top plate, and the **tail** at the end of the overhang (see Figure 22B). Most professionally designed plans, such as those available in this book, often have a template or diagram for a master or "pattern" rafter (see Figure 23B). Cut two rafters off the master and check them for accuracy before cutting the others. Use a steel carpenter's square to mark the cuts.

Raising the Roof

With the ridge board and rafters cut, you can now raise the roof. You'll need a minimum of three people. Nail an upright 2x4 for each of the end rafters flush against the middle of the end top plate. One person then lines up one end of the rafter with the end of the side top plate and ties it in with three 16d nails. The second raises and holds it at the correct slope against one of the 2x4s, while the third nails the two together. Do the same with the opposite end rafter, then align the ridge board between the top of the rafters and tie it with three 16d nails through each rafter. The ridge board must be level, and the rafter ends must be flush with the sides of the ridge board. Repeat the process at the opposite end for a single-piece ridge board. For a two-piece ridge board, tie the rafters to the last spacing mark at the opposite end.

Figure 22A - Making Rafter Patterns

For those of us not familiar with a square, lay out the initial pair of rafters on the slab. Snap chalk lines to represent the bottom of the rafters and the plate line. Use the rise in 12" to establish the angle (for example, 4" in 12"). If they fit, use them as patterns for all other rafters.

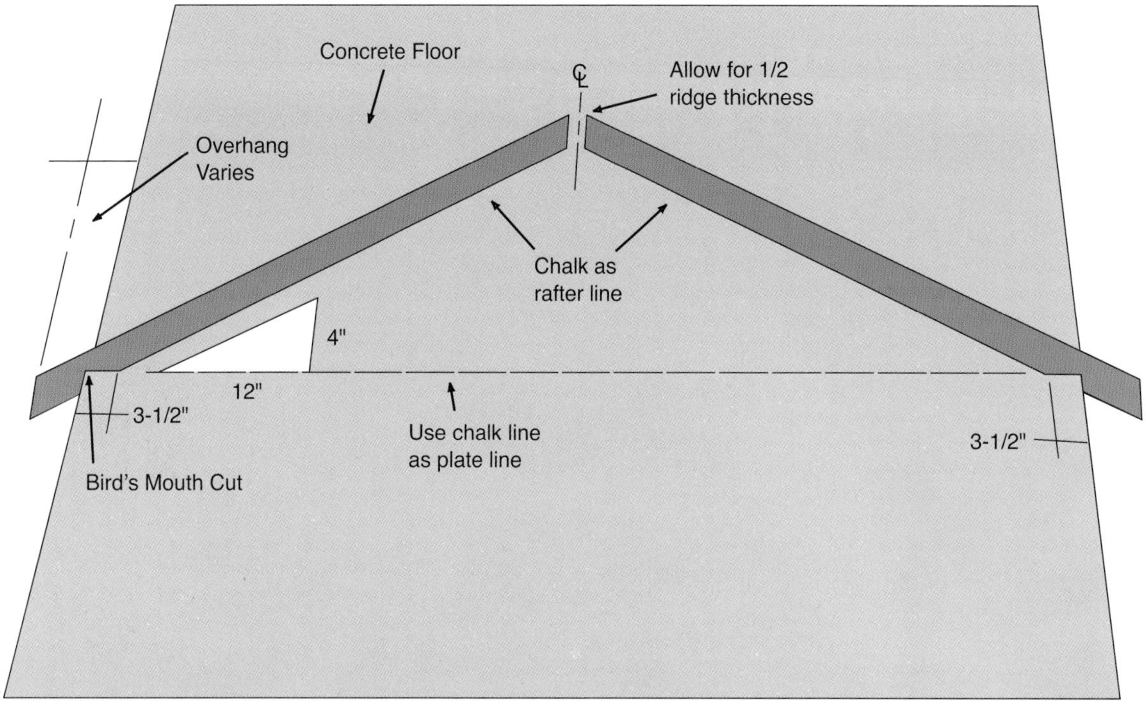

Leveling and Bracing

Make sure the end rafters are plumb, and the ridge board is level and centered mid-span, then attach a diagonal brace between the ridge board and the 2x4 nailed to the top plate. Run the remaining rafters in pairs, attaching them to the ridge board first, then to the top plate. If a second ridge board is used, the process is repeated from the opposite end of the building. The junction of the ridge boards must be covered by two rafters. Use three 16d nails to tie rafters to rafter ties (joists) and cut ties to match the slope of the rafters.

Be sure to add collar ties and hangers before removing any shoring or bracing. Blocks may be needed on the eaves for extended overhangs.

Figure 22B - Rafter Cuts

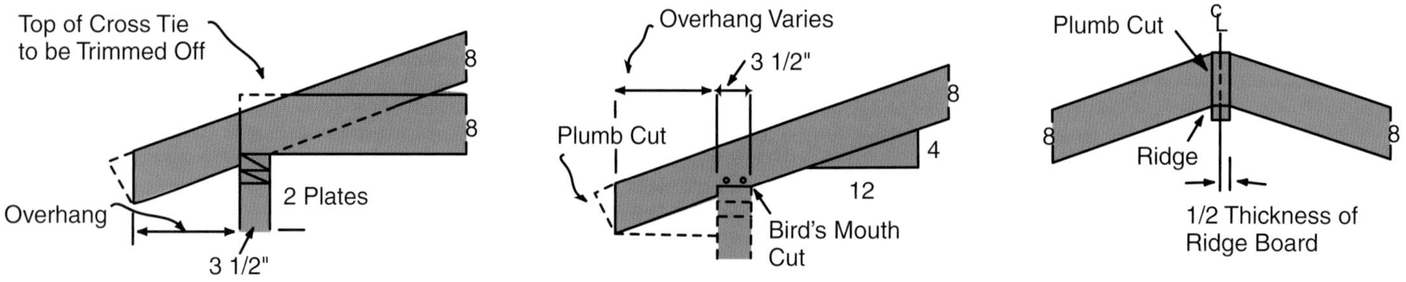

Figure 23A - Rafter Framing

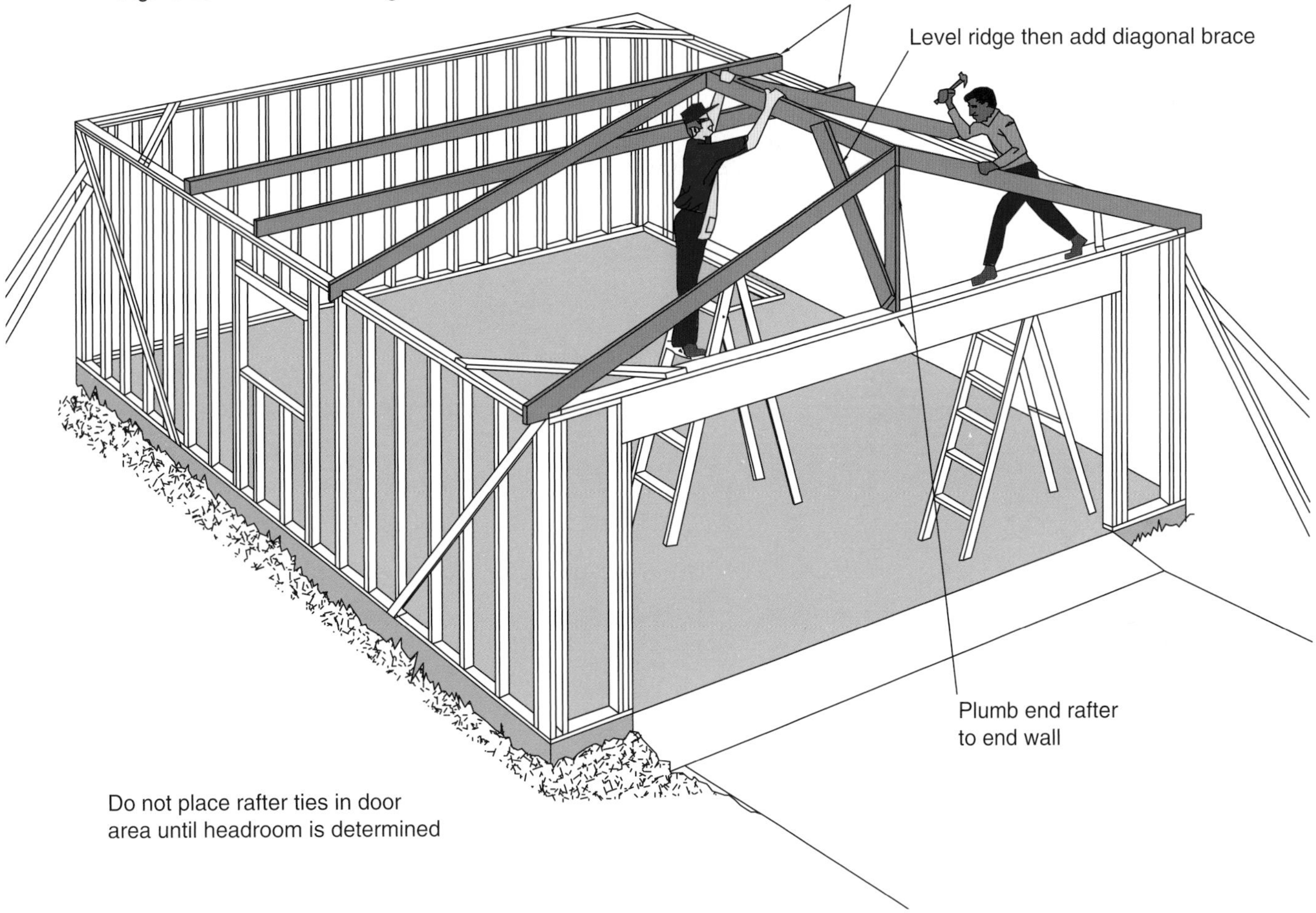
Rafter Ties
Level ridge then add diagonal brace
Plumb end rafter
to end wall
Do not place rafter ties in door
area until headroom is determined

Figure 23B - Typical Rafter Cutting Diagram

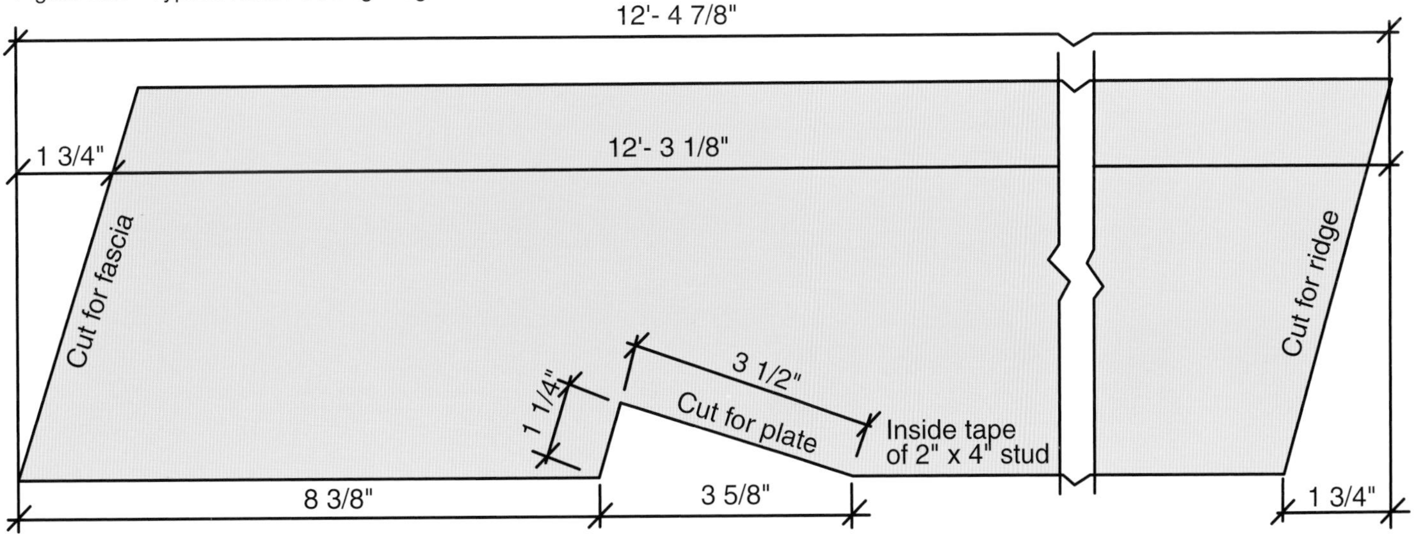
12'- 4 7/8"
1 3/4"
12'- 3 1/8"
Cut for fascia
Cut for ridge
3 1/2"
1 1/4"
Cut for plate
Inside tape
of 2" x 4" stud
8 3/8"
3 5/8"
1 3/4"

Figure 24A - Typical Garage Wall Section

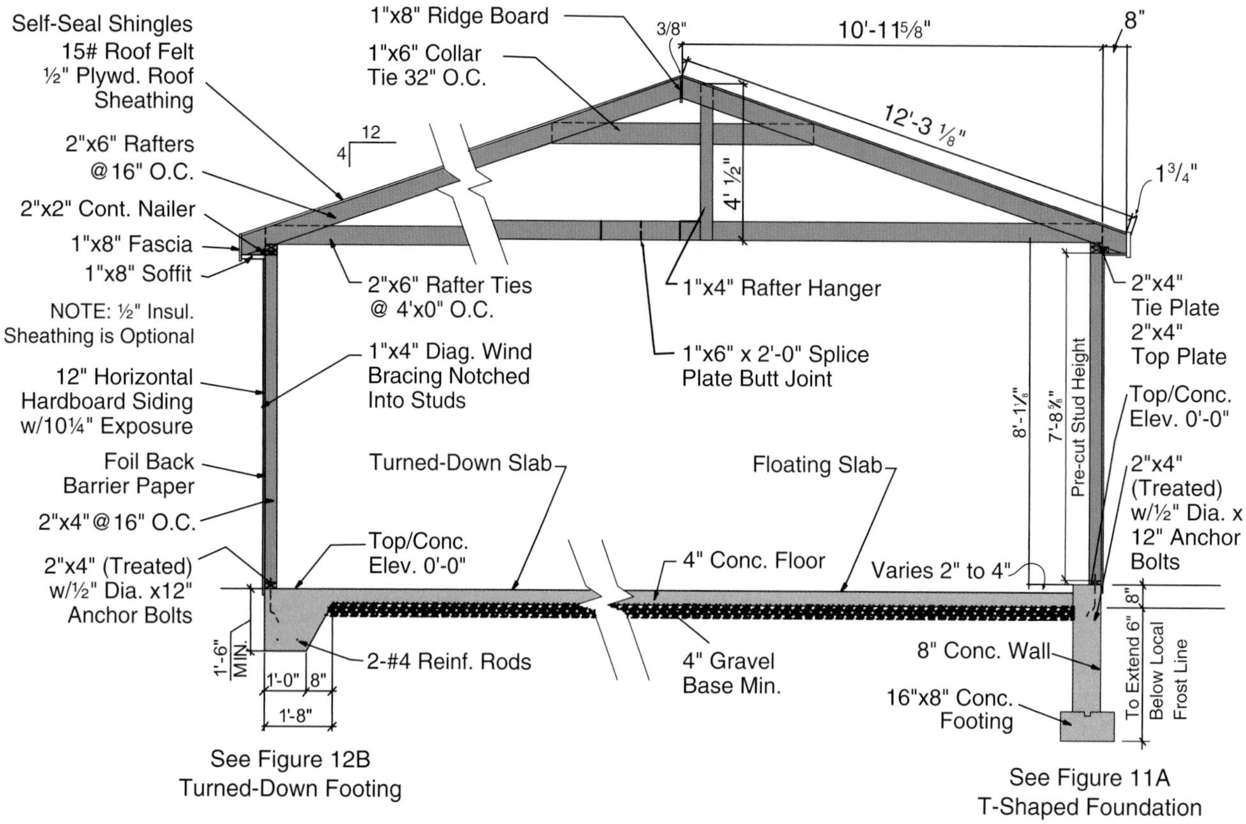
Self-Seal Shingles
15# Roof Felt
½" Plywd. Roof Sheathing
2"x6" Rafters @16" O.C.
2"x2" Cont. Nailer
1"x8" Fascia
1"x8" Soffit
NOTE: ½" Insul. Sheathing is Optional
12" Horizontal Hardboard Siding w/10¼" Exposure
Foil Back Barrier Paper
2"x4"@16" O.C.
2"x4" (Treated) w/½" Dia. x12" Anchor Bolts
1"x8" Ridge Board
1"x6" Collar Tie 32" O.C.
12
4
2"x6" Rafter Ties @ 4'x0" O.C.
1"x4" Diag. Wind Bracing Notched Into Studs
Turned-Down Slab
Top/Conc. Elev. 0'-0"
2-#4 Reinf. Rods
1'-6" MIN.
1'-0"
8"
1'-8"
See Figure 12B Turned-Down Footing
3/8"
10'-11⅝"
8"
12'-3 ⅛"
1¾"
4' ½"
1"x4" Rafter Hanger
1"x6" x 2'-0" Splice Plate Butt Joint
Floating Slab
4" Conc. Floor
4" Gravel Base Min.
Varies 2" to 4"
8'-1⅛"
7'-8⅝"
Pre-cut Stud Height
2"x4" Tie Plate
2"x4" Top Plate
Top/Conc. Elev. 0'-0"
2"x4" (Treated) w/½" Dia. x 12" Anchor Bolts
8"
To Extend 6" Below Local Frost Line
8" Conc. Wall
16"x8" Conc. Footing
See Figure 11A T-Shaped Foundation

Figure 31 - Metal Roof Framing Connectors

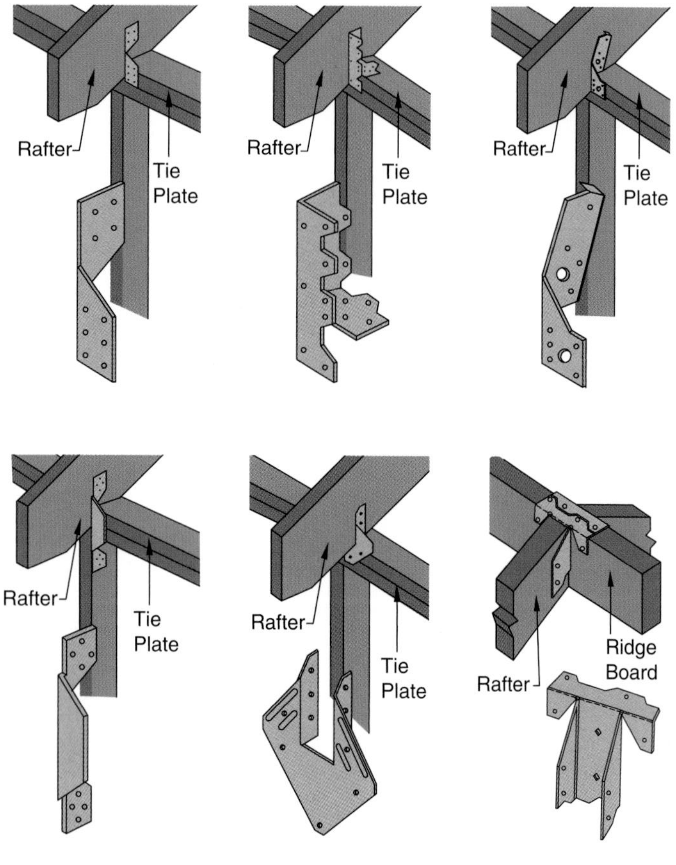
Rafter
Tie Plate
Rafter
Tie Plate
Rafter
Tie Plate
Rafter
Tie Plate
Rafter
Tie Plate
Rafter
Ridge Board

As mentioned earlier, metal fasteners provide the strength nails alone cannot provide. They also avoid the irritation of watching angled nails split the lumber which you have so carefully cut and fitted. Certain metal connectors allow the rafter to rest directly on the tie or top plate and eliminate the difficult and time-consuming bird's mouth cut.

Other connectors are designed to join the rafter to the ridge board without toenailing. As illustrated, many different types of metal connectors are available for roof framing work. While metal roof framing connectors will add some additional expense to your project, they will save you time and create a more durable garage.

Roof Trusses

Pre-engineered trusses are often available from local lumber dealers. They are designed to span the full width of a structure from one exterior wall to the other. This leaves a large room free of supports. The use of preassembled trusses speeds the erection of the roof. Be certain to obtain your trusses from a reliable source who will custom design and build them to your needs. Refer to truss manufacturer's installation and bracing requirements prior to erecting trusses.

Erecting Trusses

It is advisable to have at least two other persons assisting you when erecting roof trusses. Have all walls securely braced.

Here are the steps:

1. With one person at each side wall of the structure and one at the center, place the trusses onto the top plate of the outside walls, upside down, Figure 25A.
2. Move the first gable end truss into position at the end of the building and swing it up into position with the man in the center working from the ground with a pole to push the center up, Figure 25B.
3. Center truss between side walls. Plumb truss and temporarily toenail in place. Brace gable truss down to ground stake to keep it plumb.
4. Repeat Step 3 at opposite gable end.
5. Place nails at peak of each gable truss. Run a string line from one end to the other and draw tight.
6. Tilt up one truss at a time. Be sure that the peak is exactly under string line. Space trusses 24" apart measured from center to center. Laterally brace all trusses to keep them from tipping over. A 2x nailed to the top of each truss after it is plumb will keep them in line until the roof sheathing is applied, Figure 25C.
7. Remove temporary bracing from the top of the trusses only after roof sheathing has been applied. Note: Refer to truss manufacturing specifications for truss bracing.
8. Fasten each truss to the top plate using metal framing anchors, use one at each end of the truss. (See page 24).
9. Often construction blueprints call for a different size rafter than the top chord of trusses. If this is so, adjust the trim boards to accommodate the variance.

Roof Sheathing

Using 4'x8' plywood panels covers large roof areas quickly, although 1x8s laid up tightly can also be used. The required thickness of the sheathing will vary with rafter spacing and local building code requirements. Generally, the wider the rafters are spaced, the thicker the sheathing needs to be.

Stagger the sheathing, starting at the bottom, so that the end joints of adjacent sheets fall on different rafters. It is advisable to use plywood clips to help secure plywood together. Space 8d nails 6" apart at sheet ends, and 12" on center at intermediate rafters. If gable eaves have an overhang, extend the sheathing to cover it.

Figure 25D - Garage Door Opener

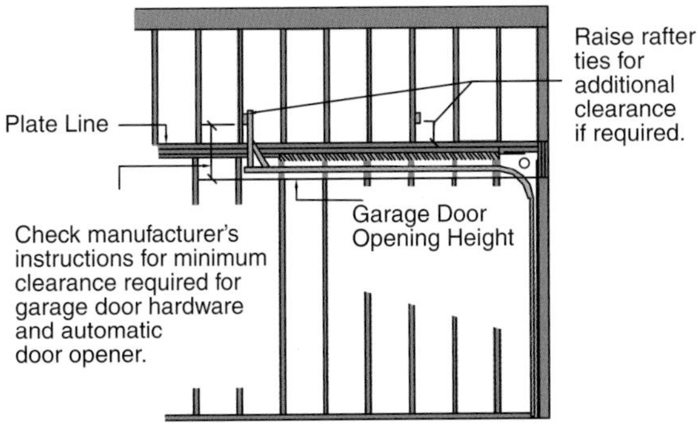

Figure 25A

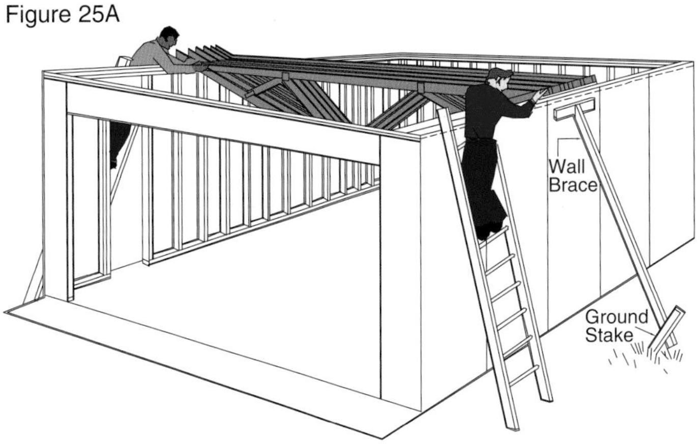

Figure 25B

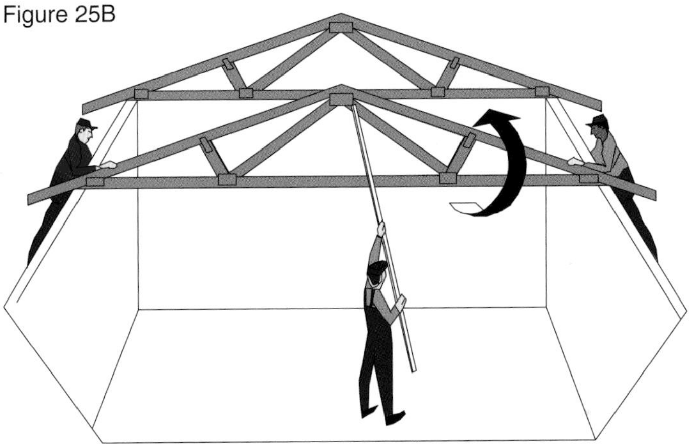

Figure 25C

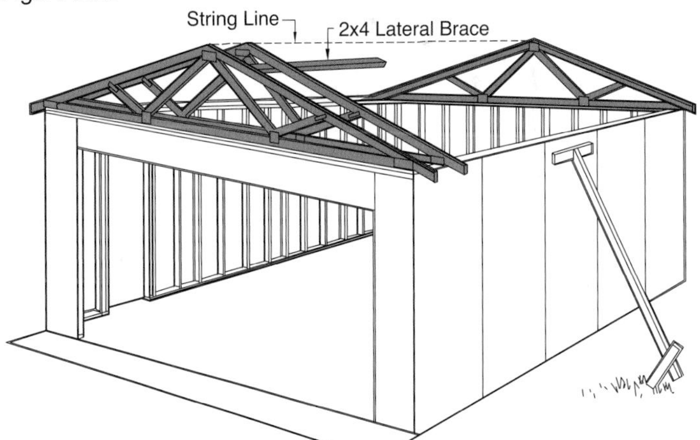

Note: Check garage door hardware and opener instructions before nailing rafter ties in place. Minimum clearance requirements between the top of the door opening and the bottom of the ties might require that the ties be set off of the top plate. See Figure 25D.

Note: Before roof sheathing is in place, determine garage door hardware headroom and then add rafter ties to clear the hardware.

Figure 26A - Roofing Diagram

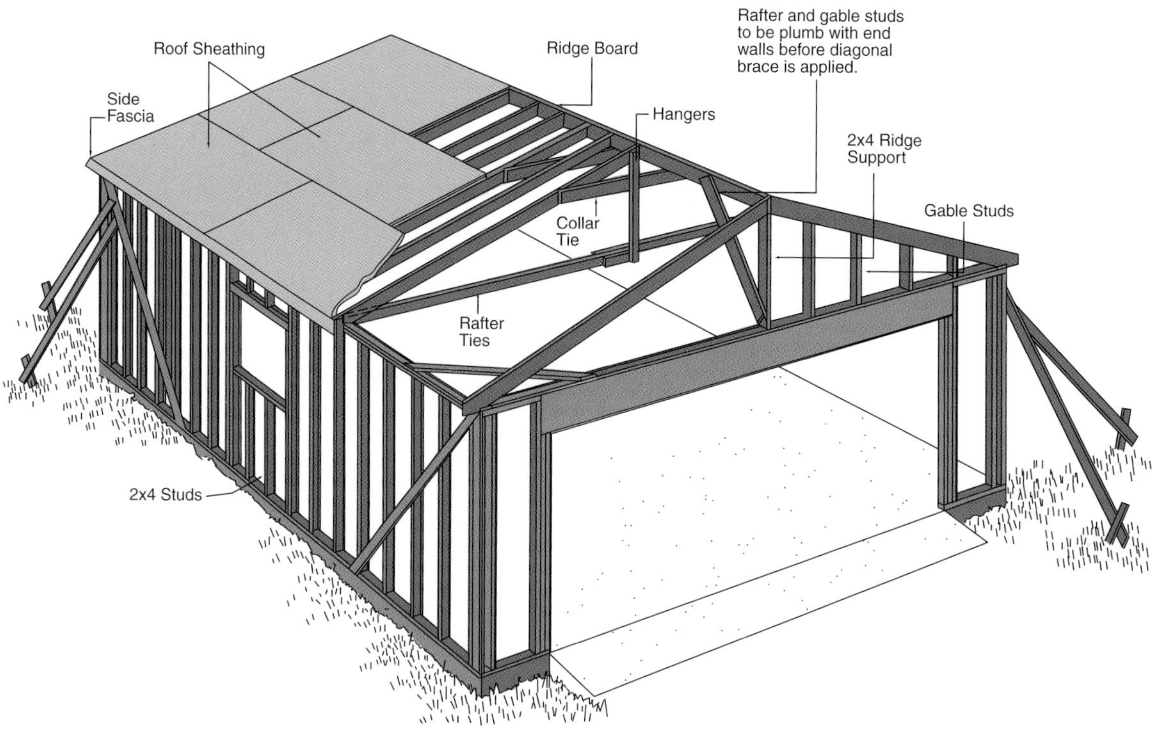

Variations of the Roof Cornice

Whatever type of roof you decide to construct, your building will have a roof overhang to protect the top of the side walls from moisture penetration. This overhang is generally known as the roof cornice. The cornice can also serve to provide ventilation and protection from the hot, overhead rays of the sun on the sidewalls. As a general rule of thumb, warmer climates tend to favor longer overhangs that offer greater shading.

An open cornice is illustrated in Figure 26B. The overhang can extend up to 24" from the edge of the building. You have the option of adding a frieze board to the rafter ends or leaving the rafter ends exposed. Remember that when you create an exposed overhang, the roof sheathing is visible from underneath. Painting or staining the sheathing can improve its appearance.

Figure 26C represents a closed cornice. Make a seat cut on the rafter at the top plate. Cut the rafter ends flush and vertical with the top plate. Bring the siding all the way up to the rafters and finish off the cornice with a trim piece that covers the slightly exposed roof sheathing.

Two variations of the boxed cornice are shown in Figures 27C and 27D. A fascia board at the rafter ends is essential for any style of boxed cornice. Figure 27B demonstrates the sloping soffit design where the rafters are used to directly attach the soffit board. Nail a 1x fascia board to the square cut rafter ends. Another frieze board covers the end portion of the soffit where it meets the wall siding.

Figure 27D portrays the level soffit design that requires 2x4 horizontal lookouts facenailed at the rafter ends and toenailed to wall siding. Level soffits generally extend no more than 12"-15" from the building wall. The lookouts help to frame the soffit construction.

Proper ventilation is essential for the boxed cornice. Install soffit vents (typically 4" x 8") at regular intervals along the soffit between the lookouts. Be sure to install the screened vents or you will have unintentionally created a birdhouse wherever you have an unscreened vent!

Figure 26B - Open Cornice

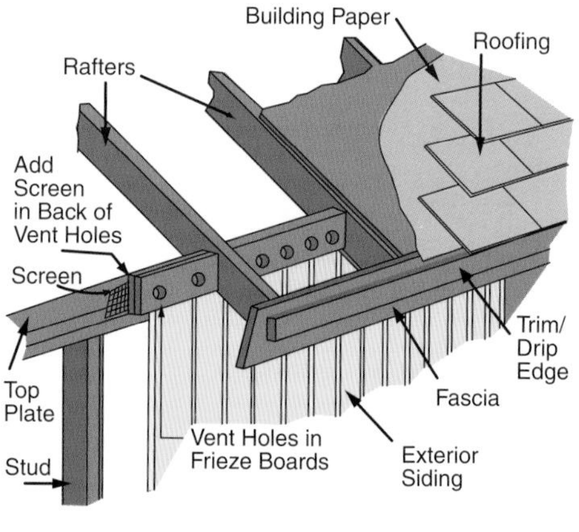

Figure 26C - Closed Cornice

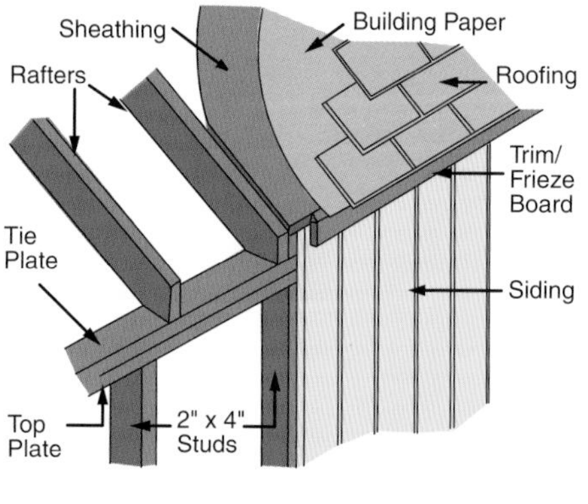

Ventilation

If you plan to use your garage as a work area or local codes require ventilation, consider installing either gable end vents or roof vents. Vents help to reduce interior temperatures during the summer months. Gable end vents should be installed at both gable ends of your roof to promote cross-ventilation.

The number of roof vents you will install depends upon the cubic footage of your building. Simply create a box frame between roof rafters and install the vent according to the manufacturer's instructions. Don't forget to flash and then caulk the vent after you have installed the roof sheathing and shingles.

Hip Roof Framing

Rafter lengths require some paperwork on hip roofs. Layout a plan view of the roof on graph paper as shown in Figure 27E. The larger the scale, the greater the accuracy, so use a minimum 1" to 1' scale.

Calculating Rafter Lengths

To determine rafter lengths, draw horizontal line A–B (Figure 27B). Locate A' by projecting up the scale height of the roof slope. A line between A' and B will give the angle for plumb and tail cuts on common and jack rafters, as well as common rafter length (except for the additional length at top for cutting angle). Lay hip roof out similarly: horizontal line A–C, and A'–C for hip length, allow enough length for angle cut.

For jack rafter lengths, lay out points X, Y, Z, and so on, along A–B and project up to A'–B. In addition to the plumb, tail, and bird's mouth cuts, jack rafters must also be cut to 45 degrees across the narrow width (Figure 27A) to line up with the hip rafter.

Erecting a Hip Roof

To erect the hip roof, begin with the common rafters along the ridge (Figure 29A), or erect four common rafters if the building is square. Nail up rafter ties as well (Figure 29B). Before nailing the rafter ties in position, it is strongly suggested that you check for proper clearance for any planned garage door and garage door opener. Most garage doors require a minimum clearance between the top of the garage door opening and the bottom of the rafter ties. The door and opener manufacturer provides these clearances and you can check them with your building supplier. To gain the clearance required, it might be necessary to set the rafter ties off the top and tie plate. See Figure 25D.

Figure 27A - Jack Rafter Cut

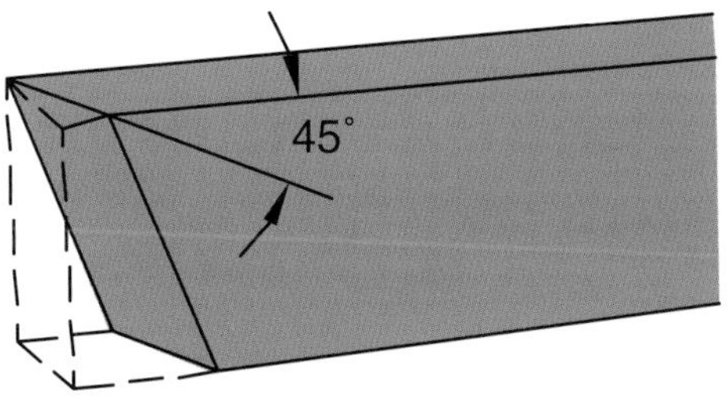

Figure 27B - Determining Rafter Lengths

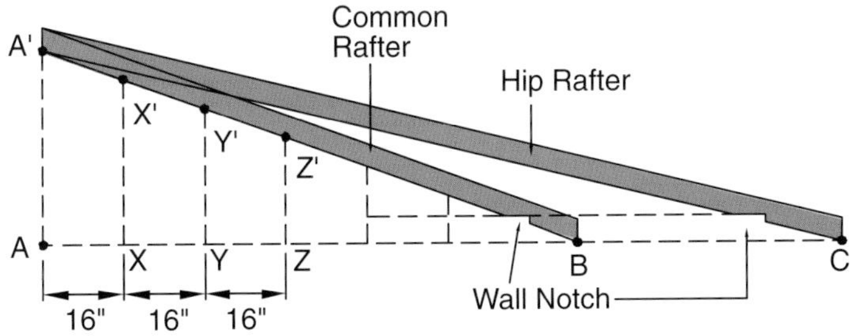

Figure 27C - Boxed Cornice/Sloping Soffit

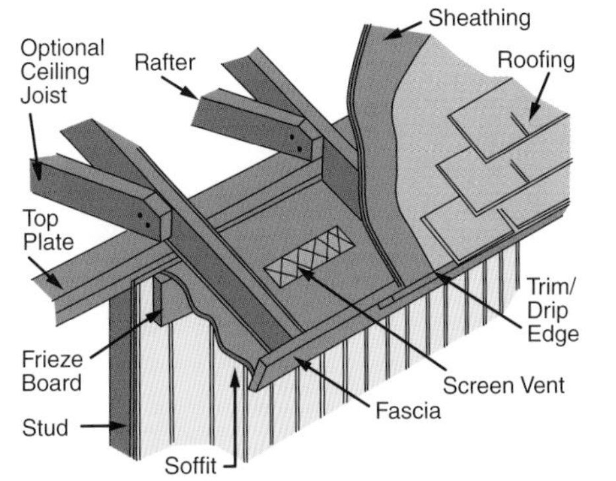

Figure 27D - Boxed Cornice/Level Soffit

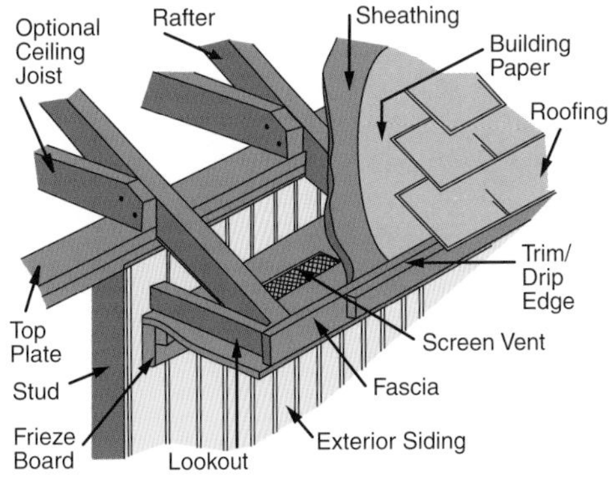

Figure 27E - Hip Roof Layout

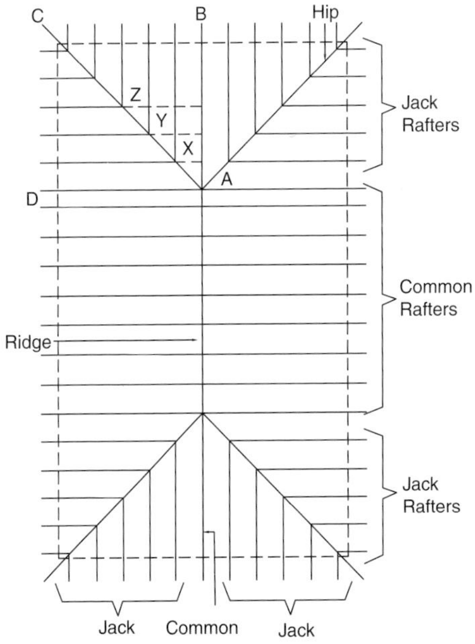

Jack Rafter Schedule

Position	A	A'	B	B'	C	C'	D	D'	E	E'	F	F'	G	G'	H	J
Overall Length = "x"	12'-1"	13'-5⅞'	10'-8⅛"	12'-1"	9'-3¼"	10'-8⅛"	7'-10⅜"	9'-3 ¼"	6'-5 ½"	7'-10⅜"	5'-0⅝"	6'-5 ½"	3'-7 ¾"	5'-0⅝"	2'-2⅞"	4'-6"
No. Required @45° Bevel	3	1	3	1	3	1	3	1	3	1	3	1	3	1	4	1
No. Required @ Reverse 45° B	3	1	3	1	3	1	3	1	3	1	3	1	3	1	4	1

Figure 28A - Rafter Peak Detail

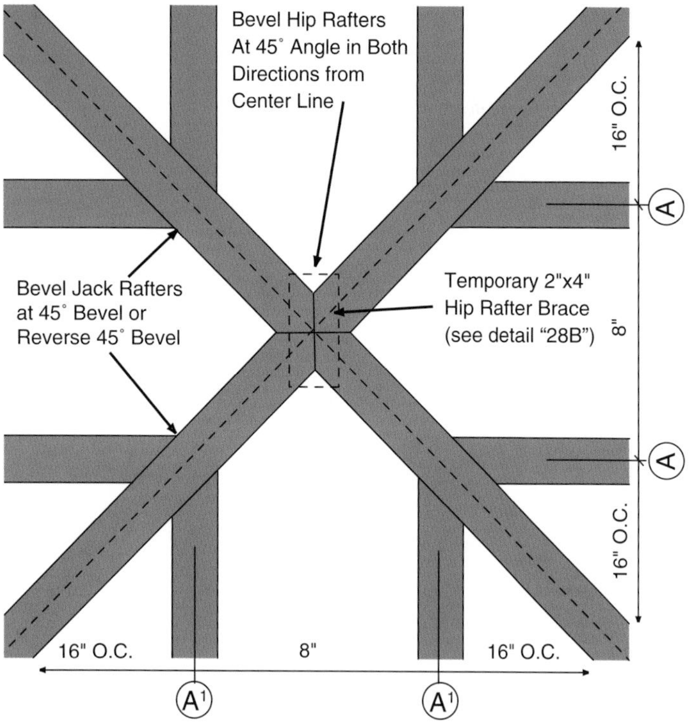
Bevel Hip Rafters
At 45˚ Angle in Both
Directions from
Center Line
Bevel Jack Rafters
at 45˚ Bevel or
Reverse 45˚ Bevel
Temporary 2"x4"
Hip Rafter Brace
(see detail "28B")
16" O.C.
8"
16" O.C.
A
A
16" O.C.
8"
16" O.C.
A1
A1

Nail hip rafters to corners, and use a temporary brace to create a slight crown in them (Figure 29B). Next, nail up jack rafters in opposing pairs connected to rafter ties. Use just one nail in each until all are in place, then adjust them to straighten the hip rafter and nail them in permanently.

Figure 28B - Hip Rafter Bracing Detail

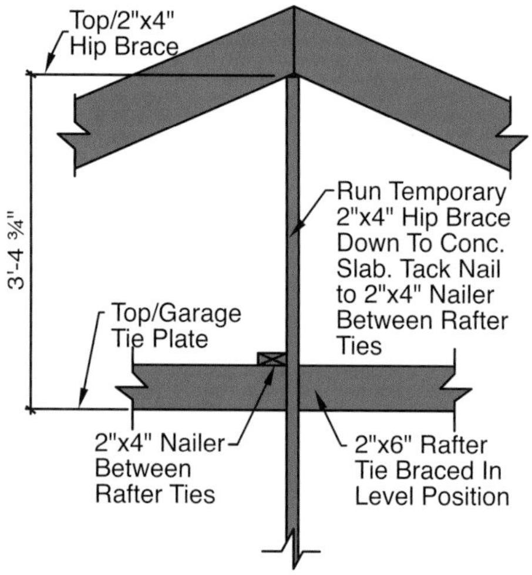
Top/2"x4"
Hip Brace
3'-4 3/4"
Run Temporary
2"x4" Hip Brace
Down To Conc.
Slab. Tack Nail
to 2"x4" Nailer
Between Rafter
Ties
Top/Garage
Tie Plate
2"x4" Nailer
Between
Rafter Ties
2"x6" Rafter
Tie Braced In
Level Position

Figure 28C - Typical Hip Rafter Cutting Templates

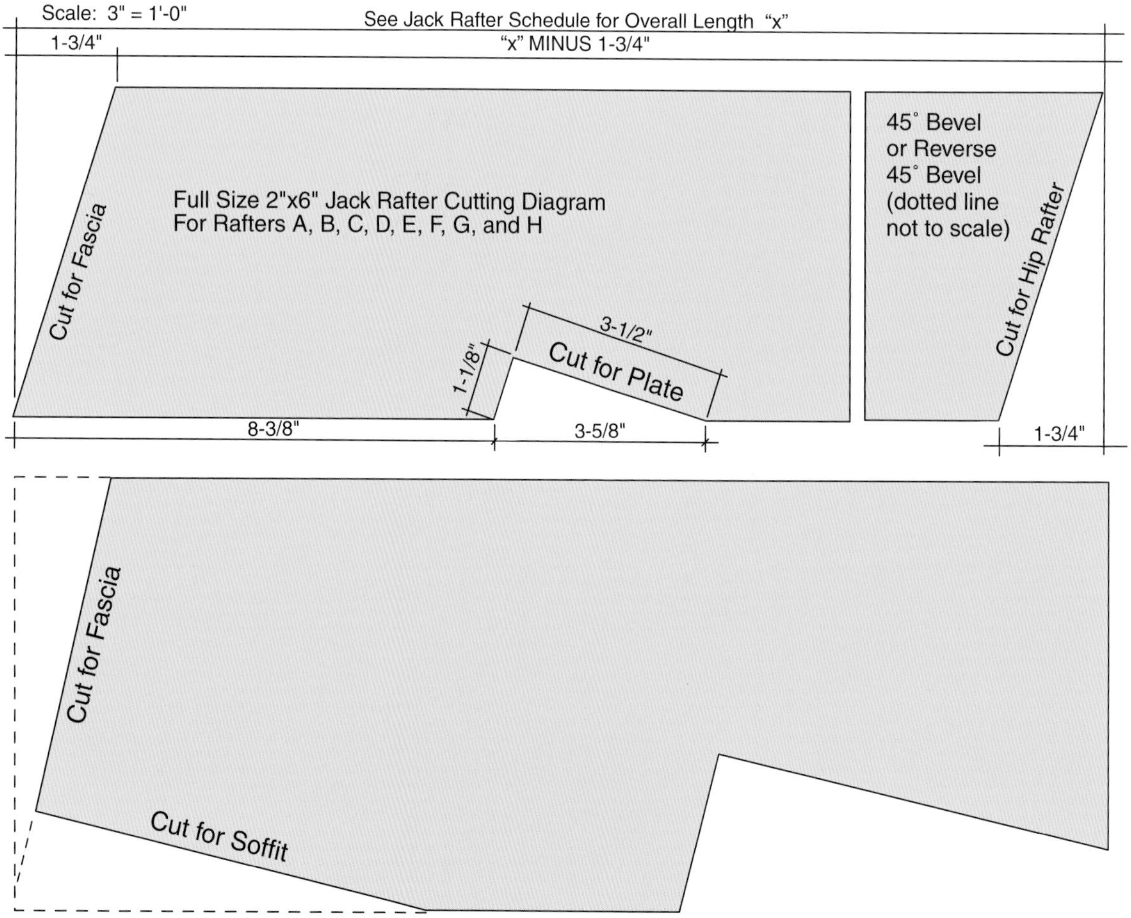
Scale: 3" = 1'-0"
See Jack Rafter Schedule for Overall Length "x"
1-3/4"
"x" MINUS 1-3/4"
Full Size 2"x6" Jack Rafter Cutting Diagram
For Rafters A, B, C, D, E, F, G, and H
Cut for Fascia
45˚ Bevel
or Reverse
45˚ Bevel
(dotted line
not to scale)
Cut for Hip Rafter
3-1/2"
Cut for Plate
1-1/8"
8-3/8"
3-5/8"
1-3/4"
Cut for Fascia
Cut for Soffit

Hip Roof Framing (continued)

Figure 29A - Hip Roof Peak Detail

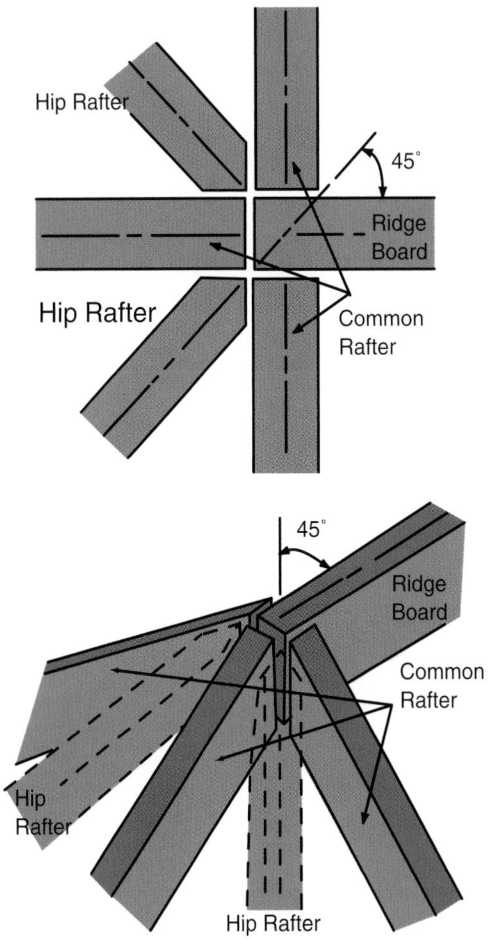

Pre-drawn garage plans are available for hip roof garages in the back of this book. To help make the job easier, most garage plans include hip roof details and rafter cutting templates like Figure 28C.

Figure 29B - Hip Roof Framing

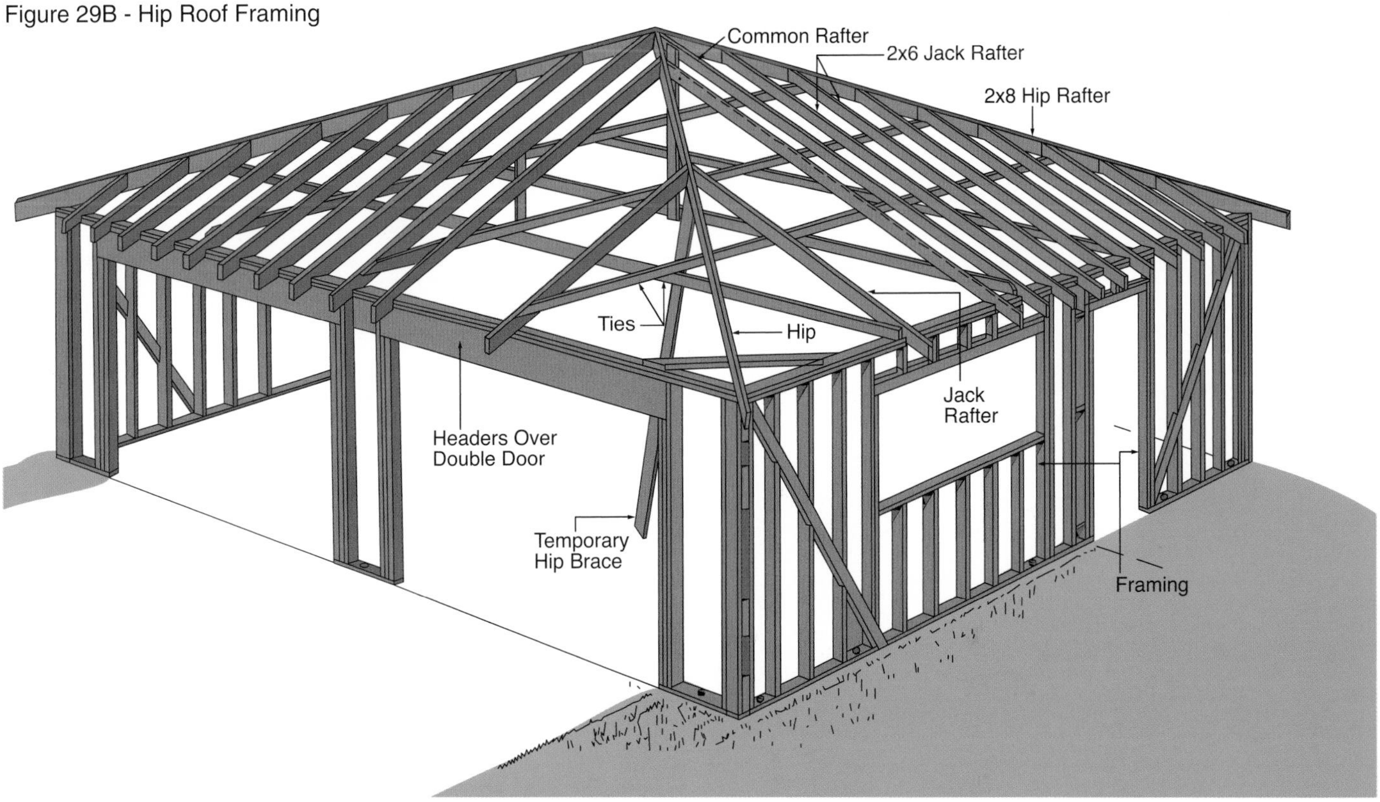

Figure 30B - Rafter Peak Detail

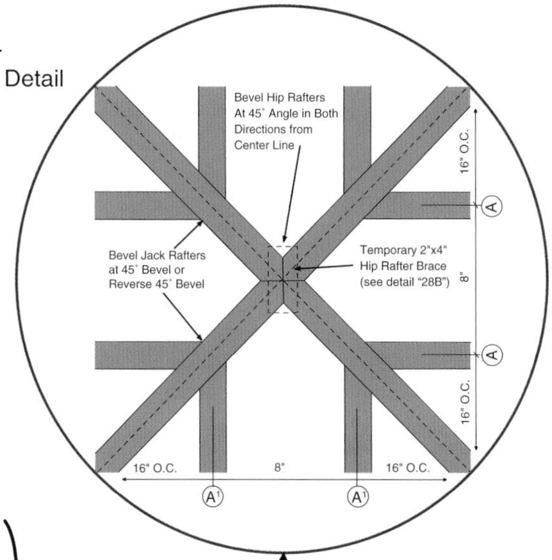
Bevel Hip Rafters At 45˚ Angle in Both Directions from Center Line
Bevel Jack Rafters at 45˚ Bevel or Reverse 45˚ Bevel
Temporary 2"x4" Hip Rafter Brace (see detail "28B")
16" O.C.
8"
16" O.C.
A
A
16" O.C.
8"
16" O.C.
A1
A1

Figure 30A - Hip Roof Details

2"x4" Tie Plate
2"x4" Jack Rafters
@16" O.C. (See schedule on page 27 for length and see figure 28C for full size cutting template.)

2"x8" Hip Rafter
(See figure 38C for full size cutting template.)

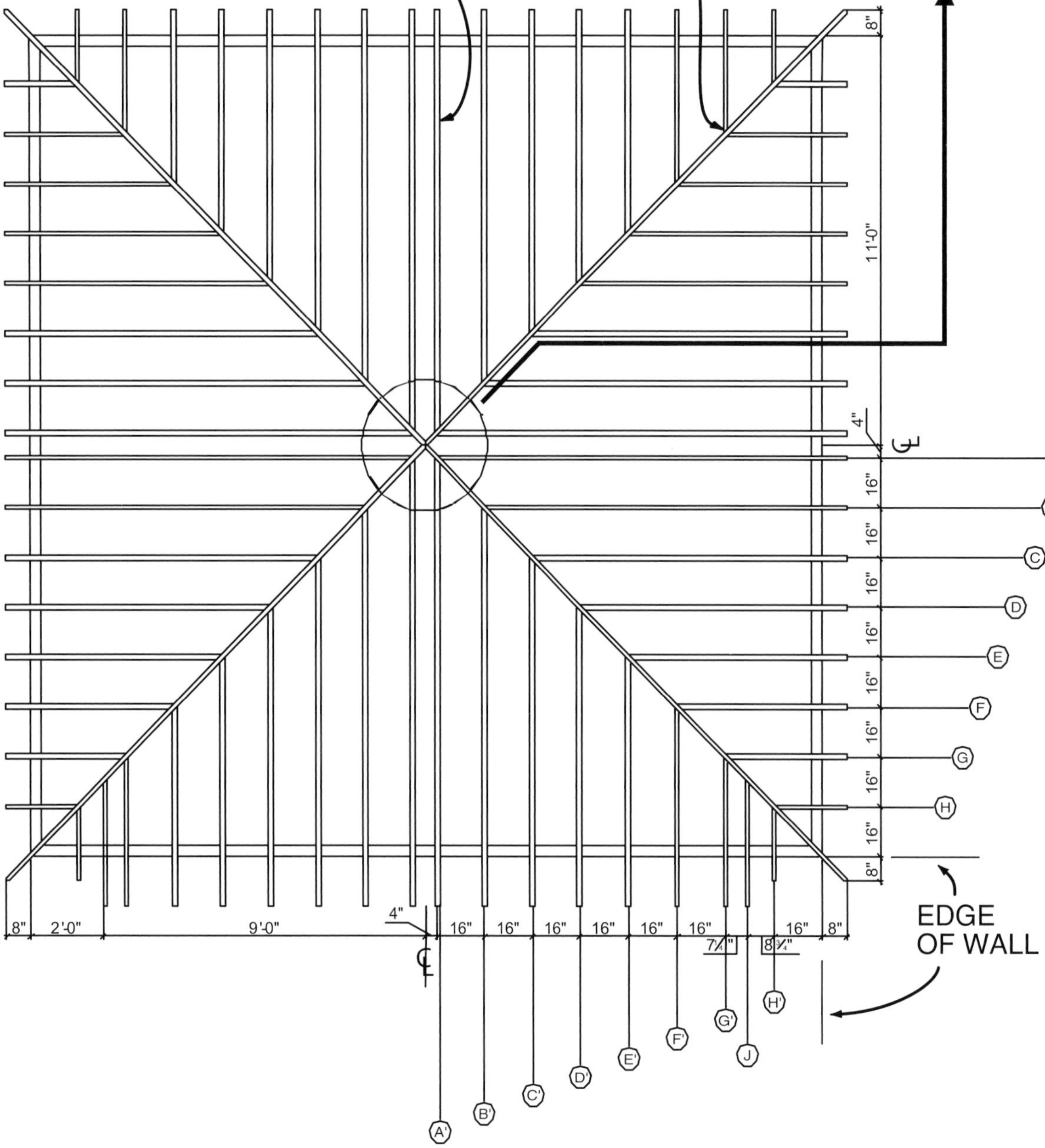
8"
11'-0"
4"
16"
16"
16"
16"
16"
16"
16"
16"
8"
A
B
C
D
E
F
G
H
8"
2'-0"
9'-0"
4"
16"
16"
16"
16"
16"
16"
16"
8"
7¼"
8¼"
A'
B'
C'
D'
E'
F'
G'
H'
J
EDGE OF WALL

Overhang and Trim Details

Before applying trim, know the nailing requirements of the siding you select. Some siding will have trim applied over the siding, but other siding will butt against trim and require extra blocking at the edges. After the roof sheathing is on, but before you install the fascia and rake boards, add soffit nailers if required. Use the longest fascia boards on the longest walls. Join all ends over the center of a rafter or nailer.

Consult Figures 31A to 31F below. At the gable end, extend the fascia (or rake board) along the edge of the roof sheathing and rafter. At the top, cut the end to the angle of the rafter and butt at the center. Be sure to prime coat both ends before butting. At the lower end, let the front rake fascia extend beyond the side fascia, then cut the ends to line up with the side fascia.

Figure 31A - Boxed Cornice Detail

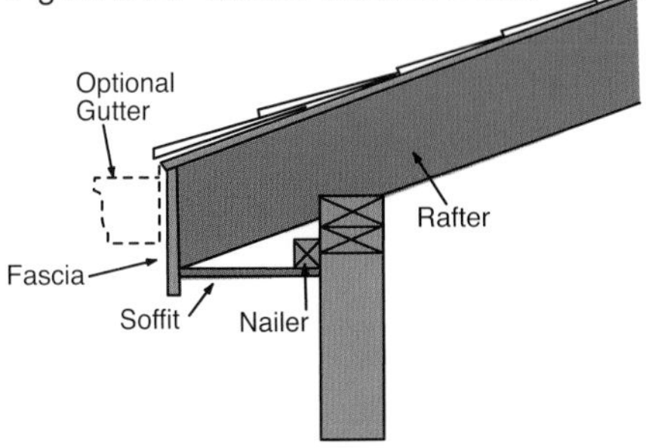

Figure 31B - Closed Cornice Detail

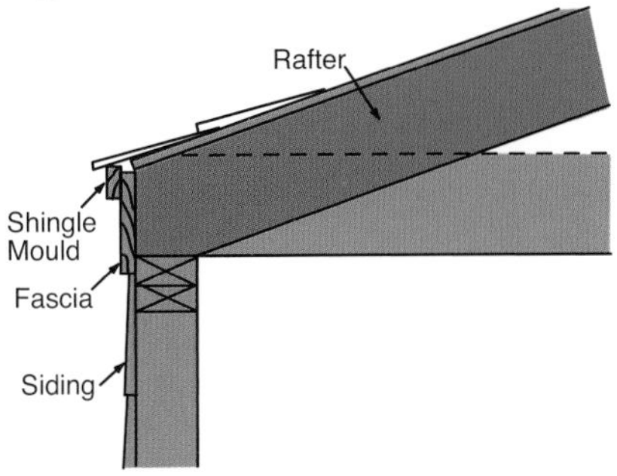

Figure 31C - Gable End Ridge Detail Box Overhang

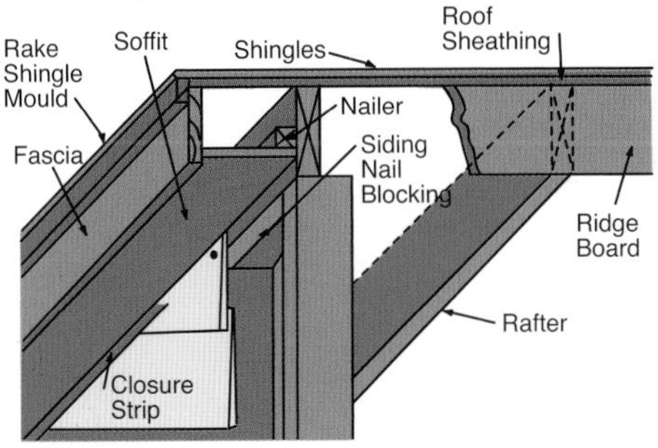

Figure 31G - Corner Tins

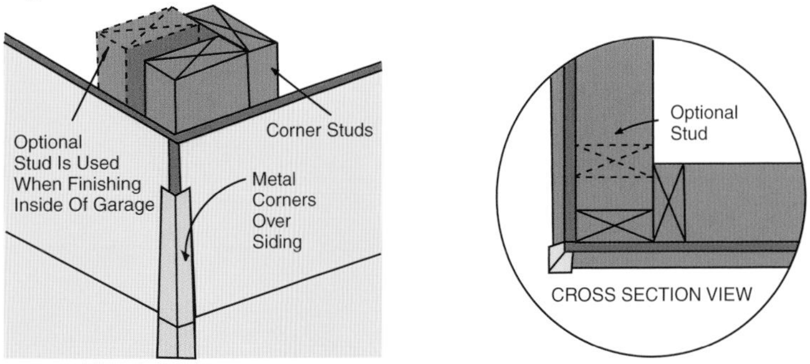

Figure 31H - Corner Boards

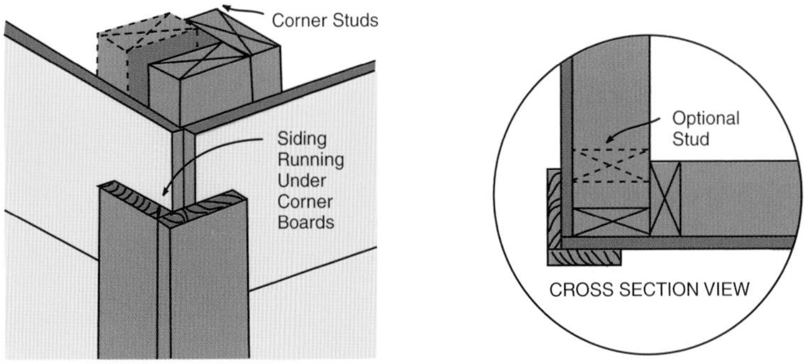

Figure 31I - Inset Corner Boards

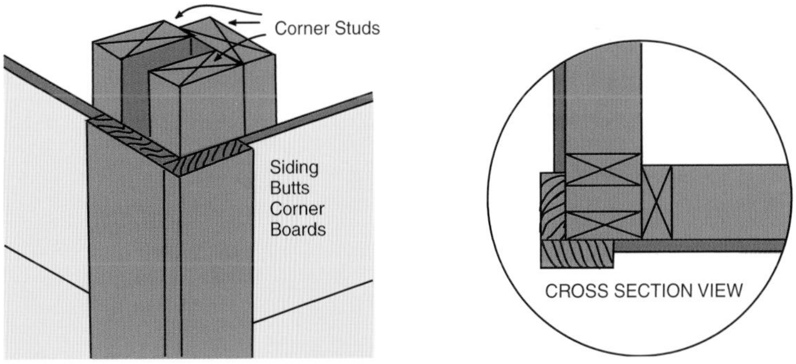

Figure 31D - Eave Detail Box Overhang

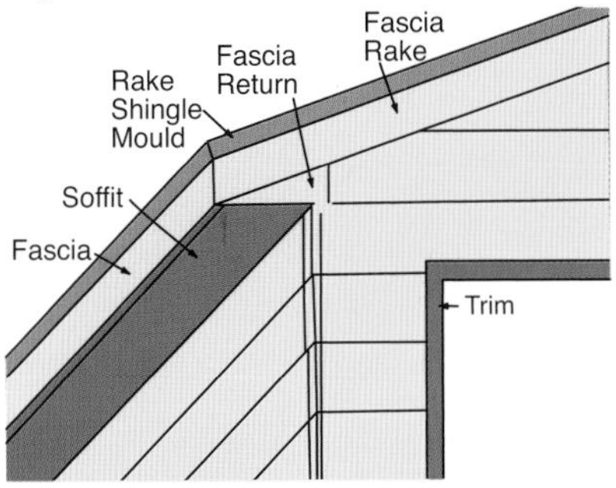

Figure 31E - Gable End Ridge Detail Open Overhang

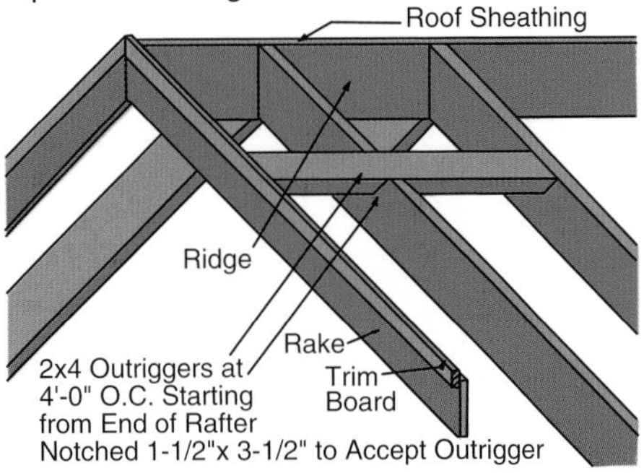

Figure 31F - Open Cornice Overhang

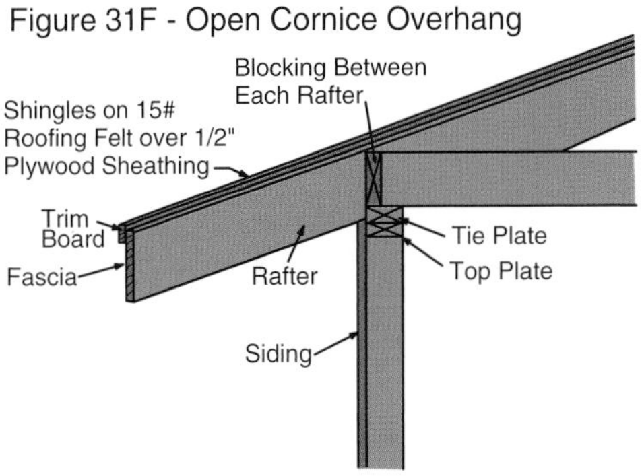

Window and Door Trim

Trim out door(s) as detailed on your garage plan. Because of the great variety in window manufacturing, it is best to study the window manufacturer's details before framing and trimming them. The service door to your garage can be ordered as a pre-hung door complete with threshold and side and head jambs. See Figures 32A to 32C for construction details on trimming on-site window and door jambs.

Garage Door Trim

Nail overhead door jambs to the cripple studs and the header according to the directions given by the garage door manufacturer. The correct installation of garage door hardware, torsion springs, and trim is critical to the safe, smooth operation of the door. This is one phase of construction where we strongly recommend the work be completed by a professional installer.

Figure 32A - Door Detail

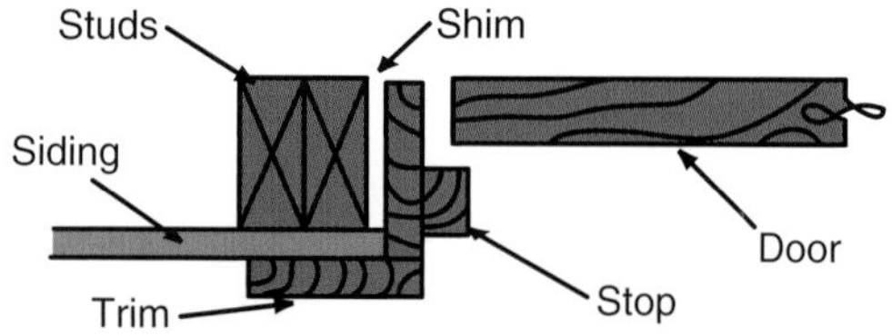

Note: Window and door jambs will move out 1/2" if 1/2" wall sheathing is used. If metal sash is used, see manufacturer's instructions before framing opening.

Figure 32B - Door Detail

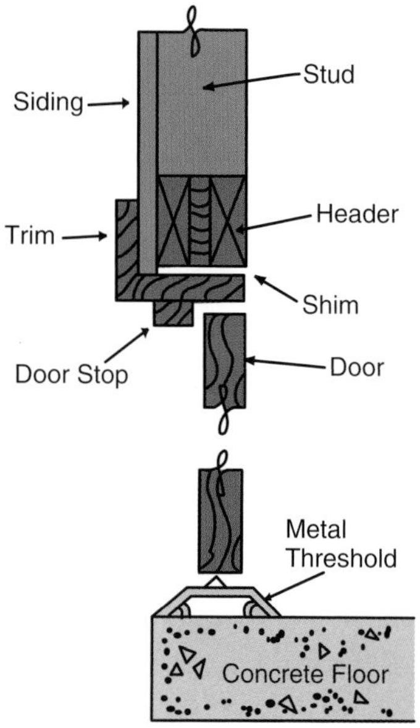

Figure 32C - Window Detail

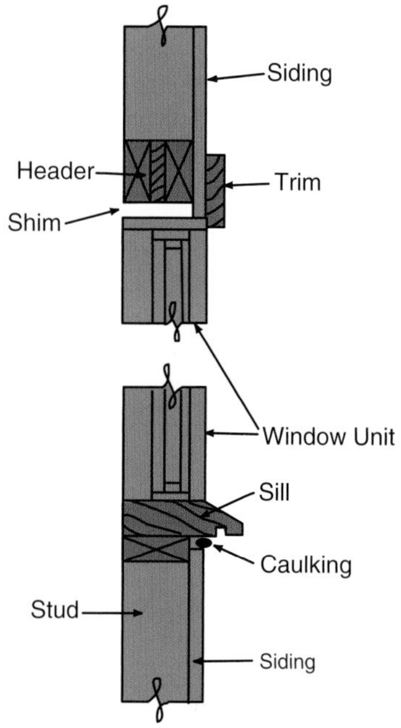

Roof Shingles

Once the roof sheathing, cornice trim, and fascia boards are in place, the roof shingles can be applied. See shingle manufacturer's instructions on bundles. Shingles, chosen to harmonize with the home, are most popular. Square butt shingles are 36" x 12" in size, have three tabs, and are normally laid with 5" exposed to the weather (Figure 32D). Start with 15# asphalt felt paper at the bottom edge of the roof. Lap each course 2". After it is on, apply a starter course of shingles (shingles turned upside down), lapping over the eave and rake fascia 1/2" to provide a drip edge. Use four nails to each shingle: apply a ridge cap at top, which is made by cutting a shingle into thirds (Figure 33A). Start at one end of the ridge and fasten with two nails to a shingle 5" exposure. Cut shingles with a utility knife. Metal drip edges are used in some locales.

When shingling a hip roof, a little more cutting is required. Use the hatchet gauge to give each hip shingle a 5" exposure.

Figure 32D - Laying Shingles

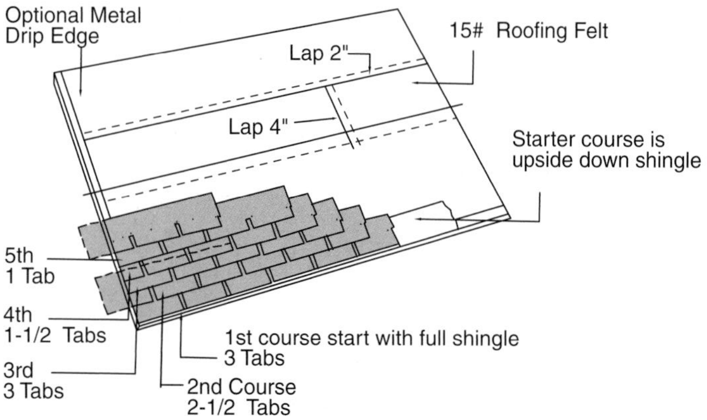

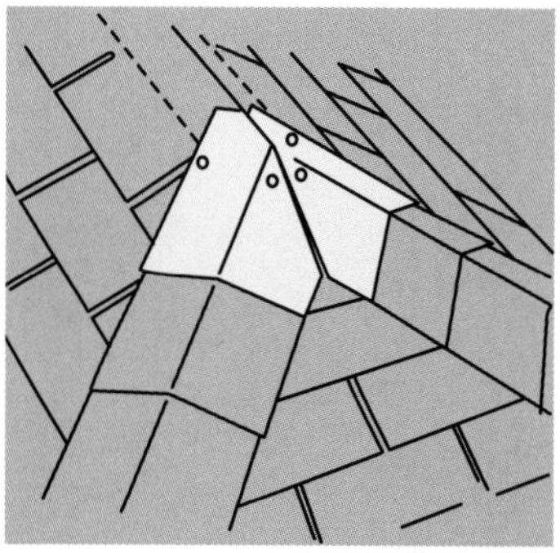

1. Trim the last hip shingles so that they meet smoothly.

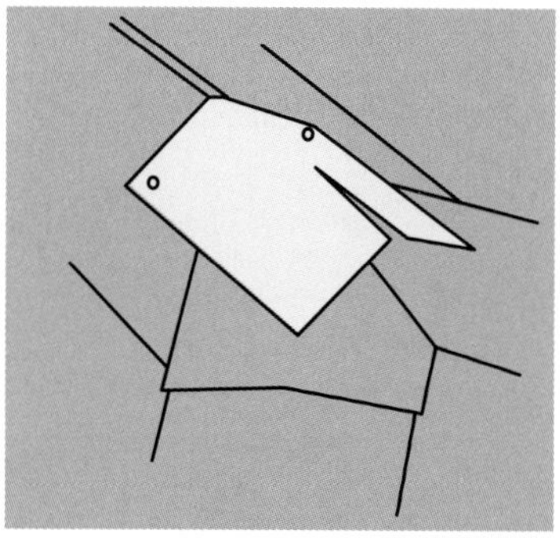

2. Cut 1st ridge shingle 4" up center; Nail over end of ridge.

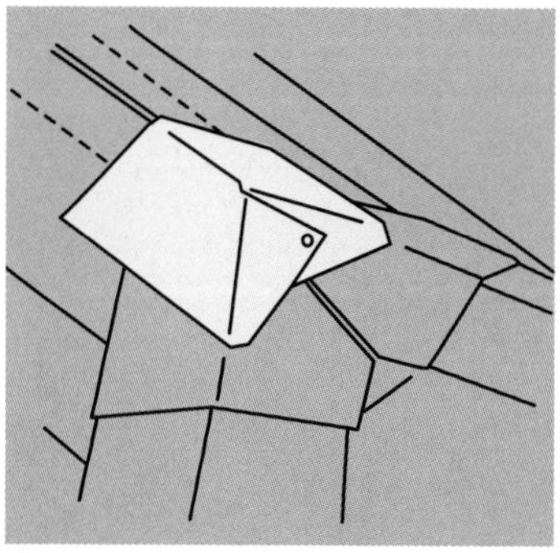

3. Fold split ends over hips and nail; Cover nails with roofing cement.

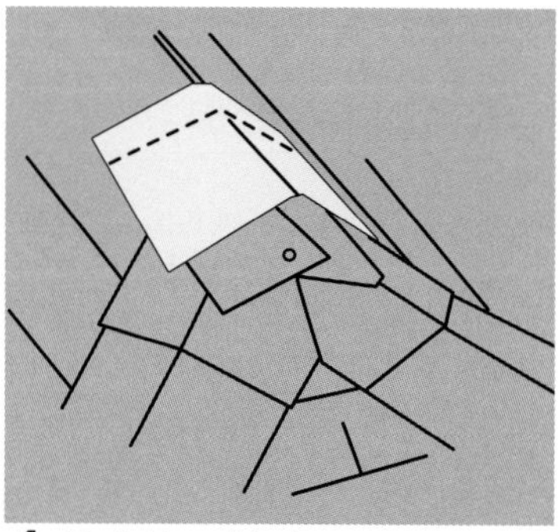

4. First ridge shingle.

Figure 33A - Cutting Shingles

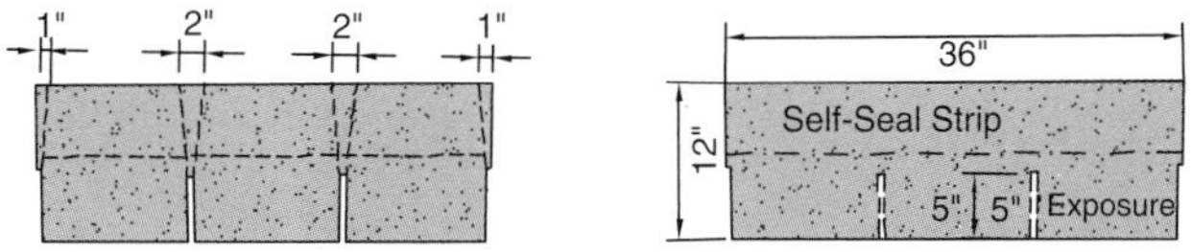
1"
2"
2"
1"
36"
Self-Seal Strip
12"
5"
5"
Exposure

To cut a shingle, score a line with your utility knife, then bend and snap off the piece. Make 3 hip or ridge shingles from one shingle.

Tab shingles are always applied so that full tab is centered over a slot below. If length of roof requires a narrow piece to finish first course, start the second row with piece of same width. Continue alternating narrow pieces in each succeeding row.

Figure 33B - Applying Ridge Cap

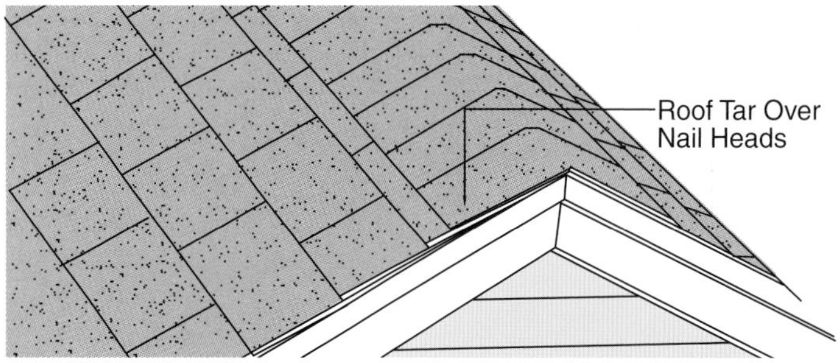
Roof Tar Over
Nail Heads

Siding

Applying Vertical Panel Siding

Before starting construction, select the siding and determine the need for wall sheathing. Wall sheathing requirements are determined by the stud spacing, the width of the door and window jambs, and the application of the trim (See Figure 33C).

A commonplace and inexpensive siding for garages, T1-11 exterior siding, does not require wall sheathing and adds structural strength. Of course you should attempt to harmonize your garage siding with your home's exterior. When you install vertical panel siding, nail 6d galvanized nails every 4"-6" at the edges of the panel and every 8"-12" inside the panel. You might be able to obtain siding nails that match the siding and thus eliminate painting both the siding and nails. If you have to add a panel above the bottom panel, use Z-bar flashing between the panels (See Figure 33E). Leave a 1/4" gap around door and window openings when cutting siding to facilitate fitting.

When plywood sheathing is used, diagonal corner bracing can often be omitted. Decide whether trim is to be applied on top of the siding or butted into it. If butted, apply trim first, then apply siding. Horizontal wood siding is more expensive than plywood panel siding but provides an attractive and durable exterior. However, horizontal wood siding requires periodic painting for preservation.

Figure 33C - Siding Alternatives

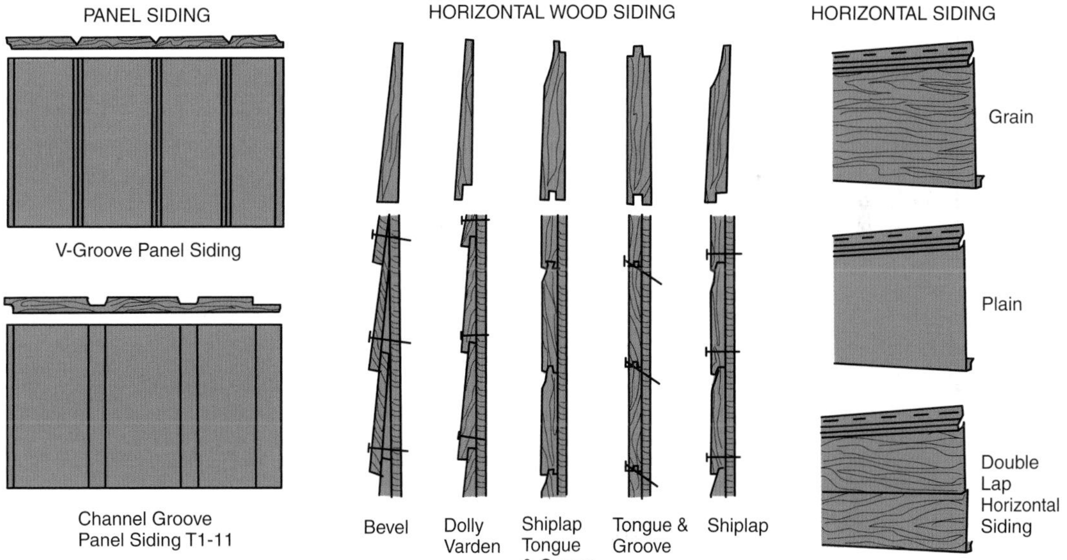
PANEL SIDING
V-Groove Panel Siding
Channel Groove
Panel Siding T1-11
HORIZONTAL WOOD SIDING
Bevel
Dolly
Varden
Shiplap
Tongue
& Groove
Tongue &
Groove
Shiplap
HORIZONTAL SIDING
Grain
Plain
Double
Lap
Horizontal
Siding

Figure 33D - Panel Siding with Batten Boards

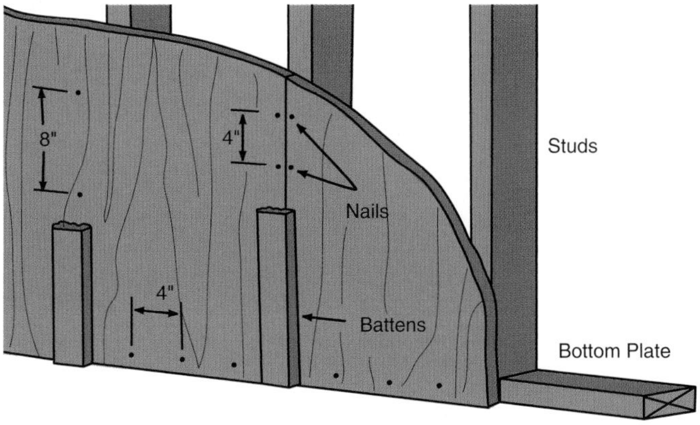
8"
4"
Nails
Studs
4"
Battens
Bottom Plate

Figure 33E - Vertical Grooved Siding Panels

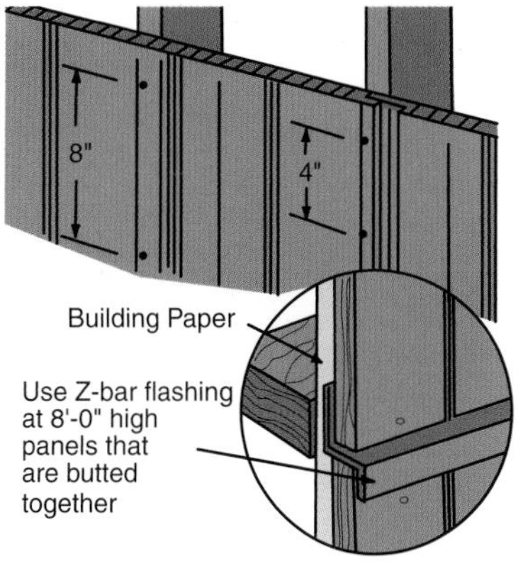
8"
4"
Building Paper
Use Z-bar flashing
at 8'-0" high
panels that
are butted
together

Horizontal Siding

Lay down various lengths of siding at each side. Apply so that joints in the succeeding course do not fall directly above each other. Butt all joints over the center of a stud. Seal by painting the edges with primer before butting. Start the bottom of the first course 1/2" below the bottom plate. Siding on all walls should be aligned and level and each course equally spaced. Be especially careful to determine the lap and exposure to the weather before applying the second and succeeding courses. Measure the distance to be covered and divide it by the desired exposure to get the total number of courses of siding. See Figure 34A below. Carefully mark these spaces on the corners of each wall, taking into consideration the overlap of the siding. Run a chalk line from one mark to another, leaving a horizontal chalk line on the building paper as a guide. If you are not applying sheathing or building paper, chalk the wall studs directly. Apply the siding and keep it consistent by checking with your level.

Figure 34B - Horizontal Siding Detail

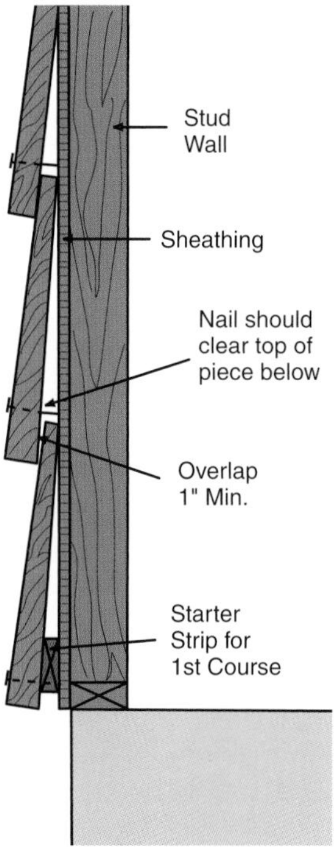

Stud Wall
Sheathing
Nail should clear top of piece below
Overlap 1" Min.
Starter Strip for 1st Course

Figure 34A - Marking Siding Courses

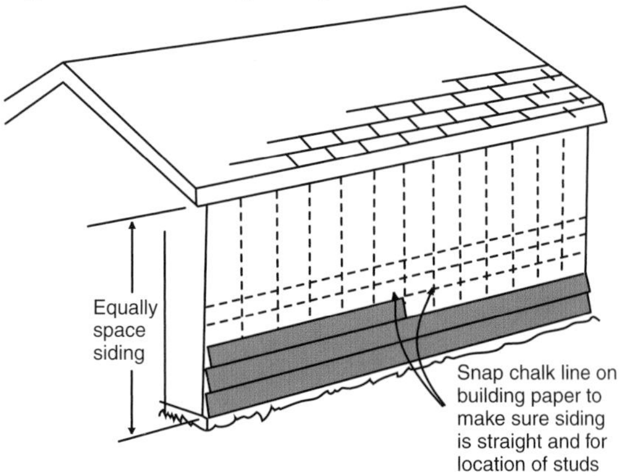

Equally space siding
Snap chalk line on building paper to make sure siding is straight and for location of studs

Final openings where siding meets the soffit, if applicable, can be closed with a piece of quarter round or shingle mould. Protect your garage by painting or staining it as soon as possible.

Vinyl Siding

Vinyl siding must be installed over a smooth surface such as wood or foam sheathing. If you are using drip-in foam backer or contoured backer make sure it meets your vinyl manufacturer's specifications. When installing vinyl siding it is recommended you use galvanized nails with smooth shank and flat heads. Remember to place nails in the center of the slot and do not nail tightly. If panels are not spaced properly allowing for expansion or nailed properly they may buckle in hot weather. No matter if you are installing siding horizontally or vertically, all corner trim, window and door trim along with starter strips are installed first. Take extra care when installing the starter strip, ensuring that it is level. Next you should install the trim for under the soffits and gable rakes. Now you are ready to install the siding panels. Snap the first panel into the starter strip and continue up the wall. Make sure to stagger joints and overlap siding ends 1" but cut nailing flange back 1-1/2" to allow for expansion. After installation is complete, caulk seams that water may penetrate but do not caulk between panel ends or trim strips. It is recommended you read the manufacturer's installation guide before starting the installation process.

Figure 34C - Applying Building Paper

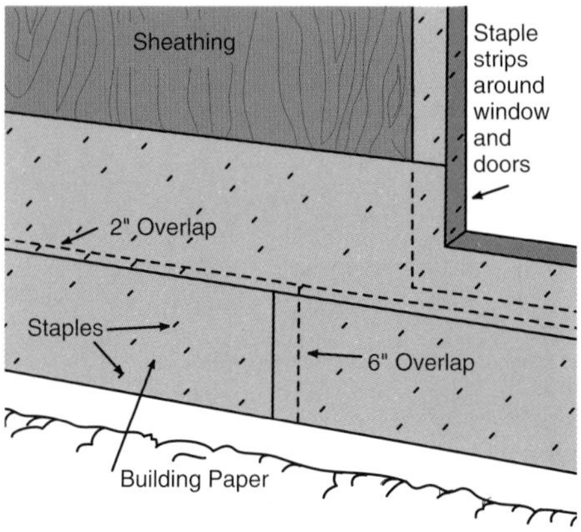

Sheathing
Staple strips around window and doors
2" Overlap
Staples
6" Overlap
Building Paper

Building Paper

Some local building codes might require that building paper be used to seal the wall from the elements. Building paper is typically felt or kraft paper impregnated with asphalt and is stapled or nailed between the siding and the sheathing or studs. Rolls are usually 36" wide and come in lengths covering between 200 to 500 square feet. Apply building paper in horizontal strips from the bottom of the wall as shown in Figure 34C. Overlaps should be 2" at horizontal joints, 6" at vertical joints, and 12" at corners. Cutting is done with a utility knife. Use just enough staples or nails to hold the paper in place. Siding nails will hold it permanently. Before you install siding, snap a level chalk line on the siding to indicate the bottom edge of the paper and work up.

Garage Doors and Mouldings

One of the most important aspects of building a garage is selecting the door. Due to the size of lots, building restrictions, and other reasons, the garage often takes an up-front position in visibility, in many cases the garage door is more prominent than the front door of the home. You will want a door that is compatible and attractive as well as utilitarian. There is a large selection of styles and patterns from which to choose in today's market.

Governing factors are usually visual appeal and budget. The door can be as plain or as ornate as you wish. It can be made of wood, fiberglass, aluminum, or steel, and it can even be insulated with a poly core. It should be solid, constructed of materials that will stand a fair amount of hard use, and it should be lightweight and balanced so that even the children in the family can operate it.

But most important are the headroom requirements and the doorjamb. If the jamb is improperly constructed, you will have nothing but grief with any door, no matter what type or quality. So, carefully check the specifications of the door manufacturer you select.

Garage Doors and Mouldings (continued)

Figure 35A - Typical Garage Door Designs

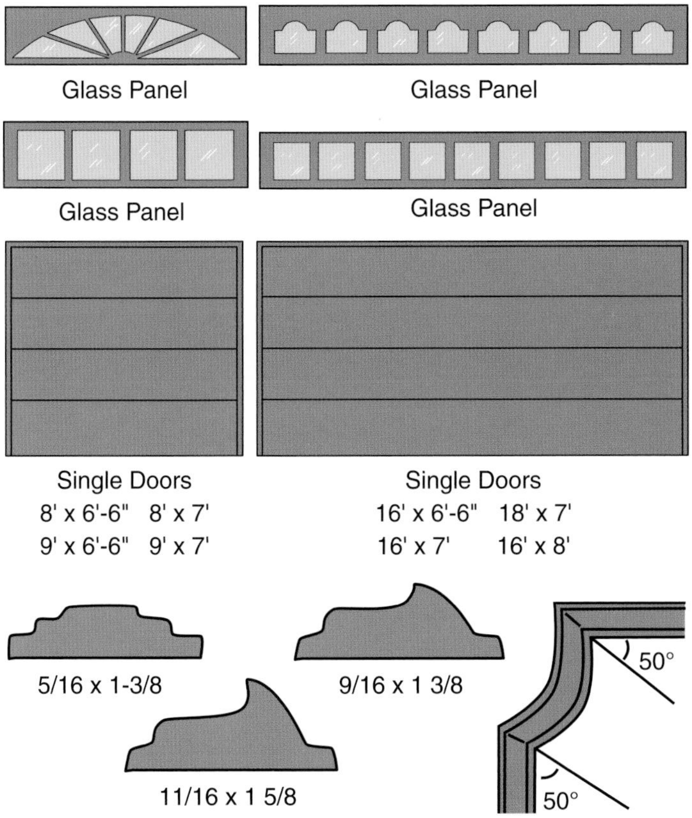
Glass Panel
Glass Panel
Glass Panel
Glass Panel
Single Doors
8' x 6'-6" 8' x 7'
9' x 6'-6" 9' x 7'
Single Doors
16' x 6'-6" 18' x 7'
16' x 7' 16' x 8'
5/16 x 1-3/8
9/16 x 1 3/8
11/16 x 1 5/8
50°
50°

Figure 35B - Typical Garage Door Mouldings

Moulding patterns and layout designs are almost as varied for garage doors as they are for the door to your house and are a great way to brighten up the front of your garage. The patterns shown here are just a suggestion of the many styles there are to choose from. Choose one or a combination of patterns, but keep in mind that the style size of your door might affect the choice of moulding. What works on an upward-working solid door might not work as well or look as good on a sectional or a side-acting door.

Remember that accurate measurements are important for mitering, especially since all of the pieces should be cut to size before you are ready to attach them to the door. Also remember that the doors will be exposed to varied weather conditions, so they will need to be sealed, stained, or painted accordingly.

Sectional Garage Doors

Sectional garage doors are comprised of several horizontal sections held together with hinges. The side hinges have rollers so that the door section can roll up or down as a single unit. Rollers, track, and brackets are made to fit the sides and top of the door against the door frame for a snug weather-tight seal. The bottom of the door should be weatherstripped. Standard rubber gasket stripping provides an especially tight fit.

Installation instructions for the door and its hardware are provided by the door manufacturer, but it is strongly recommended that this work be done by a professional. The torsion springs used to help lift and balance most door designs store tremendous amounts of energy and can cause severe bodily injury and or property damage if accidentally released during installation or operation.

Figure 35C - Garage Door Sections

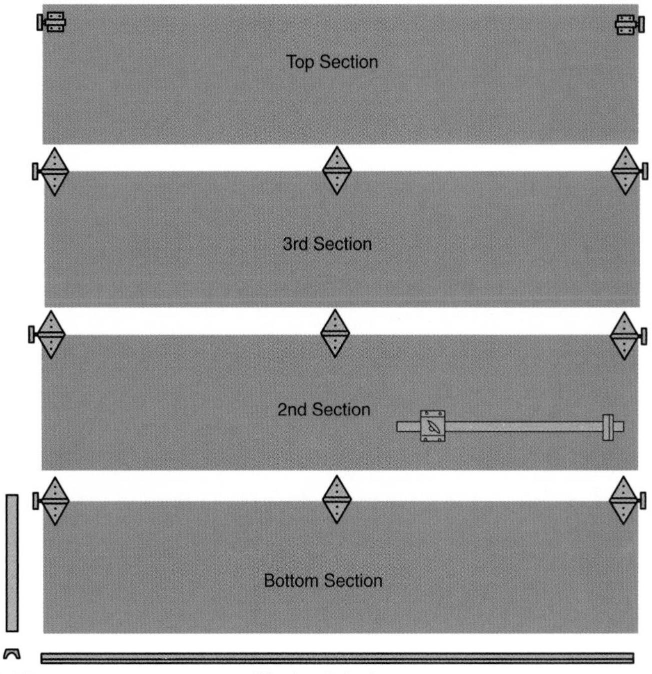
Top Section
3rd Section
2nd Section
Bottom Section
Side View
Weather Stripping

Adustable guides on each side of the door permit locking bars to glide freely. Bracket screws are tightened after adjustment.

Typical garage door lock consists of a spring-loaded bar controlled from outside with a key. Screws and plate are removed to reach latch mechanism for lubrication.

Sectional Garage Doors (continued)

Hardware Details

The torsion spring-type sectional door is operated by an assembly consisting of one or more torsion springs, a continuous torsion shaft, two lift drums, two lift cables, and associated hardware, including drum, torsion, shaft, torsion spring bearing, and bearing brackets. Track, roller bearings, and all hardware should be kept clean and lubricated. But as mentioned previously, all installation and adjustment of the system must be done by a professional.

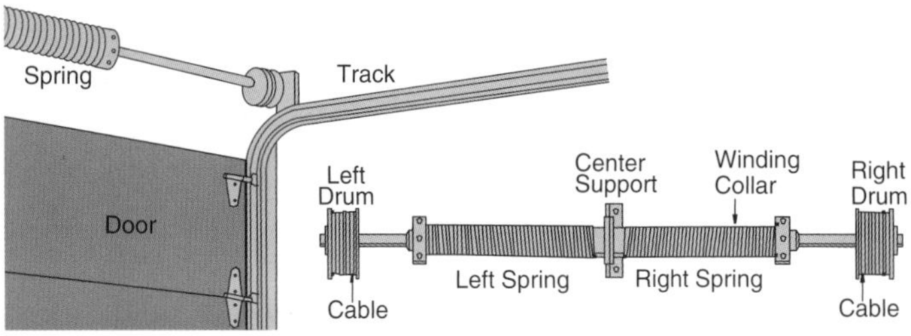

Figure 36A - Garage door with single spring across door opening. This spring winds instead of stretching. Tension is adjusted by loosening the collar locknut and winding it tighter with a bar inserted through the collar.

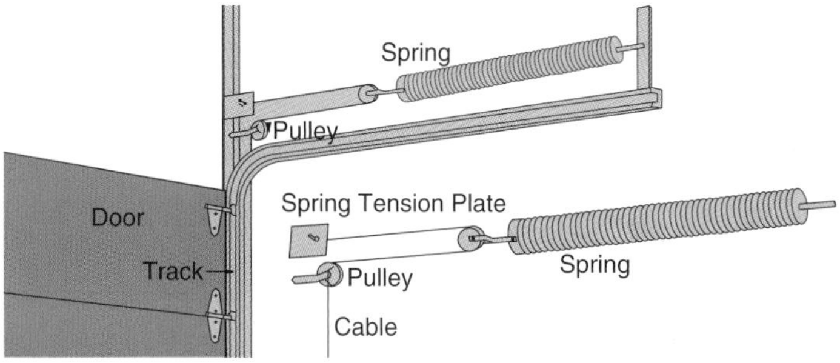

Figure 36B - The door shown here has a spring on both sides. Spring tension is adjusted by shortening or lengthening the cable length at the spring tension plate.

Installing Prehung Doors

Prehung doors are assembled at the factory. The door comes hinged and mounted on the side jamb with a hole drilled through the door for the doorknob. A right-hand door or left-hand door is determined by the side of the door on which the knob is located, viewed from inside the room into which it opens.

The door is installed by placing it into the rough opening and shimming it to make it square. Don't count on the opening being square.

After you've shimmed it so that the jamb is centered in the door opening, hold it in place by driving a 12d casing nail through the shims and into the trimmer stud near the top of the hinge-side jamb. Nail the head jamb to the header after making sure everything is square.

Again make sure the frame is centered and square, then secure the hinge side by nailing into the trimmer stud through the shims. Check that the door swings freely, then secure the other jamb. Weatherstripping is built into the threshold. The door must be removed to screw it to the existing threshold, and then measure and cut door to fit.

Figure 36C - Fitting Doors

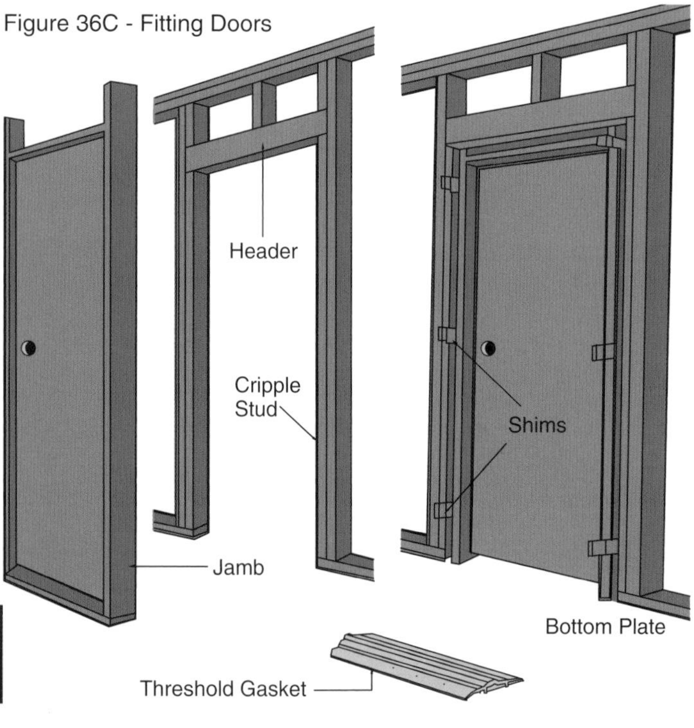

Disappearing Stairs

Folding stairways are factory-assembled for installation as a unit. The jamb is nailed to joists, and springs act as a counterbalance to the stairway and ceiling panel for easy operation. They are well suited to areas with limited head space, such as a garage loft, because the jambs and folded ladder use very little vertical space above the ceiling. Stair treads are normally painted with nonskid paint. Manufacturers provide installation instructions.

Disappearing Stair Sizes

Rough Opening	Floor To Ceiling	Ladder Width
22" x 48"	7'-10" to 8'-5"	14"
22" x 54"	8'-6" to 10'-0"	14"
30" x 60"	7'-10" to 8'-9"	22"
30" x 60"	8'-10" to 10'-0"	22"

Building the Stairway

Figure 37A - Folding Stairways

Figure 37B - Laying Out a Stringer

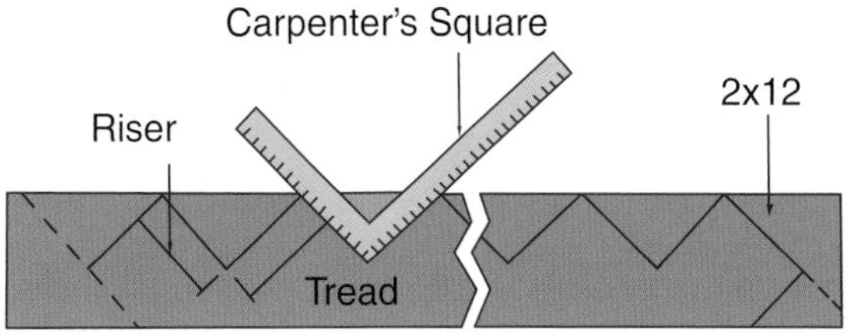

Carpenter's Square
Riser
2x12
Tread

Figure 37C - Typical Stairway

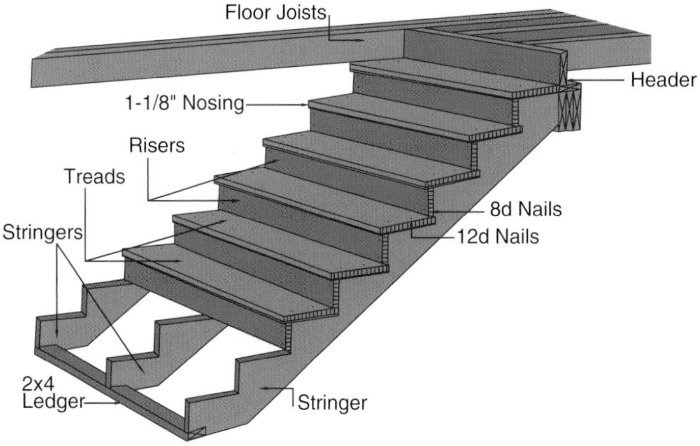

Floor Joists
Header
1-1/8" Nosing
Risers
Treads
8d Nails
12d Nails
Stringers
2x4
Ledger
Stringer

Stair assembly consists of stringers, risers, treads, and often railings. To build your stairs, begin by laying out the cut marks on the 2x12s to be used for stringers. Use a carpenter's square with the tread dimensions marked on the body of the square and the riser dimensions on the square tongue. Cuts can be made with either a handsaw or a circular saw, but final cuts should be hand-made.

Remember that the bottom edge of the riser rests on the tread beneath it, while the forward edge of the tread is flush or overhangs the riser beneath it. A 1-1/8" overhang creates a professional look.

Cut out one stringer first and check its alignment. If it is correct, use it as a master for the second stringer. A third one will also need to be cut if the stairs are 36" wide or more.

Nail the top of the stringer to trimmers or header of the rough opening. For additional strength, an extra header board, a ledger, or joist hangers can be used. The bottoms are toenailed to the floor or to a 2x4 bottom ledger.

Attach treads first with 12d nails, then nail on the riser with 8d nails. Gluing the risers and treads to the stringers, along with nailing, will help reduce noise. Check local building codes for stair construction.

Figure 37D - Typical Stair Detail

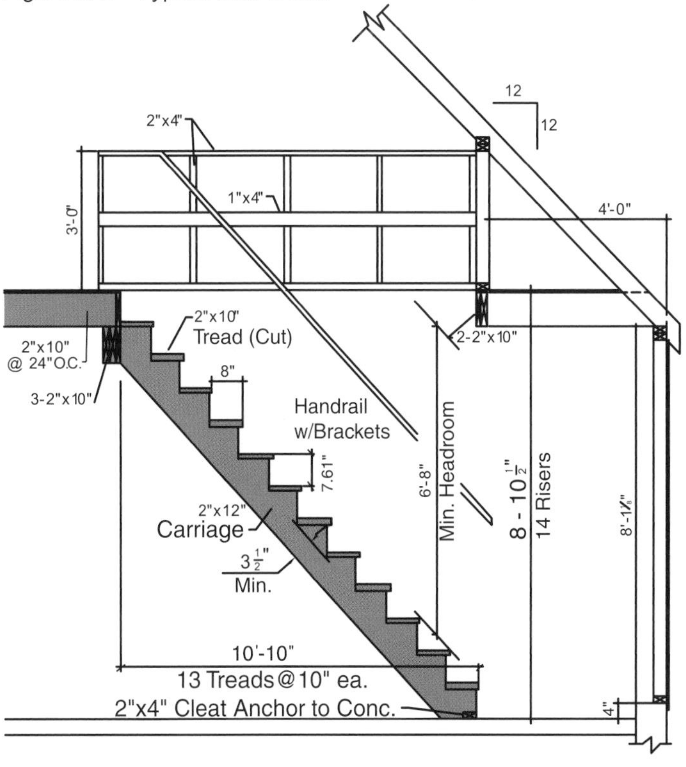

12
12
2"x4"
1"x4"
3'-0"
4'-0"
2"x10"
@ 24"O.C.
2"x10"
Tread (Cut)
2-2"x10"
8"
3-2"x10"
Handrail
w/Brackets
7.61"
6'-8"
Min. Headroom
8 - 10 1/2"
14 Risers
8'-1"
2"x12"
Carriage
3 1/2"
Min.
10'-10"
13 Treads @ 10" ea.
2"x4" Cleat Anchor to Conc.
4"

Electrical Wiring

Figure 38A - 3-Way Switch Light at End of Circuit

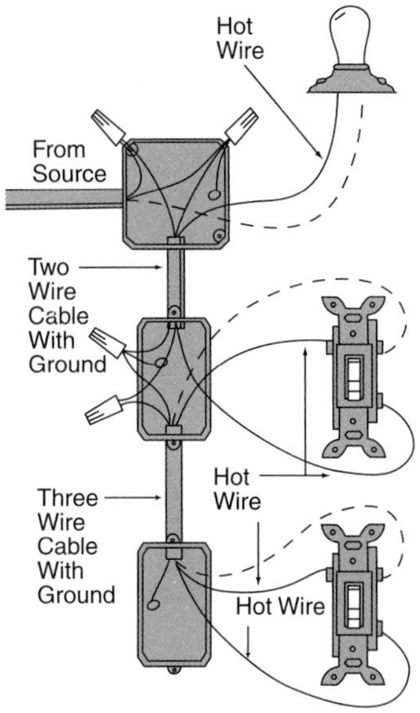
Hot Wire
From Source
Two Wire Cable With Ground
Three Wire Cable With Ground
Hot Wire
Hot Wire

Figure 38B - Light in Middle of Circuit

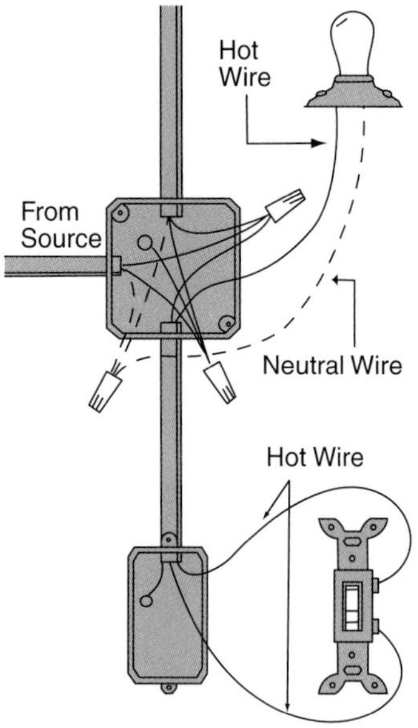
Hot Wire
From Source
Neutral Wire
Hot Wire

Figure 38C - Light at End of Circuit

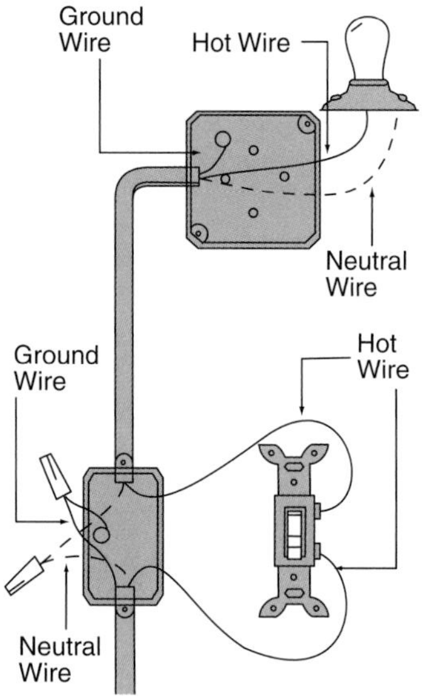
Ground Wire
Hot Wire
Neutral Wire
Ground Wire
Hot Wire
Neutral Wire

Figure 38D - Receptacle at End of Circuit

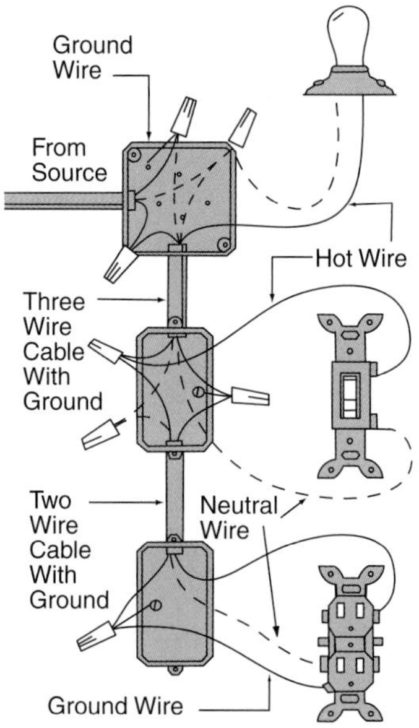
Ground Wire
From Source
Hot Wire
Three Wire Cable With Ground
Two Wire Cable With Ground
Neutral Wire
Ground Wire

If you plan on wiring your garage for electricity and are considering doing it yourself, two stops are almost mandatory: your local building code office and the power company, in that order. The code office will be able to inform you of any local wiring requirements, and they can be quite specific. They can also vary widely from one area to another. Don't bet on the code being exactly the same as it was in the last town you lived. Even though many municipalities use the National Electrical Code (NEC), which spells out uniform safety standards for wiring methods and materials, it is often modified from one municipality to another to meet local needs. Most local building departments require the use of GFCI outlets in order to obtain a building permit. Checking with the code office can advise you of those variations, as well as setting you up on permit inspection requirements. It will also advise you whether or not there are any requirements for using a professional electrician during the wiring. Remember that whether or not there are such requirements, if there's something that you're not sure of when you are putting in the wiring, it's best to have professional assistance.

The power company will be able to tell you the best or required location for a meter and service panel if the garage will be separately serviced. If you plan on running off existing home service, you can avoid trouble by making sure that the existing lines are able to carry the additional load.

Layout the location of all outlet boxes and lights on a floor plan of the garage to help in estimating material requirements. Plan on several outlets if you will use the garage as a workshop area, and be sure there is plenty of lighting for safety purposes. It is best to plan now to avoid headaches later. If you are installing an overhead garage door opener, you will also need a three-prong ceiling outlet placed in the proper position.

Keep in mind, if you plan to use an electrical outlet for charging an electric vehicle, it will require an outlet that handles a minimum of 240 volts.

Garage Door Opener

One of the most common garage accessories is the automatic garage door opener. It is available in a wide range of models from a number of manufacturers, generally at moderate expense and with a variety of features. Besides permitting you to open the garage door in stormy weather or at night without leaving your car, openers can provide interior garage lighting and a secure locking system.

Unlike the actual door and hardware, the opener itself is something you can easily install yourself. Carefully follow the manufacturer's instructions for mounting the opener at the correct height and securing it to the door header and the door.

Most openers offer a programmable remote control transmitter so you can personally select the radio frequency that opens your door. A separate wall-mounted switch is also a convenient feature to look for when selecting your opener.

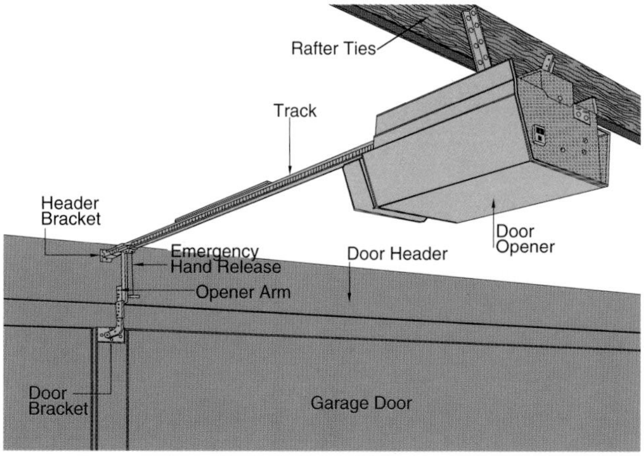
Rafter Ties
Track
Header Bracket
Emergency Hand Release
Opener Arm
Door Header
Door Opener
Door Bracket
Garage Door

Figure 38E - Installing an Automatic Garage Door Opener

Garage Storage Ideas

A. For storage of bulk goods, construction of an over-the-hood platform is an easy and worthwhile task.

B. Quick and easy storage can be found for items that don't need to be readily accessible by keeping them on boards or plywood sheets laid perpendicular to the joists.

C. Hanging cabinets keep things at hand. Use an eyehook to hold drop doors out of the way when the cabinet is being used.

D. Garages quickly become catch-alls. Hanging cabinets will give you additional storage space for less bulky items without taking up valuable floor space.

E. Smaller items can be stored on projecting shelves hung on studs or closed walls.

F. Where space is tight, a couple of blocks nailed to the studs serve as good shelf supports. All you need is some 1x4s and you can build all of the small-item storage you want.

G. Overhanging brackets are easy to make and offer out-of-the way storage for items such as lumber, pipes, etc. **Note:** Additional reinforcing of ceiling joists may be required to accommodate overhanging storage.

H. If you've got the space, deep shelves can be built quickly and simply with furring strips (1x2s), 2x4s, and plywood or 1x12s.

Figure 39A - Storage Idea A

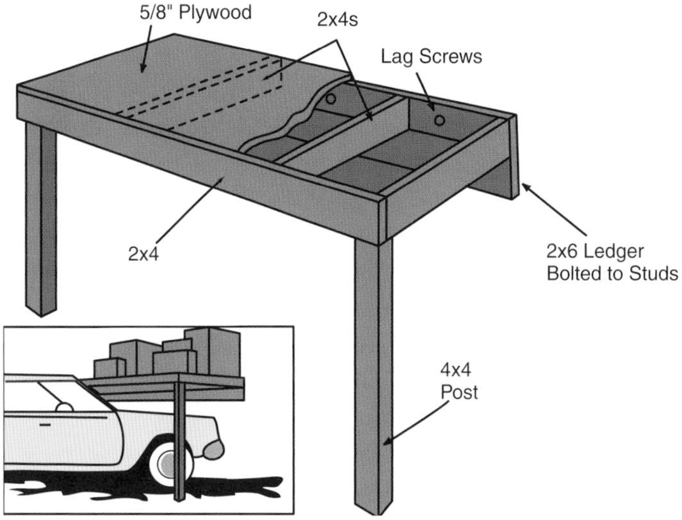

5/8" Plywood
2x4s
Lag Screws
2x4
2x6 Ledger Bolted to Studs
4x4 Post

Figure 39B - Storage Idea B

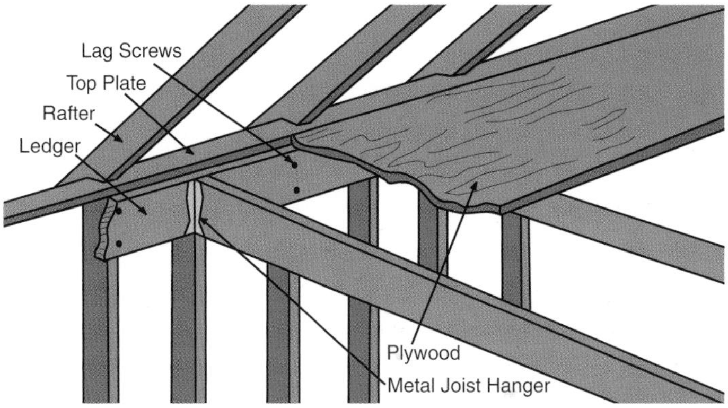

Lag Screws
Top Plate
Rafter
Ledger
Plywood
Metal Joist Hanger

Figure 39C - Storage Idea C

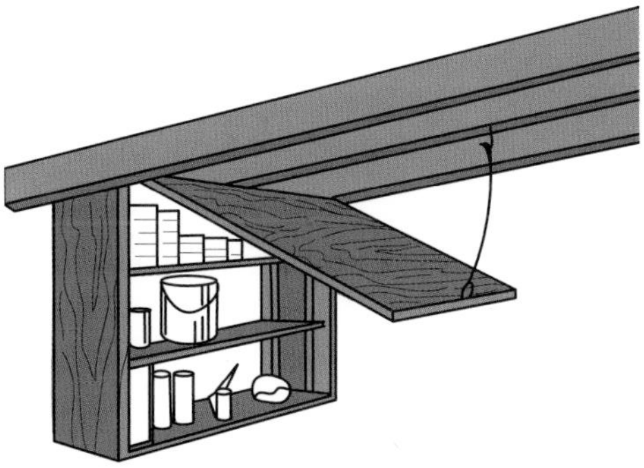

Figure 39D - Storage Idea D

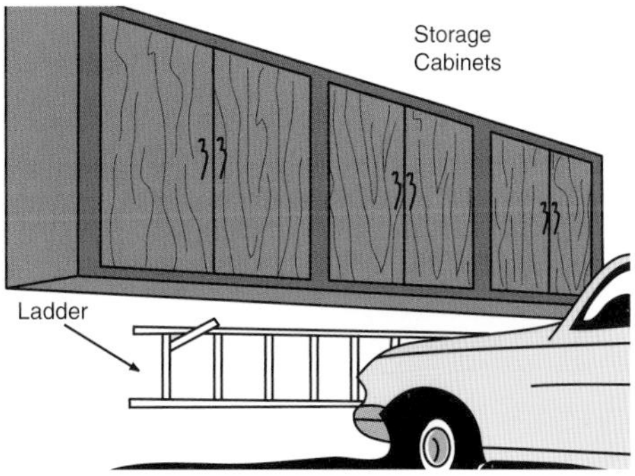

Storage Cabinets
Ladder

Figure 39E - Storage Idea E

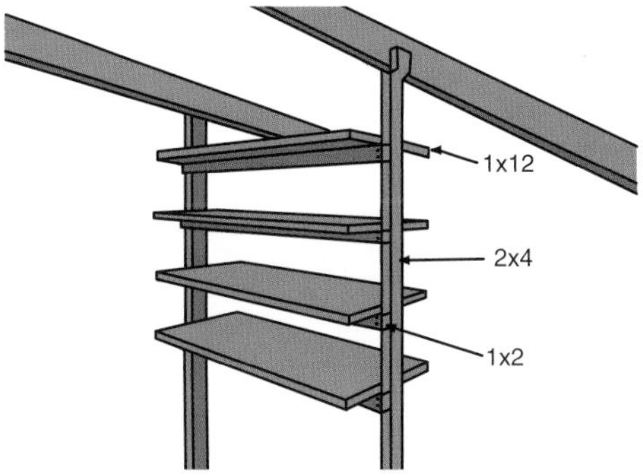

1x12
2x4
1x2

Figure 39F - Storage Idea F

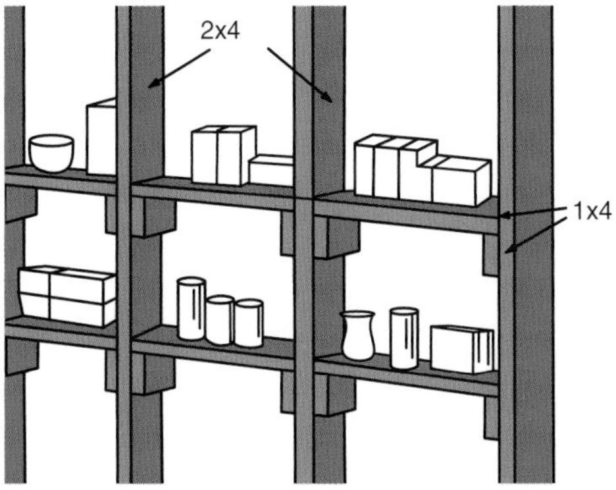

2x4
1x4

Figure 39G - Storage Idea G

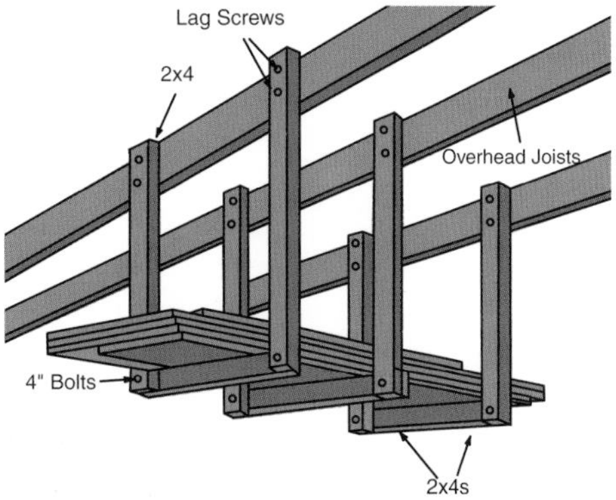

Lag Screws
2x4
Overhead Joists
4" Bolts
2x4s

Figure 39H - Storage Idea H

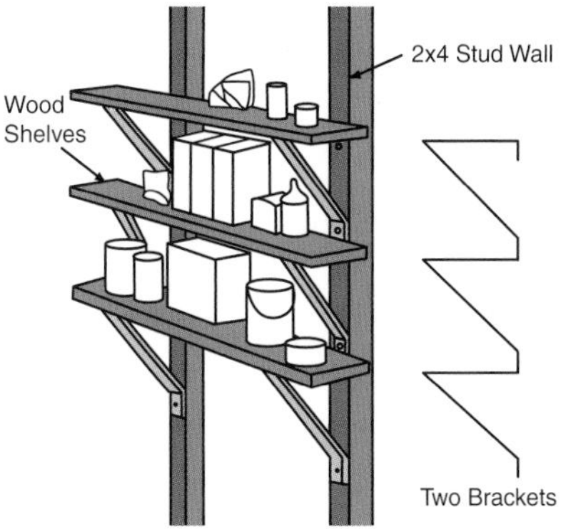

2x4 Stud Wall
Wood Shelves
Two Brackets

Garage Storage Ideas (continued)

I. Small storage compartments made of plywood or similar material can be hung from the ceiling joists to keep seasonal items organized and clean. **Note:** Additional reinforcing of ceiling joists may be required to accommodate storage compartments.

J. Spikes, dowels, or wall brackets make great hangers on studs.

K. You've got to put a ladder somewhere. The garage is long enough, so hang it from the ceiling rather than leaving it on the floor where somebody is bound to trip over it or knock it down.

L. Screw jar lids to the bottoms of shelves, and the jars become conveniently stored, portable clutter containers.

M. Be creative. One of a garage's big advantages is that there are very few storage rules. A set-up like this is made out of 2x4s and plywood gets not only the bikes out of the way, but other items as well.

N. Pegboards and spring clips keep things visible, handy, and produce a tidy, organized effect.

Figure 40A - Storage Idea I

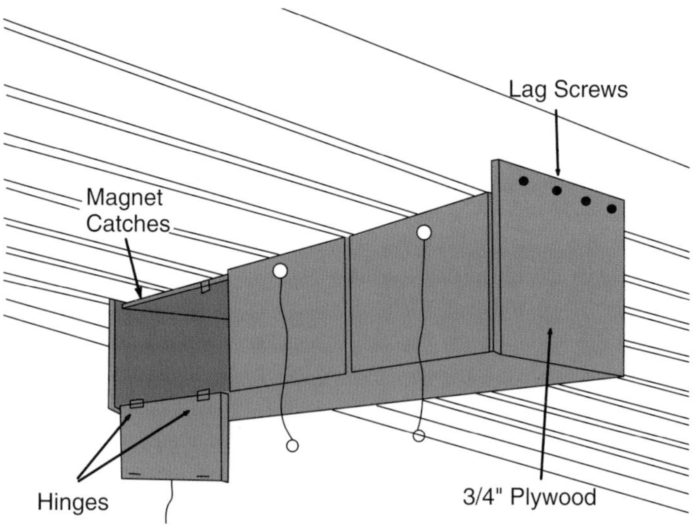

Figure 40B - Storage Idea J

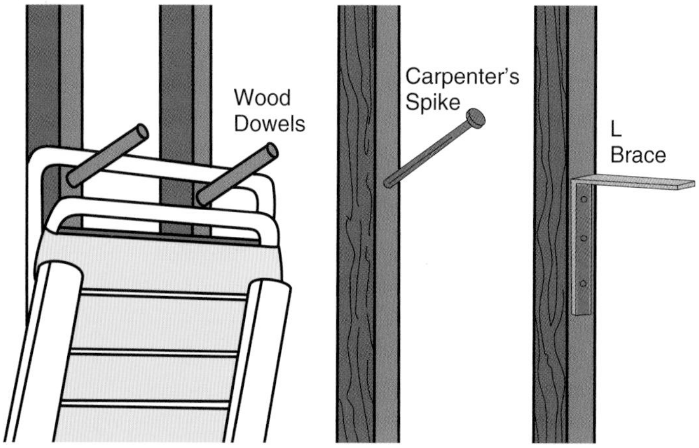

Figure 40C - Storage Idea K

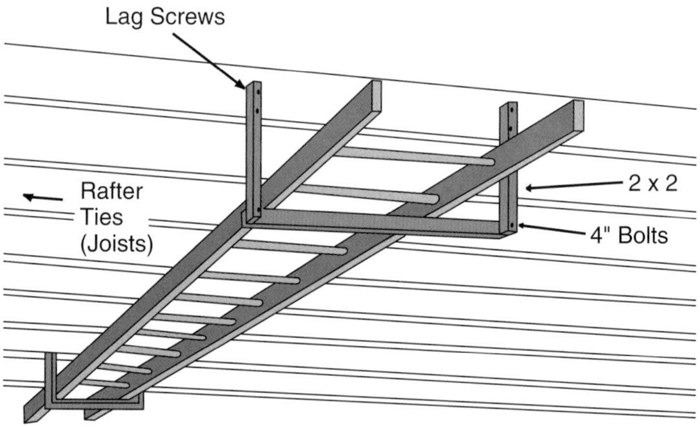

Figure 40D - Storage Idea L

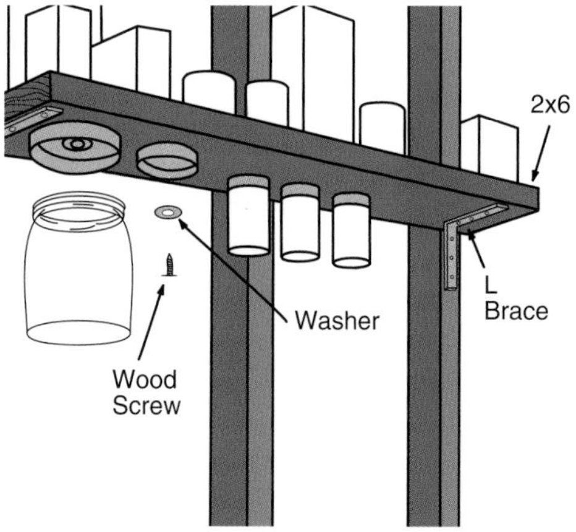

Figure 40E - Storage Idea M

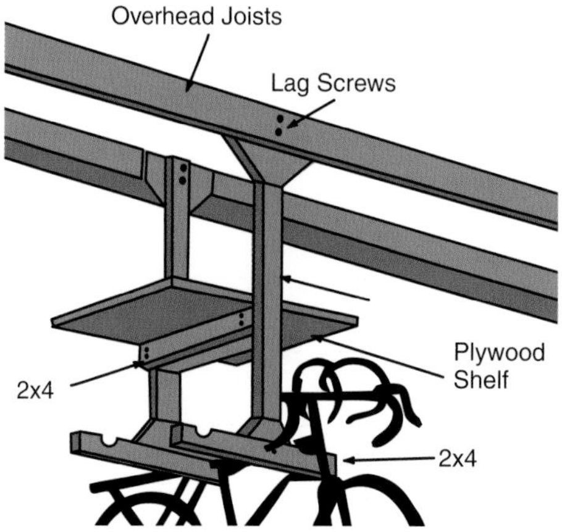

Figure 40F - Storage Idea N

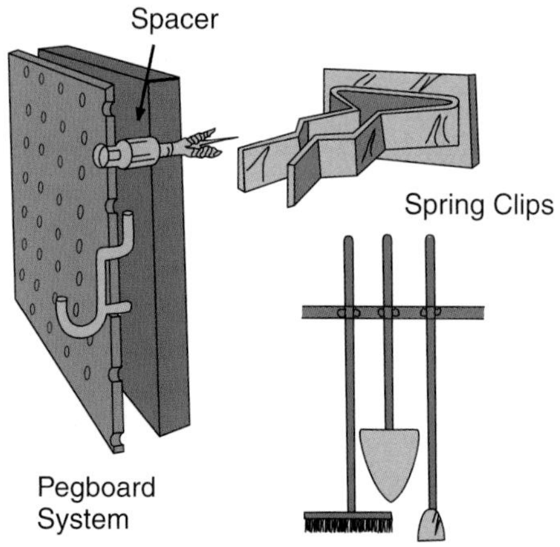

Finishing the Inside of Your Garage

You can either finish the interior of your garage with drywall or leave the wall studs exposed and use blocking to build shelving between the studs. Some garage builders will want to take advantage of the extra storage space afforded by the open wall sections. Use your imagination to create additional storage space by nailing or screwing 1x2 cleats to the studs and then installing extended horizontal shelving over the cleats.

If you elect to install 4'x8' drywall panels (also known as wallboard) in your garage, study the illustrations below for suggestions on nailing or gluing drywall to wall studs. There are many different thicknesses available for drywall panel installation. Although 1/2" drywall is common, 5/8" drywall is being required for most residential municipalities. Check with your local building department before drywall installation.

A variety of fasteners are available for wallboard. Consult with your local home improvement store, or building material supplier for suggestions. After you have installed the panels, you can tape and fill the joints with joint compound or simply cover the joints with tape if the final appearance is not a major concern.

Figure 41 - Nailing Wallboard

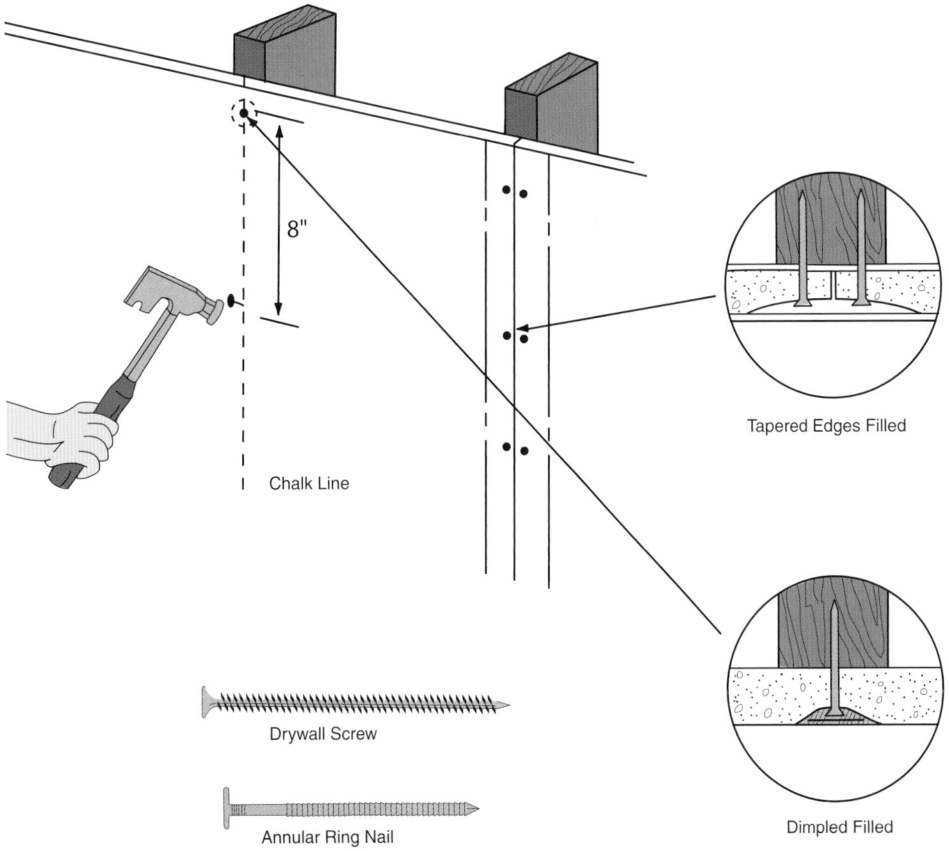
8"
Chalk Line
Tapered Edges Filled
Drywall Screw
Annular Ring Nail
Dimpled Filled

For Notes

Glossary

Anchor Bolt - A metal connector device used to connect a wood mudsill to a concrete wall or slab.

Batterboards - Scrap lumber nailed horizontally to stakes driven near each corner of the foundation excavation. Stretch nylon strings between batterboards to transfer reference points and to measure elevation.

Beam - Beams are horizontal structural members that are supported by vertical posts. Beams are typically constructed from 2 or more 2xs, 4x material, or engineered lumber.

Bottom Plate - In stud wall framing, the bottom horizontal member of the wall. Also known as the soleplate.

Bridging - Wood or metal cross pieces fastened between floor joists to provide structural strength.

Cantilever - Refers to the end portion of a joist that extends beyond the beam.

Casing - Molding around door and window openings.

Codes - Regulations implemented by your local building department which control the design and construction of buildings and other structures. Consult your local building department for applicable codes before you begin your construction project.

Collar Beam - A connecting member used between rafters to strengthen the roof structure.

Cornice - The structure created at the eave overhang which typically consists of fascia board, soffit, and moldings.

Cripple Studs - Short studs that strengthen window and door openings or the gable end of a roof. Also known as jack studs.

Darby - A flat tool with two handles used for spreading concrete, plaster or stucco.

Defect - Any defect in lumber whether a result of a manufacturing imperfection or an irregularity in the timber from which the lumber was cut. Some defects are only blemishes while others can reduce strength and durability. Grading rules establish the extent and severity of wood defects.

Drip Edge - Angled metal or wood located on the outer edge of the roof. Drip edge prevents water penetration.

Drywall - A gypsum panel used to finish interior walls. Also known as plasterboard or sheet rock.

Eave - The roof overhang projecting beyond the exterior wall.

Edge - The narrowest side of a piece of lumber that is perpendicular to both the face and the end.

Elevation - Drawing of a structure as it will appear from the front, rear, left and right sides.

Engineered Lumber - Refers to beams or rafters constructed from wood fiber and glue such as glu-lams, micro-lams, or wood I-beams. Often superior in strength and durability to dimensional lumber.

Face - The widest side of a piece of lumber that is perpendicular to both the edge and the end.

Fascia - Trim used along the eave or gable end.

Finish - Any protective coating applied to your structure to protect against weathering. Finishes are available as stains, paints, or preservatives.

Flakeboard - A panel material made from compressed wood chips bonded with resin. Also known as oriented strand board (OSB) or chipboard.

Flashing - Metal material used on the roof and eaves to prevent moisture penetration.

Fly Rafters - Rafters at the gable end that "fly" unsupported by the tie plate. Also known as rack, barge, or verge rafters.

Footing - Concrete footings help to anchor your foundation or piers in the surrounding soil and distribute weight over a larger surface area. In climates where the soil freezes, a generous footing protects against soil heaves and structural slippage.

Frieze - A horizontal framing member that connects the siding with the soffit.

Frost Line - Measure of the maximum penetration of frost in the soil in a given geographic location. Depth of frost penetration varies with climate conditions.

Furring - Narrow strips of wood attached to walls or other surfaces that serve as a fastening base for drywall.

Gable - The triangular end of the roof structure formed by the roof framing.

Galvanized Nails - Hot-dipped galvanized nails (HDG) are dipped in zinc and will not rust.

Girder - Same as beam.

Grade Stamp - A stamp imprinted on dimensional lumber that identifies wood species, grade, texture, moisture content, and usage. Grade descriptions such as select, finish, and common signify limiting characteristics that may occur in lumber in each grade. The stamp indicates a uniform measurement of performance that permits lumber of a given grade to be used for the same purpose, regardless of the manufacturer.

Grading - The process of excavating, leveling, and compacting the soil or gravel beneath your foundation to its desired finish level. Proper grading avoids drainage problems.

Grain - Lumber shows either a flat or vertical grain depending on how it was cut from the log. To minimize warping along the face of lumber (known as cupping) and raising of the grain, you should place flat grain lumber with the bark side up or facing out.

Header - A horizontal load-bearing support member over an opening in the wall such as window or door openings.

Heartwood - Core of the log that resists decay.

Hip Rafter - A short rafter that forms the hip of a roof and runs from the corner of a wall to the ridge board. Usually set at a 45-degree angle to the walls.

Jack Rafter - A short rafter that runs from the ridge board to a hip or valley rafter or from the hip rafter to the tie plate.

Joist - Lumber that is set on edge and supports a floor, decking, or ceiling. Joists in turn are supported by beams and posts.

Joist Hanger - A metal connector available in many sizes and styles that attaches to a ledge or rim joist and makes a secure butt joint between ledger and joist.

Lag Screw - Heavy-duty fastener with hexagonal bolt head that provides extra fastening power for critical structural connections. Use galvanized lag screws to prevent rust.

Glossary

Ledger - A horizontal support member to which joists or other support members are attached.

Let-in Brace - Usually a 1x4 corner brace in a wall section that runs diagonally from the bottom to top plate.

Look-out - Blocking which extends from an inner common rafter to the fly rafters at the gable ends.

Metal Connectors - Used to augment or replace nails as fasteners, metal connectors are critical for lasting and sturdy garage construction.

Moisture Content - Moisture content of wood is the weight of water in wood expressed as a percentage of the weight of wood from which all water has been removed. The drier the lumber the less the lumber will shrink and warp. Surfaced lumber with a moisture content of 19% or less is known as dry lumber and is typically grade stamped as "S-DRY." Moisture content over 19% results in a "S-GRN" stamp to indicate surfaced green.

Mudsill - The part of the wall framing that contacts the foundation. It should be pressure-treated to resist moisture and decay. Also known as the sill plate.

Outrigger - An extension of a rafter at the eave used to form a cornice or overhang on a roof.

Pea Gravel - Approximately 1/4" round gravel material used in a 4"-6" layer to cover the soil under your concrete slab.

Perpendicular - At a 90 degree or right angle.

Pilot Hole - A slightly undersized hole drilled in lumber that prevents splitting of the wood when nailed.

Pitch - A measurement of roof slope. Expressed as the ratio of the total rise divided by the span.

Plumb - Absolutely vertical. Determined with either a plumb bob or spirit level.

Post - A vertical support member that bears the weight of the joists and beams. Typically posts are at least 4x4 lumber.

Pressure-Treated - Refers to the process of forcing preservative compounds into the fiber of the wood. Handle pressure-treated lumber with caution and do not inhale or burn its sawdust. Certain types of pressure-treated lumber are suitable for ground contact use while others must be used above ground. While more expensive than untreated lumber, pressure-treated wood resists decay and is recommended where naturally decay-resistant species like cedar or redwood are unavailable or too costly.

Purlin - A horizontal member of the roof framing that supports rafters or spans between trusses.

Rafter - A roof framing member that extends from the top plate to the ridge board and supports the roof sheathing and roofing material.

Rake - The inclined end area of a gable roof.

Redwood - Decay-resistant and stable wood for exterior use. Heartwood grades provide the greatest decay resistance.

Reinforcing Bar - A steel rod that provides internal reinforcement for concrete piers and foundations. Also known as rebar.

Ridge Board - A 1x or typically 2x member on edge at the roof's peak to which the rafters are connected.

Right Triangle, 6-8-10 or 3-4-5 - A means of insuring squareness when you lay out your foundations. Mark a vertical line at exactly 8'-0" from the angle you want to square. Then mark a horizontal line at exactly 6'-0" from the crossing vertical line. Measure the distance diagonally between both the 6'-0" and 8'-0" marks and when the distance measures 10'-0" exactly you have squared a 90 degree angle between lines.

Rise - In roof construction the vertical distance the ridge rises above the top plate at the center of the span.

Rough Sill - The lowest framing member of a door or window opening.

Scale - A system of representation in plan drawing where small dimensions represent an equivalent large dimension. Most construction plans are said to be scaled down. Scale is expressed as an equation such as 1/4"=1'-0".

Screed - A straight piece of lumber used to level wet concrete or the gravel.

Sheathing - Exterior sheet (typically 4' x 8') material fastened to the rafter or exterior stud walls.

Slope - A measurement of inclination and is expressed as a percentage of units of vertical rise per units of horizontal distance.

Soffit - The underside of the roof overhang. Soffits can either be closed or open (thus exposing the roof rafters).

Span - The distance between two opposing walls as measured from the outside of the top plates or the distance between two beam supports that are measured from center to center.

Spirit Level - A sealed cylinder with a transparent tube nearly filled with liquid forming a bubble used to indicate true vertical and horizontal alignment when the bubble is centered in the length of the tube.

String Level - A spirit level mounted in a frame with prongs at either end for hanging on a string. Determines level across string lines.

Stud - The vertical framing member of a wall.

T1-11 Siding - Exterior siding material with vertical grooves usually 8" on center.

Tie Plate - The framing member nailed to the top plates in order to connect and align wall sections. Also known as the cap plate or second top plate.

Toenail - To drive a nail at an angle. When you toenail a post to a beam for example, drive the nail so that one-half the nail is in each member.

Top Plate - The horizontal top part of the wall framing perpendicular to the wall studs.

Tongue and Groove - Refers to the milling of lumber so that adjacent parts interlock for added strength and durability.

Trimmer Stud - The stud adjacent to window or door opening studs which strengthens the opening and bears the weight of the window or door headers. Also known as a jack stud.

Truss - A triangular prefabricated unit for supporting a roof load over a span. Trusses are relatively lightweight and can offer an easier method of roof construction for the novice.

Valley Rafter - A rafter running from a tie plate at the corner of a wall along the roof valley and up to the ridge.

Ready to Start Some Serious Planning?

Now that you have read this do-it-yourself manual, you're ready to start serious planning. As you can see, there are many details to consider, and they all tie together for successful completion of your garage project.

If the procedures appear at first confusing, reread the information outlined in this book several times before deciding which phases of construction you want to handle yourself and which might require professional assistance.

Because drawing up your own plan from scratch can be time consuming and difficult for the inexperienced builder, you might want to make planning and cost estimating easier by selecting a garage plan from those shown in this book.

Often blueprints with material lists are not immediately available from your local building material dealer, but you can order a garage plan that includes a material list (see specific plan for availability) by using the order form in the back of this book. If after reviewing the blueprints you still have questions, talk them over with your lumber dealer. Most dealers are familiar with construction and will be glad to help you.

The following pages include an assortment of garage plans and other projects. Remember that construction blueprints can be ordered for all of these projects by mailing the order form on page 144, visiting houseplansandmore.com/projectplans, or by calling 1-800-373-2646.

Example of a Typical Garage Plan Sheet

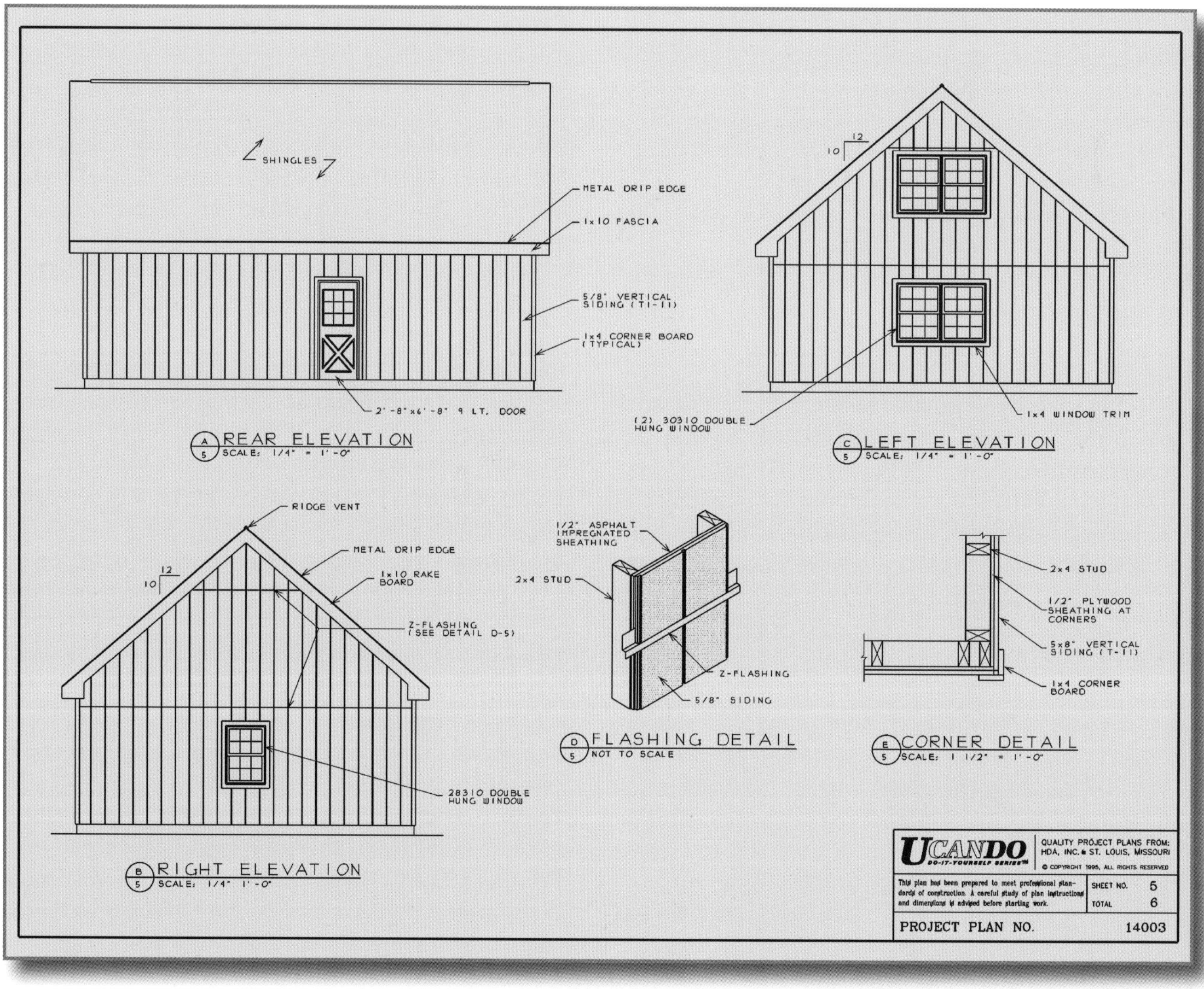

For Layout Purposes

Scale: ½" = 1'-0" per square

Scale: ¼" = 1'-0" per square

Project Plans

GARAGES, WORKSHOPS, AND MORE

1-Car Garage with Covered Porch

PLAN #F50-002D-6010

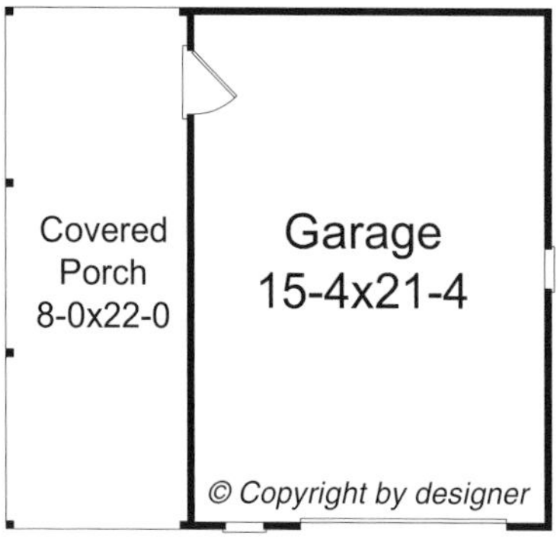
Covered
Porch
8-0x22-0
Garage
15-4x21-4
© Copyright by designer

- Width: 24'   Depth: 22'
- Building height - 13'
- Roof pitch - 5/12
- Ceiling height - 8'
- 9' x 7' overhead door
- Floating slab foundation, drawings also include slab foundation
- A distinctive covered porch provides an area for entertaining
- Complete list of materials
- Step-by-step instructions

1-Set	$175	PDF	$325
5-Set	$225	Repro	$375

1-Car Garage with Front Door

PLAN #F50-063D-6011

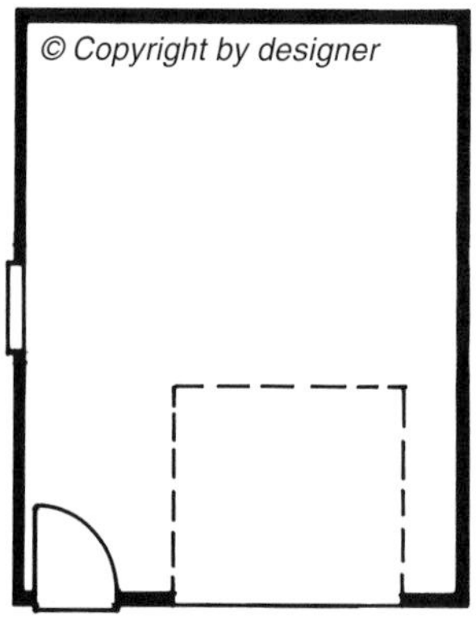
© Copyright by designer

- Width: 16'   Depth: 20'
- Building height - 12'-6"
- Roof pitch - 5/12
- Ceiling height - 8'
- 9' x 7' overhead door
- Floating slab foundation
- Complete list of materials

1-Set	$225	PDF	$375
5-Set	$375	CAD	$550

1-Car Garage with Vertical Siding

PLAN #F50-002D-6028

© Copyright by designer

- Width: 14'   Depth: 22'
- Plan includes three additional sizes: 14' x 24'   16' x 22'   16' x 24'
- Building height - 11'-2"
- Roof pitch - 4/12
- Ceiling height - 8'
- 9' x 7' overhead door
- Floating slab foundation, drawings also include slab foundation
- Complete list of materials
- Step-by-step instructions

1-Set	$125	PDF	$165
5-Set	$155	CAD	$325

PLAN #F50-059D-6009

1-Car Garage with Depth

- Width: 14' Depth: 28'
- Building height - 13'
- Roof pitch - 6/12
- Ceiling height - 8'
- 9' x 7' overhead door
- Floating slab foundation
- Side door allows easy access

1-Set	$175	CAD	$375
PDF	$260	Mat List	$40

© Copyright
by designer

PLAN #F50-002D-6022

1-Car Garage - Western Style

- Width: 14' Depth: 22'
- Building height - 10'-10"
- Roof pitch - 4/12
- Ceiling height - 8'
- 9' x 7' overhead door
- Floating slab foundation, drawings also include slab foundation
- Efficient side door provides easy access
- Complete list of materials
- Step-by-step instructions

1-Set	$125	PDF	$165
5-Set	$155	Repro	$175

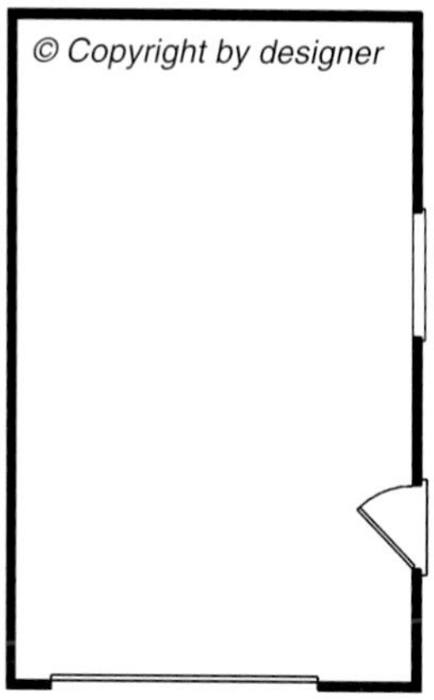
© Copyright by designer

PLAN #F50-002D-6005

1-Car Garage with Horizontal Siding

- Width: 14' Depth: 22'
- Building height - 10'-10"
- Roof pitch - 4/12
- Ceiling height - 8'
- 9' x 7' overhead door
- Floating slab foundation, drawings also include slab foundation
- Convenient side entry door
- Complete list of materials
- Step-by-step instructions

1-Set	$125	PDF	$165
5-Set	$155	CAD	$325

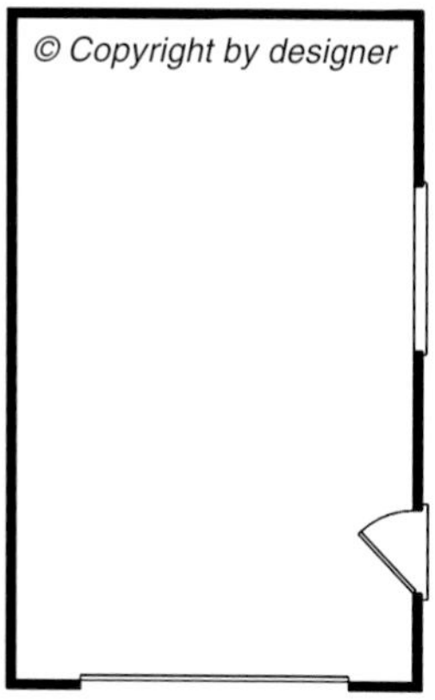
© Copyright by designer

1-Car Garage with Studio / Storage

PLAN #F50-009D-6013

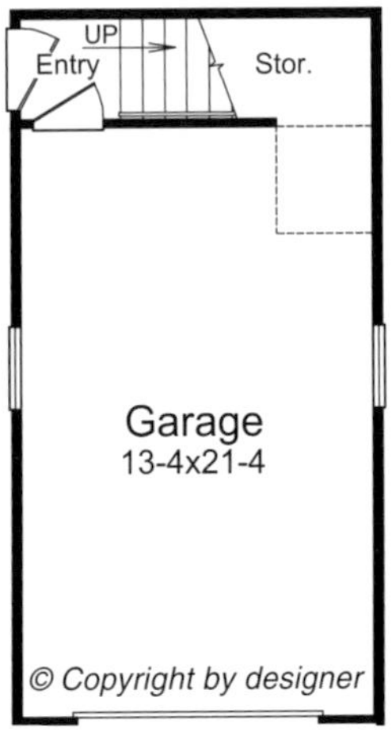

UP
Entry
Stor.
Garage
13-4x21-4
© Copyright by designer

First Floor

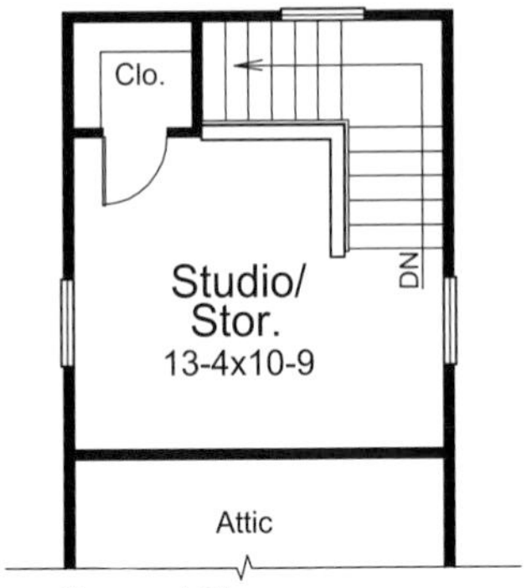

Clo.
Studio/
Stor.
13-4x10-9
DN
Attic

Second Floor

- Width: 14' Depth: 26'
- Building height - 22'
- Roof pitch - 6/12, 10/12
- Ceiling heights - First floor - 8' Second floor - 8'
- 9' x 7' overhead door
- Floating slab foundation
- Garage features a bonus storage area below the stairs
- Complete list of materials

1-Set	$225	PDF	$375
5-Set	$275	CAD	$550

Roomy 3-Car Garage

PLAN #F50-108D-6002

STORAGE
37'-4" x 23'-4"
7'-7" HIGH KNEE WALLS

Second Floor

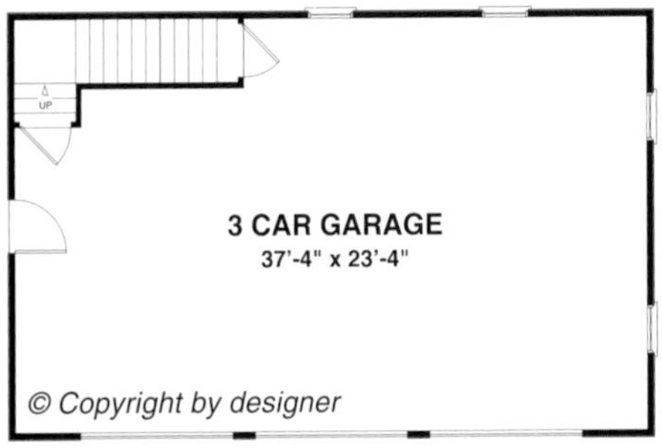

3 CAR GARAGE
37'-4" x 23'-4"
© Copyright by designer

First Floor

- Width: 38' Depth: 24'
- Building height - 24'-8"
- Roof pitch - 12/12
- Ceiling heights - First floor - 8' Second floor - 9'
- Three 9' x 7' overhead doors
- Slab foundation
- Windows illuminate the second floor storage area

PDF	$795	CAD	$1095
Repro	$945		

PLAN #F50-009D-6008

2-Car Garage with Loft

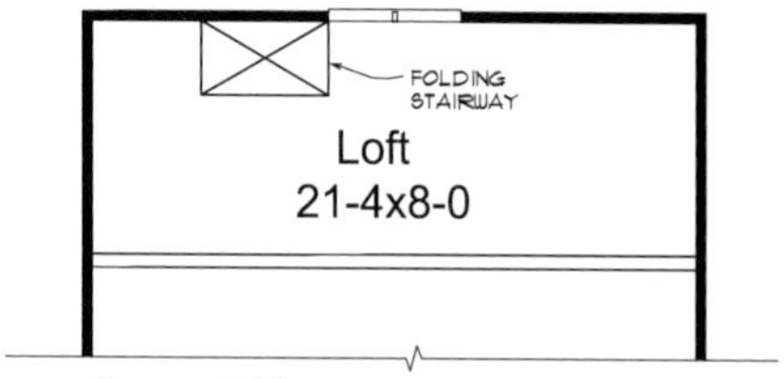
FOLDING STAIRWAY
Loft
21-4x8-0

Second Floor

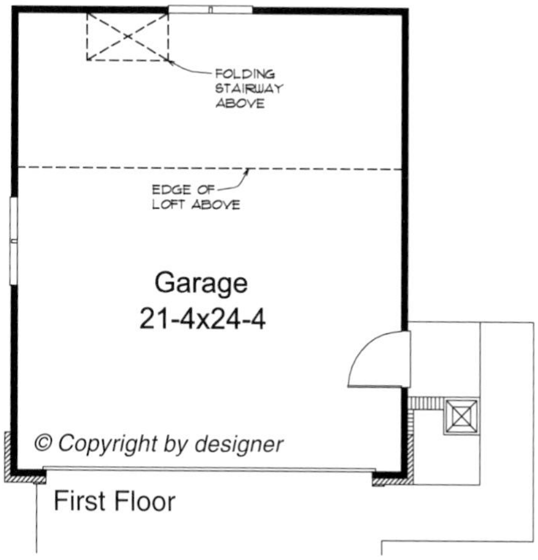
FOLDING STAIRWAY ABOVE
EDGE OF LOFT ABOVE
Garage
21-4x24-4
© Copyright by designer

First Floor

- Width: 22' Depth: 25'-4"
- Building height - 20'-6"
- Roof pitch - 3/12, 7/12
- Ceiling heights - First floor - 8' Second floor - 8'
- 18' x 7' overhead door
- Floating slab foundation
- The exterior features a roof dormer and service door
- Complete list of materials

1-Set	$275	PDF	$425
5-Set	$325	CAD	$600

PLAN #F50-117D-6001

2-Car Rustic Garage

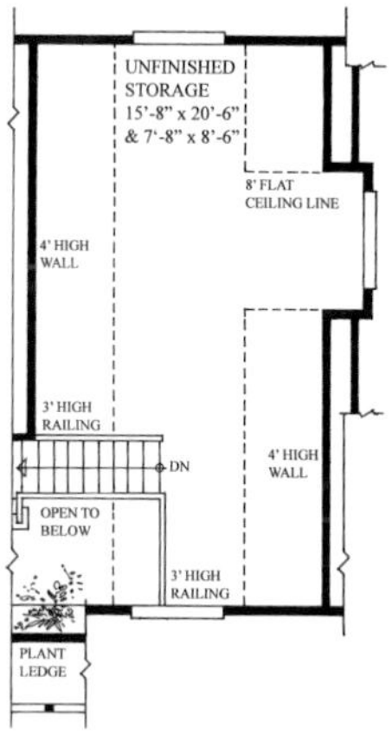
UNFINISHED STORAGE 15'-8" x 20'-6" & 7'-8" x 8'-6"
8' FLAT CEILING LINE
4' HIGH WALL
3' HIGH RAILING
DN
4' HIGH WALL
OPEN TO BELOW
3' HIGH RAILING
PLANT LEDGE

Second Floor

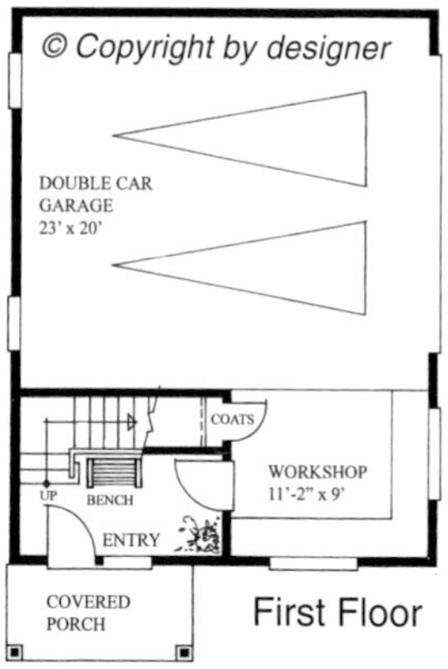
© Copyright by designer
DOUBLE CAR GARAGE 23' x 20'
COATS
WORKSHOP 11'-2" x 9'
UP
BENCH
ENTRY
COVERED PORCH

First Floor

- Width: 24' Depth: 35'
- Building height - 23'
- Roof pitch - 12/12
- Ceiling heights - First floor - 8' Second floor - 8'
- 16' x 7' overhead door
- Slab foundation
- 2" x 6" exterior walls
- The expansive second floor is perfect for storage

1-Set	$275	Repro	$475

2-Car Carport with Storage

PLAN #F50-002D-6045

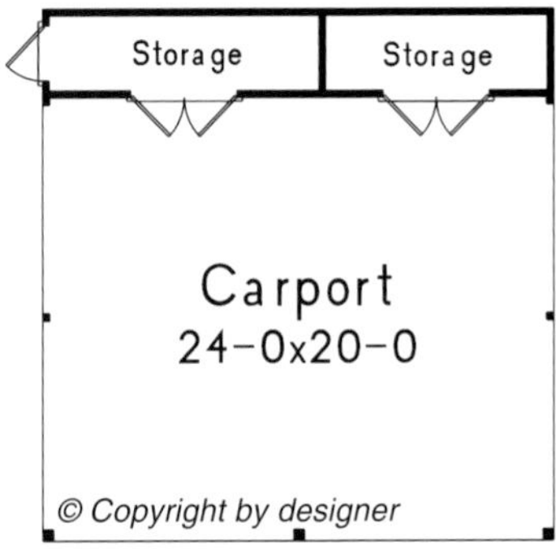
Storage
Storage
Carport
24-0x20-0
© Copyright by designer

- Width: 24' Depth: 24'
- Building height - 12'-8"
- Roof pitch - 4/12
- Ceiling height - 8'
- Slab foundation
- Unique design allows cars to enter from the front or side of the carport
- Deep storage space for long or tall items
- Complete list of materials
- Step-by-step instructions

1-Set	$175	PDF	$325
5-Set	$225	Repro	$375

Stylish European 3-Car Garage

PLAN #F50-154D-6000

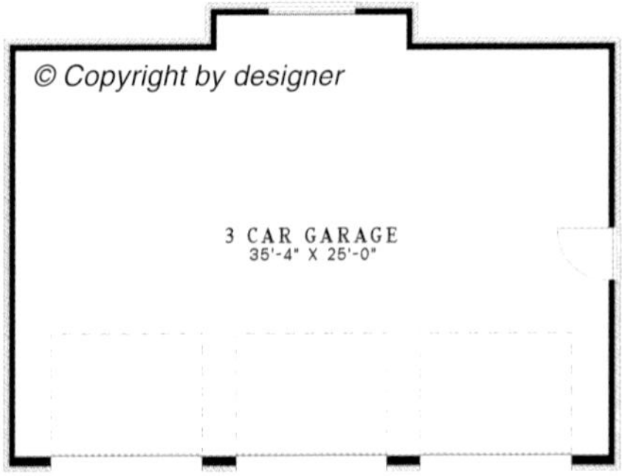
© Copyright by designer
3 CAR GARAGE
35'-4" X 25'-0"

- Width: 36' Depth: 26'
- Building height - 14'
- Roof pitch - 12/12
- Ceiling height - 10'
- Slab foundation
- Hip roof and curved wood garage doors give this garage European style

1-Set	$350	PDF	$550
5-Set	$435	CAD	$750

1-Car Garage with Flower Boxes

PLAN #F50-063D-6012

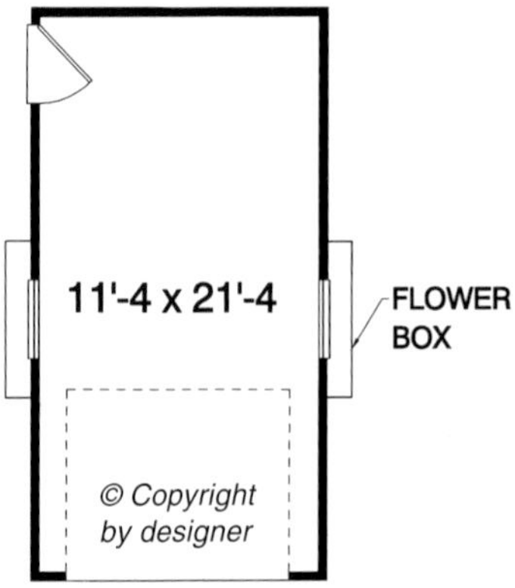
11'-4 x 21'-4
FLOWER BOX
© Copyright by designer

- Width: 12' Depth: 22'
- Building height - 11'-6"
- Roof pitch - 5/12
- Ceiling height - 8'
- 9' x 7' overhead door
- Floating slab foundation
- Charming flower boxes adorn both windows
- Complete list of materials

1-Set	$225	PDF	$375

PLAN #F50-002D-6043

1-Car Garage with Gambrel Roof & Loft

- Width: 16' Depth: 24'
- Building height - 18'-9"
- Roof pitch - 6/12
- Ceiling heights - First floor - 8' Loft - 6'-7"
- 9' x 7' overhead door
- Floating slab foundation
- Complete list of materials
- Step-by-step instructions

1-Set	$175	PDF	$325
5-Set	$225	CAD	$500

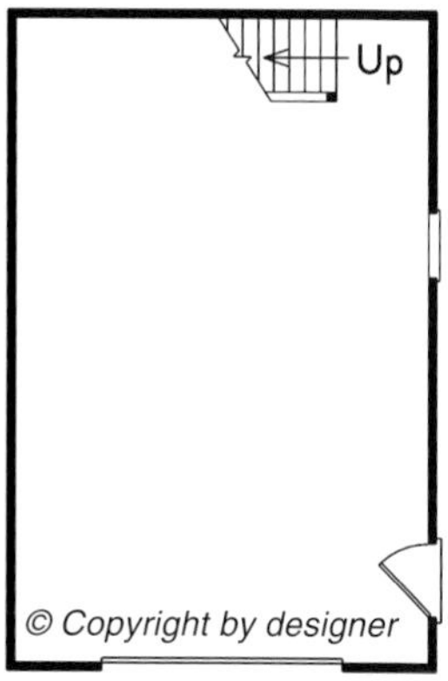
Up
© Copyright by designer

PLAN #F50-002D-6030

2-Car Garage To Add To An Existing Home

- Width: 22' Depth: 24'
- Building height - 12'-8"
- Roof pitch - 4/12
- Ceiling height - 8'
- 16' x 7' overhead door
- Floating slab foundation, drawings also include slab foundation
- Traditionally style looks great
- Complete list of materials
- Step-by-step instructions

1-Set	$225	PDF	$375
5-Set	$275	CAD	$550

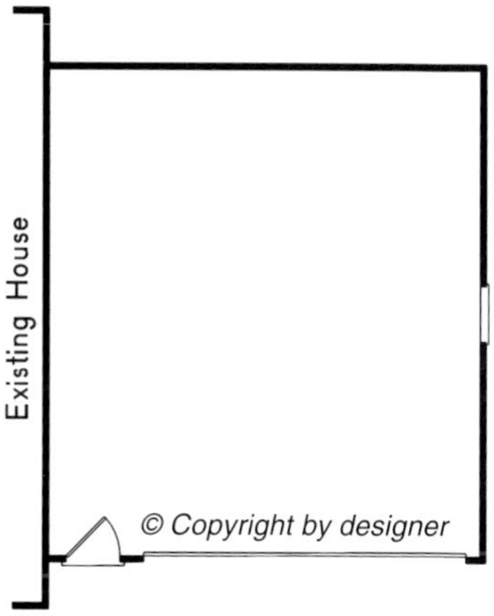
Existing House
© Copyright by designer

PLAN #F50-009D-6004

2-Car Carport with Shop / Storage

- Width: 28' Depth: 22'
- Building height - 19'
- Roof pitch - 8/12
- Ceiling height - 8'
- Slab foundation
- Storage/shop is 7'-4" x 11'-4"
- Attractive exterior complements any home
- Complete list of materials

1-Set	$175	PDF	$325
5-Set	$225	CAD	$500

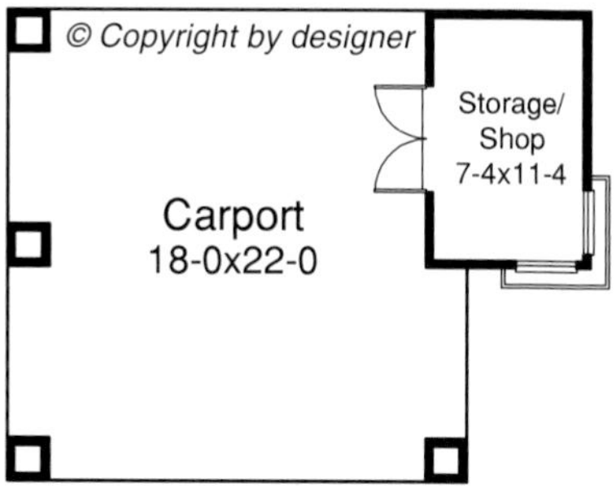
© Copyright by designer
Storage/ Shop 7-4x11-4
Carport 18-0x22-0

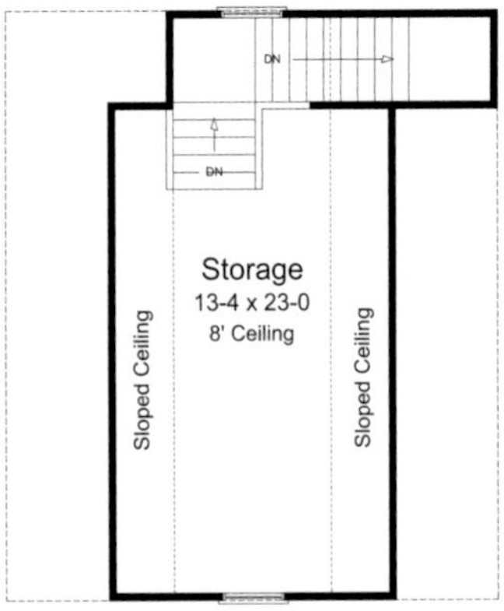

Second Floor

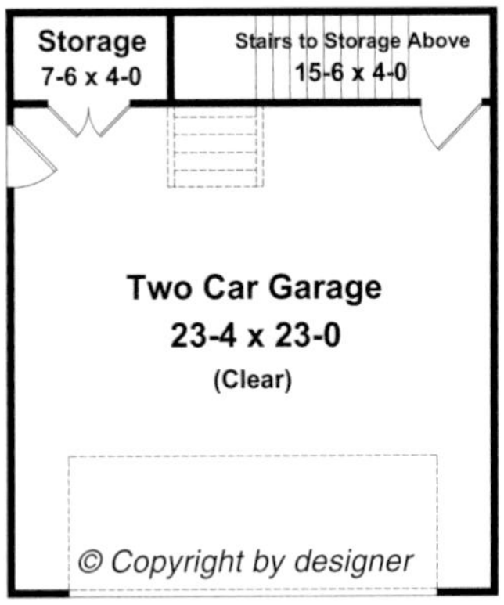

First Floor

- Width: 24' Depth: 26'
- Building height - 23'
- Roof pitch - 12/12
- Ceiling heights - First floor - 9' Second floor - 8'
- Slab foundation
- Great storage capability on the second floor

5-Set	$335	Repro	$460
PDF	$435	CAD	$655

1-Car Garage with Plenty of Room

PLAN #F50-113D-6011

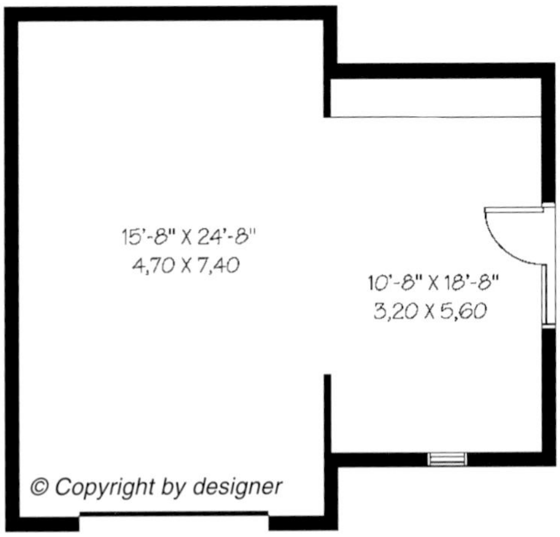

- Width: 28' Depth: 26'
- Building height - 20'
- Roof pitch - 8/12
- Ceiling height - 10'
- 2" x 6" exterior walls
- 10' x 7' overhead door
- Slab foundation

3-Set	$225	PDF	$295
5-Set	$245	CAD	$495

PLAN #F50-113D-6017

2-Car Garage with Gable Front

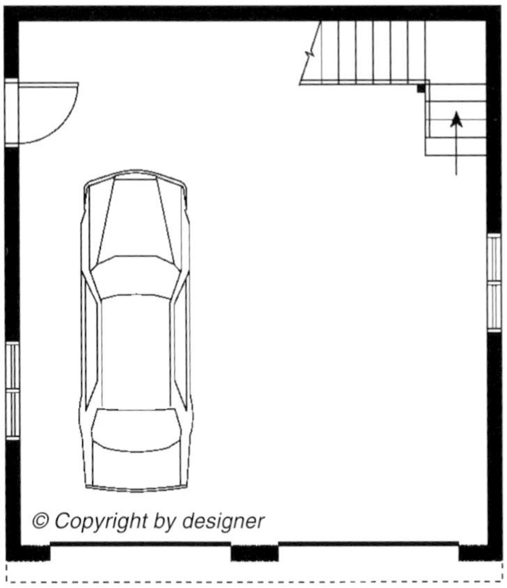
© Copyright by designer

- Width: 24' Depth: 26'
- Building height - 21'-6"
- Roof pitch - 10/12
- Two 9 x 7' overhead doors
- Ceiling heights - First floor - 9'-6" Second floor - 7'-6"
- 2" x 6" exterior walls
- Floating slab foundation

3-Set	$285	PDF	$355
5-Set	$305	CAD	$555

PLAN #F50-059D-6014

2-Car Garage with Western Flair

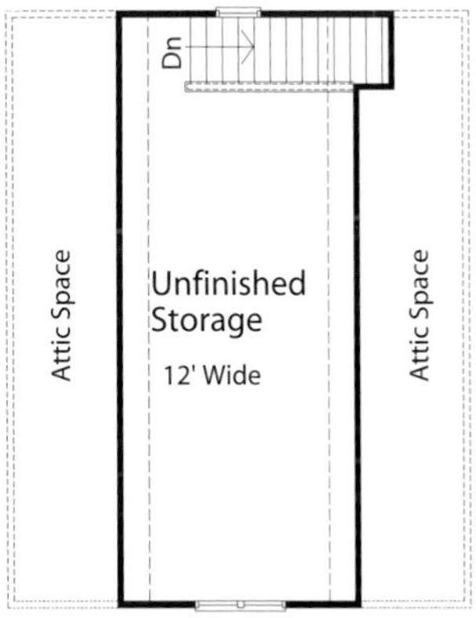
Dn
Attic Space
Unfinished Storage
12' Wide
Attic Space

Second Floor

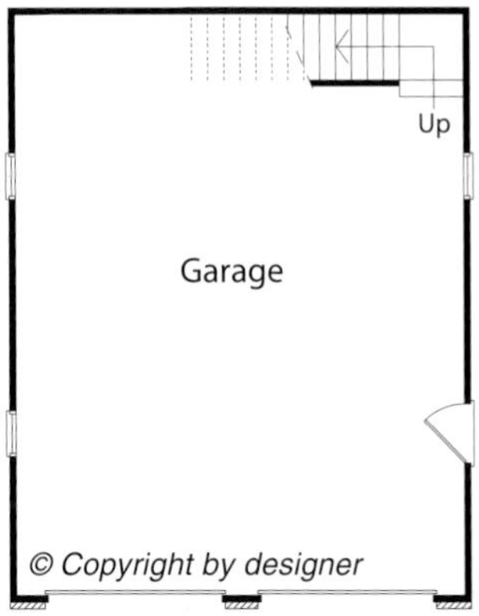
Up
Garage
© Copyright by designer

First Floor

- Width: 24' Depth: 30'-4"
- Building height - 25'
- Roof pitch - 12/12
- Ceiling heights - First floor - 9' Second floor - 8'
- Two 9' x 8' overhead doors
- 2" x 6" exterior walls available for an additional fee of $50, please specify when ordering
- Floating slab foundation

1-Set	$200	CAD	$475
PDF	$295	Mat List	$50

Stylish Carport Perfect for Any Home

PLAN #F50-124D-6003

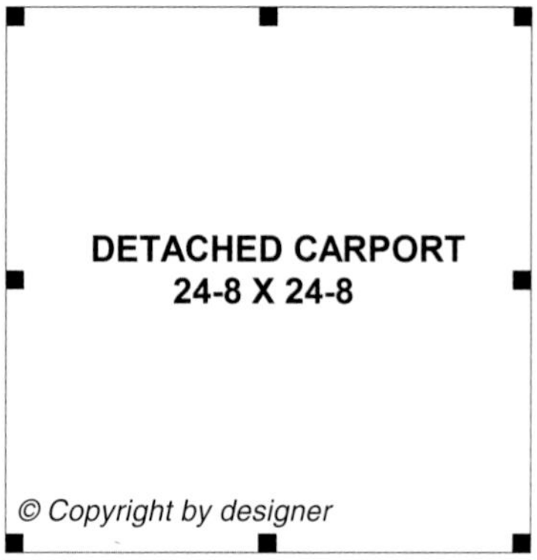
DETACHED CARPORT
24-8 X 24-8
© Copyright by designer

- Width: 24'-8" Depth: 24'-8"
- Building height - 19'-6"
- Roof pitch - 10/12
- Ceiling height - 8'
- Slab foundation

5-Set	$335	Repro	$460
PDF	$435	CAD	$655

2-Car Garage with Sun Deck

PLAN #F50-064D-6002

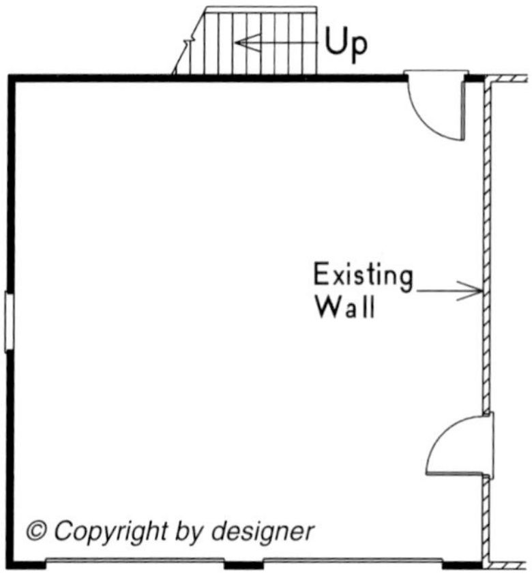
Up
Existing Wall
© Copyright by designer

- Width: 24' Depth: 24'
- Plan includes two additional sizes: 24' x 26' 26' x 26'
- Building height - 12'-6"
- Roof pitch - .125/12
- Ceiling height - 8'
- Two 9' x 7' overhead doors
- Slab foundation
- Complete list of materials
- Step-by-step instructions

1-Set	$125	Repro	$175
PDF	$165		

Classic 2-Car Economy Garage

PLAN #F50-113D-6004

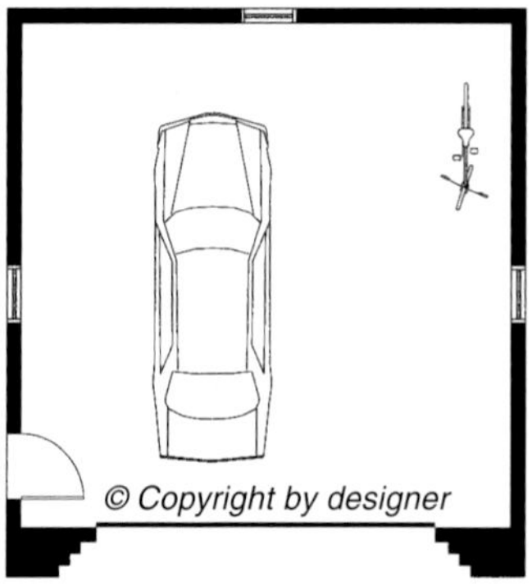
© Copyright by designer

- Width: 24' Depth: 24'
- Building height - 17'-6"
- Roof pitch - 7/12
- Ceiling height - 9'
- 10' x 7' overhead door
- 2" x 6" exterior walls
- Floating slab foundation
- Convenient side door
- Windows provide natural light

3-Set	$265	PDF	$335
5-Set	$285	CAD	$535

PLAN #F50-009D-6015

Carport with Storage

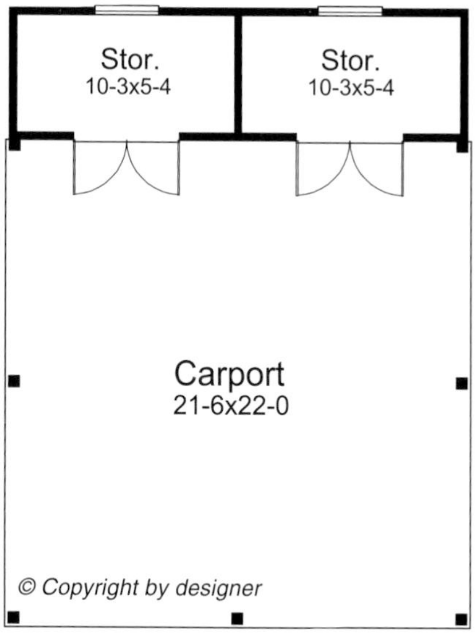

Stor.
10-3x5-4
Stor.
10-3x5-4
Carport
21-6x22-0
© Copyright by designer

- Width: 21'-6" Depth: 28'-0"
- Building height - 16'-7"
- Roof pitch - 6/12
- Ceiling height - 9'
- Slab foundation
- Eye-catching design includes roof dormers with cathedral top louvers and cross-buck doors
- Located to the rear of the carport are two very functional storage rooms
- Complete list of materials

1-Set	$225	PDF	$375
5-Set	$275	CAD	$550

PLAN #F50-059D-6021

Compact 2-Car Garage with Gable Front

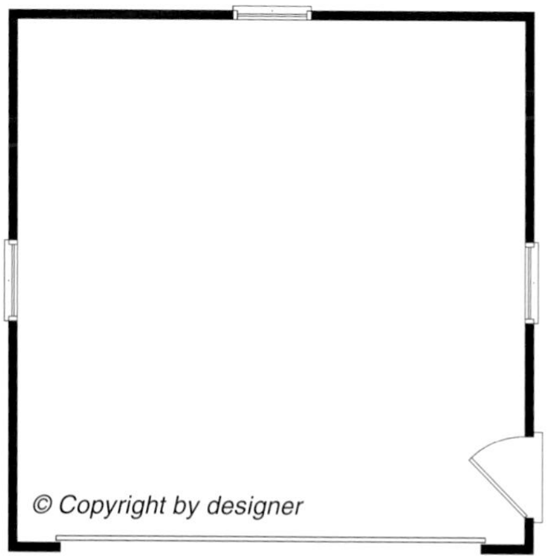

© Copyright by designer

- Width: 20' Depth: 20'
- Building height - 14'
- Roof pitch - 5/12
- Ceiling height - 8'
- 16' x 7' overhead door
- Floating slab foundation
- Excellent small garage for many different home styles

1-Set	$175	CAD	$375
PDF	$260	Mat List	$40

1-Car Garage with Storage & Porch

PLAN #F50-107D-6004

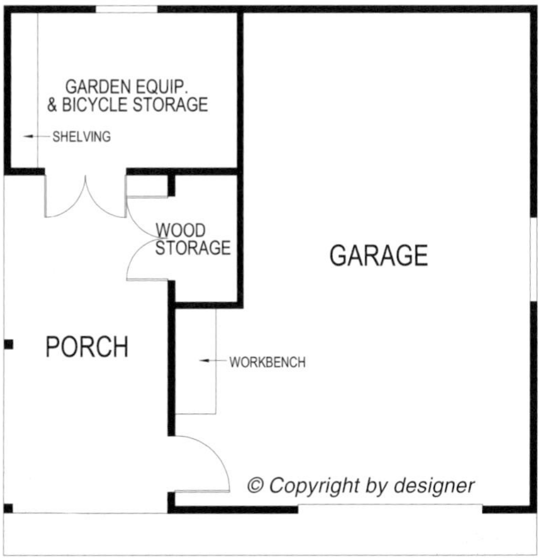
GARDEN EQUIP.
& BICYCLE STORAGE
SHELVING
WOOD
STORAGE
GARAGE
PORCH
WORKBENCH
© Copyright by designer

- Width: 26' Depth: 24'
- Building height - 14'-3"
- Roof pitch - 4/12
- Ceiling height - 8'
- 9' x 7' overhead door
- Slab foundation
- Charming garage features two storage rooms and covered porch
- Complete list of materials
- Step-by-step instructions

1-Set	$125	PDF	$165
5-Set	$155	Repro	$175

2-Car Garage with Loft / Studio

PLAN #F50-063D-6002

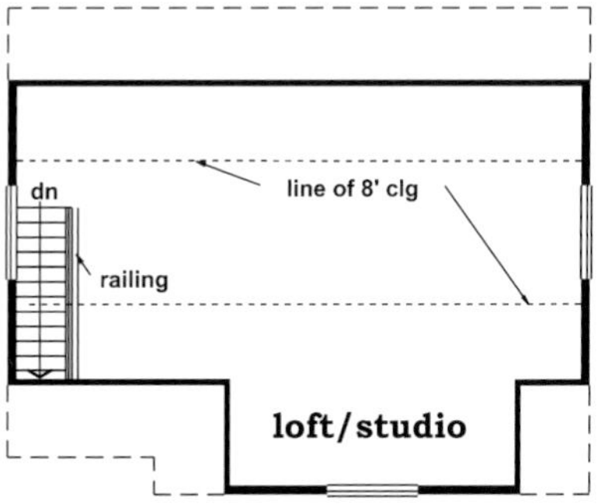
dn
line of 8' clg
railing
loft/studio

Second Floor

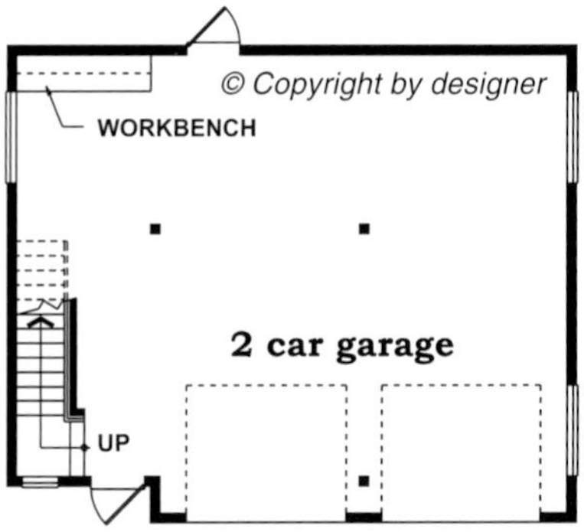
© Copyright by designer
WORKBENCH
2 car garage
UP

First Floor

- Width: 32' Depth: 26'
- Building height - 23'
- Roof pitch - 12/12
- Ceiling heights - First floor - 8' Second floor - 8'
- Two 9' x 7' overhead doors
- Slab foundation
- Additional storage available in the loft/studio
- Complete list of materials

1-Set	$420	Repro	$620
PDF	$570	CAD	$900

PLAN #F50-113D-6012

Country Style 1-Car Garage

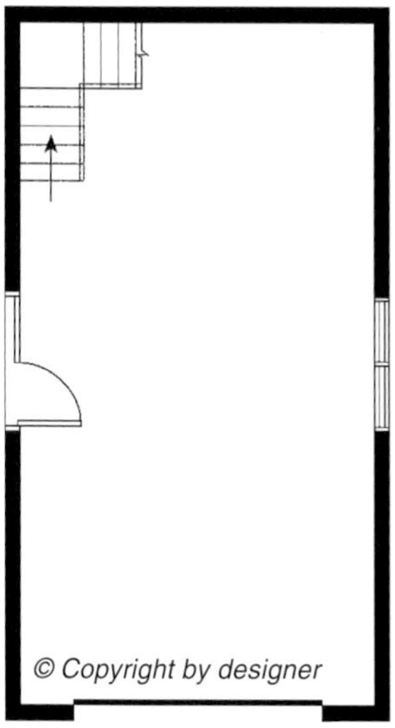
© Copyright by designer

- Width: 18'   Depth: 32'
- Building height - 24'-8"
- Roof pitch - 18/12
- Ceiling heights - First floor - 8'   Second floor - 8'
- 12' x 7' overhead door
- 2" x 6" exterior walls
- Floating slab foundation
- Excellent garage for large equipment, an RV, or boat storage

3-Set	$245	PDF	$315
5-Set	$265	CAD	$515

PLAN #F50-009D-6018

2-Car Garage with Studio Loft

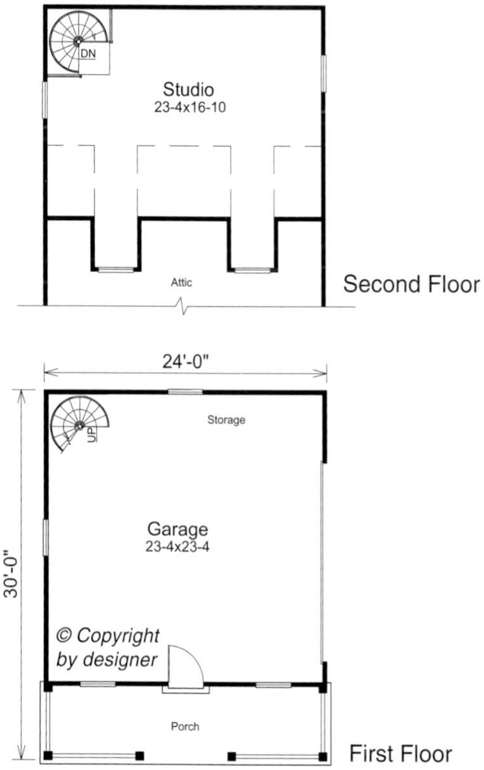
DN
Studio
23-4x16-10
Attic
Second Floor
24'-0"
30'-0"
UP
Storage
Garage
23-4x23-4
© Copyright
by designer
Porch
First Floor

- Width: 24'   Depth: 30'
- Building height - 21'-4"
- Roof pitch - 4/12, 8/12
- Ceiling height - 8'
- 16' x 7' overhead door
- Floating slab foundation, drawings also include slab foundation
- Complete list of materials

1-Set	$275	PDF	$425
5-Set	$325	CAD	$600

2-Car Garage

PLAN #F50-113D-6028

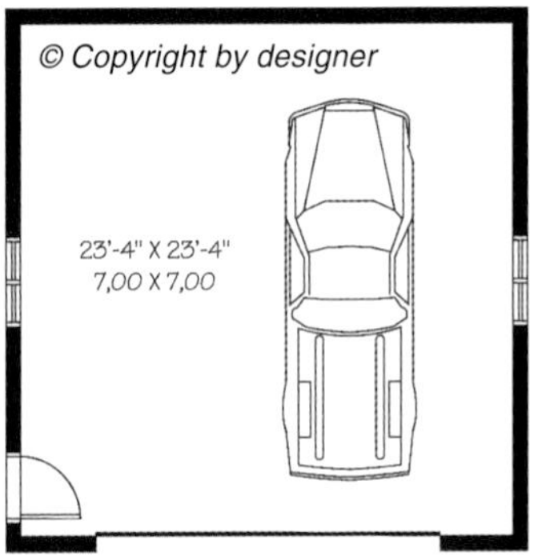

© Copyright by designer
23'-4" X 23'-4"
7,00 X 7,00

- Width: 24'   Depth: 24'
- Building height - 13'
- Roof pitch - 4/12
- Ceiling height - 8'-6"
- 16' x 7' overhead door
- Floating slab foundation
- Attractive addition to any home

3-Set	$265	PDF	$335
5-Set	$285	CAD	$535

2-Car Garage - Gambrel Roof

PLAN #F50-002D-6031

© Copyright by designer

- Width: 24'   Depth: 24'
- Building height - 15'-5"
- Roof pitch - 4/12, 8/12
- Ceiling height - 8'
- 16' x 7' overhead door
- Floating slab foundation, drawings also include slab foundation
- Attractive addition to any home
- Complete list of materials
- Step-by-step instructions

1-Set	$225	PDF	$375
5-Set	$275	Repro	$425

Stylish 2-Car Brick Garage

PLAN #F50-124D-6000

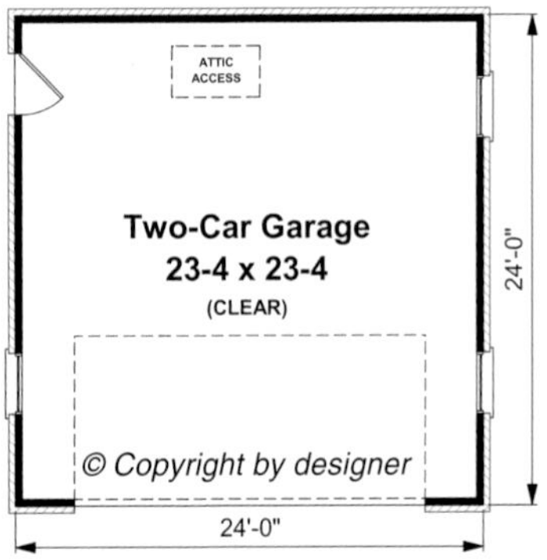

ATTIC ACCESS
Two-Car Garage
23-4 x 23-4
(CLEAR)
© Copyright by designer
24'-0"
24'-0"

- Width: 24'   Depth: 24'
- Building height - 18'-9"
- Roof pitch - 8/12
- Ceiling height - 9'
- 18' x 8' overhead door
- Slab foundation
- Plenty of room for oversized vehicles, plus easy outside access through the side door

5-Set	$335	Repro	$460
PDF	$435	CAD	$655

PLAN #F50-002D-6032

2-Car Economy Garage

- Width: 20' Depth: 20'
- Building height - 11'-10"
- Roof pitch - 4/12
- Ceiling height - 8'
- 16' x 7' overhead door
- Floating slab foundation, drawings also include slab foundation
- Complete list of materials
- Step-by-step instructions

1-Set	$225	PDF	$375
5-Set	$275	Repro	$425

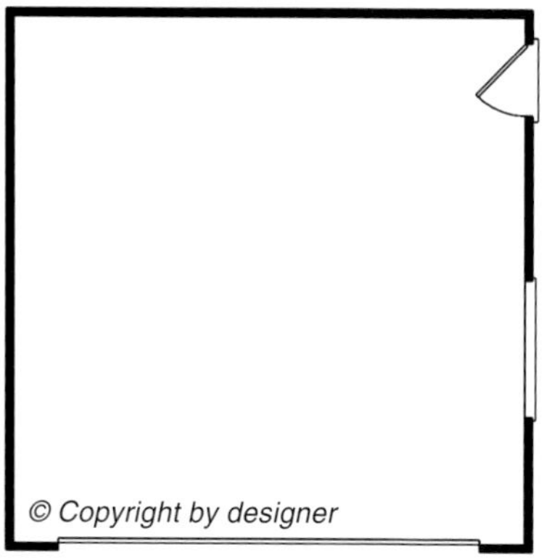
© Copyright by designer

PLAN #F50-059D-6023

Compact 2-Car Garage

- Width: 22' Depth: 22'
- Building height - 14'
- Roof pitch - 5/12
- Ceiling height - 8'
- 16' x 7' overhead door
- Floating slab foundation
- Excellent small garage perfect with many different home styles

1-Set	$175	CAD	$375
PDF	$260	Mat List	$40

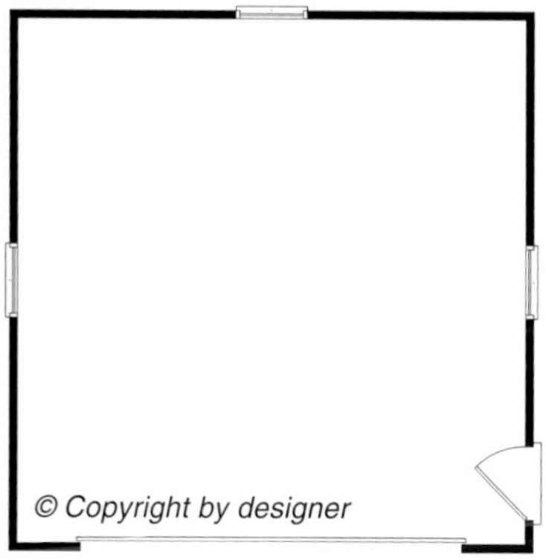
© Copyright by designer

PLAN #F50-113D-6002

1-Car Garage with Cupola

- Width: 16' Depth: 24'
- Building height - 17'-8"
- Roof pitch - 8/12
- Ceiling height - 9'
- 12' x 7' overhead door
- Floating slab foundation
- The hip roof with louvered cupola add elegance to this garage

3-Set	$205	PDF	$275
5-Set	$225	CAD	$475

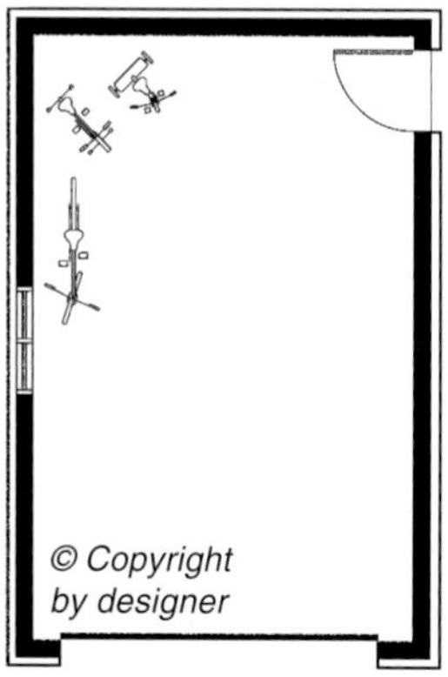
© Copyright
by designer

3-Car Garage with Gambrel Roof

PLAN #F50-113D-6032

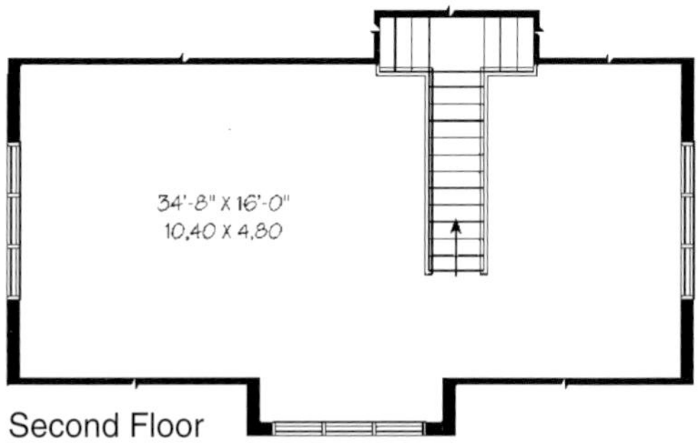
34'-8" x 16'-0"
10.40 x 4.80

Second Floor

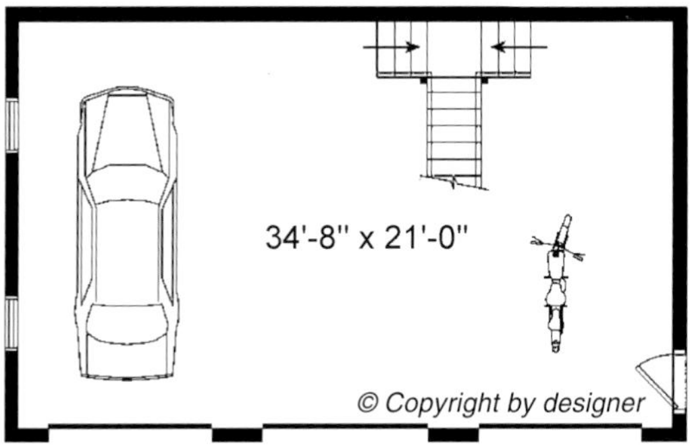
34'-8" x 21'-0"
© Copyright by designer

First Floor

- Width: 36' Depth: 22'-4"
- Building height - 25'-4"
- Roof pitch - 8/12
- Ceiling heights - First floor - 9' Second floor - 8'
- Three 9' x 8' overhead doors
- Floating slab foundation
- 2" x 6" exterior walls
- Ample amounts of light from large windows on the second floor

3-Set	$365	PDF	$435
5-Set	$385	CAD	$635

3-Car Garage with Storage

PLAN #F50-108D-6001

DN
STORAGE
37'-4" x 23'-4"
7'-7" HIGH KNEE WALLS

Second Floor

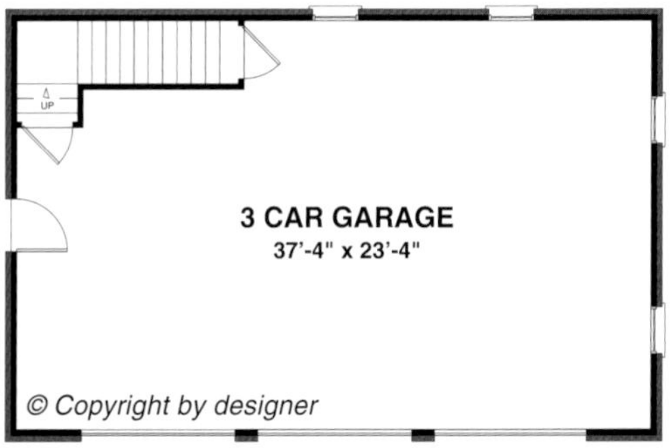
UP
3 CAR GARAGE
37'-4" x 23'-4"
© Copyright by designer

First Floor

- Width: 38' Depth: 24'
- Building height - 24'-8"
- Roof pitch - 12/12
- Ceiling heights - First floor - 8' Second floor - 9'
- Three 9' x 7' overhead doors
- Slab foundation
- Attractive brick exterior boasts curb appeal
- The second floor features an impressive storage space

PDF	$795	CAD	$1095
Repro	$945		

PLAN #F50-059D-6011

2-Car Garage with Storage

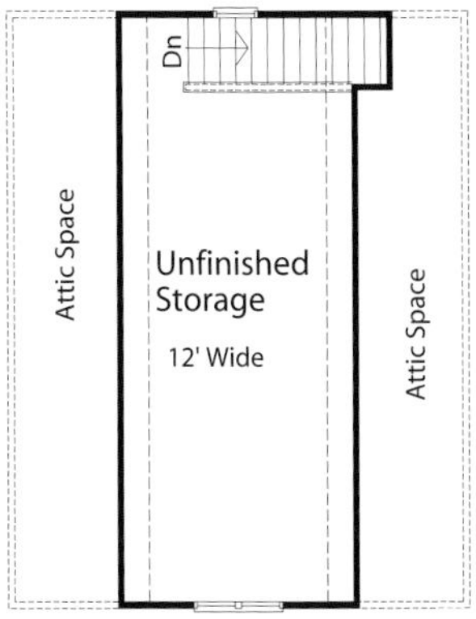

Dn
Attic Space
Unfinished Storage
12' Wide
Attic Space

Second Floor

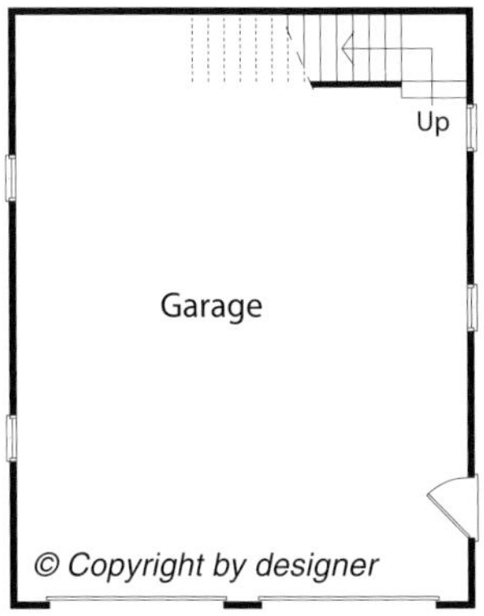

Up
Garage
© Copyright by designer

First Floor

- Width: 24' Depth: 30'
- Building height - 25'
- Roof pitch - 12/12
- Ceiling heights - First floor - 9' Second floor - 8'
- Two 9' x 8' overhead doors
- Floating slab foundation
- Attractive cupola adds country charm to the exterior

1-Set	$200	CAD	$475
PDF	$295	Mat List	$50

PLAN #F50-113D-6008

2-Car Garage with Room to Grow

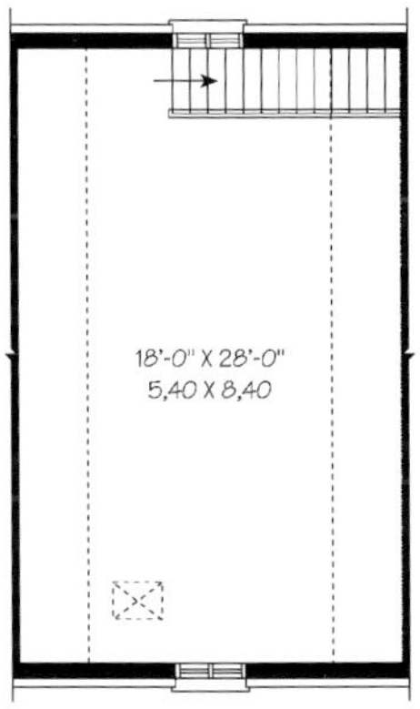

18'-0" X 28'-0"
5,40 X 8,40

Second Floor

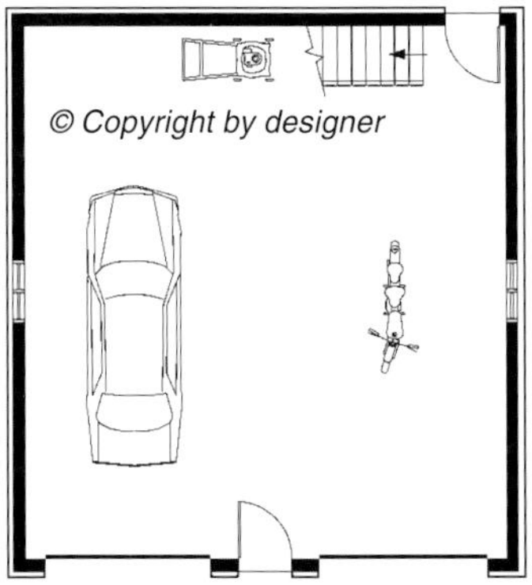

© Copyright by designer

First Floor

- Width: 28' Depth: 30'
- Building height - 25'-8"
- Roof pitch - 14/12
- Ceiling heights - First floor - 8' Second floor - 8'
- Two 9' x 7' overhead doors
- 2" x 6" exterior walls
- Floating slab foundation
- Loft above the garage provides for additional storage

3-Set	$305	PDF	$375
5-Set	$325	CAD	$575

2-Car Garage - Reverse Gable

PLAN #F50-002D-6033

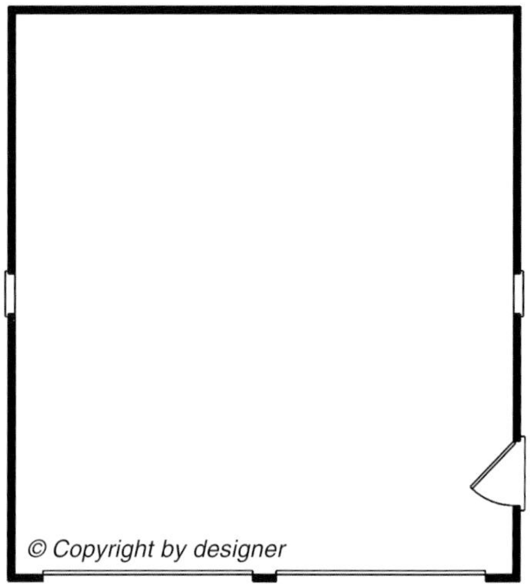
© Copyright by designer

- Width: 22' Depth: 24'
- Building height - 13'-8"
- Roof pitch - 5/12
- Ceiling height - 8'
- Two 9' x 7' overhead doors
- Floating slab foundation, drawings also include slab foundation
- Complete list of materials
- Step-by-step instructions

1-Set	$225	PDF	$375
5-Set	$275	Repro	$425

Compact 2-Car Garage

PLAN #F50-059D-6024

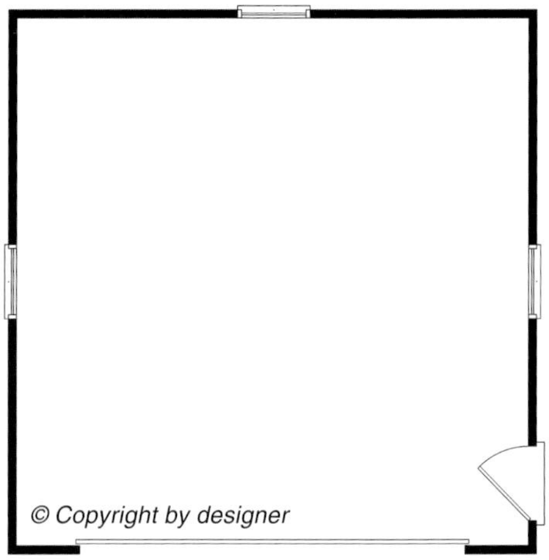
© Copyright by designer

- Width: 22' Depth: 22'
- Building height - 14'
- Roof pitch - 5/12
- Ceiling height - 9'
- 16' x 7' overhead door
- Floating slab foundation
- Excellent small garage for many different home styles

1-Set	$175	CAD	$375
PDF	$260	Mat List	$40

PLAN #F50-002D-6034

2-Car Economy Garage

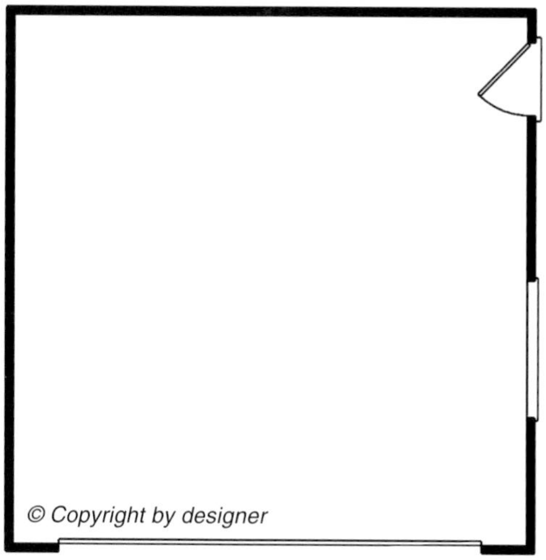
© Copyright by designer

- Width: 20'   Depth: 20'
- Building height - 12'
- Roof pitch - 4/12
- Ceiling height - 8'
- 16' x 7' overhead door
- Floating slab foundation, drawings also include slab foundation
- Hip roof design looks good on any lot
- Complete list of materials
- Step-by-step instructions

1-Set	$225	PDF	$375
5-Set	$275	Repro	$425

PLAN #F50-059D-6025

2-Car Garage

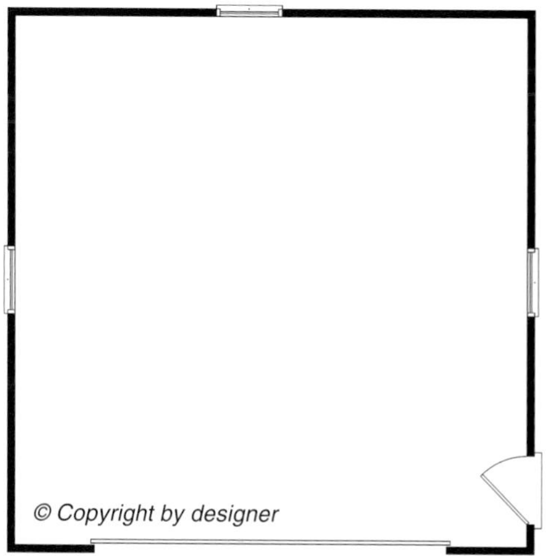
© Copyright by designer

- Width: 24'   Depth: 24'
- Building height - 15'
- Roof pitch - 5/12
- Ceiling height - 8'
- 16' x 7' overhead door
- 2" x 6" exterior walls available for an additional of $50, please specify when ordering
- Floating slab foundation

1-Set	$175	CAD	$375
PDF	$260	Mat List	$40

Spacious 2-Car Garage with Carport

PLAN #F50-124D-6001

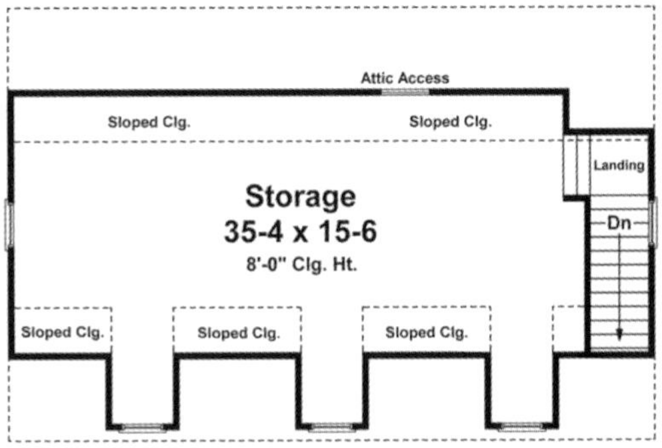

Second Floor

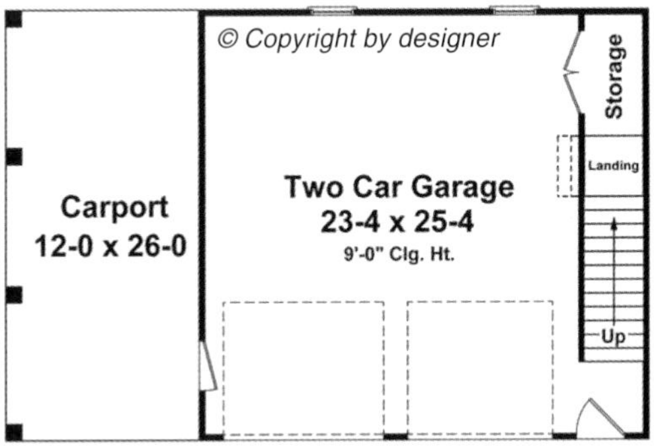

First Floor

- Width: 40' Depth: 26'
- Building height - 24'
- Roof pitch - 12/12
- Ceiling heights - First floor - 9' Second floor - 8'
- Two 9' x 7' overhead doors
- Slab foundation

5-Set	$335	Repro	$460
PDF	$435	CAD	$655

2-Car Garage with Studio / Storage

PLAN #F50-009D-6014

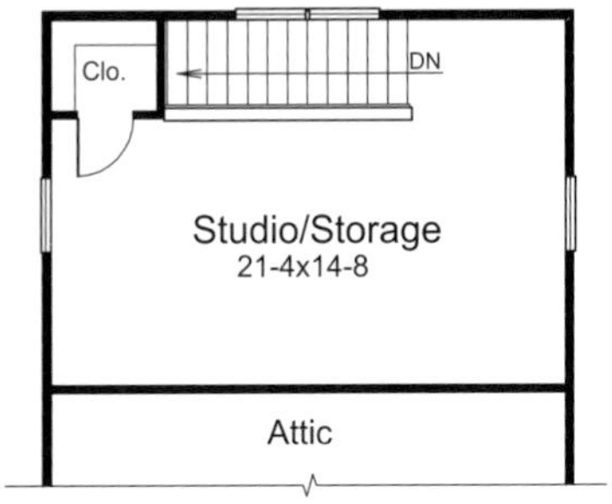

Second Floor

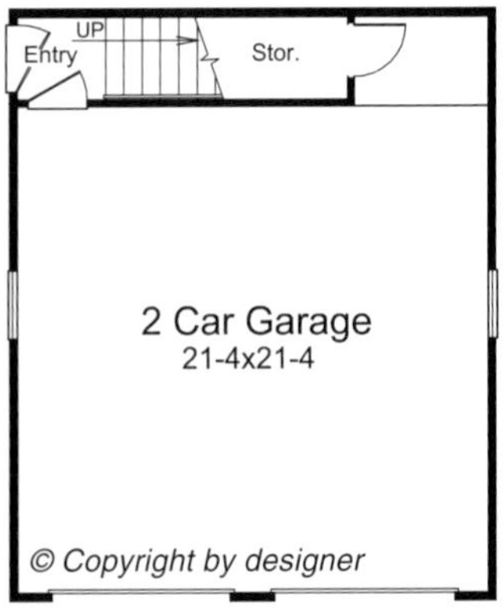

First Floor

- Width: 22' Depth: 26'
- Building height - 22'
- Roof pitch - 6/12, 10/12
- Ceiling heights - First floor - 8' Second floor - 8'
- Two 9' x 7' overhead doors
- Floating slab foundation, drawings also include slab foundation
- Complete list of materials

1-Set	$275	PDF	$425
5-Set	$325	CAD	$600

PLAN #F50-059D-6013

2-Car Garage with Dormers

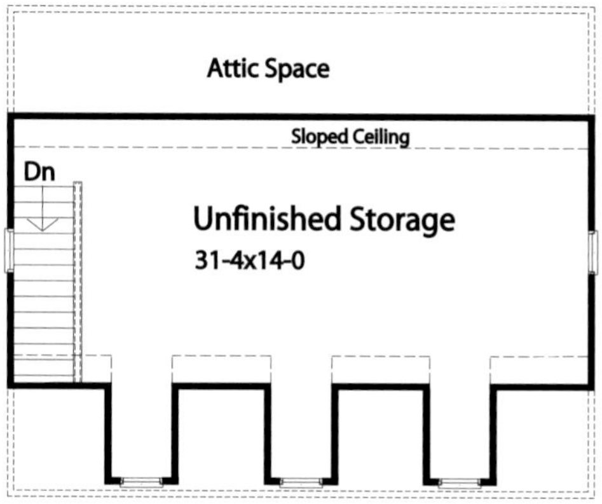
Attic Space
Sloped Ceiling
Dn
Unfinished Storage
31-4x14-0

Second Floor

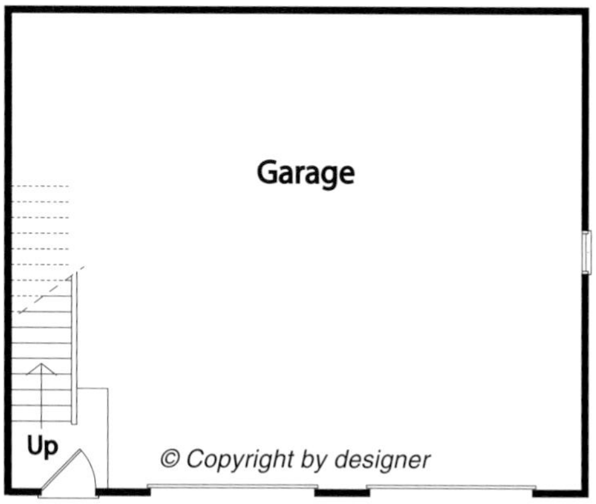
Garage
Up
© Copyright by designer

First Floor

- Width: 32' Depth: 26'
- Building height - 26'
- Roof pitch - 12/12
- Ceiling heights - First floor - 9' Second floor - 8'
- Two 9' x 8' overhead doors
- Floating slab foundation
- Trio of dormers fills unfinished storage with natural light

1-Set	$200	CAD	$475
PDF	$295	Mat List	$50

PLAN #F50-107D-6001

2-Car Garage with Work Area

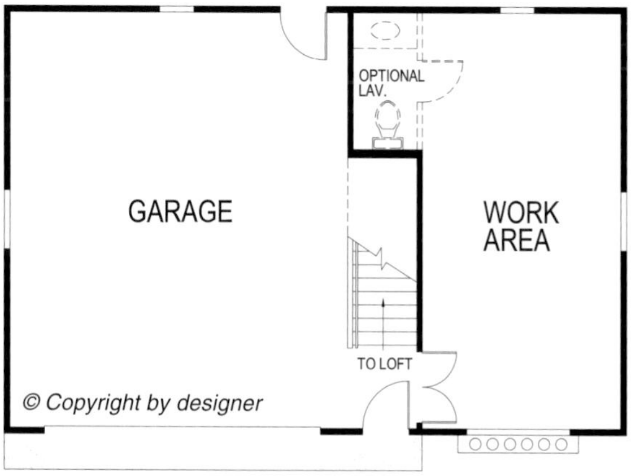
OPTIONAL LAV.
GARAGE
WORK AREA
TO LOFT
© Copyright by designer

- Width: 36' Depth: 24'
- Building height - 19'
- Roof pitch - 10/12
- Ceiling heights - First floor - 8' Loft - 6'-8"
- 16' x 7' overhead door
- Floating slab foundation, drawings also include slab foundation
- Complete list of materials
- Step-by-step instructions

1-Set	$175	PDF	$325
5-Set	$225	Repro	$375

2-Car Side Garage with Shop

PLAN #F50-009D-6001

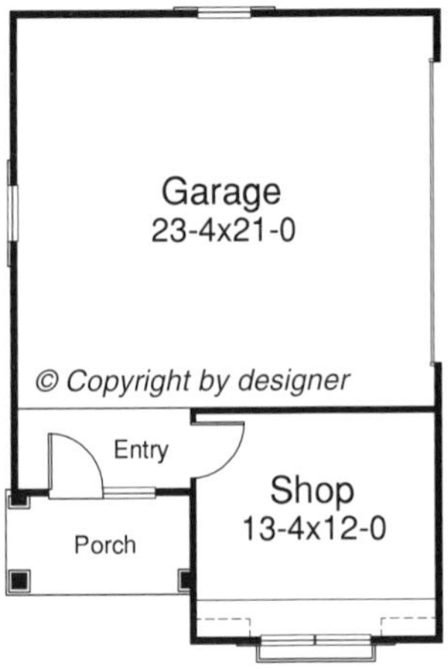
Garage
23-4x21-0
© Copyright by designer
Entry
Porch
Shop
13-4x12-0

- Width: 24'   Depth: 34'
- Building height - 21'
- Roof pitch - 3/12, 8/12
- Ceiling height - 9'
- 16' x 8' overhead door
- Floating slab foundation
- Shop is 13'-4" x 12' with built-in cabinetry
- Porch, roof dormer and shuttered window with planter box provide character
- Complete list of materials

1-Set	$325	PDF	$475
5-Set	$375	CAD	$650

Garage with Porch

PLAN #F50-114D-6001

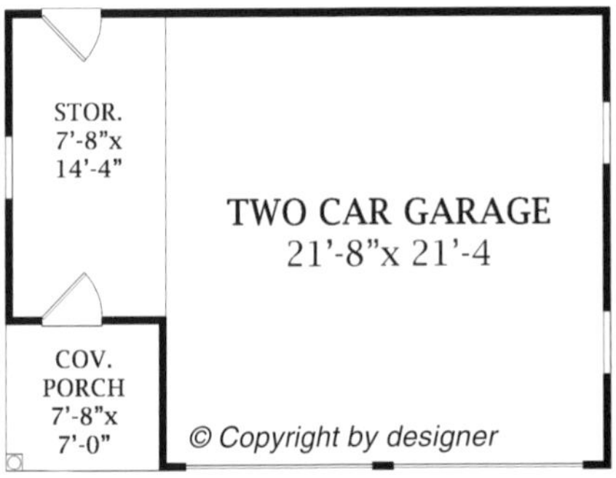
STOR.
7'-8"x
14'-4"
TWO CAR GARAGE
21'-8"x 21'-4
COV.
PORCH
7'-8"x
7'-0"
© Copyright by designer

- Width: 30'   Depth: 22'
- Building height - 21'
- Roof pitch - 7/12
- Ceiling height - 9'
- Two 9' x 8' overhead doors
- Slab foundation
- Structure is very appealing with the covered porch
- Plenty of windows provide natural light
- One-story garage has charming shingle siding and arched garage doors

PDF	$645	CAD	$1295
Repro	$675		

2-Car Garage with Shop & Storage

PLAN #F50-009D-6009

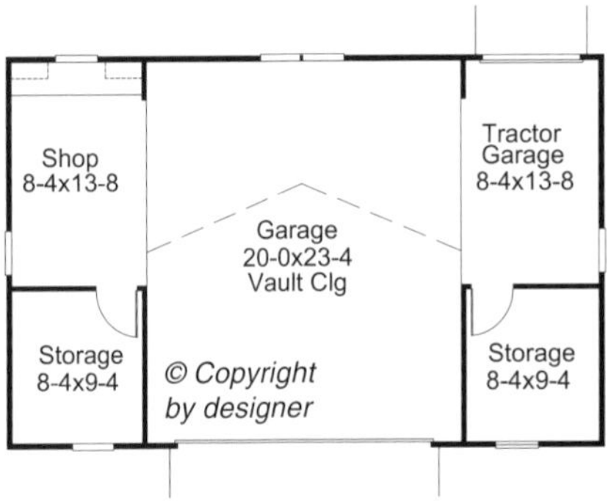
Shop
8-4x13-8
Garage
20-0x23-4
Vault Clg
Tractor
Garage
8-4x13-8
Storage
8-4x9-4
© Copyright
by designer
Storage
8-4x9-4

- Width: 38'   Depth: 24'
- Building height - 21'-6"
- Roof pitch - 8/12
- Ceiling heights -
  Garage - 14' Other - 8'
- 16' x 9', 6' x 7' overhead doors
- Floating slab foundation
- Complete list of materials

1-Set	$275	PDF	$425
5-Set	$325	Repro	$475

PLAN #F50-002D-6035

2-Car Economy Garage

- Width: 20' Depth: 20'
- Building height - 12'
- Roof pitch - 4/12
- Ceiling height - 8'
- 16' x 7' overhead door
- Floating slab foundation, drawings also include slab foundation
- Convenient side door
- Complete list of materials
- Step-by-step instructions

1-Set	$225	PDF	$375
5-Set	$275	Repro	$425

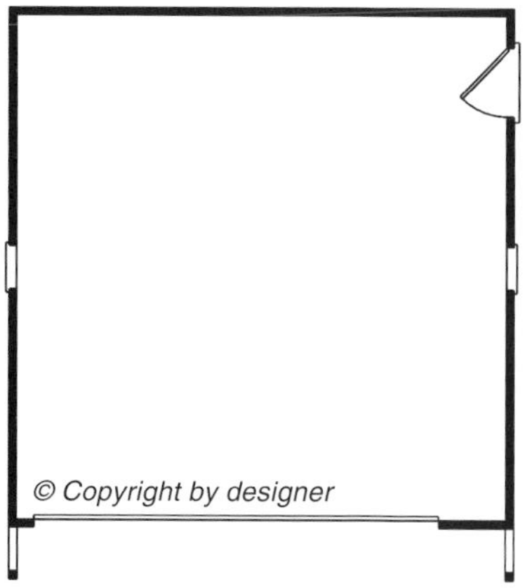
© Copyright by designer

PLAN #F50-002D-6036

2-Car Garage - Reverse Gable

- Width: 24' Depth: 22'
- Building height - 13'
- Roof pitch - 5/12
- Ceiling height - 8'
- Two 9' x 7' overhead doors
- Floating slab foundation, drawings also include slab foundation
- Convenient side door
- Complete list of materials
- Step-by-step instructions

1-Set	$225	PDF	$375
5-Set	$275	Repro	$425

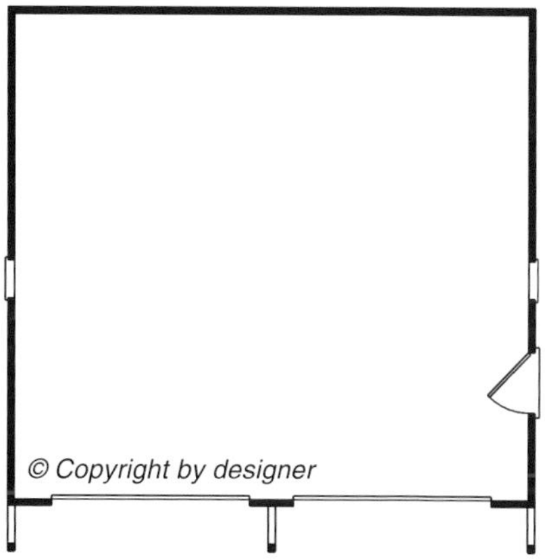
© Copyright by designer

PLAN #F50-059D-6026

2-Car Garage

- Width: 24' Depth: 24'
- Building height - 15'
- Roof pitch - 5/12
- Ceiling height - 8'
- 16' x 7' overhead door
- Floating slab foundation
- Design complements any home

1-Set	$175	CAD	$375
PDF	$260	Mat List	$40

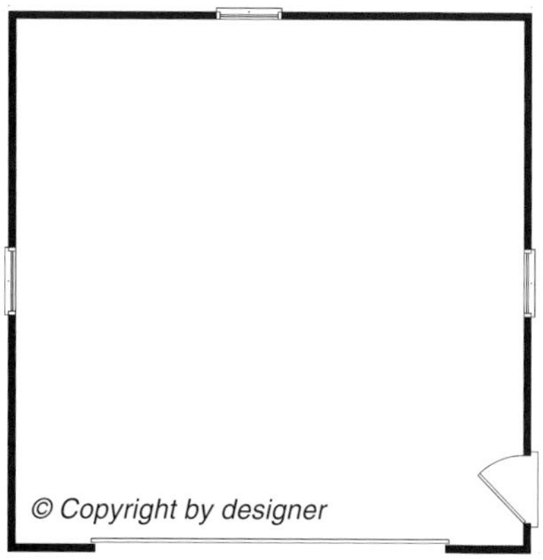
© Copyright by designer

Garage with Shop & Bonus Room

PLAN #F50-009D-6006

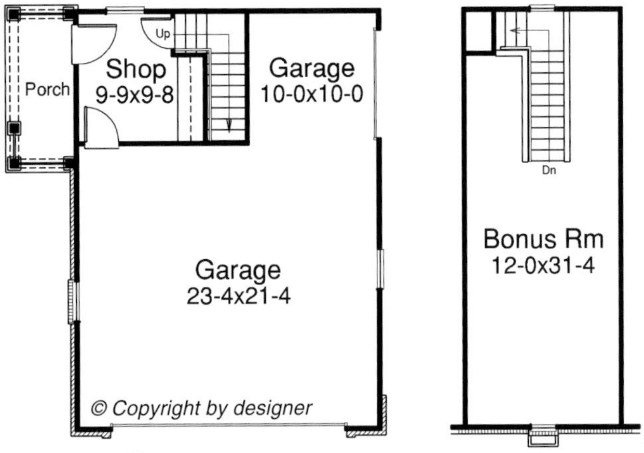

First Floor

Second Floor

- Width: 29' Depth: 32'
- Building height - 22'
- Roof pitch - 10/12
- Ceiling heights - First floor - 8' Second floor - 8'
- 16' x 8' overhead door
- Floating slab foundation
- Shop is 9'-9" x 9'-8" with built-in cabinetry
- Complete list of materials

1-Set	$325	PDF	$475
5-Set	$375	CAD	$650

2-Car Garage with Porch & Shop

PLAN #F50-009D-6005

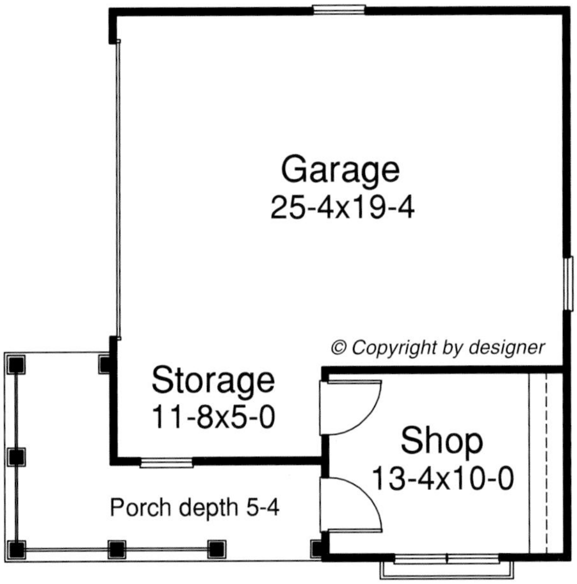

- Width: 31'-8" Depth: 30'-4"
- Building height - 19'-4"
- Roof pitch - 8/12, 9/12
- Ceiling height - 8'
- 16' x 7' overhead door
- Floating slab foundation
- Shop is 13'-4" x 10' with built-in cabinetry
- Complete list of materials

1-Set	$275	PDF	$425
5-Set	$325	CAD	$600

PLAN #F50-113D-6009

Country Style 2-Car Garage

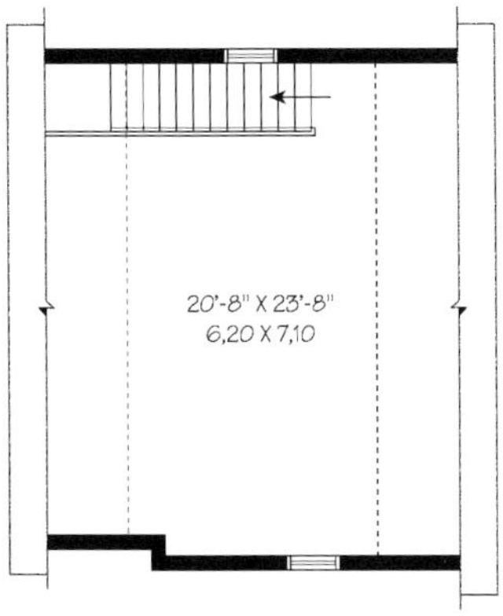

Second Floor

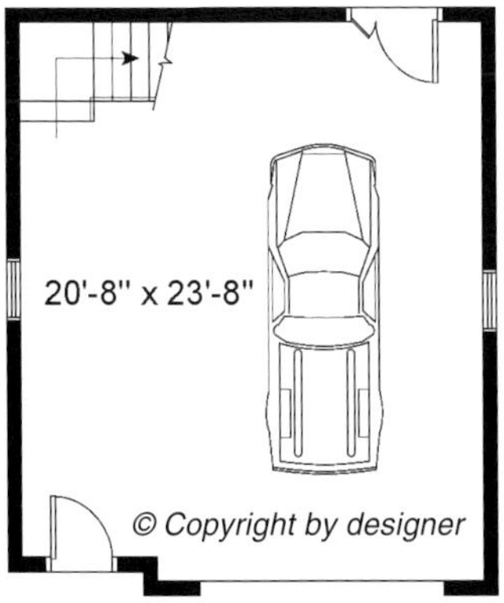

First Floor

- Width: 22'   Depth: 25'
- Building height - 25'-10"
- Roof pitch - 12/12
- Ceiling heights - First floor - 8'-4"   Second floor - 8'
- 11' x 7' overhead door
- Floating slab foundation
- Attractive gable roof design looks good on any lot
- Windows and doors add natural light to the garage
- Convenient service door in front and rear

3-Set	$245	PDF	$315
5-Set	$265	CAD	$515

PLAN #F50-059D-6015

2-Car & RV Garage with Loft

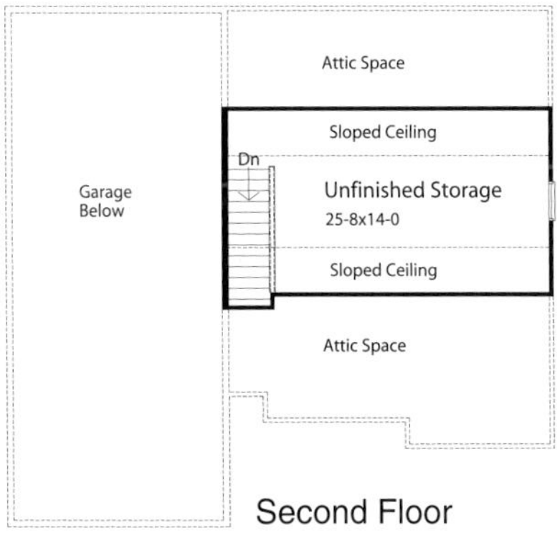

Second Floor

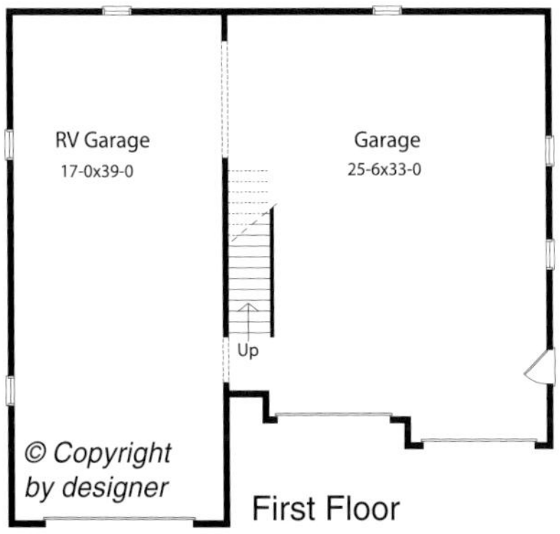

First Floor

- Width: 44'   Depth: 40'
- Building height - 25'
- Roof pitch - 9/12, 10/12
- Ceiling heights - First floor - 9' and 16'   Second floor - 8'
- Two 9' x 8', one 12' x 14' overhead doors
- Floating slab foundation
- Unfinished storage is ideal for extra camping equipment

1-Set	$200	CAD	$475
PDF	$295	Mat List	$50

2-Car Garage with Loft

PLAN #F50-002D-6001

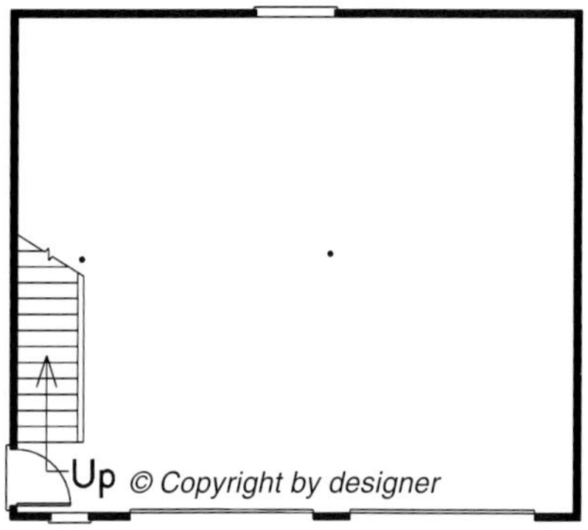
Up
© Copyright by designer

- Width: 28'   Depth: 24'
- Building height - 20'-8"
- Roof pitch - 12/12
- Ceiling heights -
  First floor - 8' Loft - 7'-6"
- Two 9' x 7' overhead doors
- Floating slab foundation, drawings also include slab foundation
- Complete list of materials
- Step-by-step instructions

1-Set	$275	PDF	$425
5-Set	$325	Repro	$600

2-Car Carport with Storage Rooms

PLAN #F50-009D-6010

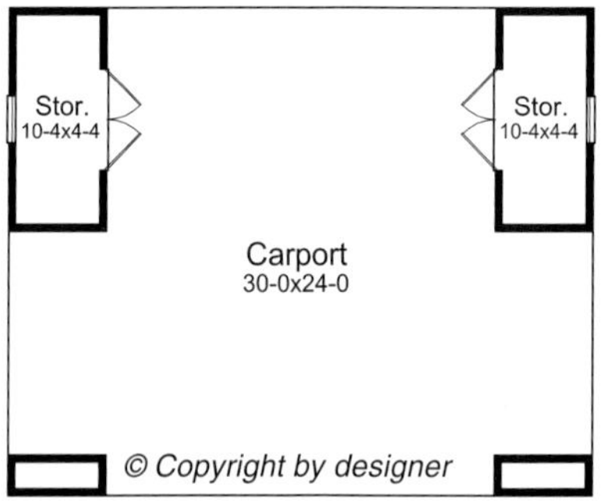
Stor.
10-4x4-4
Stor.
10-4x4-4
Carport
30-0x24-0
© Copyright by designer

- Width: 30'   Depth: 24'
- Building height - 19'-9"
- Roof pitch - 8/12
- Ceiling height - 9'
- Slab foundation
- Two convenient storage rooms with wide double-entry doors are located at the rear, each brightly lit with a double-hung window
- Complete list of materials

1-Set	$225	PDF	$375
5-Set	$275	CAD	$550

1-Car Garage with RV Storage

PLAN #F50-063D-6003

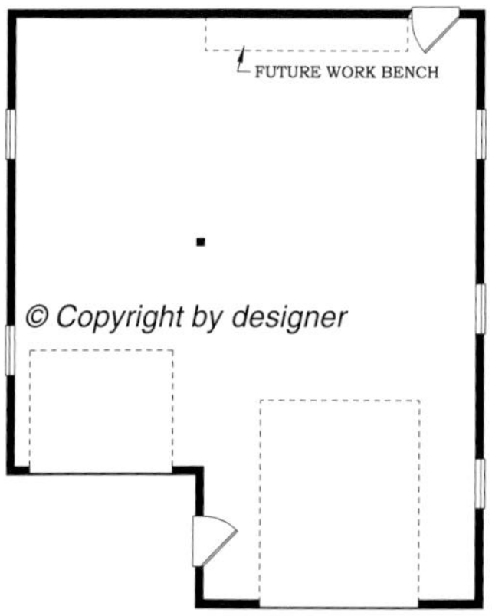
FUTURE WORK BENCH
© Copyright by designer

- Width: 30'   Depth: 36'
- Building height - 21'
- Roof pitch - 7/12
- Ceiling heights - 9' and 14'
- 9' x 7', 10' x 12' overhead doors
- Floating slab foundation
- Easily accessible side and rear entry doors
- Complete list of materials

1-Set	$420	Repro	$620
PDF	$570		

PLAN #F50-113D-6036

2-Car Garage with Side Access Door

- Width: 24' Depth: 26'
- Building height - 13'-8"
- Roof pitch - 2/12
- Ceiling height - 8'
- 9' x 8' overhead doors
- 2" x 6" exterior walls
- Monolithic slab foundation

3-Set	$205	PDF	$275
5-Set	$225	CAD	$475

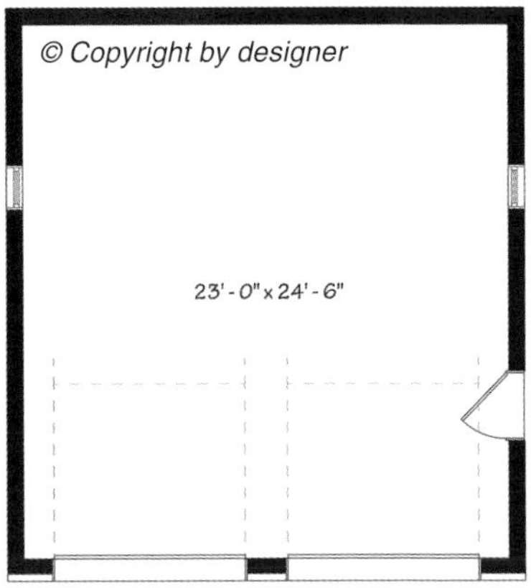
© Copyright by designer
23'-0" x 24'-6"

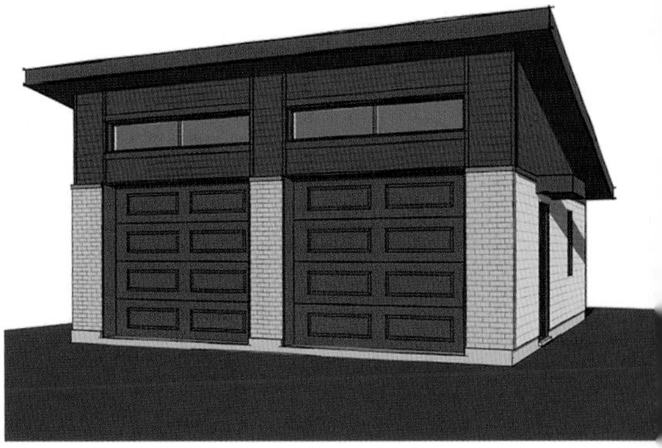

PLAN #F50-113D-6015

2-Car Garage with Country Flair

- Width: 28' Depth: 28'
- Building height - 22'-8"
- Roof pitch - 10/12
- Ceiling heights -
  First floor - 8'-6" Second floor - 8'
- Two 9' x 7' overhead doors
- Floating slab foundation

3-Set	$305	PDF	$375
5-Set	$325	CAD	$575

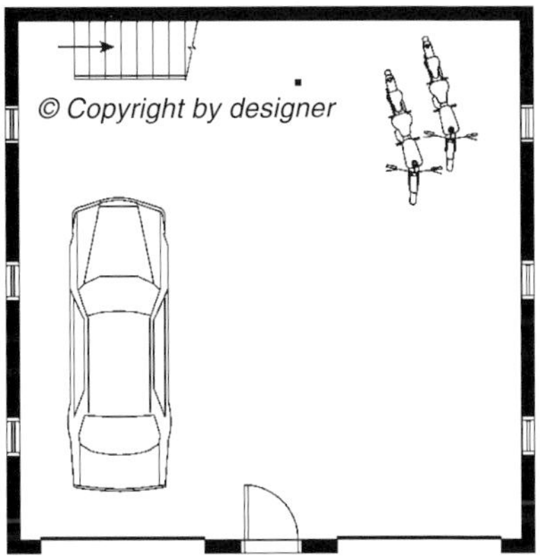
© Copyright by designer

PLAN #F50-059D-6027

2-Car Garage with Front Gable

- Width: 24' Depth: 24'
- Building height - 14'
- Roof pitch - 5/12
- Ceiling height - 8'
- Two 9' x 7' overhead doors
- Floating slab foundation

1-Set	$175	CAD	$375
PDF	$260	Mat List	$40

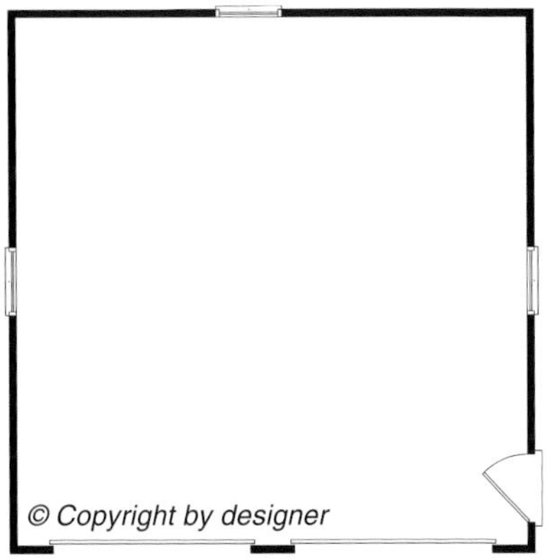
© Copyright by designer

1-Car Garage

PLAN #F50-113D-6006

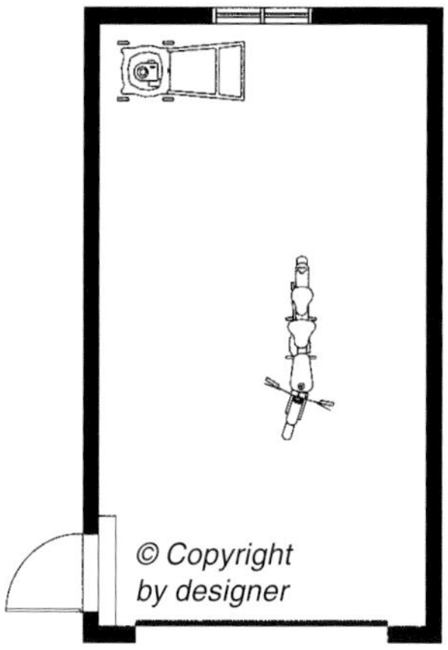
© Copyright
by designer

- Width: 14' Depth: 24'
- Building height - 17'-10"
- Roof pitch - 12/12
- Ceiling height - 9'
- 10' x 7' overhead door
- Floating slab foundation
- 2" x 6" exterior walls
- Decorative and appealing style designed for any home

3-Set	$205	PDF	$275
5-Set	$225	CAD	$475

2-Car Garage - Western Style

PLAN #F50-002D-6023

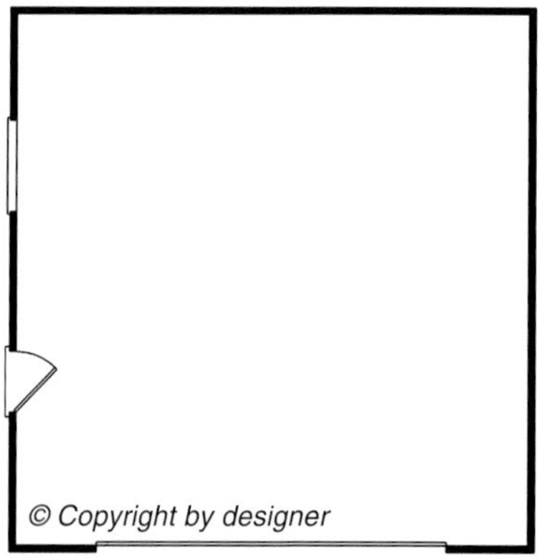
© Copyright by designer

- Width: 24' Depth: 24'
- Building height - 12'-8"
- Roof pitch - 4/12
- Ceiling height - 8'
- 16' x 7' overhead door
- Floating slab foundation, drawings also include slab foundation
- Side-entry door and window are functional extras
- Complete list of materials
- Step-by-step instructions

1-Set	$225	PDF	$375
5-Set	$275	Repro	$425

Lovely 2-Car Garage

PLAN #F50-113D-6010

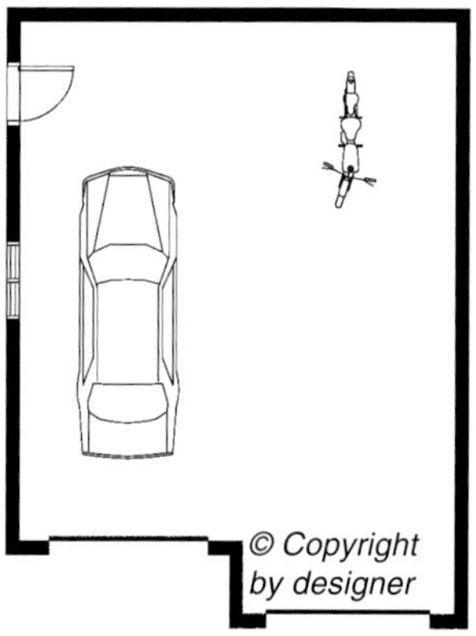
© Copyright
by designer

- Width: 24'-8" Depth: 32'
- Building height - 20'-6"
- Roof pitch - 12/12
- Ceiling height - 9'-8"
- Two 9' x 7' overhead doors
- Floating slab foundation
- 2" x 6" exterior walls
- Excellent garage for large equipment or workshop

3-Set	$265	PDF	$335
5-Set	$285	CAD	$535

PLAN #F50-002D-6039

2-Car Garage with Loft

- Width: 28' Depth: 24'
- Building height - 21'
- Roof pitch - 12/12
- Ceiling heights -
  First floor - 8' Loft - 7'-6"
- Two 9' x 7' overhead doors
- Floating slab foundation
- Charming dormers add character
- Handy side door accesses stairs to loft
- Complete list of materials

1-Set	$275	PDF	$425
5-Set	$325	Repro	$475

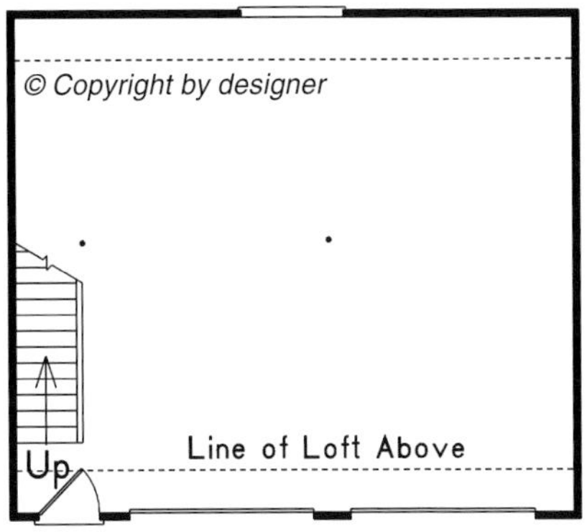
© Copyright by designer
Line of Loft Above
Up

PLAN #F50-059D-6028

2-Car Garage with Side Entrance

- Width: 24' Depth: 24'
- Building height - 14'
- Roof pitch - 5/12
- Ceiling height - 8'
- Two 9' x 7' overhead doors
- Floating slab foundation
- Doors add style to this compact garage design

1-Set	$175	CAD	$375
PDF	$260	Mat List	$40

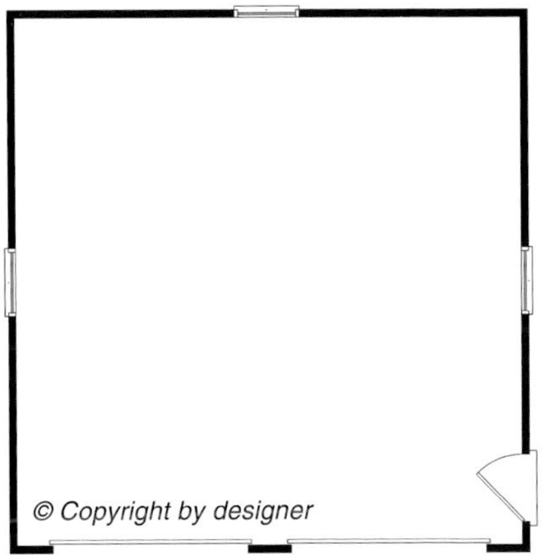
© Copyright by designer

PLAN #F50-002D-6040

2-Car Garage - Reverse Gable

- Width: 24' Depth: 22'
- Building height - 14'-8"
- Roof pitch - 5/12, 8.5/12
- Ceiling height - 8'
- Two 9' x 7' overhead doors
- Floating slab foundation, drawings also include slab foundation
- Handy side door
- Complete list of materials
- Step-by-step instructions

1-Set	$225	PDF	$375
5-Set	$275	Repro	$425

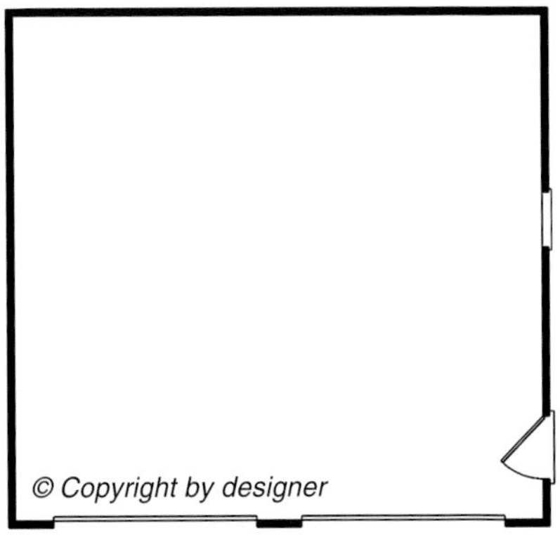
© Copyright by designer

2-Car Garage with Covered Porch

PLAN #F50-108D-6000

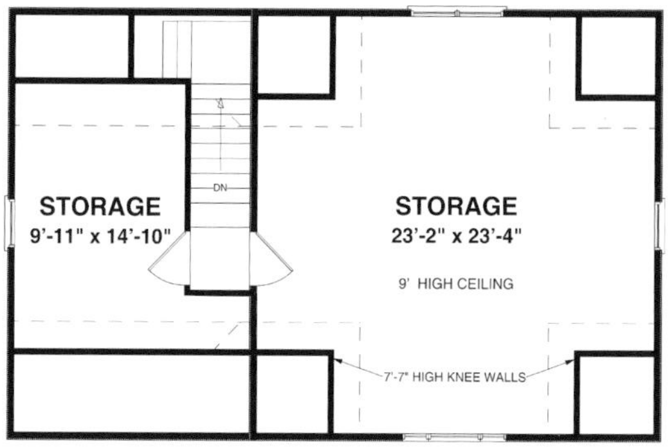
STORAGE
9'-11" x 14'-10"
DN
STORAGE
23'-2" x 23'-4"
9' HIGH CEILING
7'-7" HIGH KNEE WALLS

Second Floor

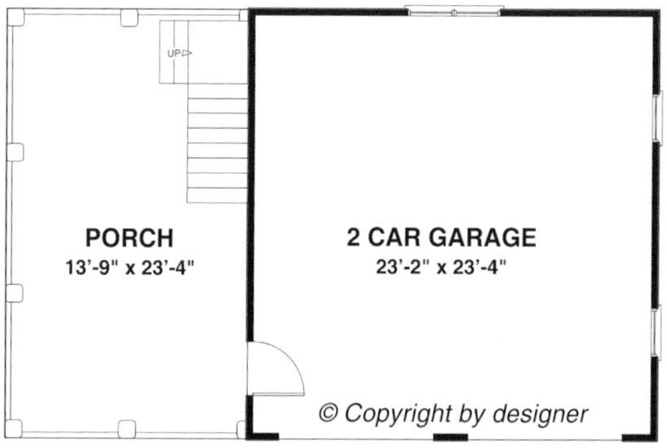
UP
PORCH
13'-9" x 23'-4"
2 CAR GARAGE
23'-2" x 23'-4"
© Copyright by designer

First Floor

- Width: 38'   Depth: 24'
- Building height - 24'-8"
- Roof pitch - 12/12
- Ceiling heights - First floor - 8'   Second floor - 9'
- Two 9' x 7' overhead doors
- Slab foundation
- A sizable covered porch offers the perfect place for outdoor dining and relaxation

PDF $795	CAD $1095
Repro $945	

3-Car Economy Garage

PLAN #F50-113D-6030

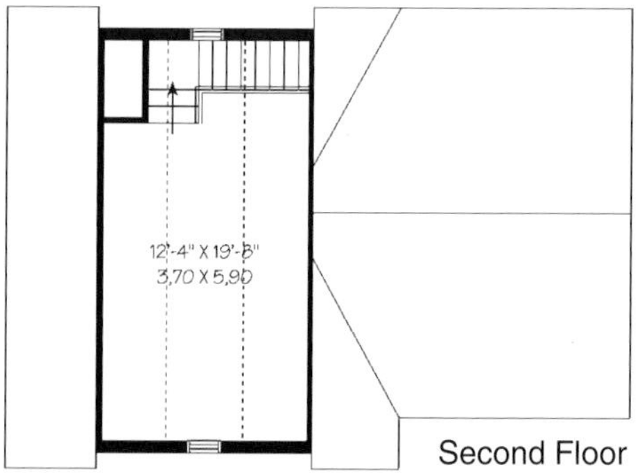
12'-4" X 19'-8"
3,70 X 5,90

Second Floor

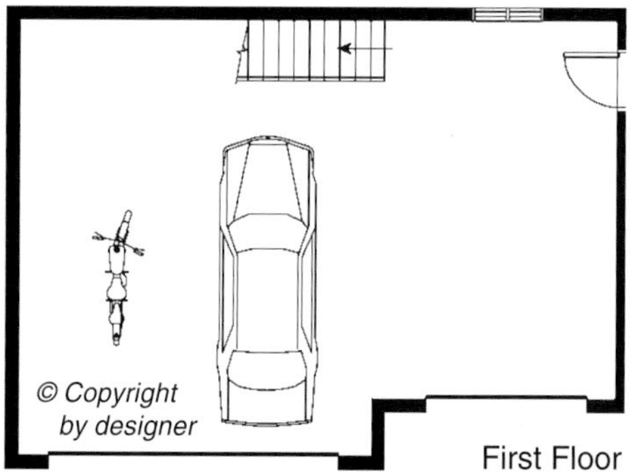
© Copyright
by designer

First Floor

- Width: 34'   Depth: 24'
- Building height - 22'-6"
- Roof pitch - 12/12
- Ceiling heights - First floor - 9'   Second floor - 8'
- 16' x 8', 9' x 8' overhead doors
- Floating slab foundation
- 2" x 6" exterior walls
- Loft provides extra storage area or workshop space

3-Set	$345	PDF	$415
5-Set	$365	CAD	$615

PLAN #F50-009D-6019

4-Car Garage with RV Storage

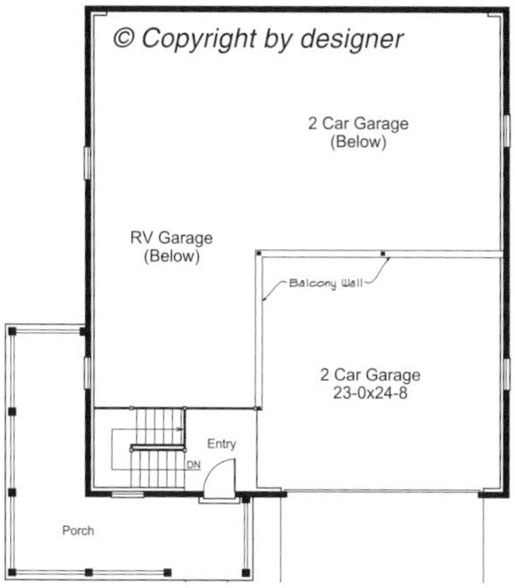
© Copyright by designer
2 Car Garage
(Below)
RV Garage
(Below)
Balcony Wall
2 Car Garage
23-0x24-8
Entry
DN
Porch

First Floor

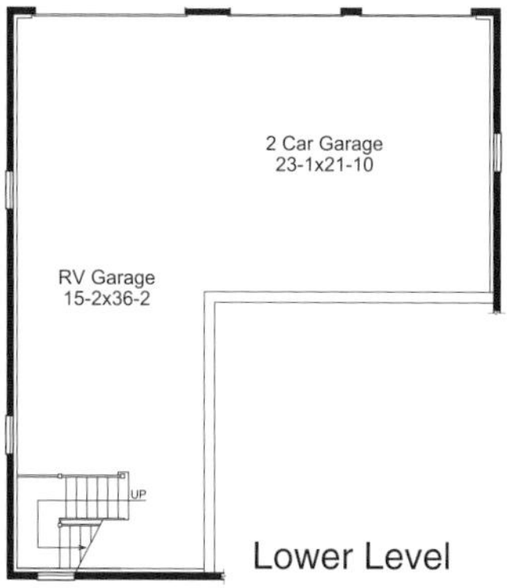
2 Car Garage
23-1x21-10
RV Garage
15-2x36-2
UP

Lower Level

- Width: 47'-4" Depth: 52'-4"
- Building height - 20'-10"
- Roof pitch - 5/12
- Ceiling heights - First floor - 9' Lower level - 17'-8"
- Two 9' x 9' overhead doors, one 12' x 14' overhead door, one 18' x 8' overhead door
- Walk-out basement foundation
- Complete list of materials

1-Set	$325	PDF	$475
5-Set	$375	CAD	$650

PLAN #F50-110D-7500

3-Car Craftsman Style Garage

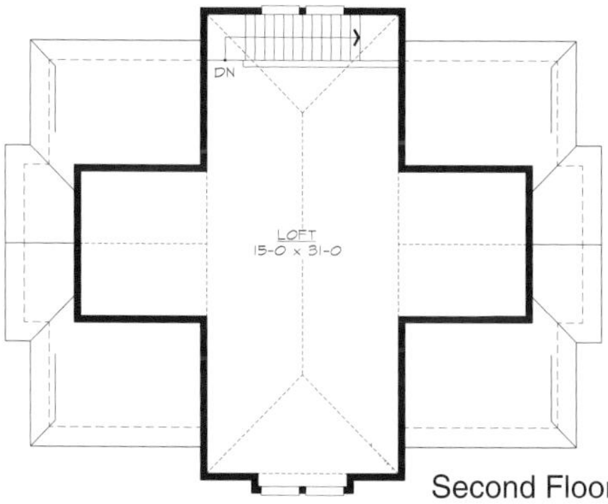
DN
LOFT
15-0 x 31-0

Second Floor

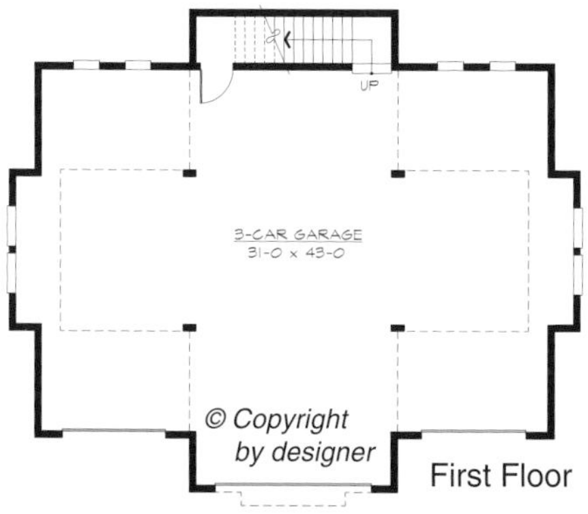
UP
3-CAR GARAGE
31-0 x 43-0
© Copyright
by designer

First Floor

- Width: 44' Depth: 36'
- Building height - 23'
- Roof pitch - 8/12
- Ceiling heights - First floor - 9'-1" Second Floor - 7'-1"
- Two 8' x 7' overhead doors, one 12' x 18' overhead door
- Slab foundation

5-Set	$700	PDF	$1050
8-Set	$800	CAD	$1550

2-Car Garage with Greenhouse

PLAN #F50-002D-6029

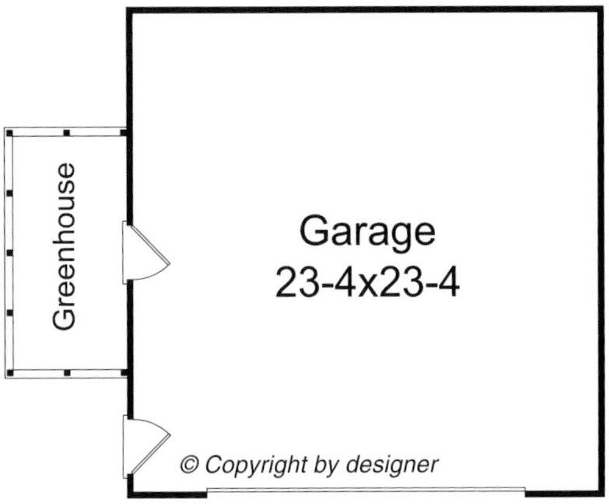
Greenhouse
Garage
23-4x23-4
© Copyright by designer

- Width: 30' Depth: 24'
- Building height - 12'-8"
- Roof pitch - 4/12
- Ceiling height - 8'
- 16' x 7' overhead door
- Floating slab foundation
- Additional space is perfect for storing lawn equipment
- Complete list of materials
- Step-by-step instructions

1-Set	$275	PDF	$425
5-Set	$325	Repro	$475

2-Car Garage with Workshop

PLAN #F50-002D-6002

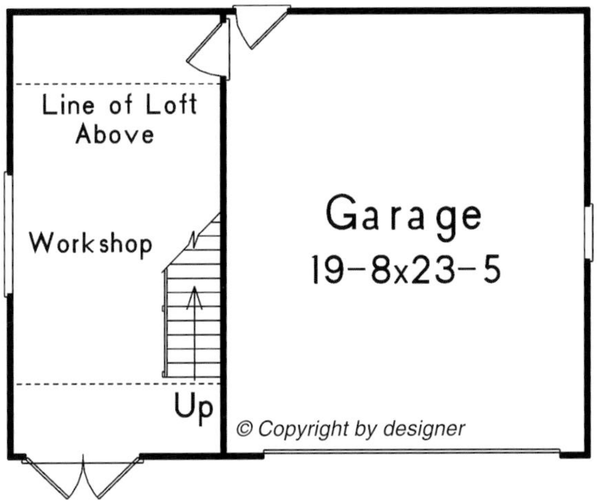
Line of Loft
Above
Workshop
Up
Garage
19-8x23-5
© Copyright by designer

- Width: 32' Depth: 24'
- Building height - 20'-2"
- Roof pitch - 10/12
- Ceiling heights - First floor - 9'-8" Loft - 8'
- Floating slab foundation
- Plans include vertical siding (not pictured)
- Complete list of materials
- Step-by-step instructions

1-Set	$275	PDF	$475
5-Set	$325	Repro	$600

PLAN #F50-059D-6019

Stylish 2-Car Garage

- Width: 30'   Depth: 26'-4"
- Building height - 17'
- Roof pitch - 6/12, 7/12
- Ceiling height - 9'
- Two 9' x 7' overhead doors
- Floating slab foundation
- Plenty of room for vehicles and storage
- Brick veneer adds elegance to this garage plan

1-Set	$175	CAD	$375
PDF	$260	Mat List	$40

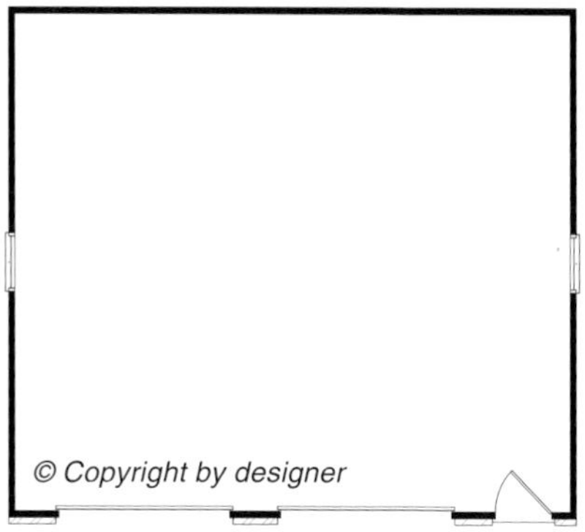
© Copyright by designer

PLAN #F50-002D-6000

2-Car Garage with Loft

- Width: 22'   Depth: 26'
- Building height - 20'-7"
- Roof pitch - 7/12, 22/12
- Ceiling heights -
  First floor - 8'   Loft - 7'-4"
- Two 9' x 7' overhead doors
- Floating slab foundation
- Complete list of materials
- Step-by-step instructions

1-Set	$275	PDF	$425
5-Set	$325	Repro	$475

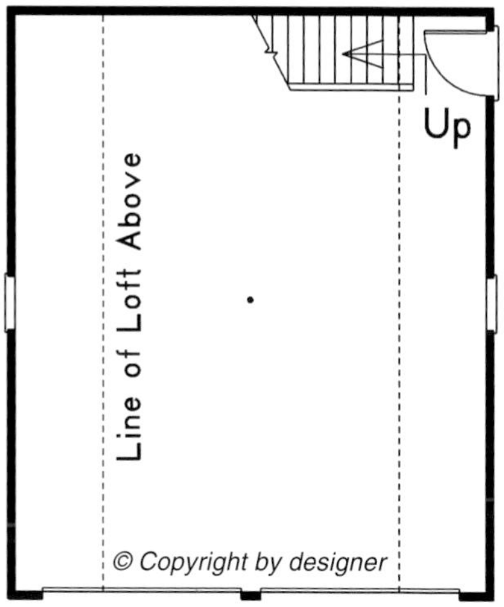
Up
Line of Loft Above
© Copyright by designer

PLAN #F50-002D-6027

2-Car Garage - Reverse Gable

- Width: 24'   Depth: 24'
- Building height - 16'-7"
- Roof pitch - 8/12
- Ceiling height - 8'
- Two 9' x 7' overhead doors
- Floating slab foundation, drawings also include slab foundation
- Complete list of materials
- Step-by-step instructions

1-Set	$225	PDF	$375
5-Set	$275	Repro	$425

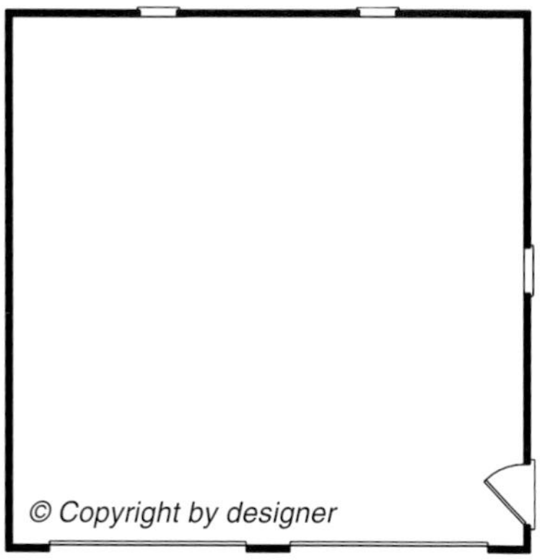
© Copyright by designer

Two-Story 2-Car Garage

PLAN #F50-114D-6002

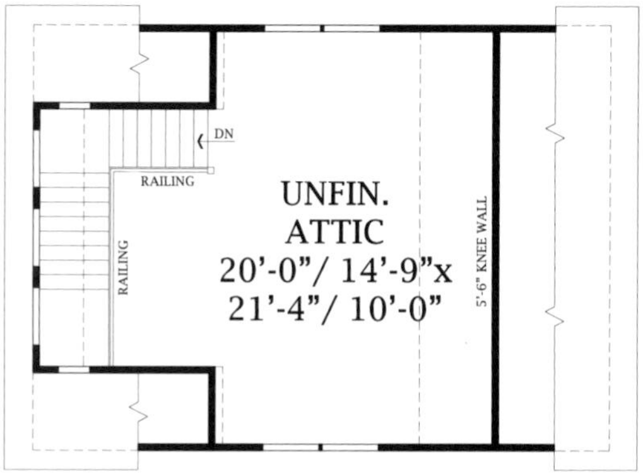

Second Floor

- Width: 30'-8" Depth: 22'
- Building height - 26'-2"
- Roof pitch - 11/12
- Ceiling heights - First floor - 9' Second floor - 9'
- Two 9' x 8' overhead doors
- Slab foundation
- The garage has 611 square feet on the first floor and 397 square feet on the second floor

PDF $645	CAD $1295
Repro $675	

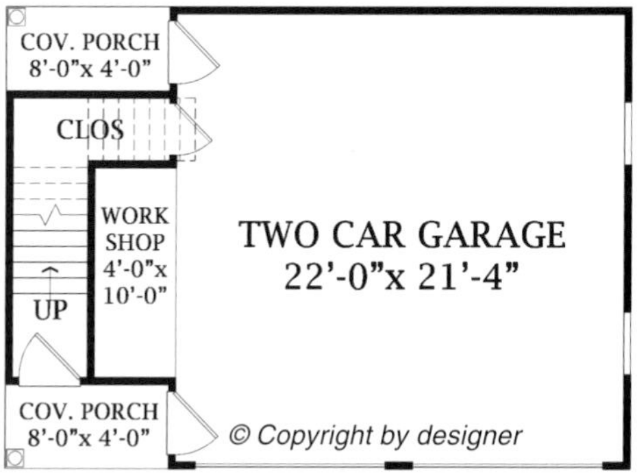

First Floor

2-Car Garage with Covered Entry

PLAN #F50-059D-6010

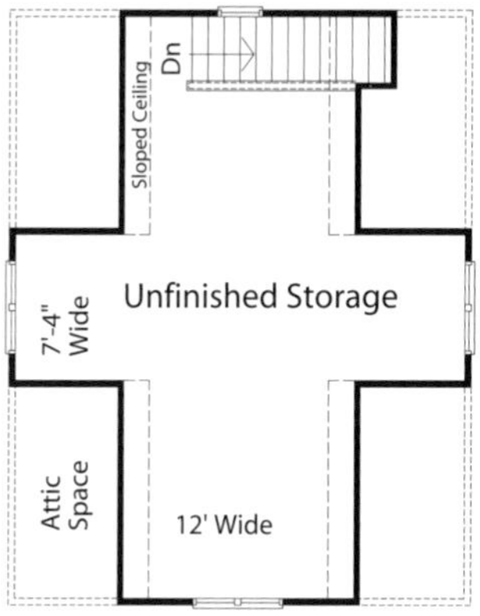

Second Floor

- Width: 28' Depth: 30'
- Building height - 25'
- Roof pitch - 12/12
- Ceiling heights - First floor - 9' Second floor - 8'
- Two 9' x 8' overhead doors
- Floating slab foundation
- 2" x 6" exterior walls available for an additional fee of $50, please specify when ordering

1-Set $200	CAD $475
PDF $295	Mat List $50

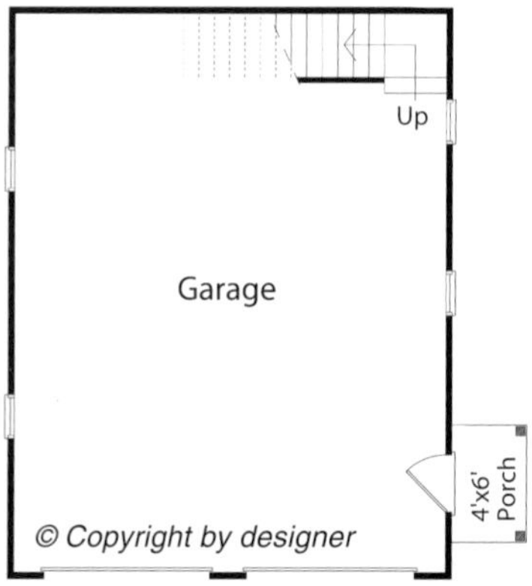

First Floor

PLAN #F50-114D-6000

2-Car Victorian Garage

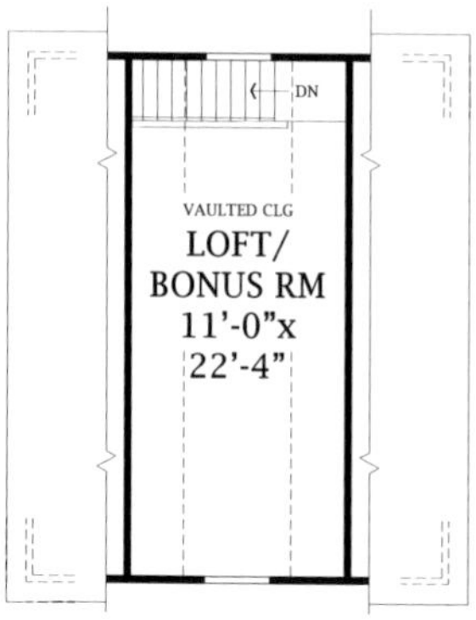
DN
VAULTED CLG
LOFT/
BONUS RM
11'-0"x
22'-4"

Second Floor

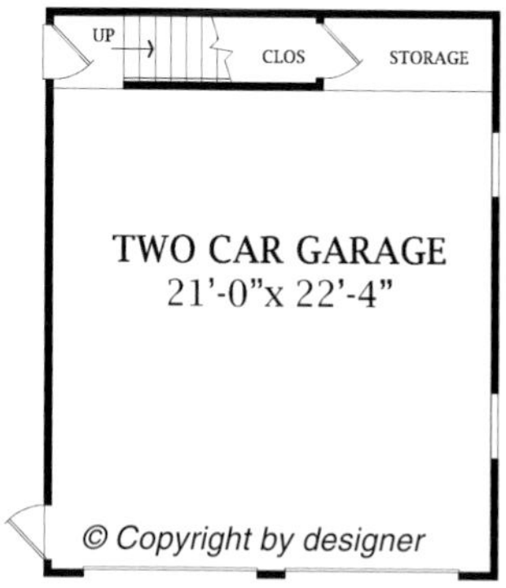
UP
CLOS
STORAGE
TWO CAR GARAGE
21'-0"x 22'-4"
© Copyright by designer

First Floor

- Width: 21'-8" Depth: 26'
- Building height - 21'-6"
- Roof pitch - 12/12
- Ceiling heights - First floor - 8' Second floor - 8'
- Two 8' x 7' overhead doors
- Slab foundation
- This attractive and compact structure provides a second floor loft/bonus room that can be finished

PDF $645	CAD $1295
Repro $675	

PLAN #F50-107D-6003

2- or 3-Car Garage with Loft

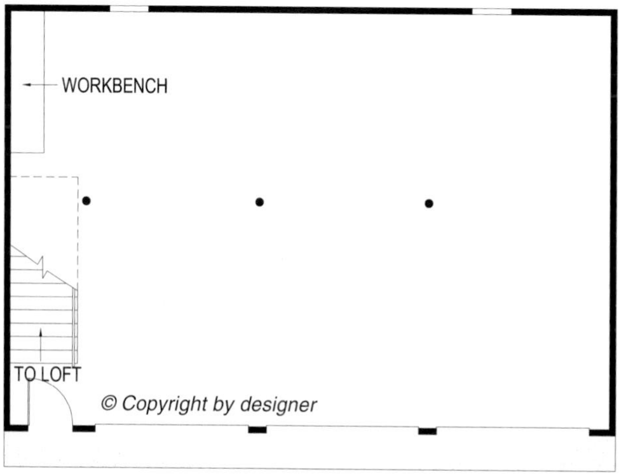
WORKBENCH
TO LOFT
© Copyright by designer

- Width: 36' Depth: 24'
- Plan includes two additional sizes:
  26' x 24' 30' x 24'
- Building height - 21'
- Ceiling height - 8'-6"
- Slab foundation, drawings also include floating slab foundation
- Two or three 9' x 7' overhead doors
- Step-by-step directions

1-Set $225	PDF $375
5-Set $275	Repro $425

Basic 1-Car Garage

PLAN #F50-113D-6023

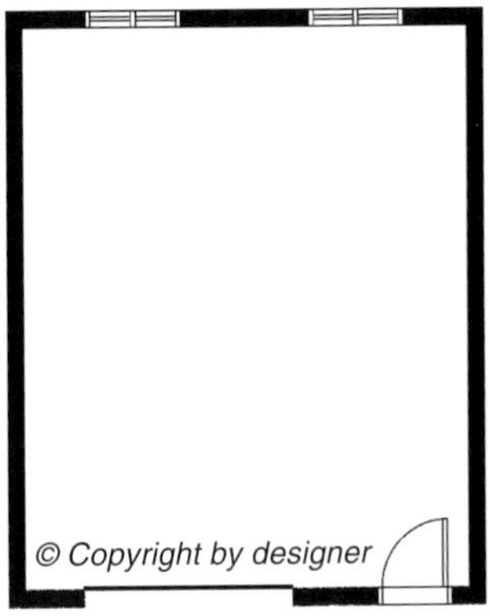
© Copyright by designer

- Width: 20' Depth: 24'
- Building height - 13'
- Roof pitch - 4/12
- Ceiling height - 8'-8"
- 9' x 7' overhead door
- Floating slab foundation
- 2" x 6" exterior walls
- Wonderful versatility with this design

3-Set	$225	PDF	$295
5-Set	$245	CAD	$495

2-Car Carport with Storage

PLAN #F50-009D-6002

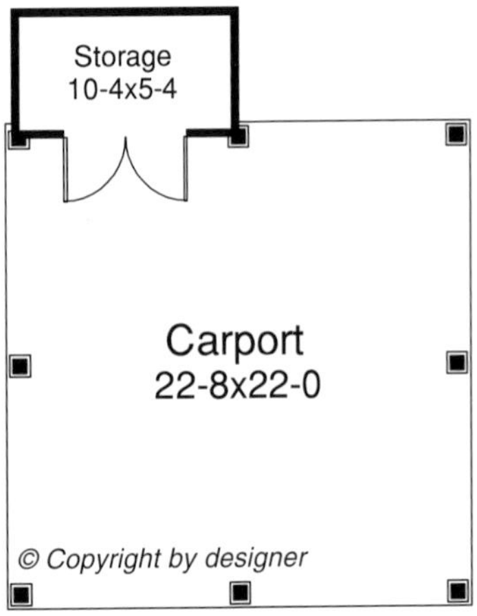
Storage
10-4x5-4
Carport
22-8x22-0
© Copyright by designer

- Width: 22'-8" Depth: 27'-8"
- Building height - 18'
- Roof pitch - 8/12
- Ceiling height - 9'
- Slab foundation
- Storage shed is 10'-4" x 5'-4" with double-door access
- Stylish details include attic louver, special trim and column moldings
- Complete list of materials

1-Set	$175	PDF	$325
5-Set	$225	CAD	$500

1-Car Garage with Gable Front

PLAN #F50-113D-6001

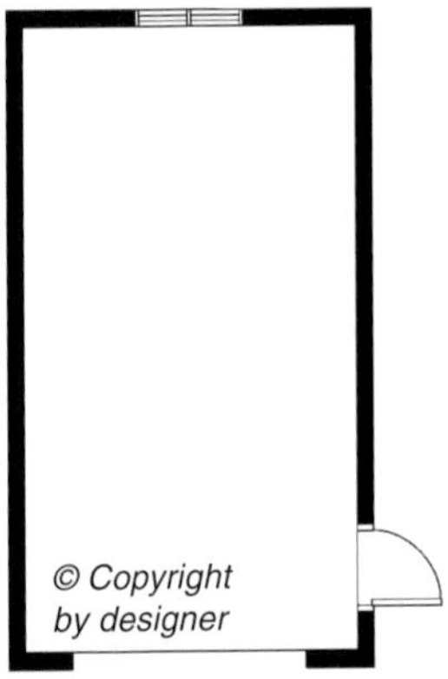
© Copyright
by designer

- Width: 14' Depth: 24'
- Building height - 14'
- Roof pitch - 8/12
- Ceiling height - 8'-4"
- 9' x 7' overhead door
- Floating slab foundation
- Excellent small garage for any home style
- Additional space is perfect for yard equipment storage

3-Set	$205	PDF	$275
5-Set	$225	CAD	$475

PLAN #F50-059D-6031

Compact 2-Car Garage

- Width: 22' Depth: 22'
- Building height - 14'
- Roof pitch - 5/12
- Ceiling height - 8'
- 16' x 7' overhead door
- Floating slab foundation
- Brick veneer adds elegance to this garage plan
- Excellent small garage for many different home styles

1-Set	$175	CAD	$375
PDF	$260	Mat List	$40

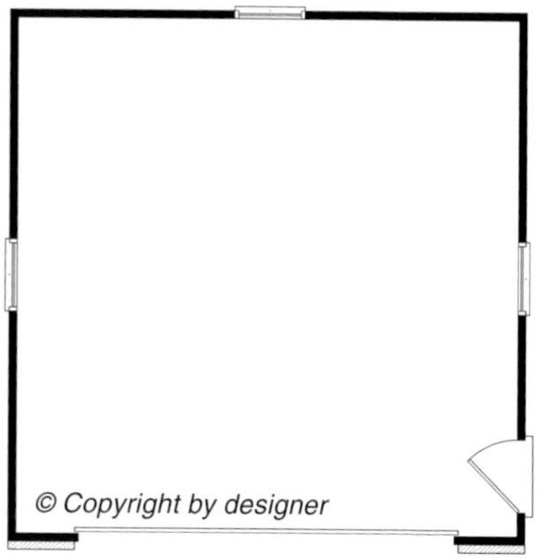
© Copyright by designer

PLAN #F50-002D-6021

2-Car Garage

- Width: 22' Depth: 24'
- Building height - 12'-2"
- Roof pitch - 4/12
- Ceiling height - 8'
- 16' x 7' overhead door
- Floating slab foundation, drawings also include slab foundation
- Appealing side entry
- Complete list of materials
- Step-by-step instructions

1-Set	$225	PDF	$375
5-Set	$275	Repro	$425

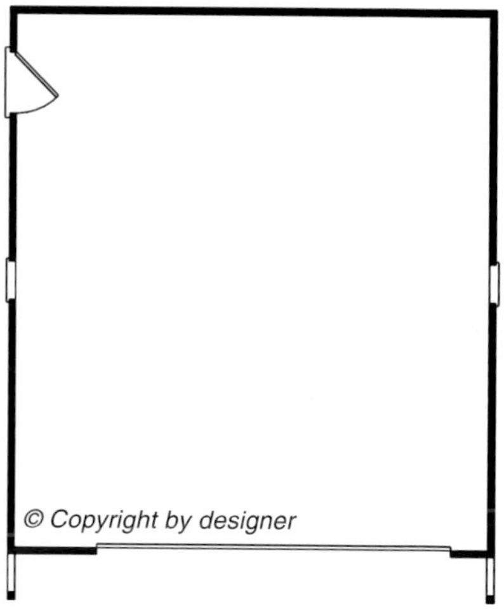
© Copyright by designer

PLAN #F50-059D-6033

2-Car Garage

- Width: 24' Depth: 24'
- Building height - 14'
- Roof pitch - 5/12
- Ceiling height - 8'
- 16' x 7' overhead door
- Floating slab foundation
- Brick veneer adds elegance to this garage plan

1-Set	$175	CAD	$375
PDF	$260	Mat List	$40

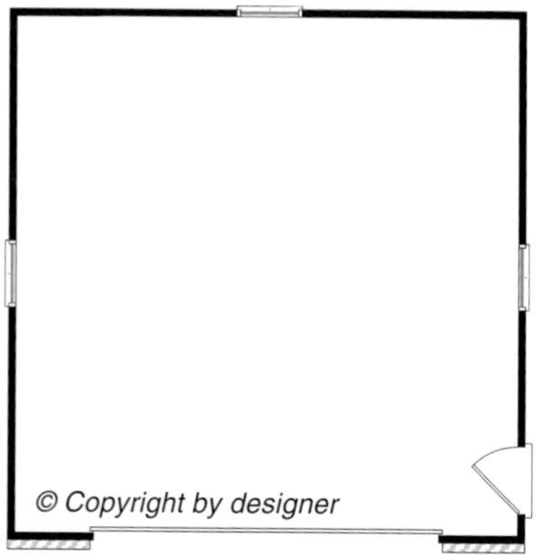
© Copyright by designer

1-Car Garage - Western Style

PLAN #F50-113D-6005

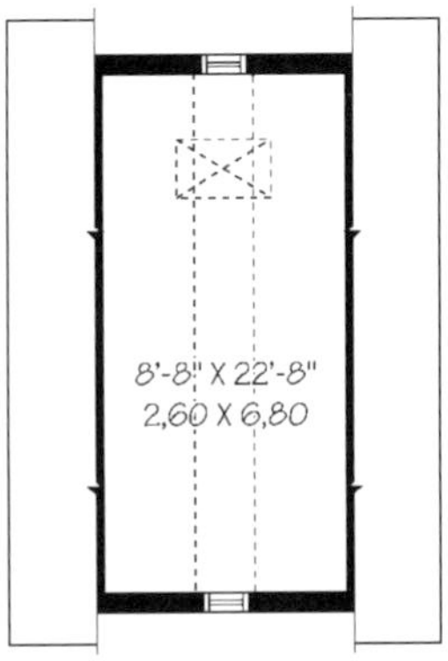
8'-8" X 22'-8"
2,60 X 6,80

Second Floor
272 sq. ft.

© Copyright
by designer

First Floor
384 sq. ft.

- Width: 16' Depth: 24'
- Building height - 18'-2"
- Roof pitch - 12/12
- Ceiling heights - First floor - 9'-2" Second floor - 6'
- 10' x 7' overhead door
- Floating slab foundation
- 2" x 6" exterior walls
- A pull-down, foldable ladder provides access to a convenient storage loft

3-Set	$225	PDF	$295
5-Set	$245	CAD	$495

RV Garage with Rear Entry

PLAN #F50-009D-7526

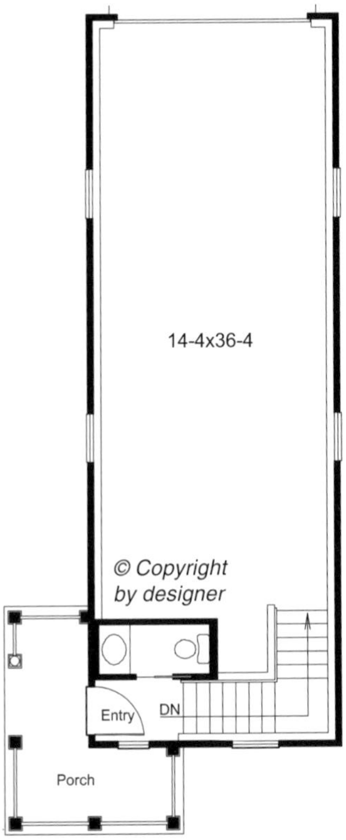
14-4x36-4
© Copyright
by designer
Entry
DN
Porch

- Width: 16' Depth: 50'
- Building height - 15'
- Roof pitch - 5/12, 8/12
- Ceiling heights - Bath and Entry - 8' Garage - 16'-8"
- 12' x 14' overhead door
- Walk-out basement foundation
- Covered porch leads to foyer with half bath and stairs to the lower level
- Complete list of materials

1-Set	$275	PDF	$425
5-Set	$325	Repro	$475

PLAN #F50-009D-7506

RV & 2-Car Garage with Shop

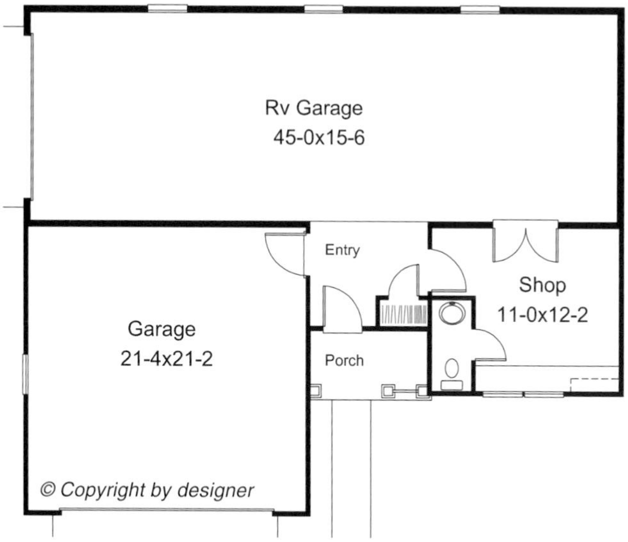
Rv Garage
45-0x15-6
Entry
Shop
11-0x12-2
Garage
21-4x21-2
Porch
© Copyright by designer

- Width: 46'   Depth: 38'
- Building height - 21'-4"
- Roof pitch - 7/12, 8/12
- Ceiling heights - 9' and 16'
- 16' x 7', 12' x 14' overhead doors
- Floating slab foundation
- Shop is 11' x 12'-2" and includes built-in cabinets and half bath
- Pleasing exterior disguises RV side-garage with a one-story look
- Complete list of materials

1-Set	$325	PDF	$475
5-Set	$375	CAD	$650

PLAN #F50-113D-6003

1-Car Garage with Gambrel Roof

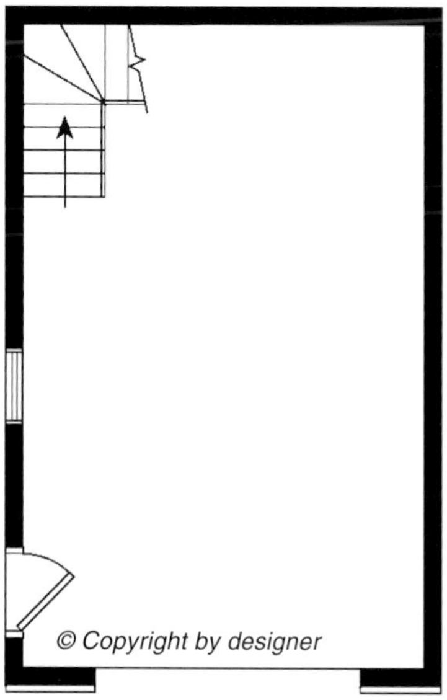
© Copyright by designer

- Width: 16'   Depth: 24'
- Building height - 18'
- Roof pitch - 10/12
- Ceiling heights - First floor - 8'-6"'   Second floor - 6'
- 10' x 7' overhead door
- Floating slab foundation

3-Set	$225	PDF	$295
5-Set	$245	CAD	$495

3-Car Garage

PLAN #F50-002D-6025

© Copyright by designer

- Width: 30'   Depth: 24'
- Building height - 13'-8"
- Roof pitch - 5/12
- Ceiling height - 8'
- 9' x 7', 16' x 7' overhead doors
- Floating slab foundation, drawings also include slab foundation
- Handy side entry door
- Complete list of materials
- Step-by-step instructions

1-Set	$325	PDF	$475
5-Set	$375	Repro	$525

2-Car Garage

PLAN #F50-113D-6025

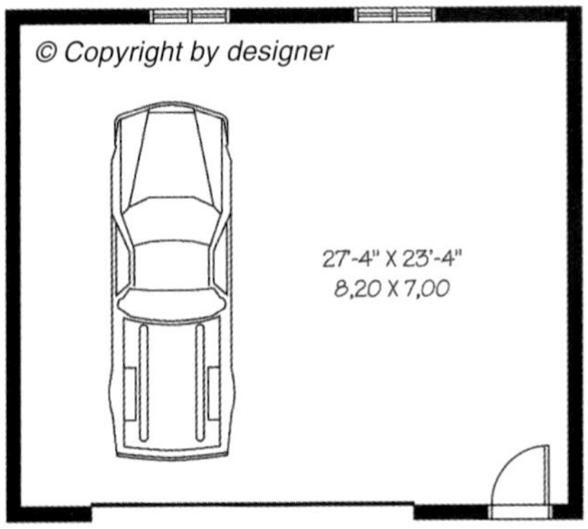
© Copyright by designer
27'-4" X 23'-4"
8,20 X 7,00

- Width: 28'   Depth: 24'
- Building height - 13'
- Roof pitch - 4/12
- Ceiling height - 8'-6"
- 16' x 7' overhead door
- Floating slab foundation
- 2" x 6" exterior walls

3-Set	$265	PDF	$335
5-Set	$285	CAD	$535

2-Car Garage with Loft

PLAN #F50-002D-6015

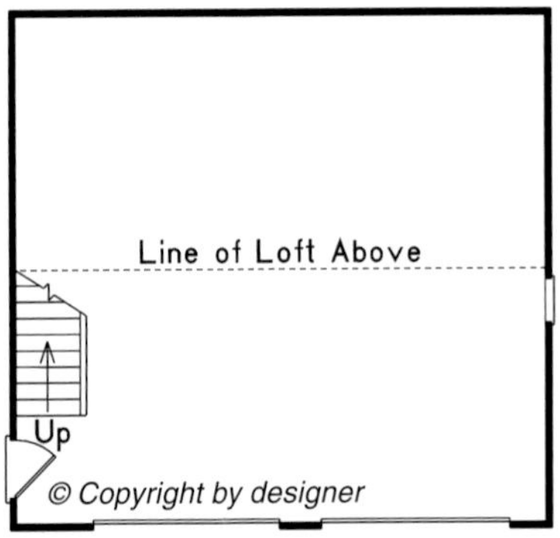
Line of Loft Above
Up
© Copyright by designer

- Width: 26'   Depth: 24'
- Building height - 20'
- Roof pitch - 6/12
- Ceiling heights -
  First floor - 8' Loft - 10'
- Two 9' x 7' overhead doors
- Floating slab foundation
- Complete list of materials
- Step-by-step instructions

1-Set	$275	PDF	$475
5-Set	$325	CAD	$600

PLAN #F50-002D-6014

2-Car Garage

- Width: 24' Depth: 22'
- Building height - 14'
- Roof pitch - 6/12
- Ceiling height - 8'
- 16' x 7' overhead door
- Floating slab foundation, drawings also include slab foundation
- Wonderful versatility with this design
- Complete list of materials
- Step-by-step instructions

1-Set	$225	PDF	$375
5-Set	$275	Repro	$425

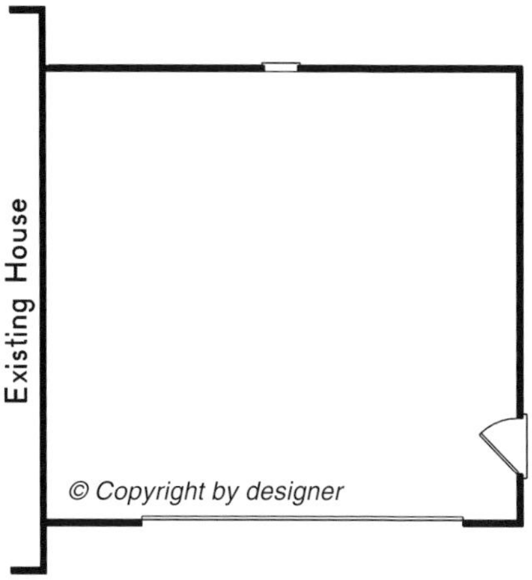

Existing House
© Copyright by designer

PLAN #F50-059D-6037

2-Car Garage with Front Door

- Width: 30' Depth: 26'
- Building height - 17'
- Roof pitch - 6/12, 7/12
- Ceiling height - 9'
- Two 9' x 7' overhead doors
- Floating slab foundation
- Front entrance provides easy access

1-Set	$175	CAD	$375
PDF	$260	Mat List	$40

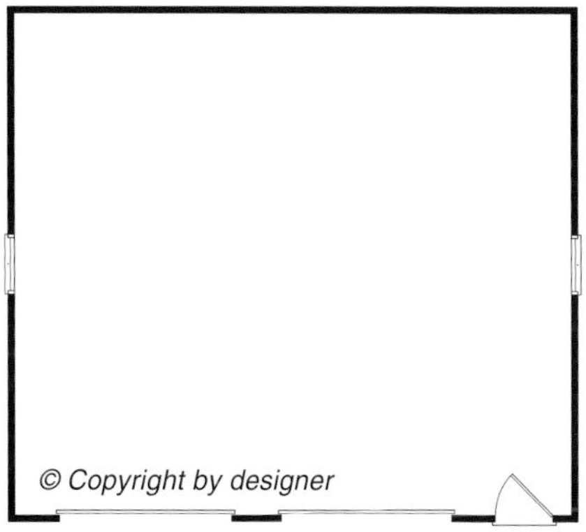

© Copyright by designer

PLAN #F50-064D-6004

2-Car Garage with Loft

- Width: 24' Depth: 26'
- Plan includes two additional sizes:
  26' x 26' 26' x 28'
- Building height - 22'-4"
- Roof pitch - 10/12 or 12/12
- Ceiling height - 8'
- 16' x 7' overhead door
- Floating slab foundation, drawings also include slab
- Complete list of materials
- Step-by-step instructions

1-Set	$125	Repro	$175
PDF	$165		

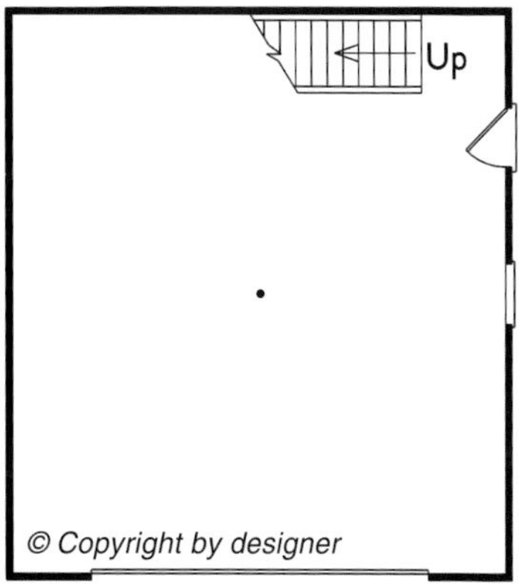

Up
© Copyright by designer

RV & 2-Car Garage with Loft

PLAN #F50-059D-6012

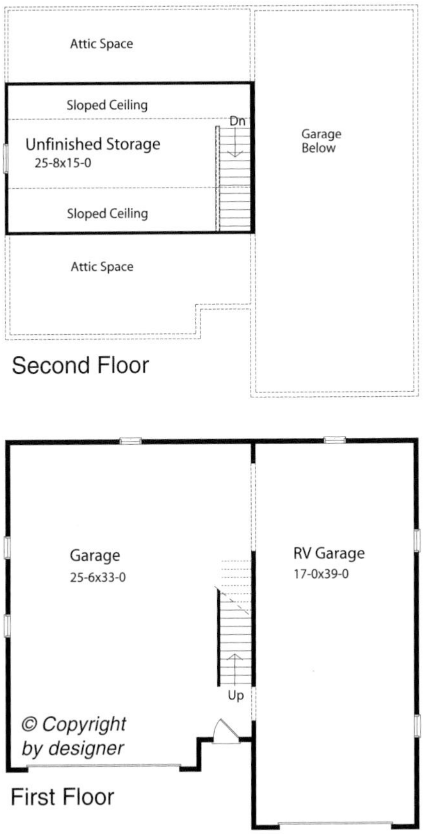

- Width: 44'   Depth: 40'
- Building height - 25'
- Roof pitch - 9/12, 10/12
- Ceiling heights - First floor - 9' and 16'   Second floor - 8'
- 16' x 8', 12' x 14' overhead doors
- Unfinished storage could easily be converted to an office or workshop

1-Set	$200	CAD	$475
PDF	$295	Mat List	$50

4-Car Garage with Shop

PLAN #F50-009D-6007

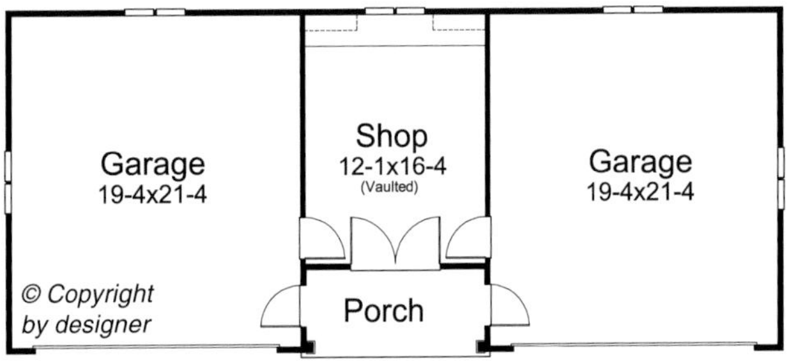

- Width: 52'   Depth: 22'
- Building height - 19'
- Roof pitch - 8/12
- Ceiling heights - Shop - 17'-6"   Garage - 9'
- Two 16' x 7' overhead doors
- Slab foundation
- Complete list of materials

1-Set	$325	PDF	$475
5-Set	$375	Repro	$525

PLAN #F50-113D-6034

1-Car Garage with Storage

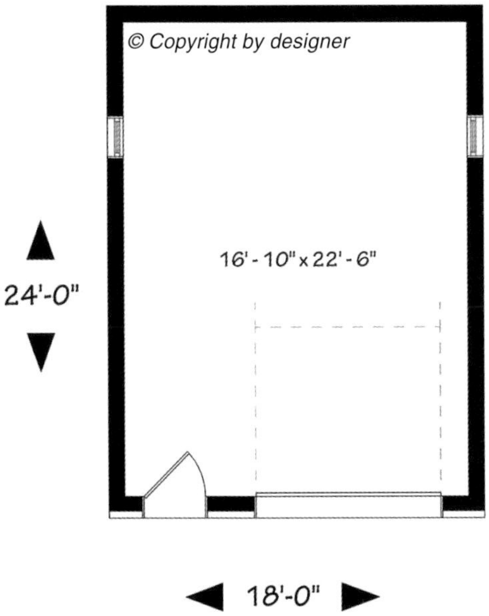

© Copyright by designer
16'-10" x 22'-6"
24'-0"
18'-0"

- Width: 18' Depth: 24'
- Building height - 14'-4"
- Roof pitch - 2/12
- Ceiling height - 8'
- 9' x 8' overhead door
- 2" x 6" exterior walls
- Plenty of sunlight streams through the large window above the garage door
- Monolithic slab foundation

3-Set	$205	PDF	$275
5-Set	$225	CAD	$475

PLAN #F50-059D-6002

4-Car Garage with Office

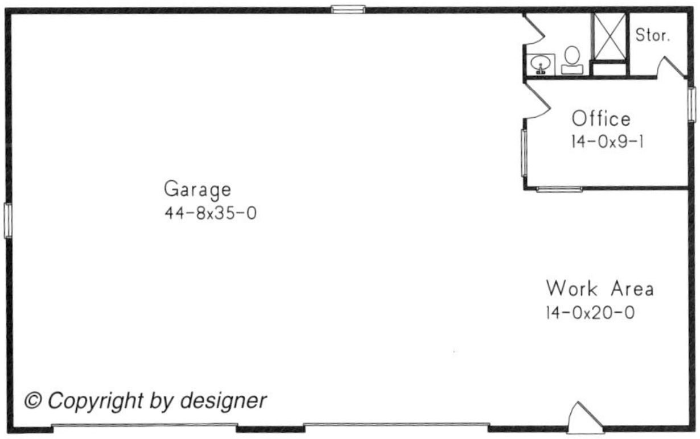

Stor.
Office
14-0x9-1
Garage
44-8x35-0
Work Area
14-0x20-0
© Copyright by designer

- Width: 60' Depth: 36'
- Building height - 20'
- Roof pitch - 5/12
- Ceiling height - 10'
- Two 16' x 8' overhead doors
- Floating slab foundation
- Convenient office area with storage is secluded for privacy and includes a half bath nearby

1-Set	$190	CAD	$425
PDF	$280	Mat List	$40

2-Car Garage with RV Storage

PLAN #F50-063D-6004

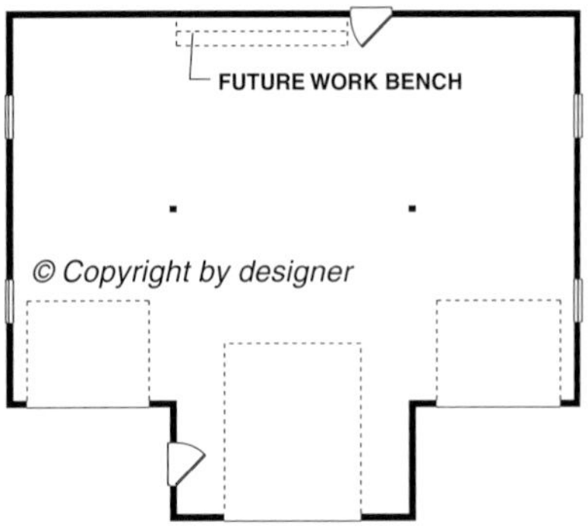
FUTURE WORK BENCH
© Copyright by designer

- Width: 42'   Depth: 36'
- Building height - 21'
- Roof pitch - 7/12
- Ceiling heights - 9' and 14'
- Two 9' x 7', one 10' x 12' overhead doors
- Floating slab foundation
- Offers perfect storage options
- Complete list of materials

1-Set	$420	PDF	$570
5-Set	$470	Repro	$620

2-Car Garage with Shop

PLAN #F50-009D-6000

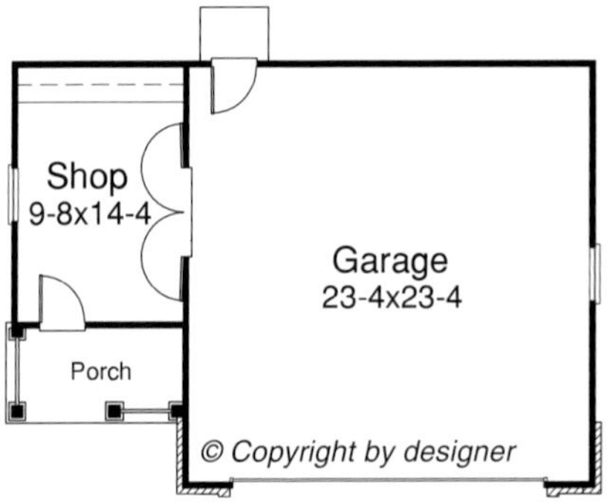
Shop
9-8x14-4
Garage
23-4x23-4
Porch
© Copyright by designer

- Width: 34'   Depth: 24'
- Building height - 24'
- Roof pitch - 10/12
- Ceiling height - 9'
- 18' x 8' overhead door
- Floating slab foundation
- Shop is 9'-8" x 14'-4" with built-in cabinetry
- Porch, stonework, and shuttered window create charming exterior
- Complete list of materials

1-Set	$275	PDF	$425
5-Set	$325	CAD	$600

2-Car Garage - Victorian Style

PLAN #F50-002D-6018

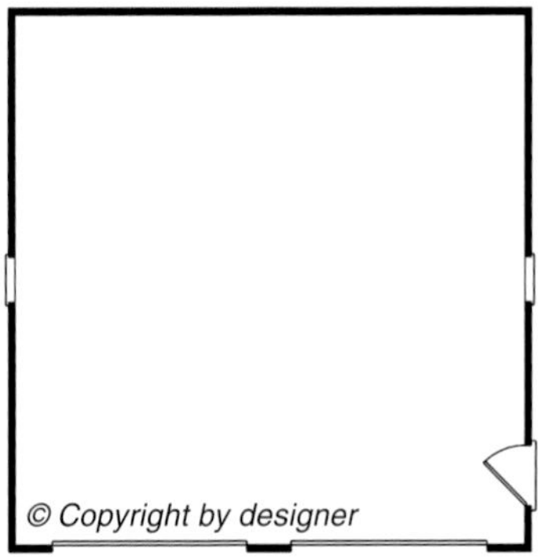
© Copyright by designer

- Width: 24'   Depth: 24'
- Building height - 16'-7"
- Roof pitch - 8/12
- Ceiling height - 8'
- Two 9' x 7' overhead doors
- Floating slab foundation, drawings also include slab foundation
- Complete list of materials
- Step-by-step instructions

1-Set	$225	PDF	$375
5-Set	$275	Repro	$425

PLAN #F50-107D-6005

3-Car Garage with Vaulted Loft

- Width: 36'   Depth: 24'
- Building height - 22'-8"
- Roof pitch - 11/12, 4/12
- Ceiling heights - First floor - 8'-10"   Loft - 10'
- Three 9' x 7' overhead doors
- Slab foundation, drawings also include floating slab foundation
- Complete list of materials
- Step-by-step instructions

1-Set	$275	PDF	$425
5-Set	$325	CAD	$600

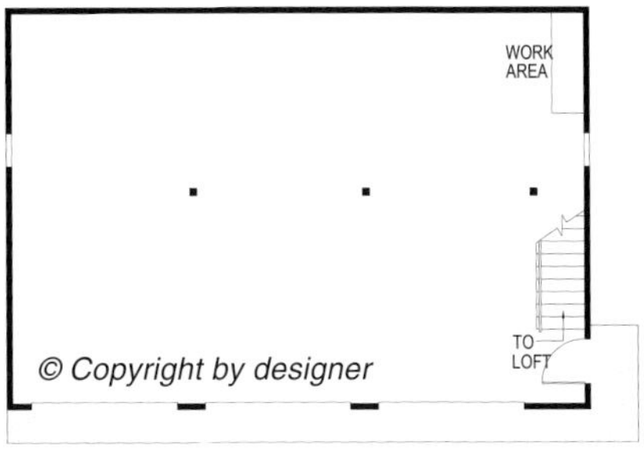
WORK AREA
TO LOFT
© Copyright by designer

PLAN #F50-059D-6007

Deep 2-Car Garage

- Width: 30'   Depth: 30'
- Building height - 15'
- Roof pitch - 4/12
- Ceiling height - 9'
- Two 9' x 7' overhead doors
- Floating slab foundation
- Roomy two-car garage has convenient entry door

1-Set	$175	CAD	$375
PDF	$260	Mat List	$40

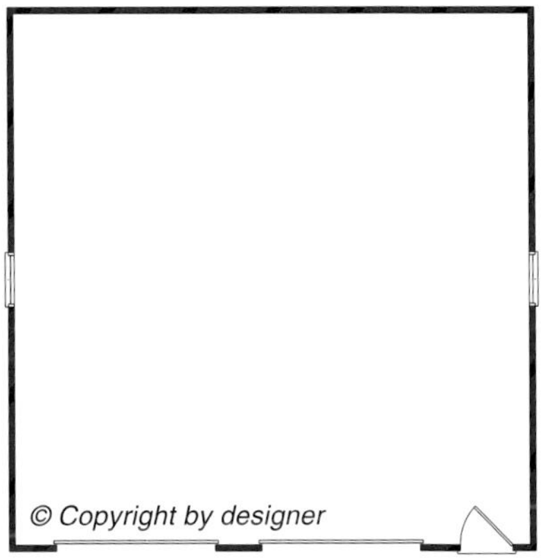
© Copyright by designer

PLAN #F50-002D-6019

2-Car Garage with 8' High Door

- Width: 24'   Depth: 26'
- Building height - 13'-8"
- Roof pitch - 4/12
- Ceiling height - 9'
- 16' x 8' overhead door
- Floating slab foundation, drawings also include slab foundation
- Side window adds light
- Complete list of materials
- Step-by-step instructions

1-Set	$225	PDF	$375
5-Set	$275	CAD	$550

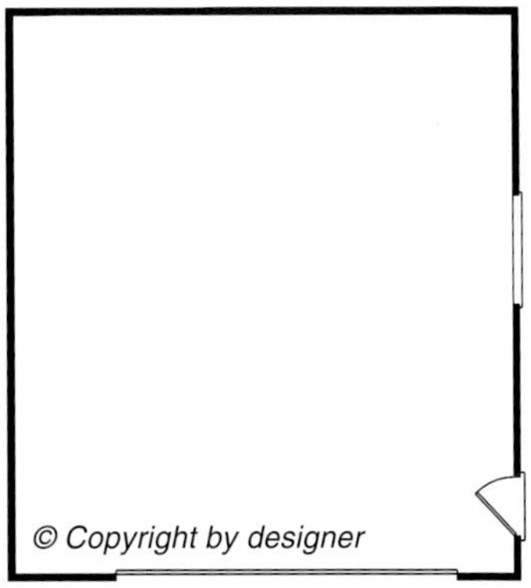
© Copyright by designer

2-Car Charming Garage

PLAN #F50-117D-6000

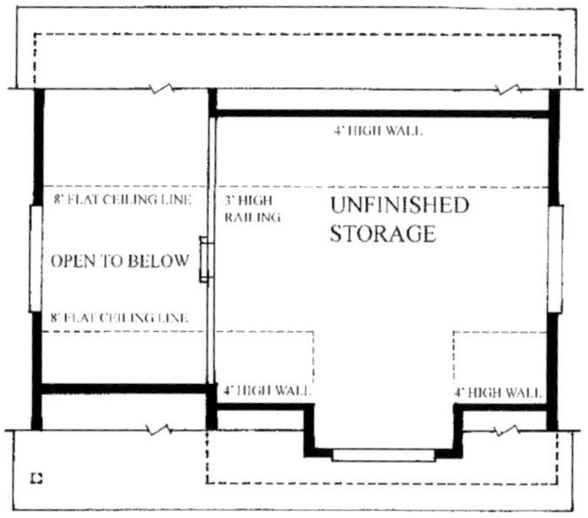

Second Floor

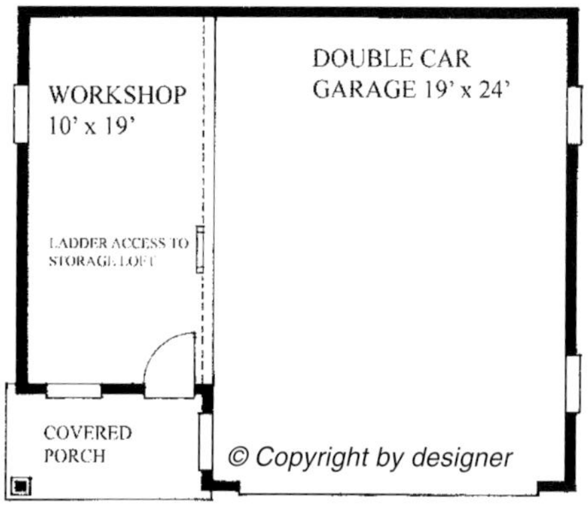

First Floor

- Width: 30' Depth: 25
- Building Height - 24'
- Roof pitch - 12/12
- Ceiling heights - First floor - 9' Second floor - 8'
- 16' x 8' overhead door
- Floating slab foundation
- 2" x 6" exterior walls
- The workshop includes ladder access to the loft above
- A quaint covered front porch offers a great place for relaxing

1-Set	$420	Repro	$620
PDF	$570	CAD	$900

Attractive 2-Car Garage

PLAN #F50-113D-6016

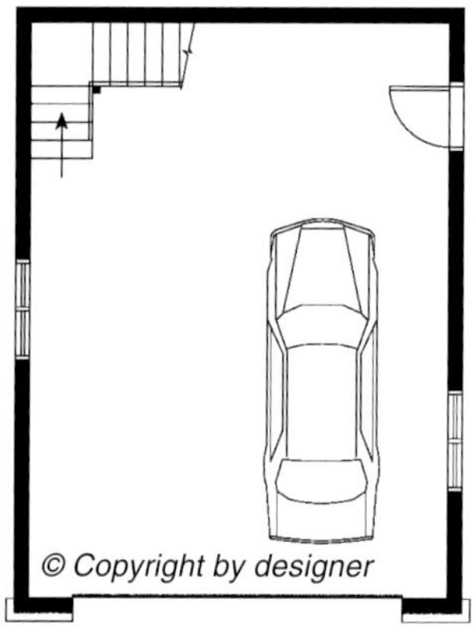

First Floor
606 sq. ft.

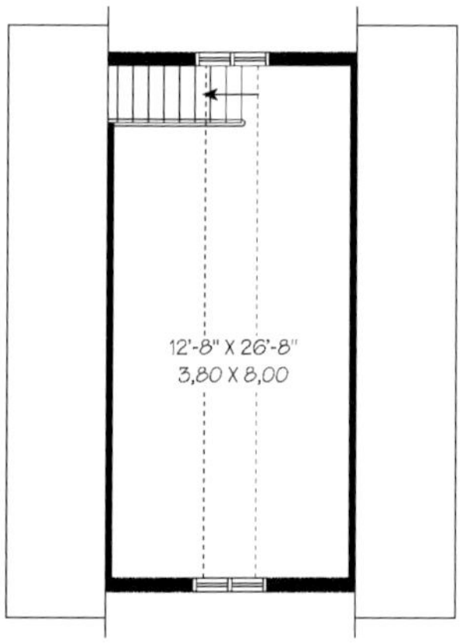

Second Floor
374 sq. ft.

- Width: 21'-4" Depth: 28'-4"
- Building height - 20'-8"
- Roof pitch - 10/12
- Ceiling heights - First floor - 8'-4" Second floor - 8'
- 16' x 7' overhead door
- Floating slab foundation
- 2" x 6" exterior walls

3-Set	$285	PDF	$355
5-Set	$305	CAD	$555

PLAN #F50-113D-6029

3-Car Garage with Gable

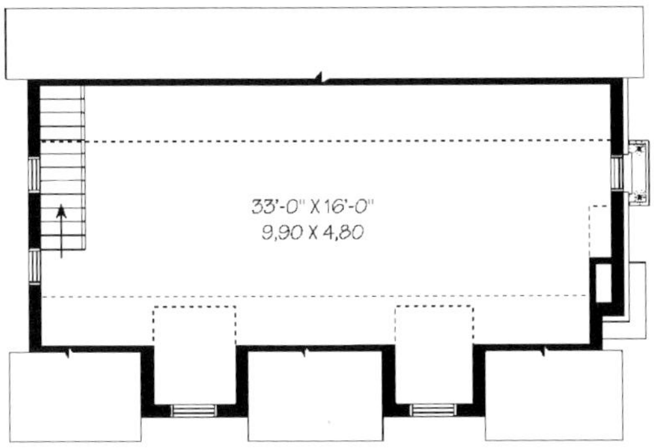

33'-0" X 16'-0"
9,90 X 4,80

Second Floor

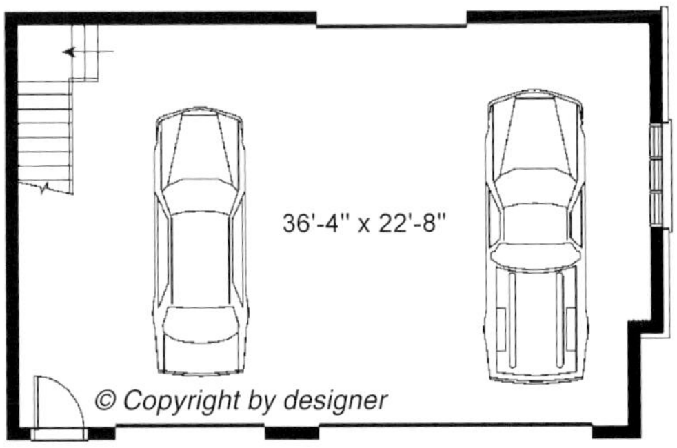

36'-4" x 22'-8"
© Copyright by designer

First Floor

- Width: 38'   Depth: 24'
- Building height - 25'-6"
- Roof pitch - 14/12
- Ceiling heights - First floor - 8'   Second Floor - 8'
- 9' x 7',16' x 7' overhead doors
- Floating slab foundation
- 2" x 6" exterior walls
- Loft is perfect for a home office or extra storage

3-Set	$365	PDF	$435
5-Set	$385	CAD	$635

PLAN #F50-059D-6001

2-Car Garage with Storage

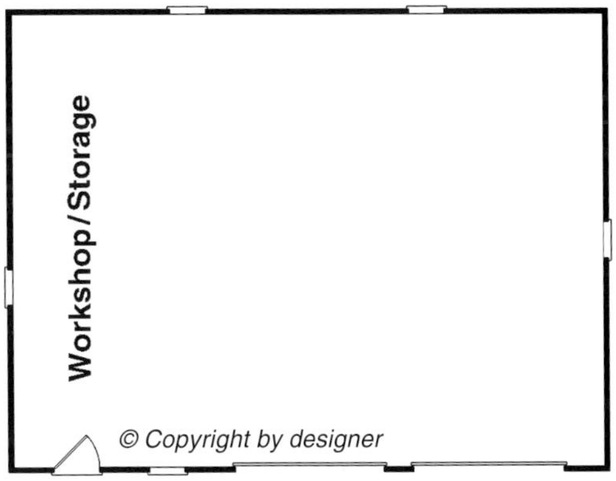

Workshop/Storage
© Copyright by designer

- Width: 40'   Depth: 30'
- Building height - 16'-7"
- Roof pitch - 5/12
- Ceiling height - 10'
- Two 10' x 9' overhead doors
- Floating slab foundation
- Oversized garage is ideal as a workshop or boat storage

1-Set	$175	CAD	$375
PDF	$260	Mat List	$40

2-Car Garage with Hip Roof

PLAN #F50-002D-6009

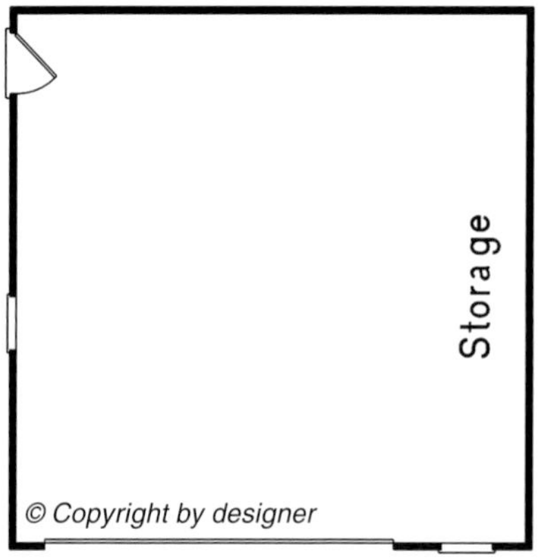

Storage
© Copyright by designer

- Width: 24'   Depth: 24'
- Building height - 12'-6"
- Roof pitch - 4/12
- Ceiling height - 8'
- 16' x 7' overhead door
- Floating slab foundation, drawings also include slab foundation
- Side entry provides easy access
- Complete list of materials
- Step-by-step instructions

1-Set	$225	PDF	$375
5-Set	$275	Repro	$425

2-Car Garage with Workshop

PLAN #F50-063D-6010

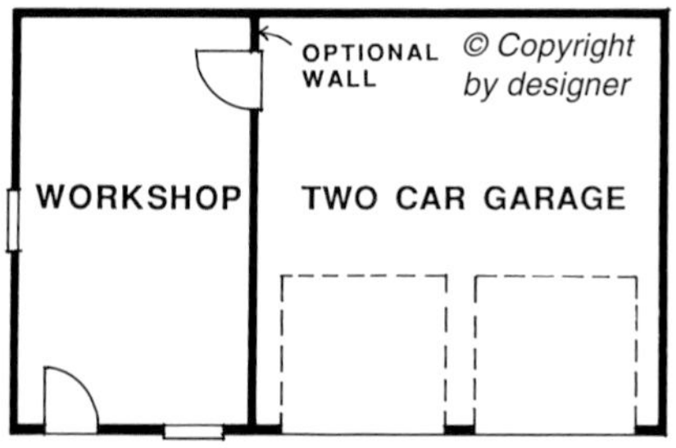

OPTIONAL WALL
© Copyright by designer
WORKSHOP
TWO CAR GARAGE

- Width: 32'   Depth: 20'
- Building height - 13'
- Roof pitch - 5/12
- Ceiling height - 8'
- Two 9' x 7' overhead doors
- Floating slab foundation
- Workshop is ideal for storage, gardening or hobbies
- Outdoor entrance provides quick access
- Complete list of materials

1-Set	$225	PDF	$375
5-Set	$275	Repro	$425

2-Car Garage with Storage

PLAN #F50-002D-6008

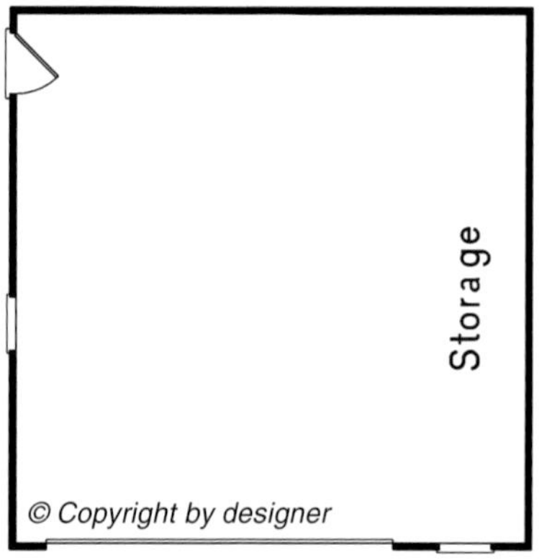

Storage
© Copyright by designer

- Width: 24'   Depth: 24'
- Building height - 12'-8"
- Roof pitch - 4/12
- Ceiling height - 8'
- 16' x 7' overhead door
- Floating slab foundation, drawings also include slab foundation
- Extra space is perfect for storage
- Complete list of materials
- Step-by-step instructions

1-Set	$225	PDF	$375
5-Set	$275	Repro	$425

PLAN #F50-059D-6006

Deep 2-Car Garage

- Width: 24'   Depth: 30'
- Building height - 15'
- Roof pitch - 4/12
- Ceiling height - 9'
- Two 9' x 7' overhead doors
- Floating slab foundation
- Side entry and window brighten interior

1-Set	$175	CAD	$375
PDF	$260	Mat List	$40

© Copyright by designer

PLAN #F50-113D-6035

Stylish Contemporary Garage

- Width: 20'   Depth: 24'
- Building height - 14'-4"
- Roof pitch - 2/12
- Ceiling height - 8'
- 2" x 6" exterior walls
- 9' x 8' overhead door
- Sunlight fills the interior thanks to the large window above the garage door
- Monolithic slab foundation

3-Set	$205	PDF	$275
5-Set	$225	CAD	$475

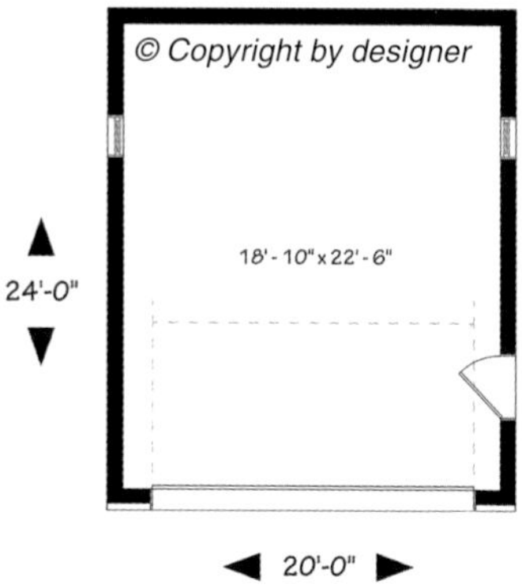
© Copyright by designer
18'-10" x 22'-6"
24'-0"
20'-0"

PLAN #F50-059D-6003

Oversized 2-Car Garage

- Width: 24'   Depth: 38'
- Building height - 14'
- Roof pitch - 4/12
- Ceiling height - 9'
- 16' x 7' overhead door
- 2" x 6" exterior walls available for an additional fee of $50, please specify when ordering
- Floating slab foundation
- Convenient side entrance door

1-Set	$175	CAD	$375
PDF	$260	Mat List	$40

© Copyright
by designer

Stylish Garage

PLAN #F50-113D-6000

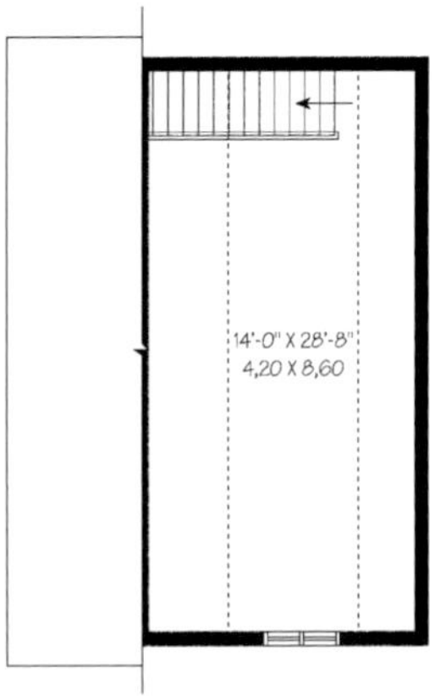
14'-0" X 28'-8"
4,20 X 8,60

Second Floor
450 sq. ft.

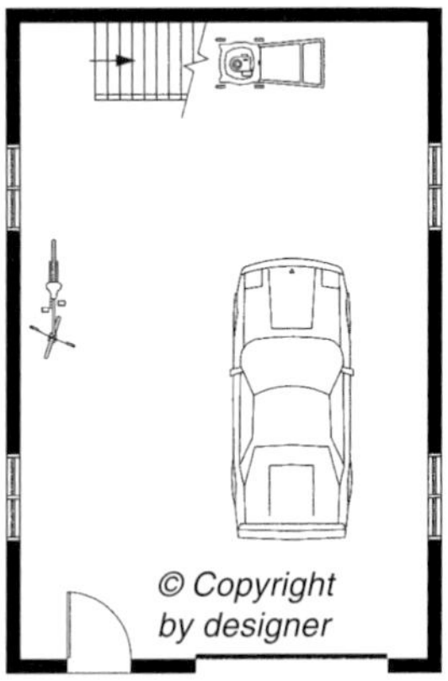
© Copyright
by designer

First Floor
600 sq. ft.

- Width: 20' Depth: 30'
- Building height - 23'-8"
- Roof pitch - 12/12
- Ceiling heights - First floor - 8'-4" Second floor - 8'
- 9' x 7' overhead door
- Floating slab foundation
- 2" x 6" exterior walls
- Unique and appealing design
- Additional space is perfect for yard equipment storage

3-Set	$245	PDF	$315
5-Set	$265	CAD	$515

2-Car Garage with Office

PLAN #F50-009D-7507

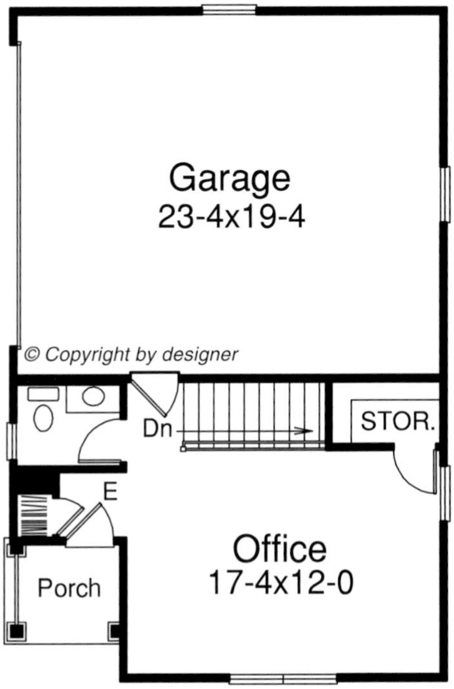
Garage
23-4x19-4
© Copyright by designer
Dn
STOR.
E
Office
17-4x12-0
Porch

- 350 square feet of living area
- Width: 24' Depth: 36'
- Building height - 18'
- Roof pitch - 8/12
- Ceiling height - 8'
- 16' x 7' overhead door
- Basement foundation
- Complete list of materials

1-Set	$275	PDF	$425
5-Set	$325	CAD	$600

PLAN #F50-009D-6012

Garage with Shop and Safety Shelter

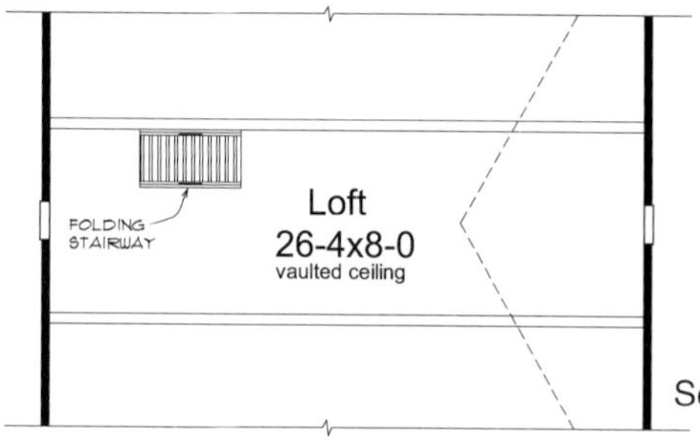
FOLDING STAIRWAY
Loft
26-4x8-0
vaulted ceiling

Second Floor

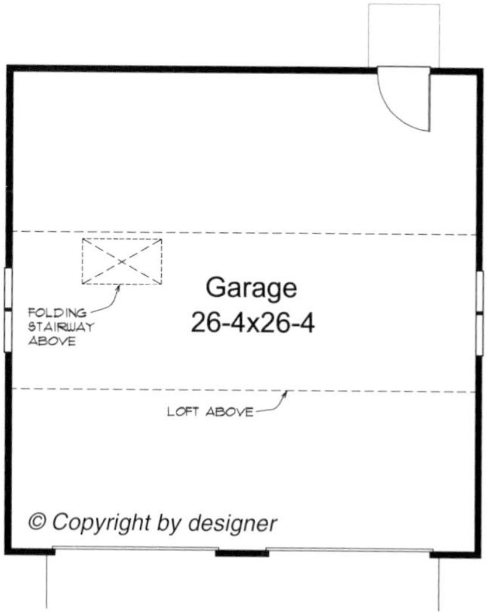
FOLDING STAIRWAY ABOVE
Garage
26-4x26-4
LOFT ABOVE
© Copyright by designer

First Floor

- Width: 27' Depth: 27'
- Building height - 21'
- Roof pitch - 8/12
- Ceiling heights - First floor - 9' Second Floor - 8'-6"
- Two 9' x 7' overhead doors
- Floating slab foundation
- A pull-down foldable ladder provides access to a convenient vaulted storage loft, well-lit wall and clerestory windows
- Complete list of materials

1-Set	$275	PDF	$425
5-Set	$325	Repro	$475

PLAN #F50-009D-7533

2-Car Rear Entry Garage & Bar

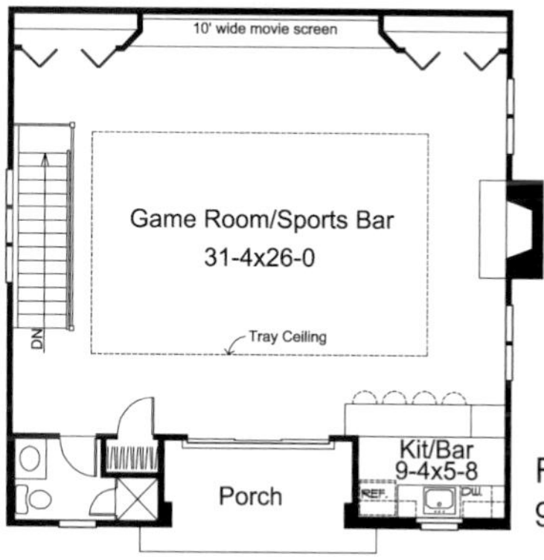
10' wide movie screen
Game Room/Sports Bar
31-4x26-0
Tray Ceiling
DN
Kit/Bar
9-4x5-8
Porch

First Floor
960 sq. ft.

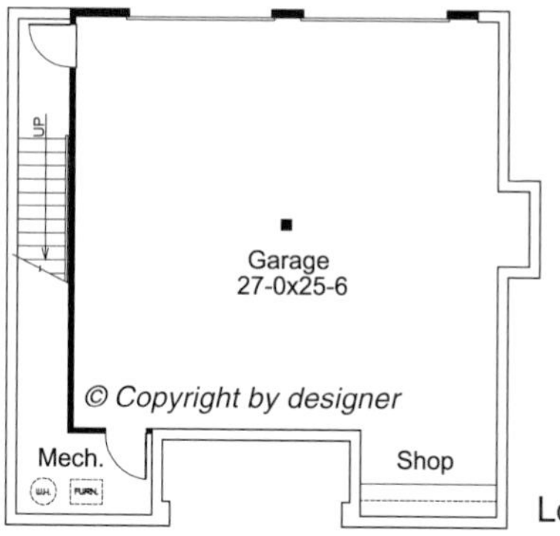
UP
Garage
27-0x25-6
© Copyright by designer
Mech.
Shop

Lower Level

- 960 square feet of living area
- Width: 34' Depth: 32'
- Building height - 17'
- Roof pitch - 5/12, 8/12
- Ceiling heights - First floor - 8' Lower level - 7'-10"
- Two 9' x 7' overhead doors
- Walk-out basement foundation
- Complete list of materials

1-Set	$420	PDF	$570
5-Set	$470	CAD	$620

2-Car Garage with Lots of Room

PLAN #F50-059D-6005

© Copyright by designer

- Width: 30' Depth: 28'
- Building height - 17'
- Roof pitch - 4/12
- Ceiling height - 9'
- 16' x 8' overhead door
- Floating slab foundation
- Two side windows brighten interior

1-Set	$175	CAD	$375
PDF	$260	Mat List	$40

RV & Tandem Garage

PLAN #F50-009D-6011

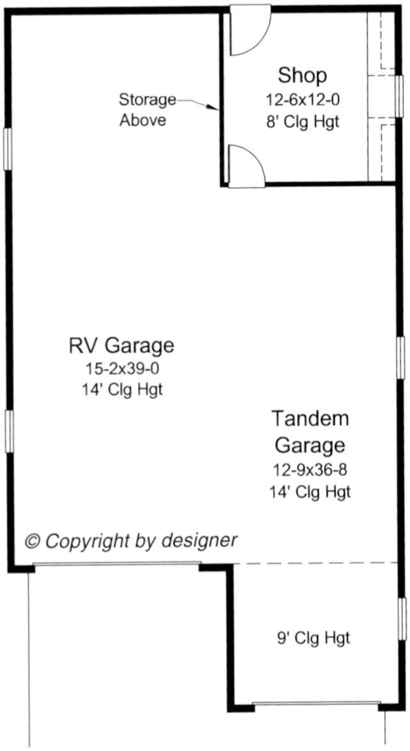
Shop
12-6x12-0
8' Clg Hgt
Storage Above
RV Garage
15-2x39-0
14' Clg Hgt
Tandem Garage
12-9x36-8
14' Clg Hgt
© Copyright by designer
9' Clg Hgt

- Width: 29' Depth: 50'
- Building height - 24'-3"
- Roof pitch - 6/12
- Ceiling heights - Garage - 9' and 14' Shop - 8'
- 9' x 8' and 12' x 12' overhead doors
- Floating slab foundation
- The shop has additional storage above the shop ceiling
- Complete list of materials

1-Set	$275	PDF	$425
5-Set	$325	CAD	$600

PLAN #F50-113D-6021

Simple 2-Car Garage

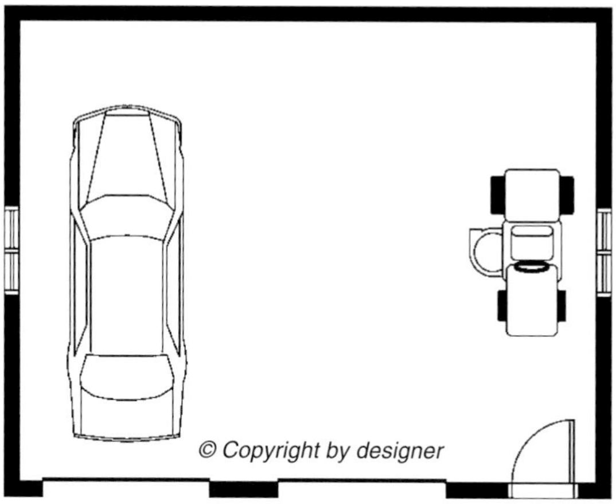
© Copyright by designer

- Width: 28' Depth: 22'
- Building height - 16'-10"
- Roof pitch - 8/12
- Ceiling height - 10'
- Two 8' x 7' overhead doors
- 2" x 6" exterior walls
- Floating slab foundation

3-Set	$265	PDF	$335
5-Set	$285	CAD	$535

PLAN #F50-002D-6041

2 1/2-Car Garage / Roadside Stand

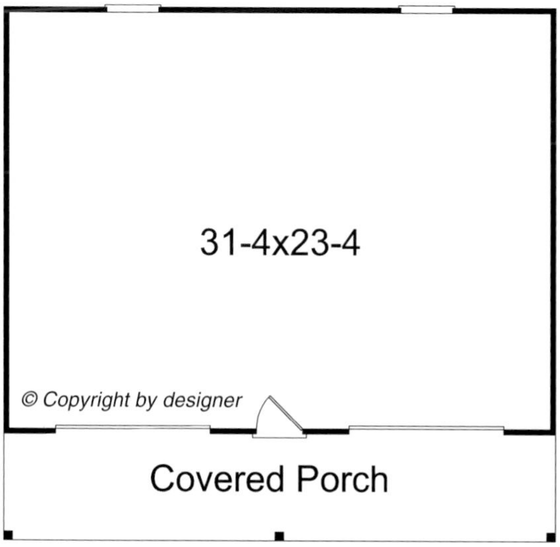
31-4x23-4
© Copyright by designer
Covered Porch

- Width: 32' Depth: 30'
- Building height - 15'-7"
- Roof pitch - 4/12
- Ceiling height - 10'
- Two 9' x 8' overhead doors
- Floating slab foundation, drawings also include slab foundation
- Complete list of materials
- Step-by-step instructions

1-Set	$275	PDF	$425
5-Set	$325	Repro	$475

3-Car Garage with Bonus Room

PLAN #F50-009D-7517

Second Floor
564 sq. ft.

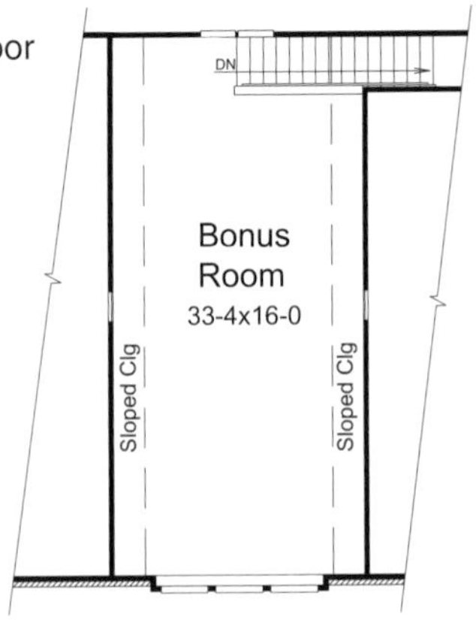
DN
Bonus
Room
33-4x16-0
Sloped Clg
Sloped Clg

- 967 square feet of living area
- Width: 32'-8" Depth: 34'-4"
- Building height - 25'
- Roof pitch - 10/12
- Ceiling heights - First floor - 9' Second floor - 8'
- Three 9' x 8' overhead doors
- Slab foundation
- Hall from garage provides access to office or workshop, a half bath, stairs to second floor bonus room and door to exterior
- Complete list of materials

1-Set	$325	PDF	$475
5-Set	$375	CAD	$650

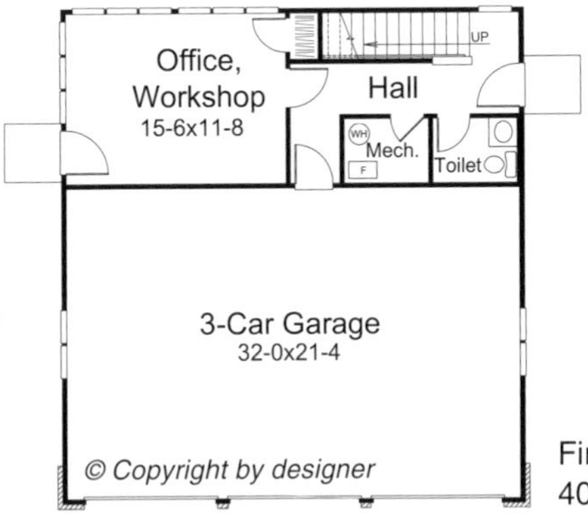
UP
Office,
Workshop
15-6x11-8
Hall
WH
Mech.
F
Toilet
3-Car Garage
32-0x21-4
© Copyright by designer

First Floor
403 sq. ft.

Stylish 2-Car Garage

PLAN #F50-113D-6014

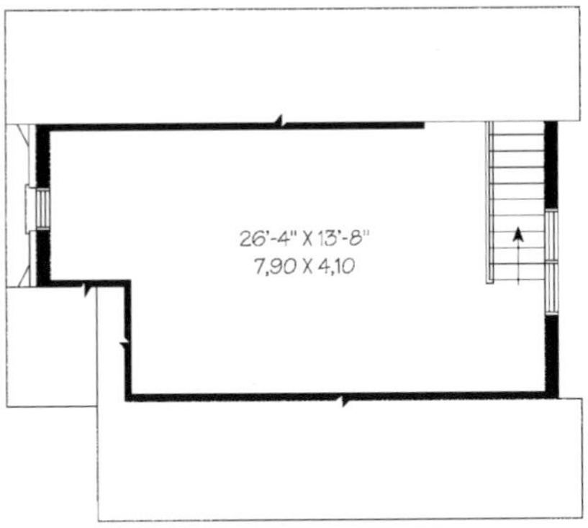
26'-4" X 13'-8"
7,90 X 4,10

Second Floor
403 sq. ft.

- Width: 28' Depth: 24'
- Building height - 23'-4"
- Roof pitch - 12/12
- Ceiling heights - First floor - 9'-2" Second floor - 8'
- 16' x 7' overhead door
- Floating slab foundation
- 2" x 6" exterior walls

3-Set	$305	PDF	$375
5-Set	$325	CAD	$575

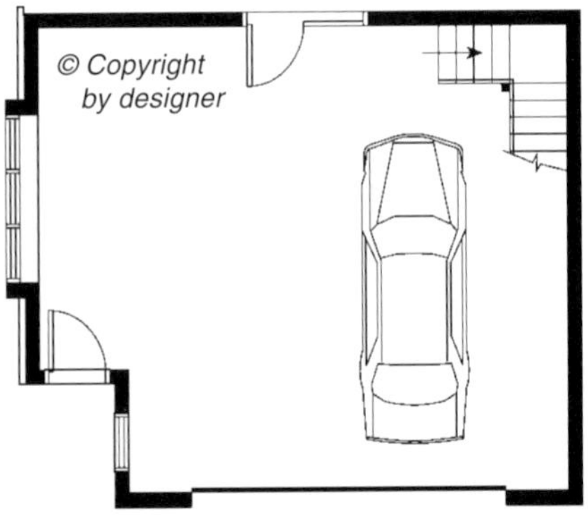
© Copyright
by designer

First Floor
645 sq. ft.

PLAN #F50-002D-7527

2-Car Garage Studio Apartment

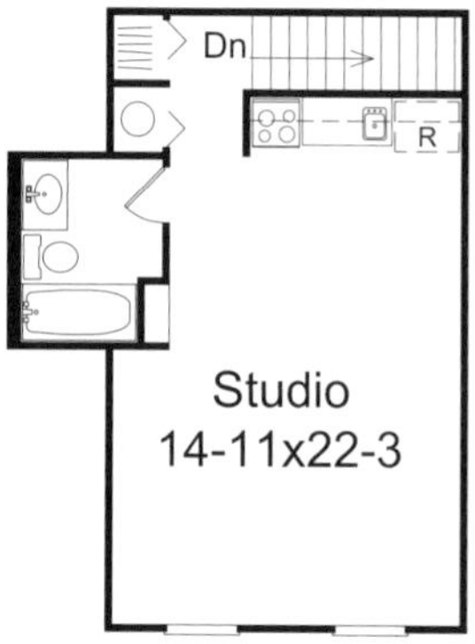

Dn
R
Studio
14-11x22-3

Second Floor
438 sq. ft.

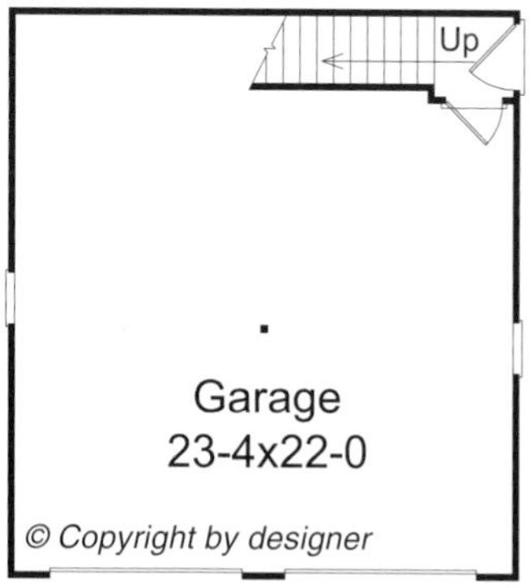

Up
Garage
23-4x22-0
© Copyright by designer

First Floor

- 438 square feet of living area
- Width: 24' Depth: 26'
- Building height - 21'-3"
- Roof pitch - 6/12, 24/12
- Ceiling heights - First floor - 8' Second floor - 7'-9"
- Two 9' x 7' overhead doors
- Studio, 1 bath
- Floating slab foundation
- Complete list of materials
- Step-by-step instructions

1-Set	$420	PDF	$570
5-Set	$470	Repro	$620

PLAN #F50-002D-7525

2-Car Garage Apartment - Studio

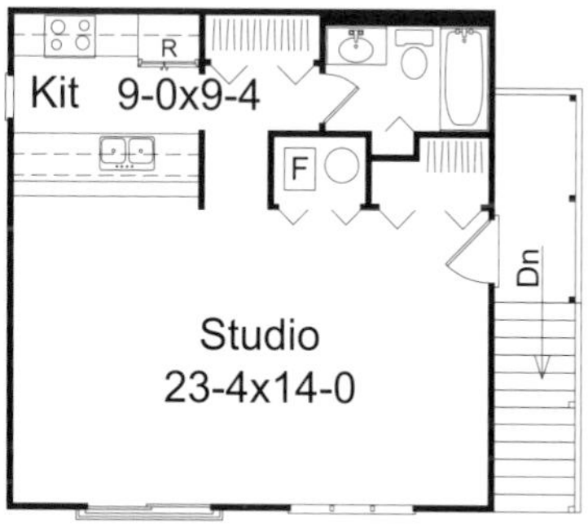

R
Kit 9-0x9-4
F
Dn
Studio
23-4x14-0

Second Floor
576 sq. ft.

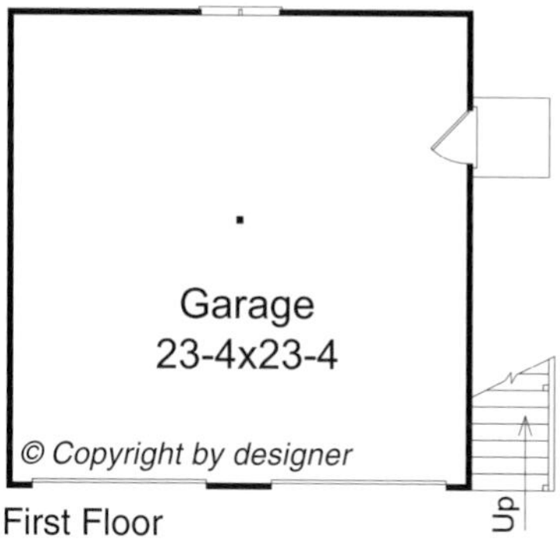

Garage
23-4x23-4
© Copyright by designer
Up

First Floor

- 576 square feet of living area
- Width: 28' Depth: 24'
- Building height - 21'-6"
- Ceiling heights - First floor - 8' Second floor - 8'
- Studio, 1 bath
- Floating slab foundation
- Complete list of materials
- Step-by-step instructions

1-Set	$420	PDF	$570
5-Set	$470	Repro	$620

2 1/2-Car Garage

PLAN #F50-002D-6007

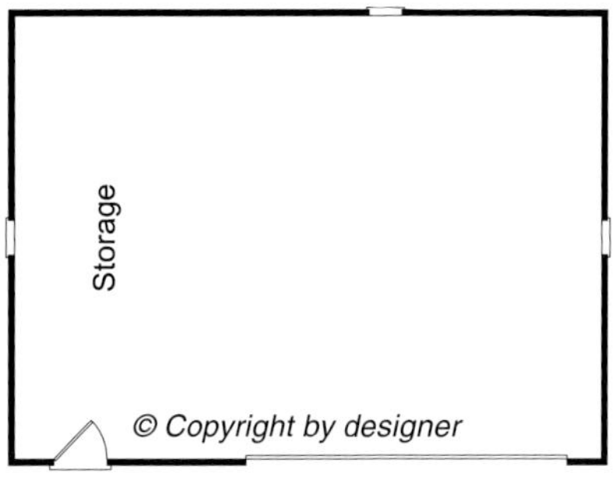

Storage
© Copyright by designer

- Width: 30' Depth: 22'
- Building height - 12'-2"
- Roof pitch - 4/12
- Ceiling height - 8'
- 16' x 7' overhead door
- Floating slab foundation, drawings also include slab foundation
- Additional space is perfect for yard equipment storage
- Complete list of materials
- Step-by-step instructions

1-Set	$225	PDF	$375
5-Set	$275	Repro	$425

2 1/2-Car Garage - Western Style

PLAN #F50-002D-6024

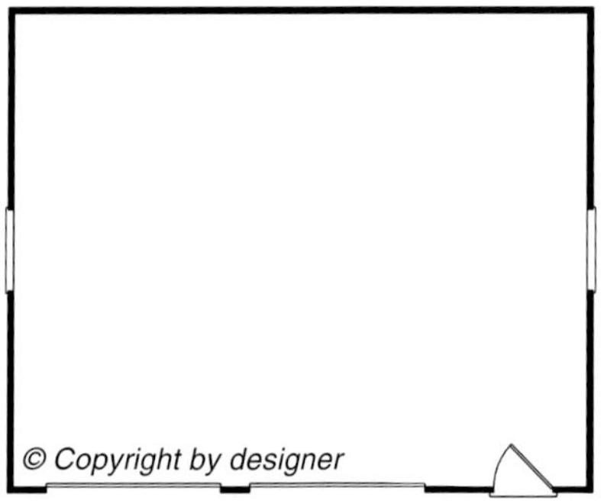

© Copyright by designer

- Width: 30' Depth: 24'
- Building height - 12'-6"
- Roof pitch - 4/12
- Ceiling height - 8'
- Two 9' x 7' overhead doors
- Floating slab foundation, drawings also include slab foundation
- Complete list of materials
- Step-by-step instructions

1-Set	$225	PDF	$375
5-Set	$275	Repro	$425

1-Car & RV Garage

PLAN #F50-059D-6016

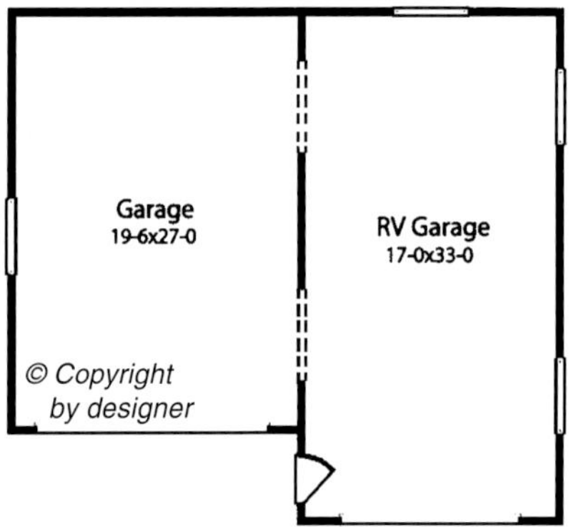

Garage
19-6x27-0
RV Garage
17-0x33-0
© Copyright by designer

- Width: 38' Depth: 34'
- Building height - 21'
- Roof pitch - 6/12
- Ceiling heights - 10' and 16'
- 16' x 8', 12' x 14' overhead doors
- Floating slab foundation
- Excellent garage for large equipment or workshop

1-Set	$190	CAD	$425
PDF	$280	Mat List	$40

PLAN #F50-002D-6011

3-Car Garage

© Copyright by designer

- Width: 32' Depth: 22'
- Building height - 12'-2"
- Roof pitch - 4/12
- Ceiling height - 8'
- 9' x 7', 16' x 7' overhead doors
- Floating slab foundation, drawings also include slab foundation
- Complete list of materials
- Step-by-step instructions

1-Set	$325	PDF	$475
5-Set	$375	Repro	$525

PLAN #F50-059D-6000

2-Car Garage with RV / Boat Area

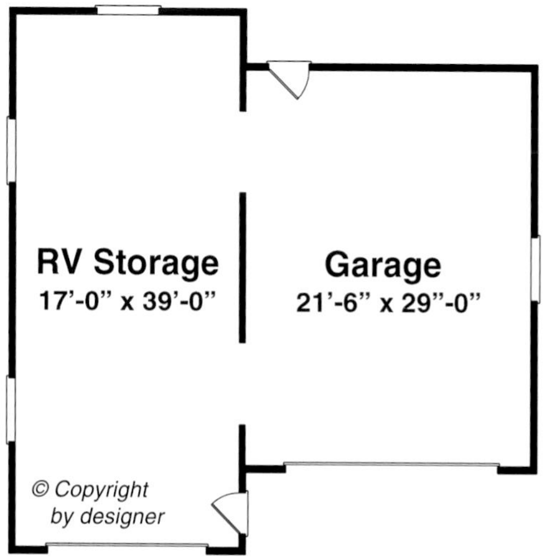
RV Storage
17'-0" x 39'-0"
Garage
21'-6" x 29"-0"
© Copyright by designer

- Width: 40' Depth: 40'
- Building height - 21'
- Roof pitch - 6/12
- Ceiling heights - 10' and 16'
- 12' x 14', 16' x 8' overhead doors
- Floating slab foundation
- Excellent garage for large equipment, RV or boat storage

1-Set	$190	CAD	$425
PDF	$280	Mat List	$40

Decorative 1-Car Garage

PLAN #F50-113D-6007

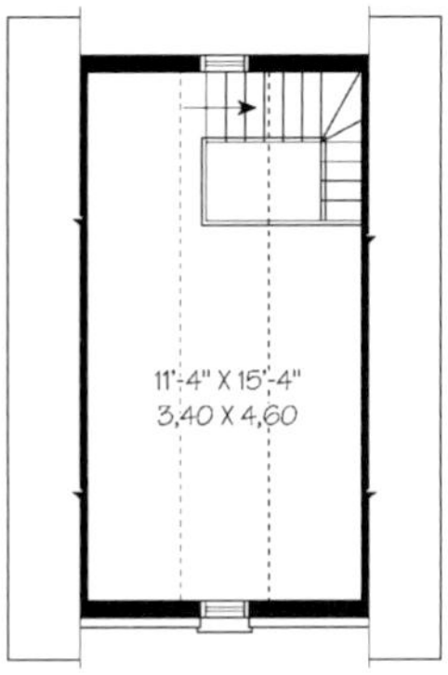
11'-4" X 15'-4"
3,40 X 4,60

Second Floor
261 sq. ft.

- Width: 15'   Depth: 23'
- Building height - 20'
- Roof pitch - 14/12
- Ceiling heights - First floor - 8'   Second floor - 7'
- 10' x 7' overhead door
- Floating slab foundation
- 2" x 6" exterior walls
- Decorative moldings and shutters add curb appeal

3-Set	$225	PDF	$295
5-Set	$245	CAD	$495

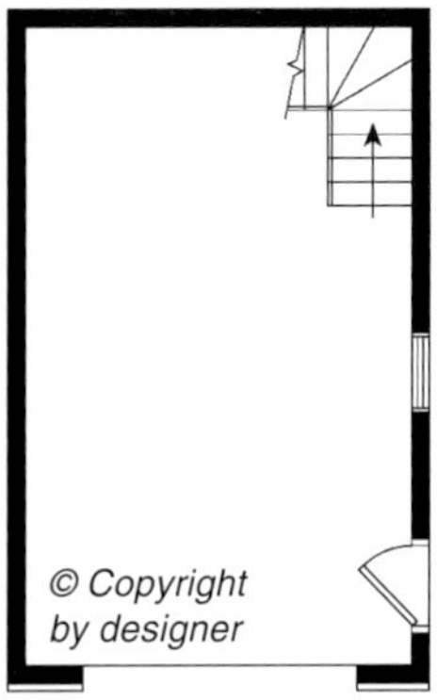
© Copyright
by designer

First Floor
345 sq. ft.

1-Car Garage

PLAN #F50-113D-6027

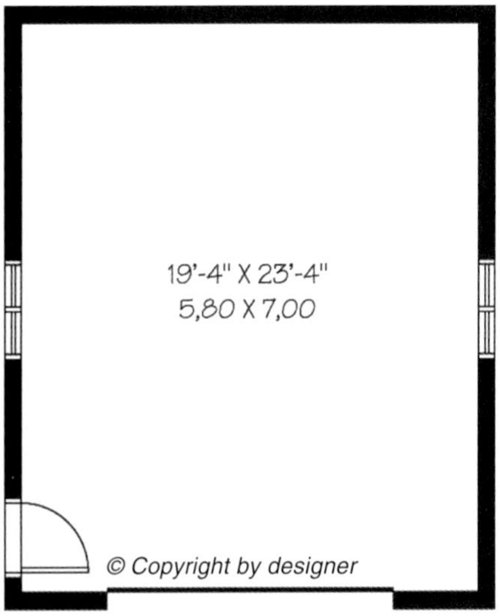
19'-4" X 23'-4"
5,80 X 7,00
© Copyright by designer

- Width: 20'   Depth: 24'
- Building height - 12'-4"
- Roof pitch - 4/12
- Ceiling height - 8'
- 12' x 7' overhead door
- Floating slab foundation
- 2" x 6" exterior walls

3-Set	$225	PDF	$295
5-Set	$245	CAD	$495

PLAN #F50-002D-7526

2-Car Garage Apartment - Cape Cod Style

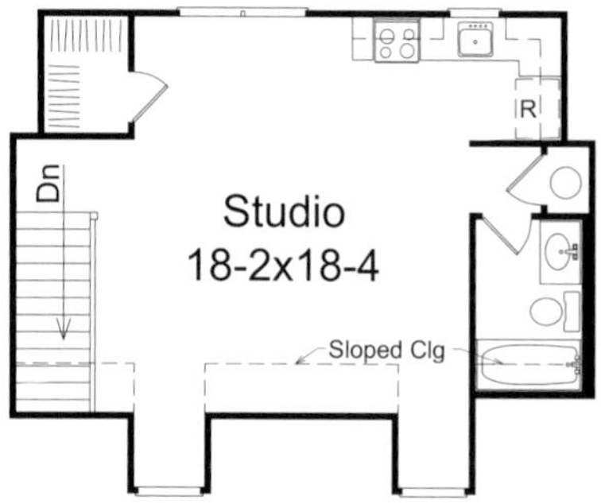
Studio
18-2x18-4
Dn
R
Sloped Clg

Second Floor
566 sq. ft.

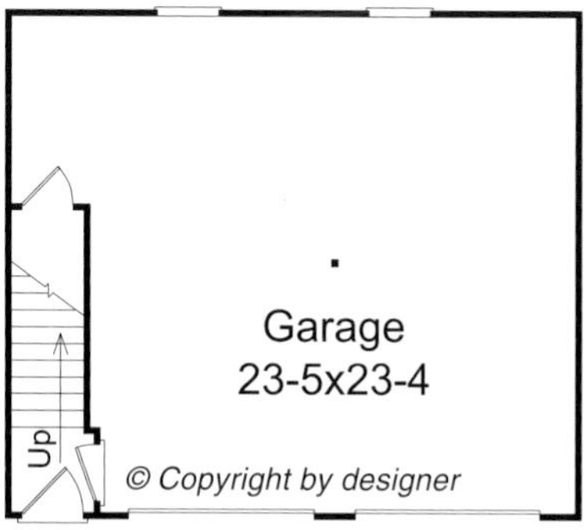
Garage
23-5x23-4
Up
© Copyright by designer

First Floor

- 566 square feet of living area
- Width: 28' Depth: 24'
- Building height - 22'
- Roof pitch - 4.5/12, 12/12
- Ceiling heights - First floor - 8' Second floor - 7'-7"
- Two 9' x 7' overhead doors
- Studio, 1 bath
- Floating slab foundation
- Complete list of materials
- Step-by-step instructions

1-Set	$420	PDF	$570
5-Set	$470	Repro	$620

PLAN #F50-002D-6042

3-Car Garage / Workshop

© Copyright by designer

- Width: 24' Depth: 36'
- Building height - 14'-6"
- Roof pitch - 4/12
- Ceiling height - 10'
- Three 9' x 8' overhead doors
- Floating slab foundation, drawings also include slab foundation
- Complete list of materials
- Step-by-step instructions

1-Set	$325	PDF	$475
5-Set	$375	CAD	$650

3-Car Garage

PLAN #F50-002D-6046

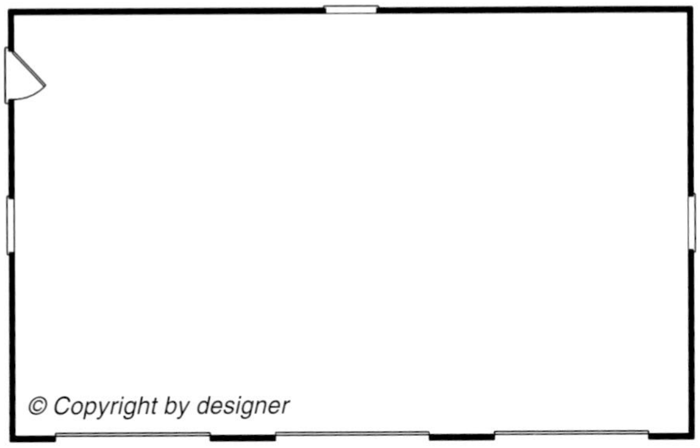
© Copyright by designer

- Width: 40' Depth: 24'
- Building height - 15'-6"
- Roof pitch - 6/12
- Ceiling height - 9'
- Three 9' x 7' overhead doors
- Floating slab foundation, drawings also include slab foundation
- Complete list of materials
- Step-by-step instructions

1-Set	$325	PDF	$475
5-Set	$375	CAD	$650

1-Car Garage

PLAN #F50-113D-6024

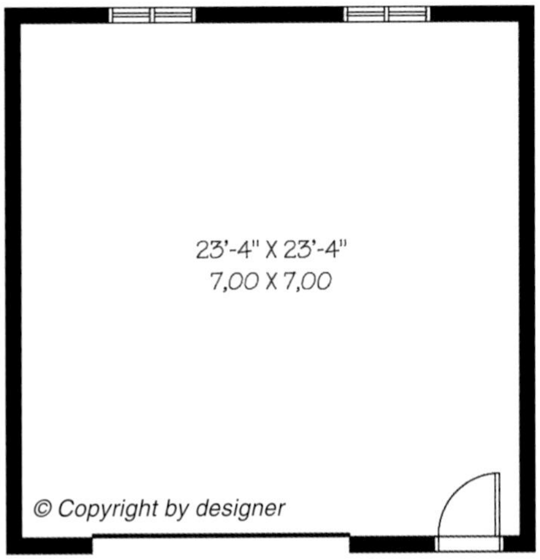
23'-4" X 23'-4"
7,00 X 7,00
© Copyright by designer

- Width: 24' Depth: 24'
- Building height - 13'
- Roof pitch - 4/12
- Ceiling height - 8'
- 16' x 7' overhead door
- Floating slab foundation
- 2" x 6" exterior walls

3-Set	$245	PDF	$315
5-Set	$265	CAD	$515

PLAN #F50-002D-6020

3-Car Garage with Workshop

Workshop Area
© Copyright by designer

- Width: 32'   Depth: 28'
- Building height - 13'-3"
- Roof pitch - 4/12
- Ceiling height - 8'
- 9' x 7', 16' x 7' overhead doors
- Floating slab foundation, drawings also include slab foundation
- Side entry door provides easy access
- Complete list of materials
- Step-by-step instructions

1-Set	$325	PDF	$475
5-Set	$375	CAD	$650

PLAN #F50-002D-6044

3-Car Garage with Loft

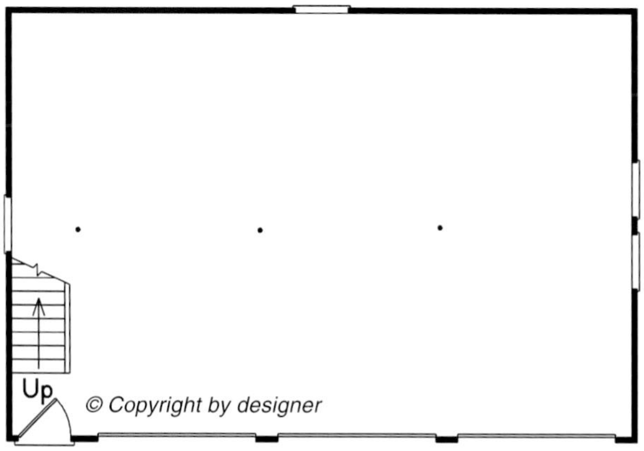
Up
© Copyright by designer

- Width: 36'   Depth: 24'
- Building height - 20'-8"
- Roof pitch - 12/12
- Ceiling heights - First floor - 8'   Loft - 7'-6"
- Three 9' x 7' overhead doors
- Floating slab foundation
- Complete list of materials
- Step-by-step instructions

1-Set	$325	PDF	$475
5-Set	$375	CAD	$650

Classic 2-Car Garage

PLAN #F50-113D-7506

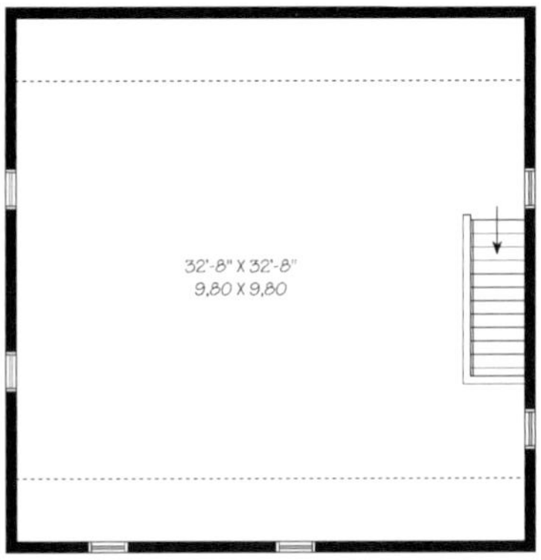
32'-8" X 32'-8"
9,80 X 9,80

Second Floor
1156 sq. ft.

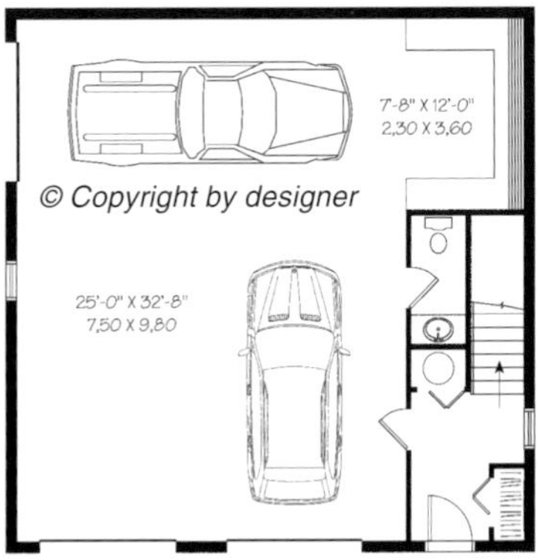
7'-8" X 12'-0"
2,30 X 3,60
© Copyright by designer
25'-0" X 32'-8"
7,50 X 9,80

First Floor
89 sq. ft.

- 1,245 total square feet
- Width: 34'   Depth: 34'
- Building height - 29'-10"
- Roof pitch - 10/12
- Ceiling heights - First floor - 8'   Second floor - 8'
- Two 9' x 7' overhead door
- Floating slab foundation
- 2" x 6" exterior walls
- The first floor includes a half bath and large U-shaped counter perfect for a workshop, while the second floor is a large open space

3-Set	$365	PDF	$435
5-Set	$385	CAD	$635

4-Car Garage

PLAN #F50-009D-6003

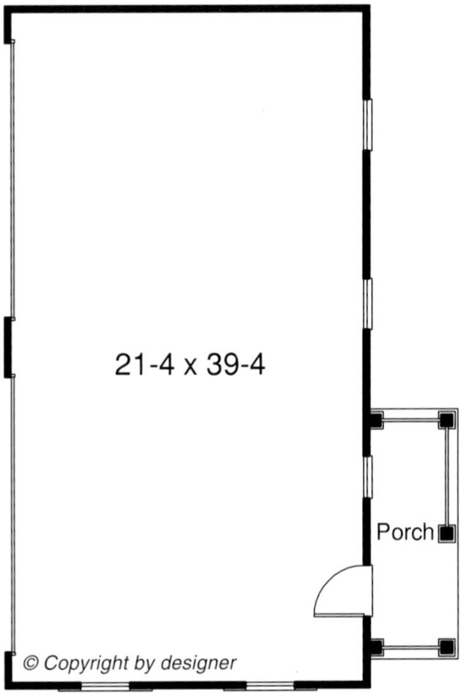
21-4 x 39-4
Porch
© Copyright by designer

- Width: 22'   Depth: 40'
- Building height - 18'
- Roof pitch - 8/12
- Ceiling height - 18'
- Two 16' x 7' overhead doors
- Floating slab foundation
- Structure is very appealing as a side or rear garage
- Complete list of materials

1-Set	$325	PDF	$475
5-Set	$375	CAD	$650

PLAN #F50-002D-7530

3-Car Garage Apartment - Cape Cod Style

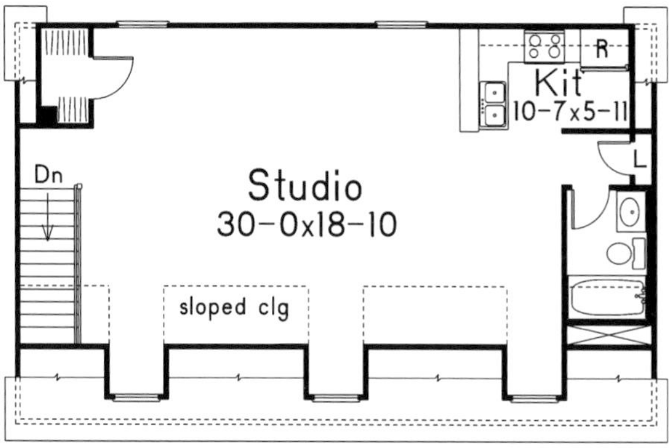

Second Floor
813 sq. ft.

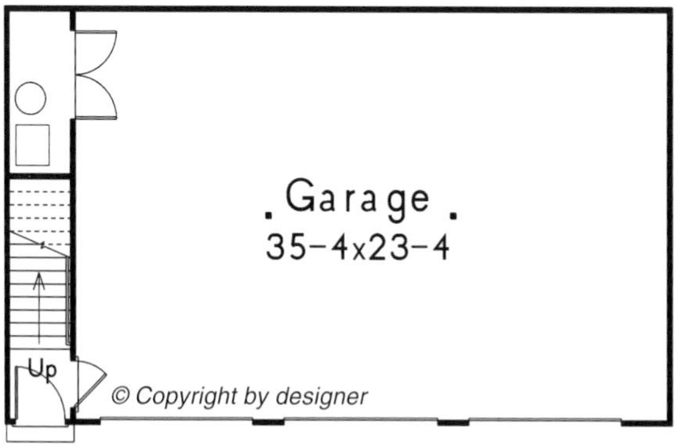

First Floor

- 813 square feet of living area
- Width: 40' Depth: 24'
- Building height - 22'
- Roof pitch - 4.25/12, 12/12
- Ceiling heights - First floor - 8' Second floor - 8'
- Three 9' x 7' overhead doors
- 1 bedroom, 1 bath
- Floating slab foundation

1-Set	$540	PDF	$720
5-Set	$590	CAD	$1110

PLAN #F50-059D-7509

3-Car Garage Apartment

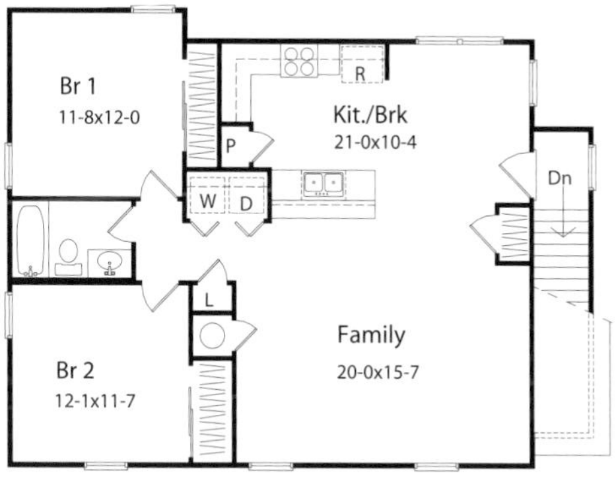

Second Floor
1,032 sq. ft.

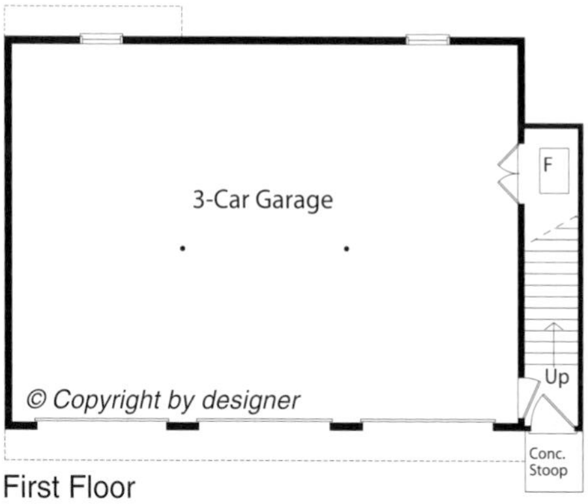

First Floor

- 1,032 square feet of living area
- Width: 40' Depth: 30'
- Building height - 23'-6"
- Roof pitch - 5/12, 10/12
- Ceiling heights - First floor - 8' Second floor - 8'
- Three 9' x 7' overhead doors
- 2 bedrooms, 1 bath
- Floating slab foundation

1-Set	$300	CAD	$575
PDF	$450	Mat List	$50

3-Car Garage

PLAN #F50-059D-6004

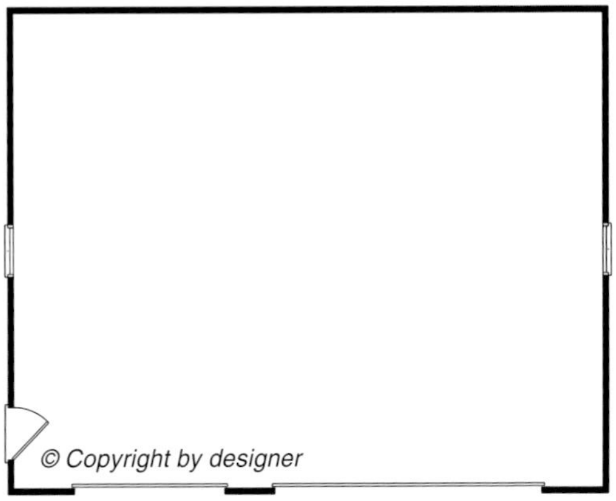
© Copyright by designer

- Width: 36' Depth: 28'
- Building height - 17'
- Roof pitch - 4/12
- Ceiling height - 9'
- 9' x 8', 16' x 8' overhead doors
- Floating slab foundation
- Versatile design looks good with many different home styles

1-Set	$175	CAD	$375
PDF	$260	Mat List	$40

2-Car Garage

PLAN #F50-063D-6009

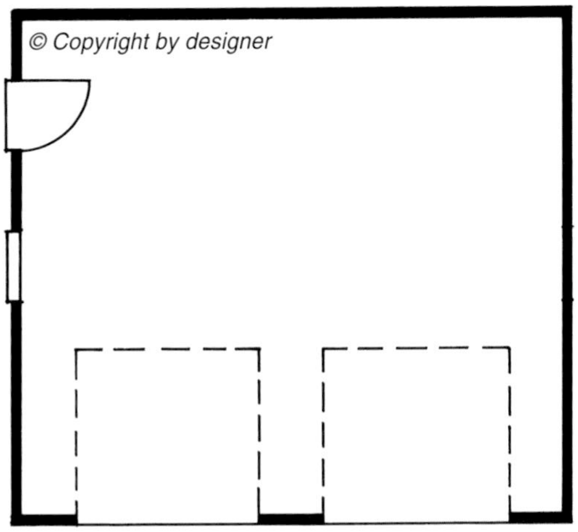
© Copyright by designer

- Width: 24' Depth: 22'
- Building height - 13'-6"
- Roof pitch - 5/12
- Ceiling height - 8'
- Two 9' x 7' overhead doors
- Floating slab foundation
- Complete list of materials

1-Set	$225	PDF	$375
5-Set	$275	Repro	$425

PLAN #F50-002D-6013

2-Car Garage

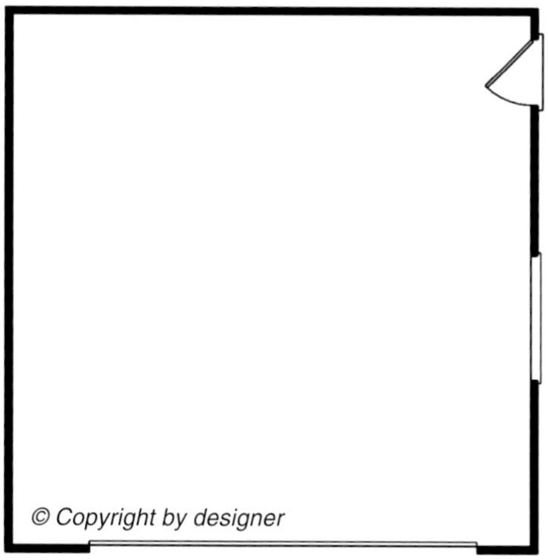
© Copyright by designer

- Width: 22' Depth: 22'
- Building height - 12'-2"
- Roof pitch - 4/12
- Ceiling height - 8'
- 16' x 7' overhead door
- Floating slab foundation, drawings also include slab foundation
- Perfect for a tractor or other lawn equipment
- Complete list of materials
- Step-by-step instructions

1-Set	$225	PDF	$375
5-Set	$275	Repro	$425

PLAN #F50-113D-6031

Spacious 3-Car Garage

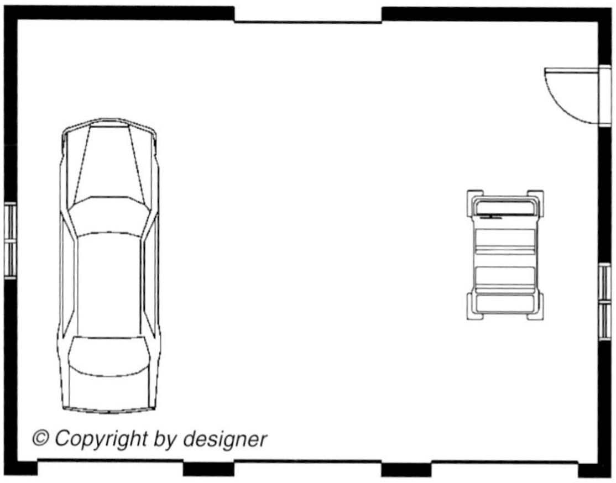
© Copyright by designer

- Width: 34' Depth: 24'
- Building height - 15'-4"
- Roof pitch - 6/12
- Ceiling height - 8'
- Three 18' x 7' overhead doors
- 2" x 6" exterior walls
- Lots of storage in this garage
- Floating slab foundation

3-Set	$325	PDF	$395
5-Set	$345	CAD	$595

3-Car Carport with Apartment

PLAN #F50-002D-7516

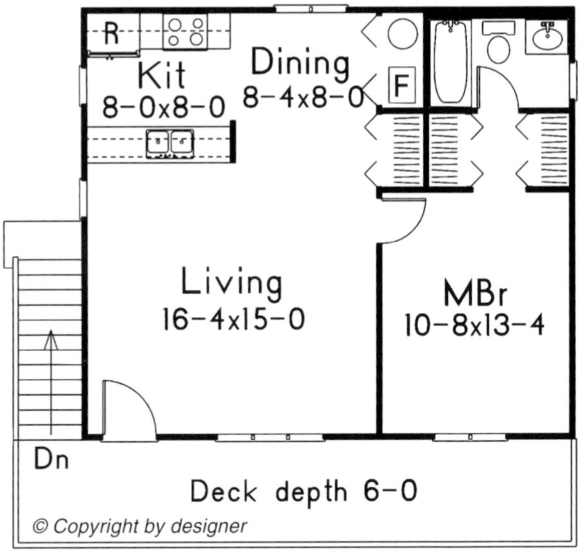

- 672 square feet of living area
- Width: 28' Depth: 24'
- Building height - 22' with 8' carport height
- Roof pitch - 4/12
- Ceiling height - 8'
- 1 bedroom, 1 bath
- Pier foundation
- Complete list of materials
- Step-by-step instructions

1-Set	$420	PDF	$570
5-Set	$470	Repro	$620

Apartment Garage & RV Storage

PLAN #F50-007D-0189

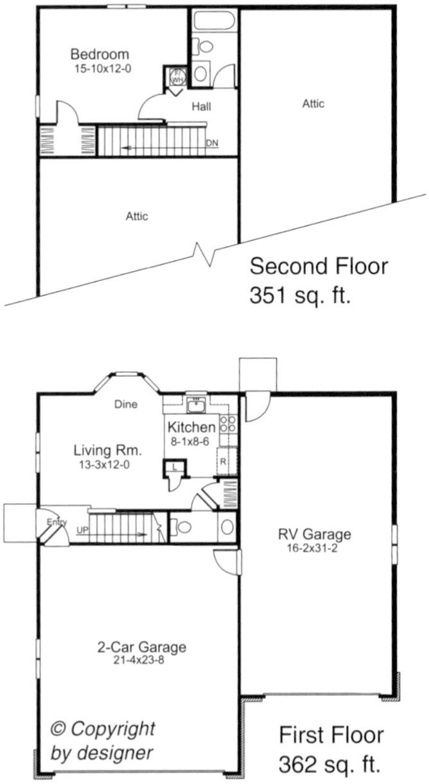

- 713 square feet of living area
- Width: 38'-8" Depth: 42'-4"
- Building height - 25'
- Roof pitch - 3.5/12, 6.5/12
- Ceiling heights - First floor - 9' Second floor - 8' RV garage - 13'-4"
- 18' x 8', 12' x 12' overhead doors
- 1 bedroom, 1 1/2 baths
- Slab foundation

1-Set	$540	PDF	$720
5-Set	$590	Repro	$760

PLAN #F50-009D-7523

2-Car Garage with Shop & Storage

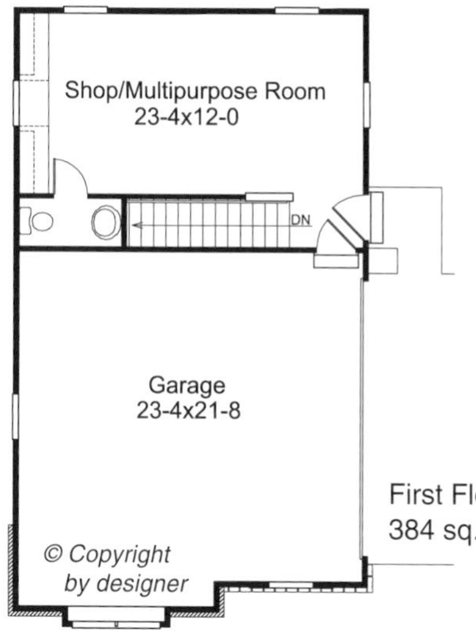

Shop/Multipurpose Room
23-4x12-0
DN
Garage
23-4x21-8
© Copyright
by designer

First Floor
384 sq. ft.

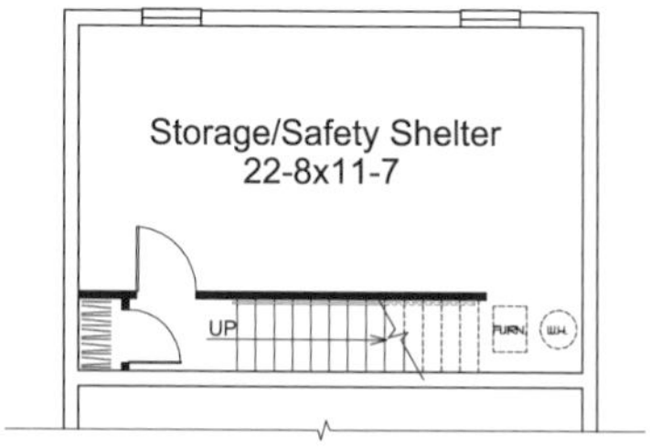

Storage/Safety Shelter
22-8x11-7
UP

Lower Level
25 sq. ft.

- 409 square feet of living area
- Width: 24' Depth: 40'-8"
- Building height - 17'-6"
- Roof pitch - 8/12
- Ceiling heights - First floor - 8' Lower level - 7'-10"
- 18' x 7' overhead door
- Basement foundation
- The storage/safety shelter is 263 square feet
- Complete list of materials

1-Set	$275	PDF	$425
5-Set	$325	CAD	$600

PLAN #F50-007D-0188

Studio Apartment Garage with Office

Second Floor
370 sq. ft.

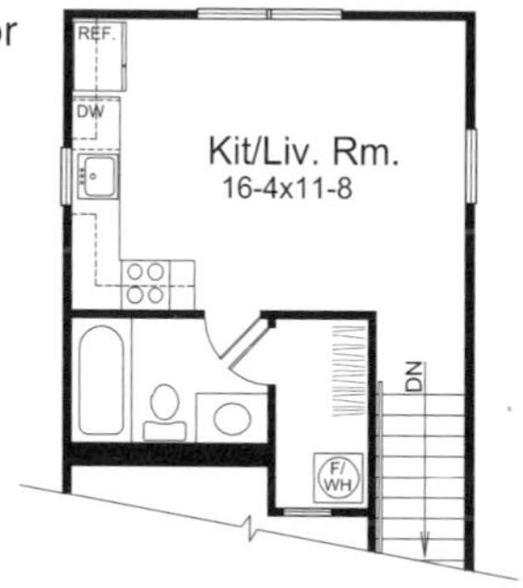

REF.
DW
Kit/Liv. Rm.
16-4x11-8
DN
F/WH

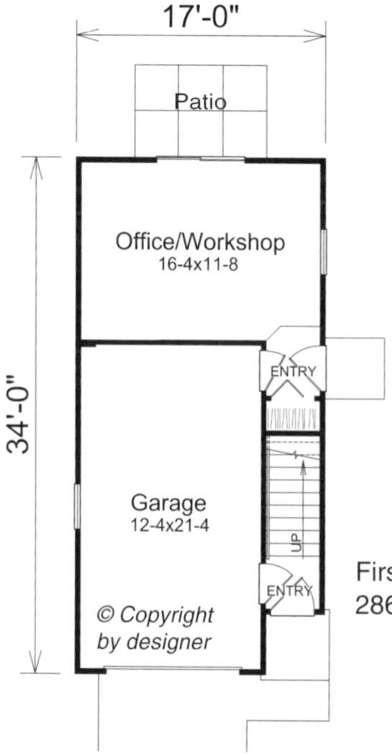

17'-0"
Patio
Office/Workshop
16-4x11-8
ENTRY
34'-0"
Garage
12-4x21-4
UP
ENTRY
© Copyright
by designer

First Floor
286 sq. ft.

- 656 square feet of living area
- Width: 17' Depth: 34'
- Building height - 23'
- Roof pitch - 7/12
- Ceiling heights - First floor - 8' Second floor - 8'
- 9'x 7' overhead door
- Slab foundation
- Complete list of materials

1-Set	$420	PDF	$570
5-Set	$470	CAD	$900

Spacious 2-Car Garage

PLAN #F50-113D-6022

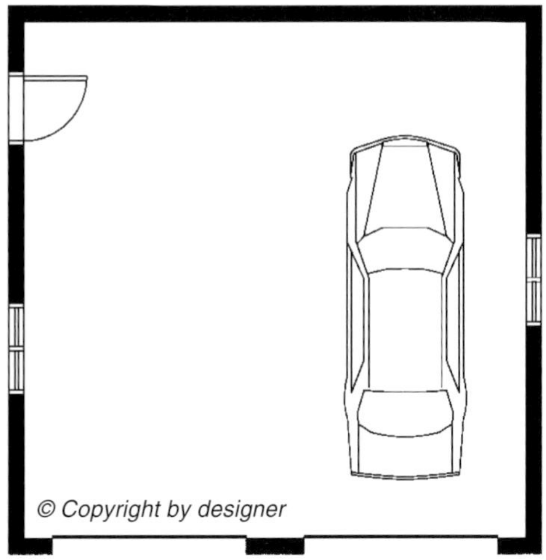
© Copyright by designer

- Width: 24' Depth: 24'
- Building height - 15'-4"
- Roof pitch - 6/12
- Ceiling height - 8'
- Two 9' x 7' overhead doors
- Floating slab foundation
- 2" x 6" exterior walls
- Attractive style for any home type

3-Set	$265	PDF	$335
5-Set	$285	CAD	$535

Roomy 2-Car Garage

PLAN #F50-113D-6018

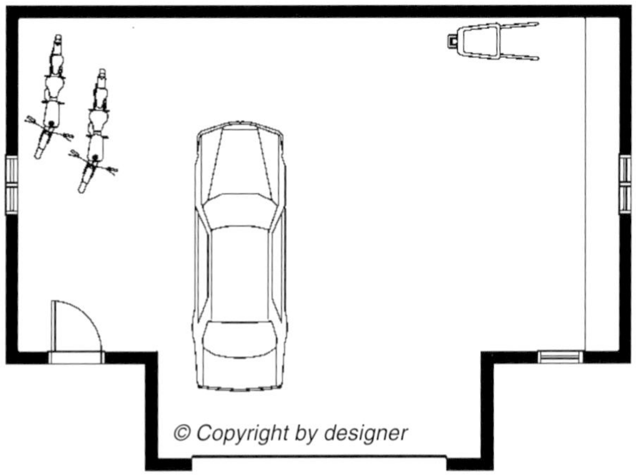
© Copyright by designer

- Width: 36' Depth: 26'
- Building height - 19'-2"
- Roof pitch - 8/12
- Ceiling height - 8'
- 15' x 7' overhead door
- Floating slab foundation
- 2" x 6" exterior walls
- Attractive styling with decorative window

3-Set	$285	PDF	$355
5-Set	$305	CAD	$555

PLAN #F50-009D-7518

Shop & Equipment Garage

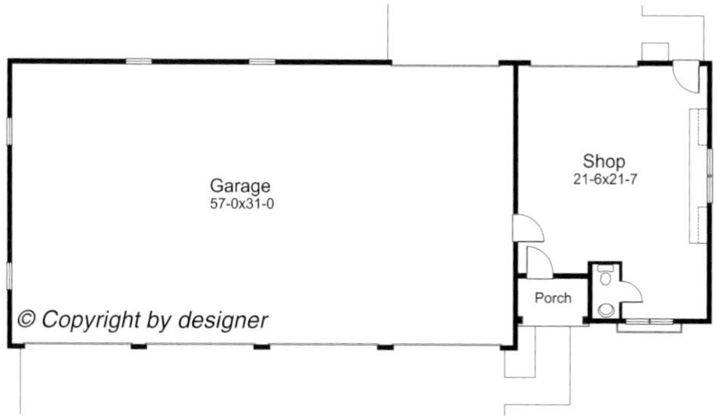
Garage
57-0x31-0
Shop
21-6x21-7
Porch
© Copyright by designer

- Width: 80' Depth: 32'
- Building height - 21'
- Roof pitch - 6/12
- Ceiling heights - Shop - 10' Garage - 12'
- Five 12' x 10' and one 12' x 8' overhead doors
- Slab foundation
- Exterior features a porch and a roof cupola
- Shop includes a convenient half bath
- Complete list of materials

1-Set	$325	PDF	$475
5-Set	$375	CAD	$650

PLAN #F50-113D-6013

Charming 2-Car Garage

12'-0" X 19'-8"
3,60 X 5,90

Second Floor
334 sq. ft.

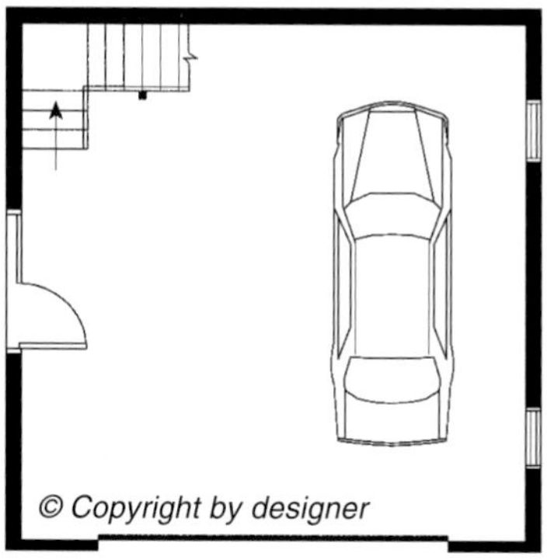
© Copyright by designer

First Floor

- Width: 284' Depth: 24'
- Building height - 22'-2"
- Roof pitch - 10/12
- Ceiling heights - First floor - 9' Second floor - 8'
- 16' x 8' overhead door
- Floating slab foundation
- 2" x 6" exterior walls

3-Set	$285	PDF	$355
PDF	$305	CAD	$555

Double Gabled 2-Car Garage

PLAN #F50-113D-6020

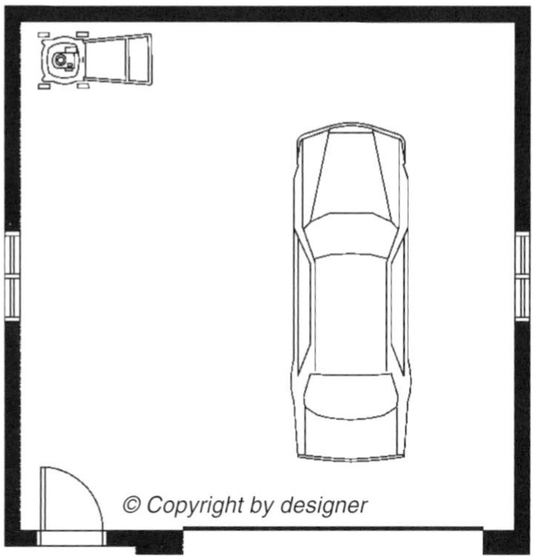
© Copyright by designer

- Width: 24' Depth: 24'
- Building height - 17'-8"
- Roof pitch - 8/12
- Ceiling height - 8'
- 14' x 7' overhead door
- Floating slab foundation
- 2" x 6" exterior walls
- Additional space is perfect for yard equipment storage

3-Set	$245	PDF	$315
5-Set	$265	CAD	$515

3-Car Garage - Western Style

PLAN #F50-002D-6026

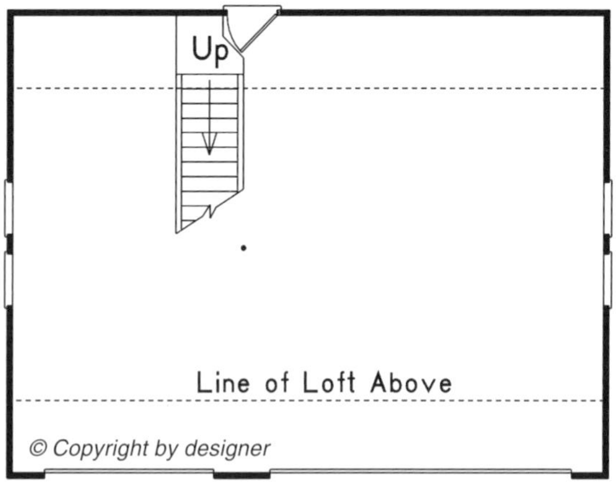
Up
Line of Loft Above
© Copyright by designer

- Width: 32' Depth: 24'
- Building height - 20'-6"
- Roof pitch - 12/12
- Ceiling heights - First floor - 8' Loft - 8'
- 9' x 7', 16' x 7' overhead doors
- Floating slab foundation, drawings also include slab foundation
- Complete list of materials
- Step-by-step instructions

1-Set	$325	PDF	$475
5-Set	$375	Repro	$525

PLAN #F50-113D-6019

1-Car Garage with Hip Roof

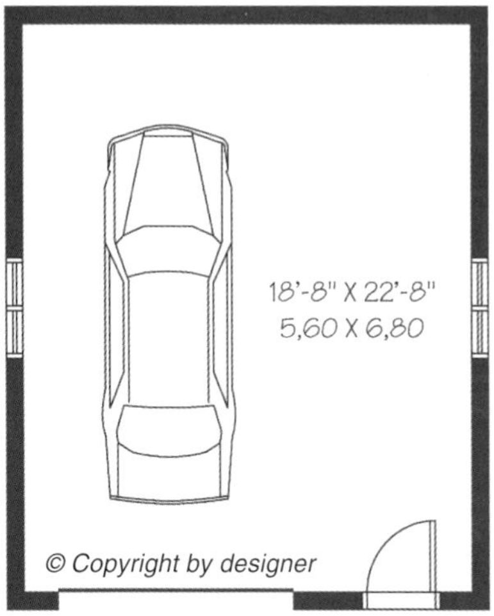
18'-8" X 22'-8"
5,60 X 6,80
© Copyright by designer

- Width: 20' Depth: 24'
- Building height - 16'-4"
- Roof pitch - 8/12
- Ceiling height - 8'
- 10' x 7' overhead door
- Floating slab foundation

3-Set	$225	PDF	$295
5-Set	$245	CAD	$495

PLAN #F50-113D-6033

1-Car Garage for a Modern Dwelling

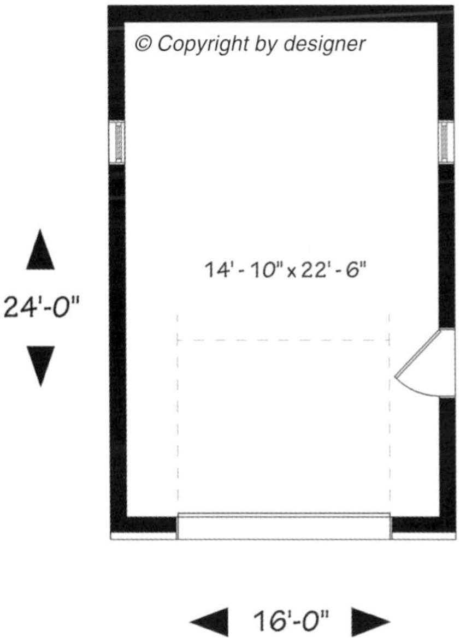
© Copyright by designer
14'-10" x 22'-6"
24'-0"
16'-0"

- Width: 16' Depth: 24'
- Building height - 14'-4"
- Roof pitch - 2/12
- Ceiling height - 8'
- 10' x 8' overhead door
- 2" x 6" exterior walls
- Practical and sleek design with a side access door
- Monolithic slab foundation

3-Set	$205	PDF	$275
5-Set	$225	CAD	$475

Country Style 2-Car Apartment Garage

PLAN #F50-124D-7503

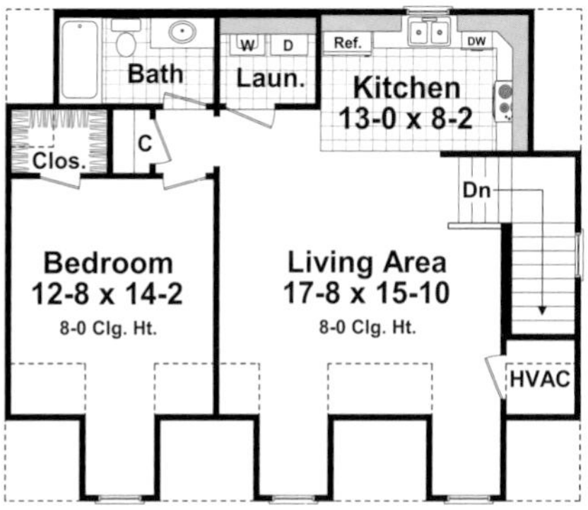

Second Floor
853 sq. ft.

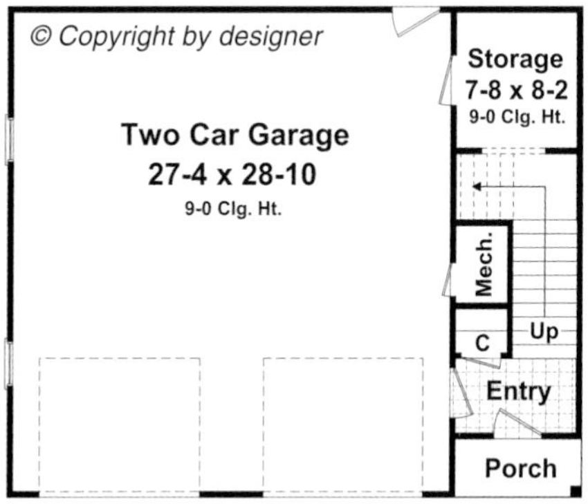

First Floor
126 sq. ft.

- 979 total square feet of living area
- Width: 36' Depth: 24'
- Building height - 29'-6"
- Roof pitch - 4/12, 12/12
- Ceiling heights - First floor - 9' Second floor - 8'
- 1 bedroom, 1 bath
- Slab foundation
- Spacious second floor apartment with first floor storage

5-Set	$335	Repro	$460
PDF	$435	CAD	$655

2-Car Garage with Workshop

PLAN #F50-002D-6004

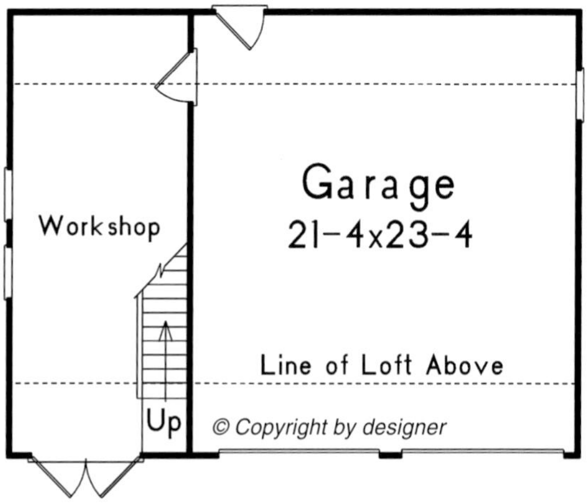

- Width: 32' Depth: 24'
- Building height - 21'
- Roof pitch - 12/12
- Ceiling heights - First floor - 8' Loft - 7'-6"
- Two 9' x 7' overhead doors
- Floating slab foundation, drawings also include slab foundation
- Complete list of materials
- Step-by-step instructions

1-Set	$275	PDF	$425
5-Set	$325	CAD	$600

PLAN #F50-117D-7500

2-Car Craftsman Apartment Garage

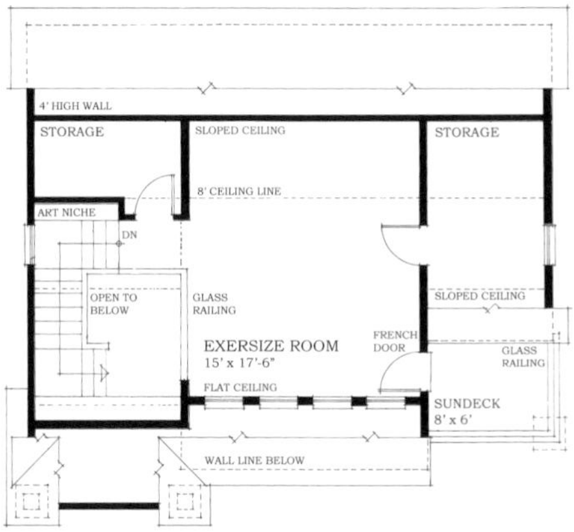

Second Floor
607 sq. ft.

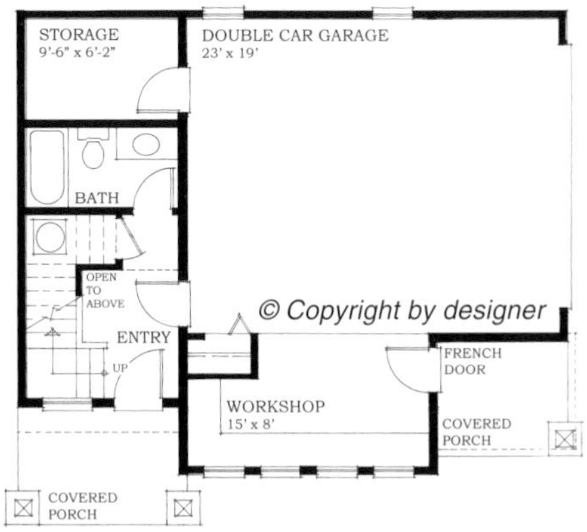

First Floor
848 sq. ft.

- 1,455 square feet of living area
- Width: 34' Depth: 31'
- Building height - 25'
- Roof pitch - 10/12
- Ceiling heights - First floor - 8', 17' Second floor - 8'
- 16' x 7' overhead door
- 2" x 6" exterior walls
- Slab foundation

1-Set	$420	PDF	$570
5-Set	$470	CAD	$900

PLAN #F50-113D-7504

2-Car Garage with Style

Second Floor
928 sq. ft.

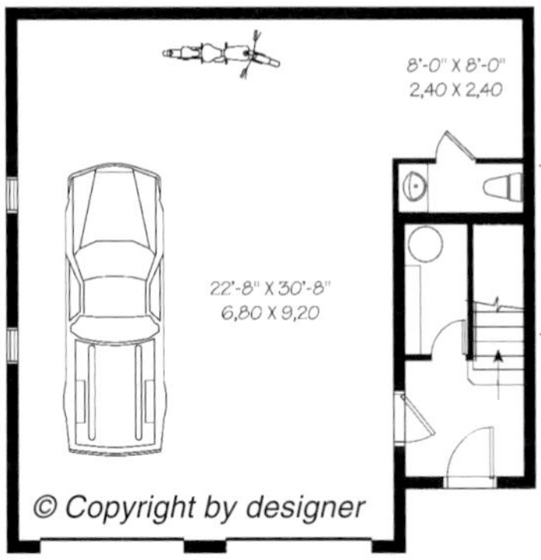

First Floor
140 sq. ft.

- 1,068 square feet of living area
- Width: 32' Depth: 32'
- Building height - 28'-8"
- Roof pitch - 10/12, 6/12
- Ceiling heights - First floor - 8' Second floor - 8'-6"
- 2 bedrooms, 1 1/2 baths
- 2" x 6" exterior walls
- Floating slab foundation

5-Set	$870	PDF	$1050
8-Set	$900	CAD	$1620

4-Car Apartment Garage with Shop

PLAN #F50-007D-0144

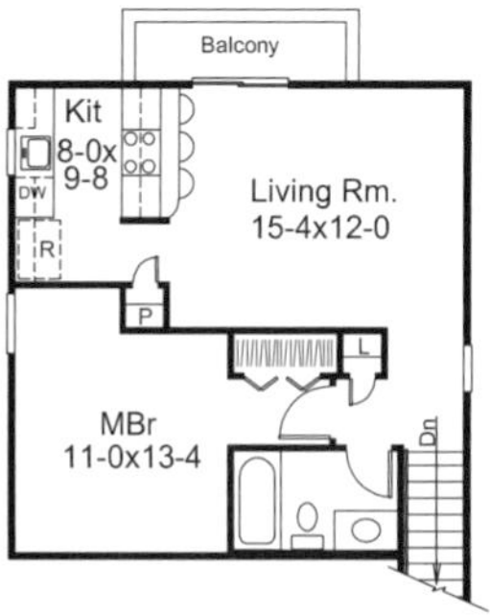

Second Floor
576 sq. ft.

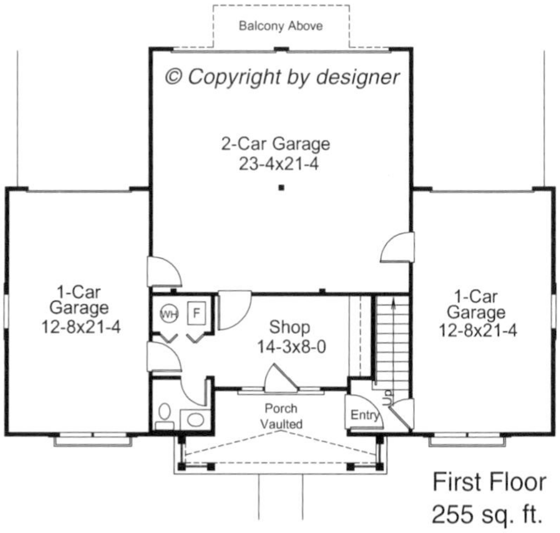

First Floor
255 sq. ft.

- 831 square feet of living area
- Width: 50' Depth: 37'-8"
- Building height - 25'-6"
- Roof pitch - 10/12, 10.5/12
- Ceiling heights - First floor - 9' Second floor - 8'
- Four 9' x 8' overhead doors
- 1 bedroom, 1 1/2 baths
- Slab foundation

1-Set	$540	PDF	$720
5-Set	$590	Repro	$760

2-Car Apartment Garage with Pizzazz

PLAN #F50-007D-0241

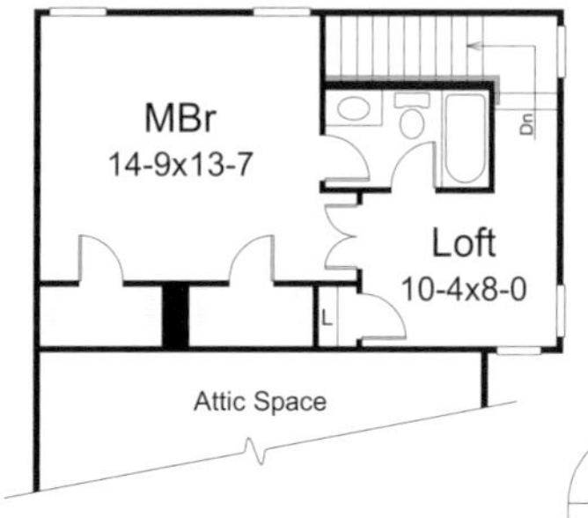

Second Floor
495 sq. ft.

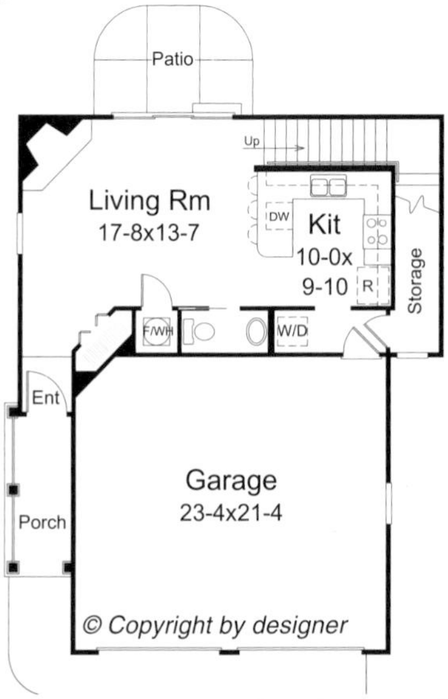

First Floor
591 sq. ft.

- 1,086 square feet of living area
- Width: 32'-8" Depth: 39'-4"
- Building height - 21'-6"
- Roof pitch - 2.5/12, 5/12
- Ceiling heights - First floor - 8' Second floor - 8'
- Two 9' x 7' overhead doors
- 1 bedroom, 1 1/2 baths
- Slab foundation

1-Set	$590	PDF	$790
5-Set	$650	Repro	$840

PLAN #F50-002D-7528

Apartment with Exterior Entrance

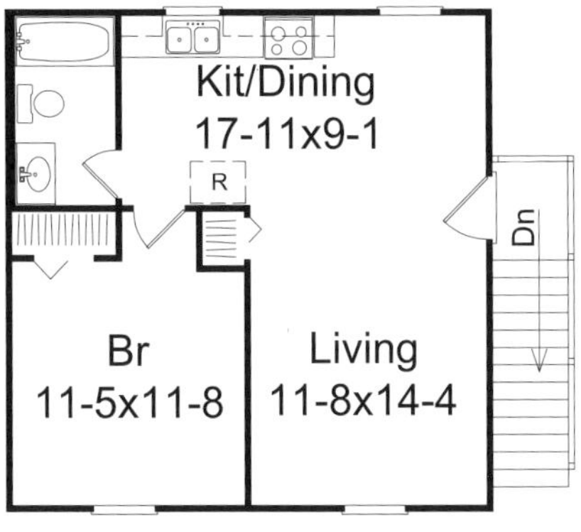

Kit/Dining
17-11x9-1
R
Dn
Br
11-5x11-8
Living
11-8x14-4

Second Floor
576 sq. ft.

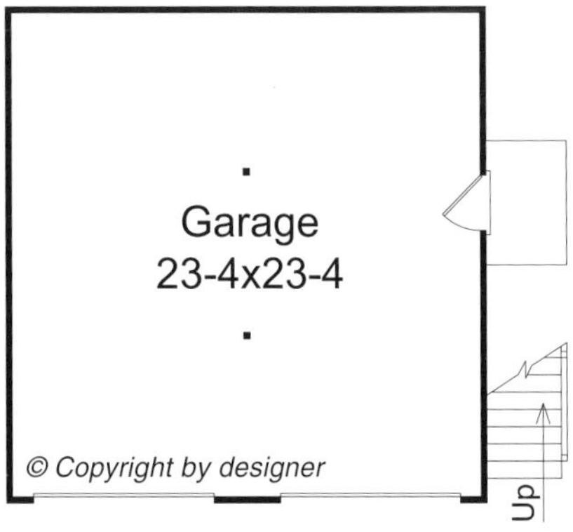

Garage
23-4x23-4
© Copyright by designer
Up

First Floor

- 576 square feet of living area
- Width: 28' Depth: 24'
- Building height - 21'-5"
- Roof pitch - 4/12
- Ceiling heights - First floor - 8' Second floor - 8'
- Two 9' x 7' overhead doors
- 1 bedroom, 1 bath
- Floating slab foundation
- Complete list of materials
- Step-by-step instructions

1-Set	$420	PDF	$520
5-Set	$470	Repro	$620

PLAN #F50-113D-7501

2-Car Garage Apartment

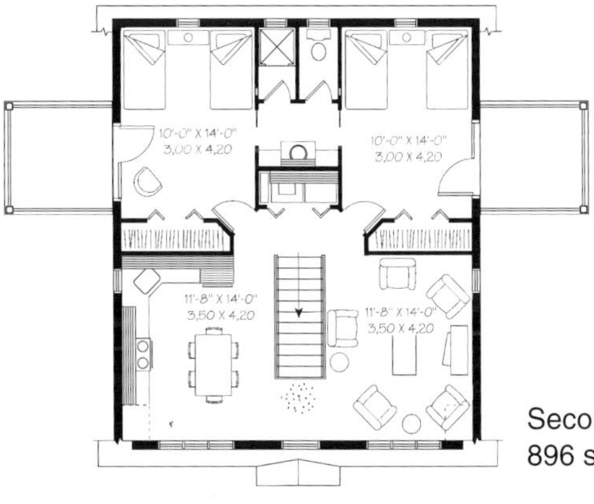

Second Floor
896 sq. ft.

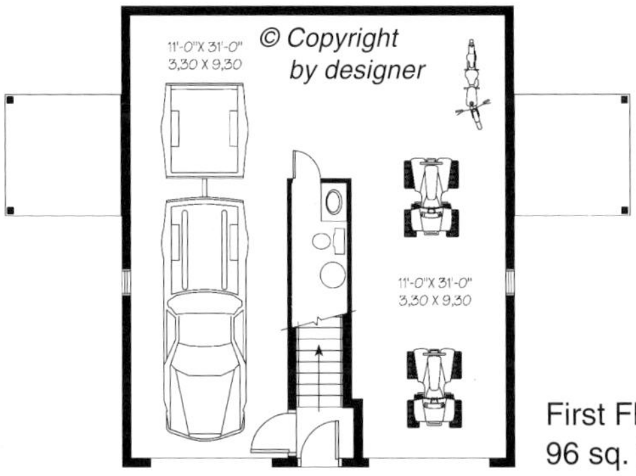

© Copyright
by designer

First Floor
96 sq. ft.

- 992 square feet of living area
- Width: 28' Depth: 32'
- Building height - 26'-8"
- Roof pitch - 6/12
- Ceiling heights - First floor - 8' Second floor - 8'
- Two 9' x 7' overhead doors
- 2 bedrooms, 1 1/2 baths
- Floating slab foundation

5-Set	$810	PDF	$990
8-Set	$840	CAD	$1560

Roomy 2-Car Garage Apartment

PLAN #F50-113D-7500

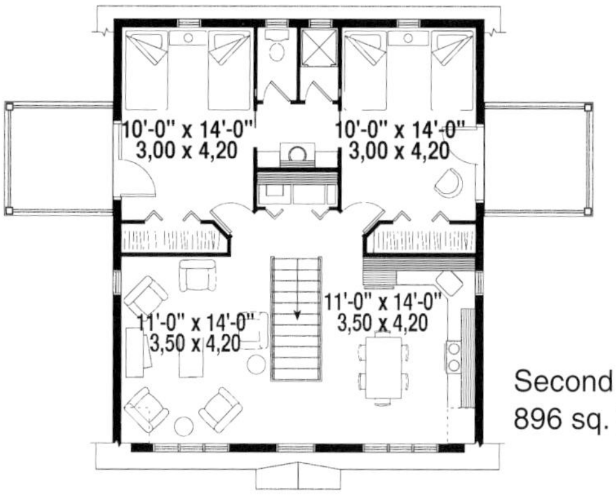
10'-0" x 14'-0"
3,00 x 4,20
10'-0" x 14'-0"
3,00 x 4,20
11'-0" x 14'-0"
3,50 x 4,20
11'-0" x 14'-0"
3,50 x 4,20

Second Floor
896 sq. ft.

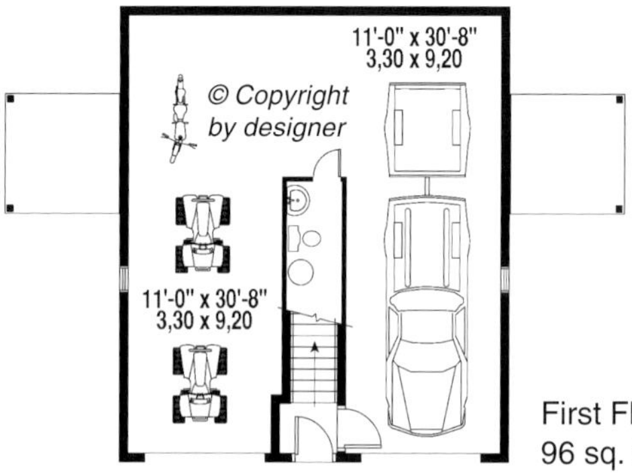
11'-0" x 30'-8"
3,30 x 9,20
© Copyright
by designer
11'-0" x 30'-8"
3,30 x 9,20

First Floor
96 sq. ft.

- 992 square feet of living area
- Width: 28' Depth: 32'
- Building height - 26'-8"
- Roof pitch - 6/12
- Ceiling heights - First floor - 8' Second floor - 8'
- Two 9' x 7' overhead doors
- 2 bedrooms, 1 1/2 baths
- Floating slab foundation
- 2" x 6" exterior walls

5-Set	$810	PDF	$990
8-Set	$840	CAD	$1560

1-Car Garage with Studio Apartment

PLAN #F50-007D-0195

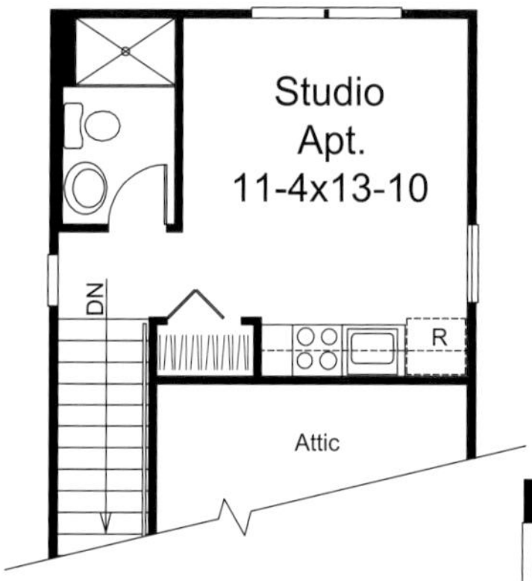
Studio
Apt.
11-4x13-10
DN
R
Attic

Second Floor
237 sq. ft.

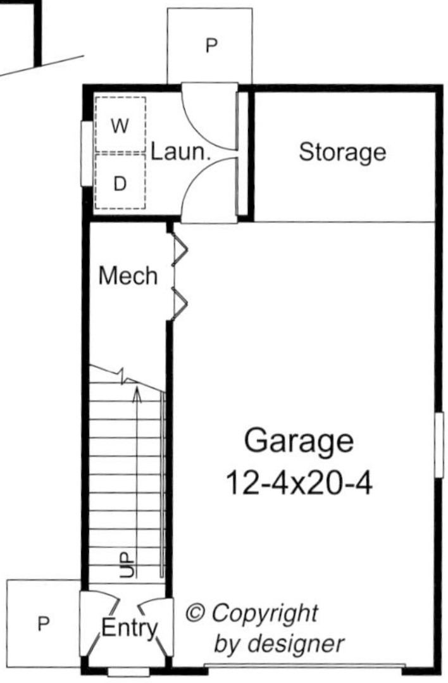
P
W
Laun.
D
Storage
Mech
Garage
12-4x20-4
UP
P
Entry
© Copyright
by designer

First Floor
105 sq. ft.

- 342 square feet of living area
- Width: 17' Depth: 27'
- Building height - 22'-5"
- Roof pitch - 4/12, 8.5/12
- Ceiling heights - First floor - 8' Second floor - 8'
- 9' x 7' overhead door
- Studio, 1 bath
- Slab foundation

1-Set	$540	PDF	$720
5-Set	$590	CAD	$1110

PLAN #F50-007D-0159

Cozy 2-Car Garage Apartment

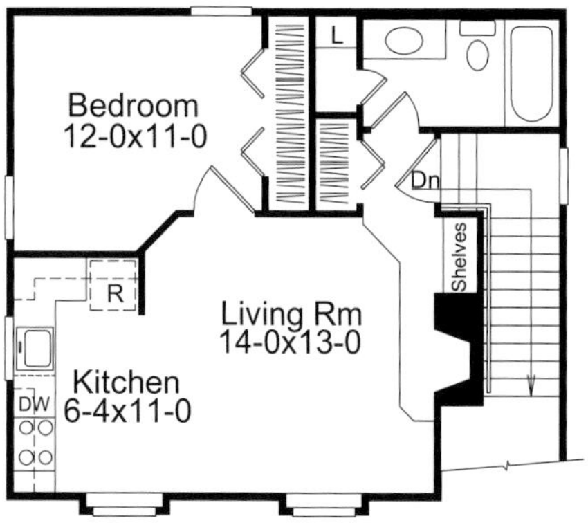
Bedroom
12-0x11-0
L
Dn
Shelves
R
Living Rm
14-0x13-0
Kitchen
6-4x11-0
DW

Second Floor
615 sq. ft.

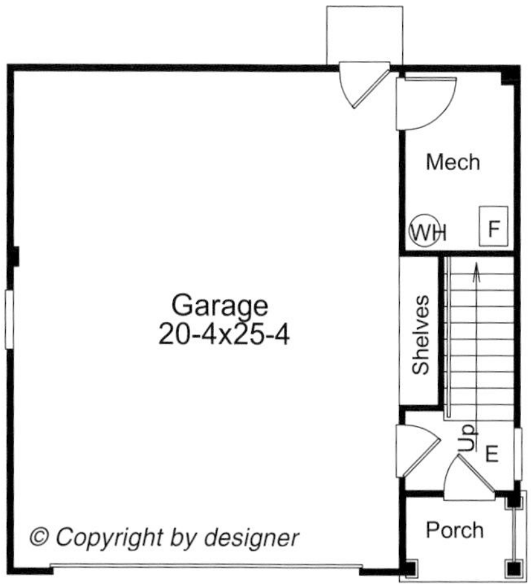
Mech
WH
F
Garage
20-4x25-4
Shelves
Up
E
Porch
© Copyright by designer

First Floor

- 615 square feet of living area
- Width: 27' Depth: 26'
- Building height - 25'-4"
- Roof pitch - 8/12, 10/12
- Ceiling heights - First floor - 8' Second floor - 8'
- 16' x 7' overhead door
- 1 bedroom, 1 bath
- Slab foundation

1-Set	$420	PDF	$570
5-Set	$470	CAD	$900

PLAN #F50-007D-0242

Apartment Garage with Outdoor Balcony

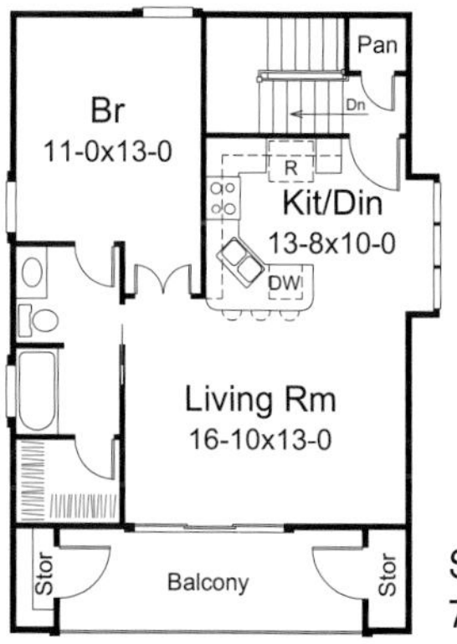
Pan
Br
11-0x13-0
Dn
R
Kit/Din
13-8x10-0
DW
Living Rm
16-10x13-0
Stor
Balcony
Stor

Second Floor
734 sq. ft.

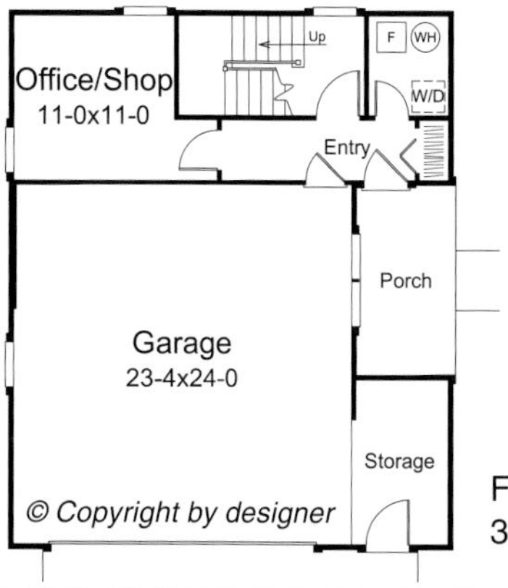
F
WH
Up
Office/Shop
11-0x11-0
W/D
Entry
Porch
Garage
23-4x24-0
Storage
© Copyright by designer

First Floor
357 sq. ft.

- 1,091 square feet of living area
- Width: 30'-8" Depth: 36'
- Building height - 25'-6"
- Roof pitch - 6/12
- Ceiling heights - First floor - 8' Second floor - 8'
- 18' x 7' overhead door
- 1 bedroom, 1 bath
- Slab foundation

1-Set	$590	PDF	$790
5-Set	$650	CAD	$1300

2-Car Garage with Country Flair

PLAN #F50-113D-7503

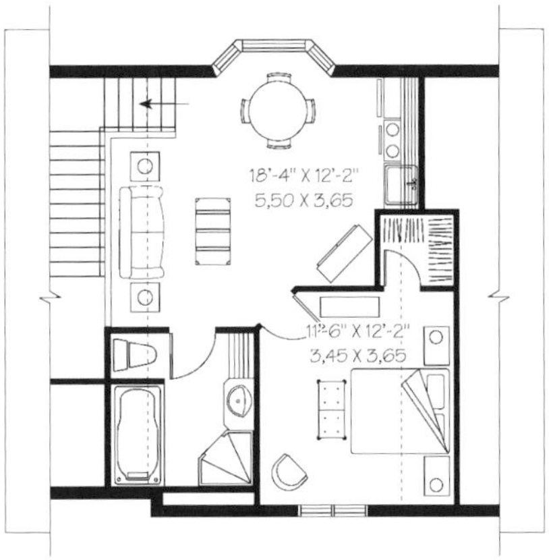
18'-4" X 12'-2"
5,50 X 3,65
11'-6" X 12'-2"
3,45 X 3,65

Second Floor
601 sq. ft.

- 713 square feet of living area
- Width: 28' Depth: 26'
- Building height - 28'-2"
- Roof pitch - 12/12
- Ceiling heights - First floor - 9'-6" Second floor - 8'
- 16' x 7' overhead door
- 1 bedroom, 1 bath
- Floating slab foundation
- 2" x 6" exterior walls

5-Set	$750	PDF	$930
8-Set	$780	CAD	$1500

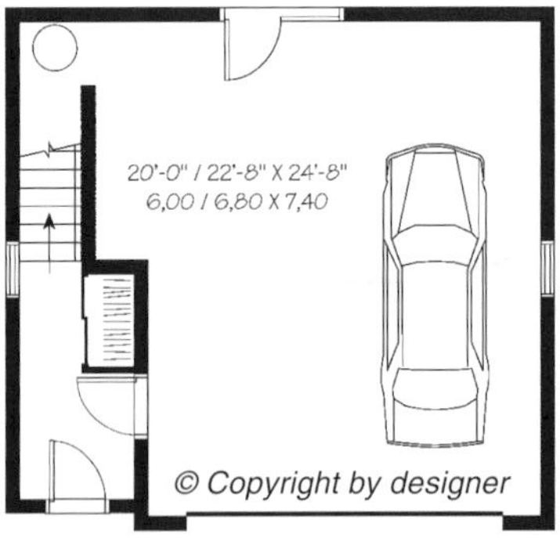
20'-0" / 22'-8" X 24'-8"
6,00 / 6,80 X 7,40
© Copyright by designer

First Floor
112 sq. ft.

2-Car Garage Apartment

PLAN #F50-063D-7506

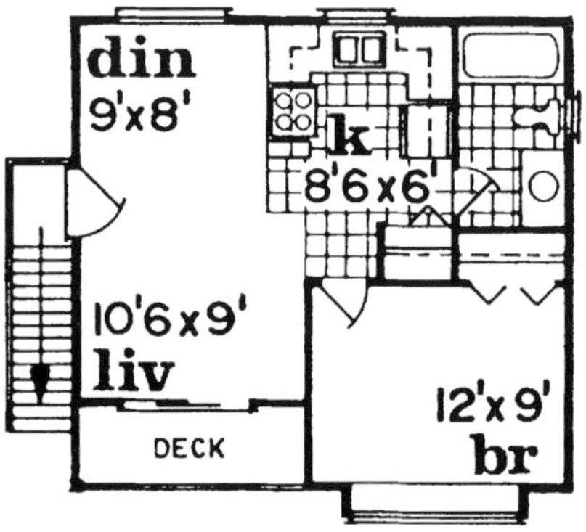
din
9'x8'
k
8'6x6'
10'6x9'
liv
DECK
12'x9'
br

Second Floor
484 sq. ft.

- 484 square feet of living area
- Width: 24' Depth: 22'
- Building height - 25'
- Roof pitch - 7/12
- Ceiling heights - First floor - 8' Second floor - 8'
- 1 bedroom, 1 bath
- Floating slab foundation
- Complete list of materials

1-Set	$420	Repro	$620
PDF	$570		

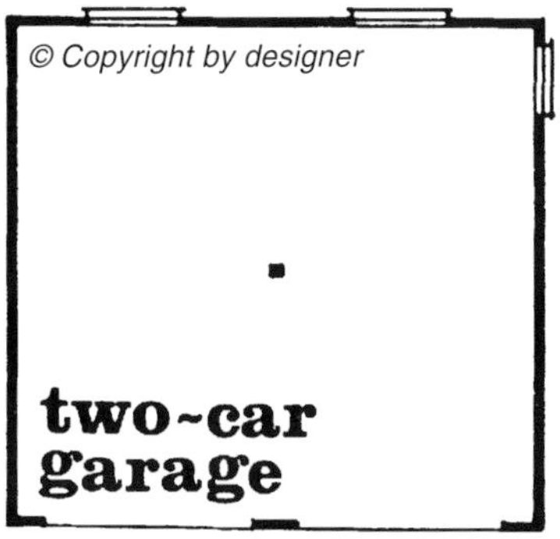
© Copyright by designer
two~car
garage

First Floor

PLAN #F50-002D-7524

2-Car Garage - Gambrel Roof

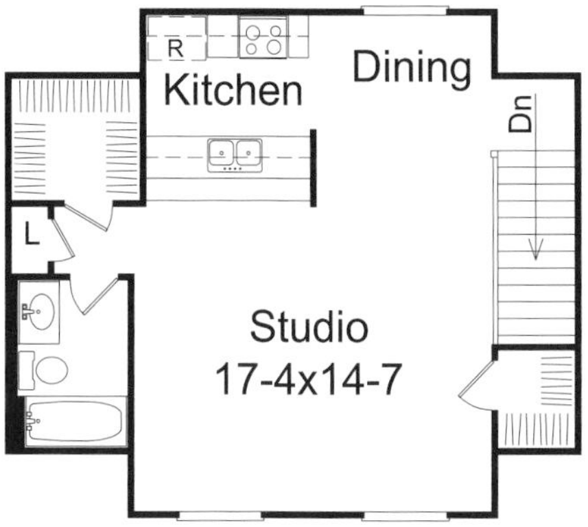

R
Kitchen
Dining
Dn
L
Studio
17-4x14-7

Second Floor
604 sq. ft.

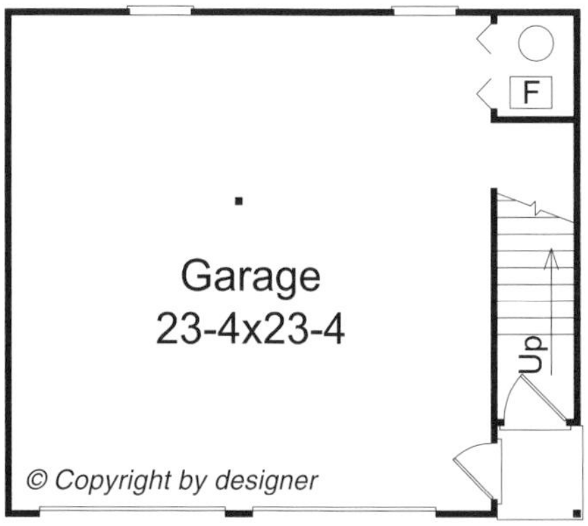

F
Garage
23-4x23-4
Up
© Copyright by designer

First Floor

- 604 square feet of living area
- Width: 28' Depth: 24'
- Building height - 21'-4"
- Roof pitch - 4/12, 12/4.75
- Ceiling heights - First floor - 8' Second floor - 8'
- Two 9' x 7' overhead doors
- Studio, 1 bath
- Floating slab foundation
- Complete list of materials
- Step-by-step instructions

1-Set	$420	PDF	$520
5-Set	$470	Repro	$620

PLAN #F50-113D-7502

1-Car Garage with Apartment

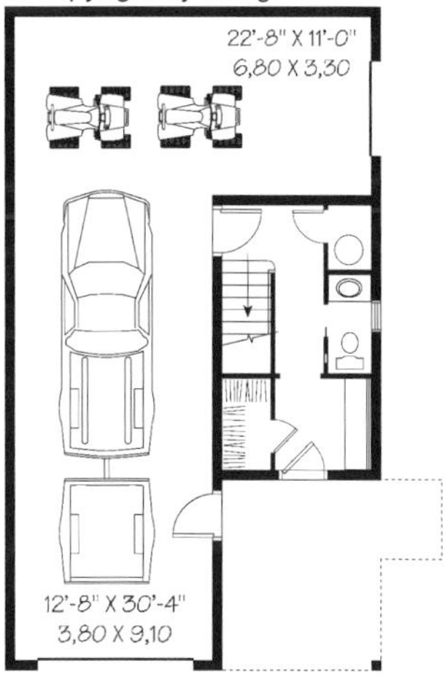

© Copyright by designer
22'-8" X 11'-0"
6,80 X 3,30
12'-8" X 30'-4"
3,80 X 9,10

First Floor
888 sq. ft.

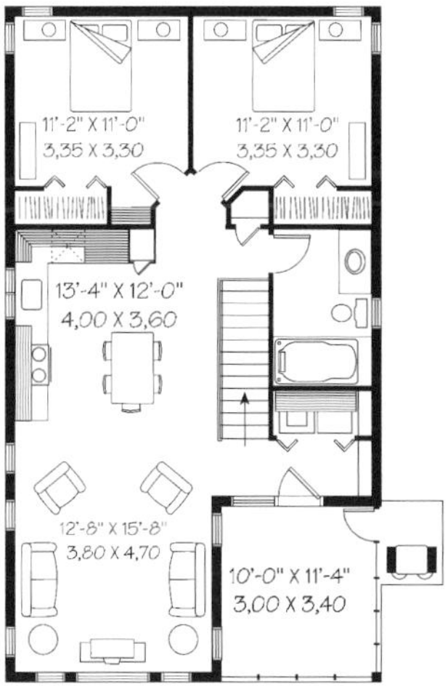

11'-2" X 11'-0"
3,35 X 3,30
11'-2" X 11'-0"
3,35 X 3,30
13'-4" X 12'-0"
4,00 X 3,60
12'-8" X 15'-8"
3,80 X 4,70
10'-0" X 11'-4"
3,00 X 3,40

Second Floor
192 sq. ft.

- 1,080 square feet of living area
- Width: 24' Depth: 42'-8"
- Building height - 27'
- Ceiling heights - First floor - 8'-6" Second floor - 8'
- 10' x 7', 6' x 7' overhead doors
- 2 bedrooms, 1 1/2 baths
- Floating slab foundation
- 2" x 6" exterior walls

5-Set	$810	PDF	$990
8-Set	$840	CAD	$1560

2-Car Garage Apartment

PLAN #F50-007D-0040

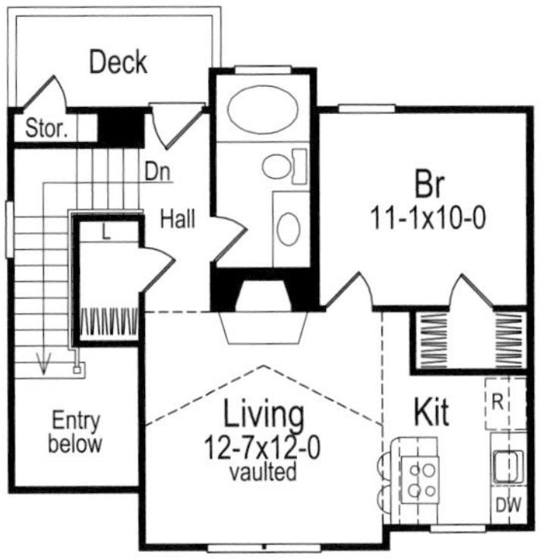

Second Floor
512 sq. ft.

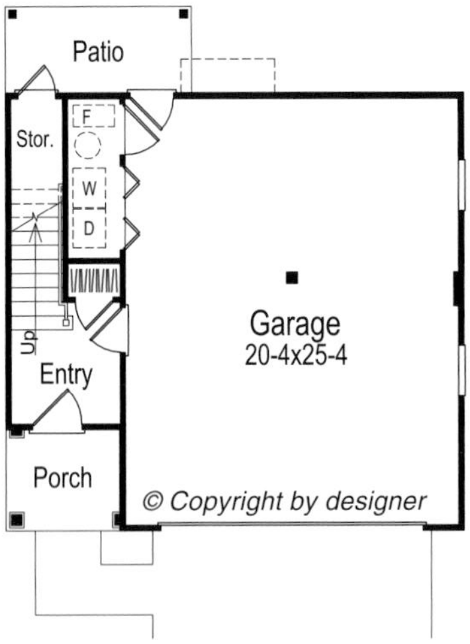

First Floor
120 sq. ft.

- 632 square feet of living area
- Width: 28' Depth: 26'
- Building height - 26'-6"
- Roof pitch - 8/12, 9/12
- Ceiling heights - First floor - 9' Second floor - 8'
- 16' x 7' overhead door
- 1 bedroom, 1 bath
- Slab foundation

1-Set	$540	PDF	$720
5-Set	$590	CAD	$1110

2-Car Western Garage Apartment

PLAN #F50-002D-7519

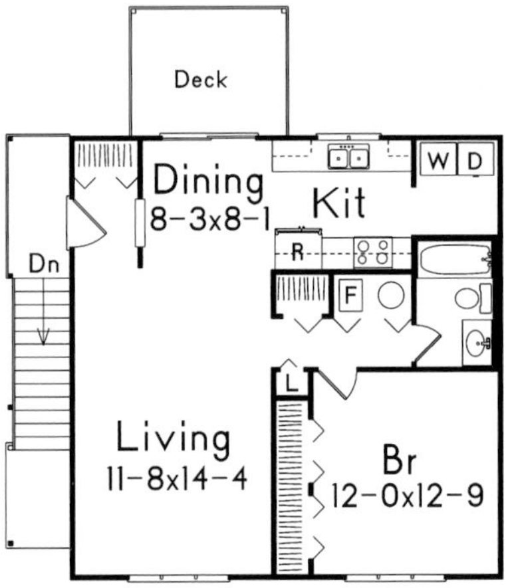

Second Floor
784 sq. ft.

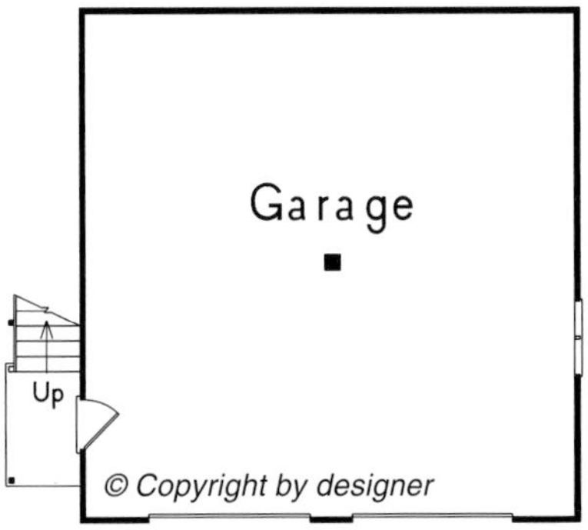

First Floor

- 784 square feet of living area
- Width: 28' Depth: 28'
- Building height - 24'-6"
- Ceiling heights - First floor - 8' Second floor - 8'
- 1 bedroom, 1 bath
- Floating slab foundation
- Complete list of materials
- Step-by-step instructions

1-Set	$540	PDF	$720
5-Set	$590	Repro	$760

PLAN #F50-063D-7503

2-Car Garage Apartment

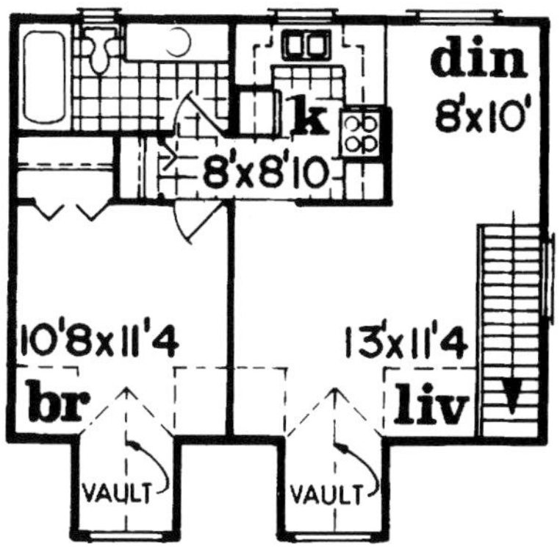
din
8'x10'
k
8'x8'10
10'8x11'4
br
13'x11'4
liv
VAULT
VAULT

Second Floor
652 sq. ft.

two-car garage

First Floor

- 652 square feet of living area
- Width: 28' Depth: 26'
- Building height - 23'
- Roof pitch - 3.5/12, 11/12
- Ceiling heights - First floor - 8' Second floor - 8'
- Two 9' x 7' overhead doors
- 1 bedroom, 1 bath
- Slab foundation
- Complete list of materials

1-Set $420		Repro $620
PDF $570		

PLAN #F50-059D-7510

2-Car Garage Apartment

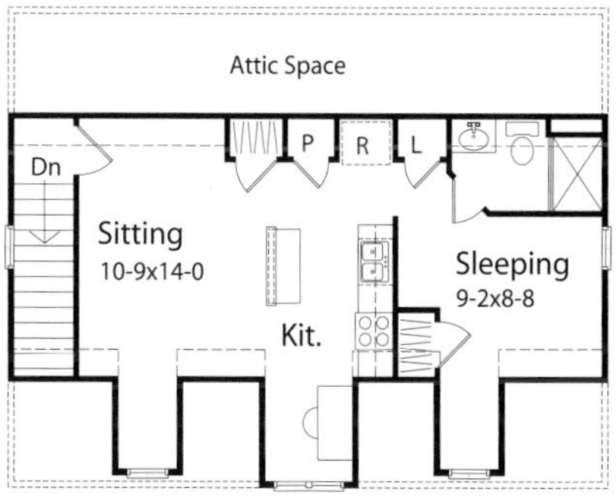
Attic Space
Dn
P
R
L
Sitting
10-9x14-0
Sleeping
9-2x8-8
Kit.

Second Floor
568 sq. ft.

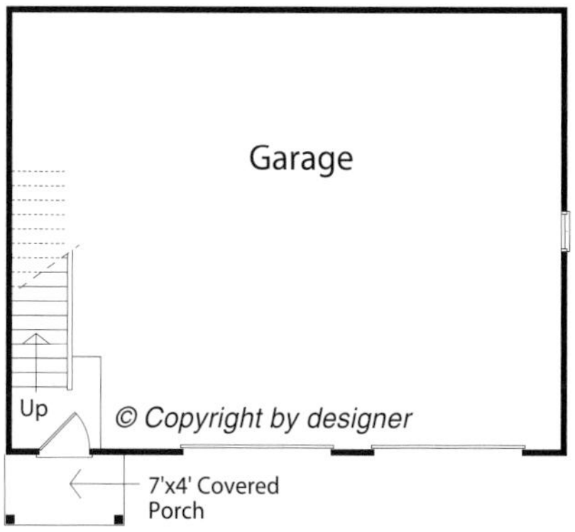
Garage
Up
7'x4' Covered
Porch

First Floor

- 568 square feet of living area
- Width: 34' Depth: 26'
- Building height - 26'
- Roof pitch - 12/12
- Ceiling heights - First floor - 9' Second floor - 8'
- Two 9' x 8' overhead doors
- 1 bedroom/sleeping area, 1 bath
- Floating slab foundation

1-Set $300	CAD $575
PDF $450	Mat List $50

2-Car Garage with Rustic Flair

PLAN #F50-113D-7505

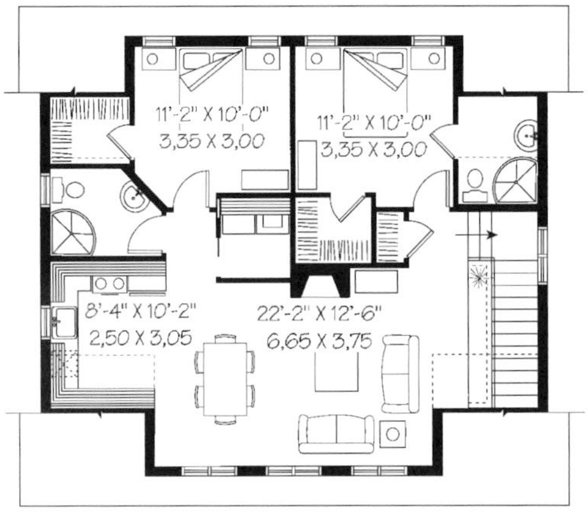

Second Floor
968 sq. ft.

- 1,096 square feet of living area
- Width: 36' Depth: 30'
- Building height - 27'
- Roof pitch - 12/12
- Ceiling heights - First floor - 9' Second floor - 8'
- 16' x 7' overhead door
- 2 bedrooms, 2 baths
- Floating slab foundation
- 2" x 6" exterior walls

5-Set	$870	PDF	$1050
8-Set	$900	CAD	$1620

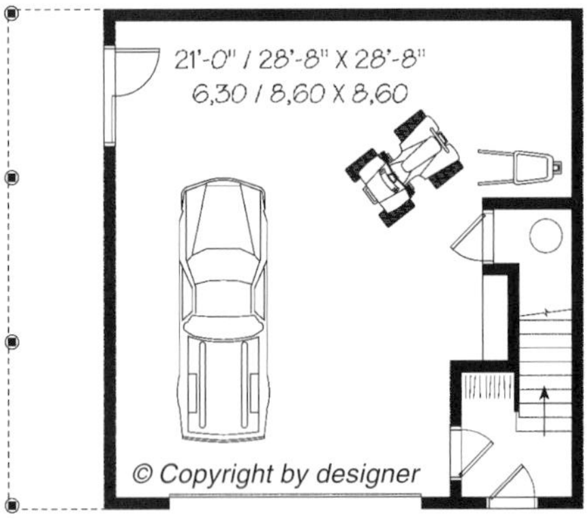

First Floor
128 sq. ft.

3-Car Garage Apartment

PLAN #F50-063D-7504

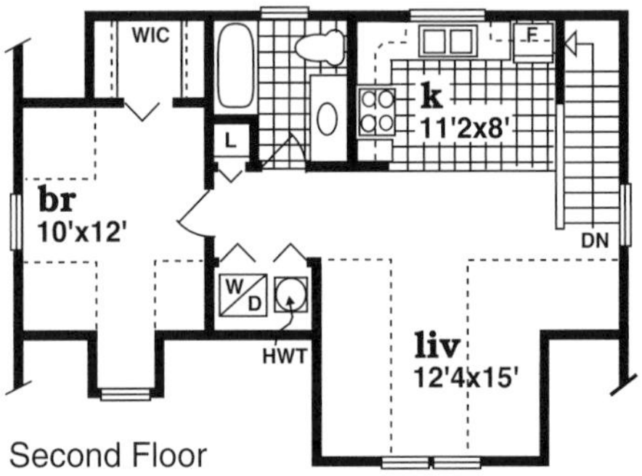

Second Floor
676 sq. ft.

- 676 square feet of living area
- Width: 34' Depth: 24'
- Building height - 21'
- Roof pitch - 12/12, 3.5/12
- Ceiling heights - First floor - 8' Second floor - 8'
- 1 bedroom, 1 bath
- Slab foundation
- Complete list of materials

1-Set	$420	Repro	$620
PDF	$570	CAD	$900

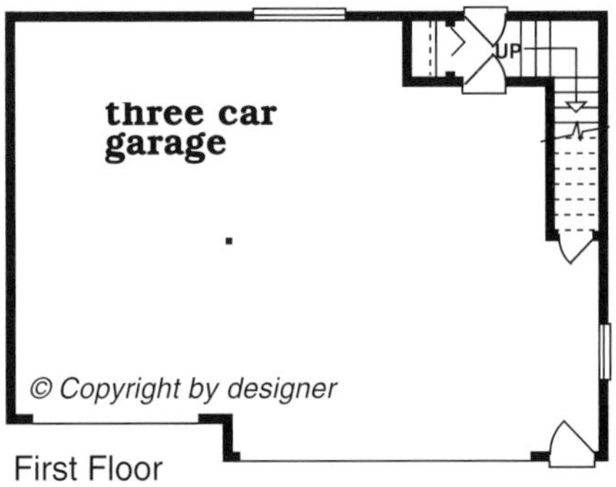

First Floor

PLAN #F50-059D-7513

Charming 2-Car Garage Apartment

Kitchen
8-4x7
Dining
13x10-4
MBr.
12x10-9
Great Room
13x11

Second Floor
701 sq. ft.

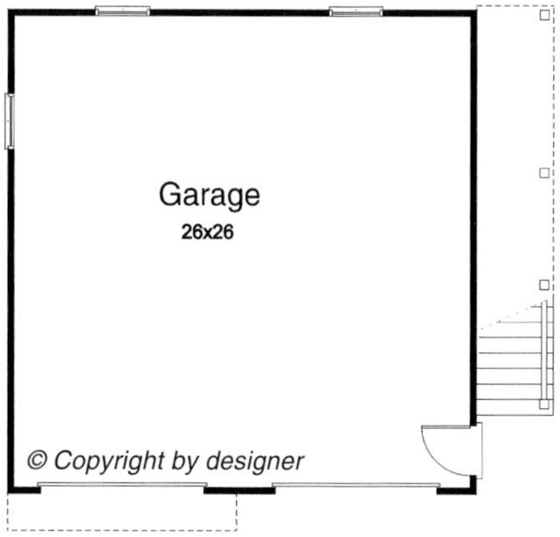
Garage
26x26
© Copyright by designer

First Floor

- 701 square feet of living area
- Width: 30' Depth: 26'
- Building height - 26'
- Roof pitch - 6/12, 8/12, 9/12
- Ceiling heights - First floor - 9' Second floor - 8'
- Two 9' x 7' overhead doors
- 1 bedroom, 1 bath
- Floating slab foundation

1-Set	$300	CAD	$575
PDF	$450	Mat List	$50

PLAN #F50-059D-7512

2-Car Garage Apartment

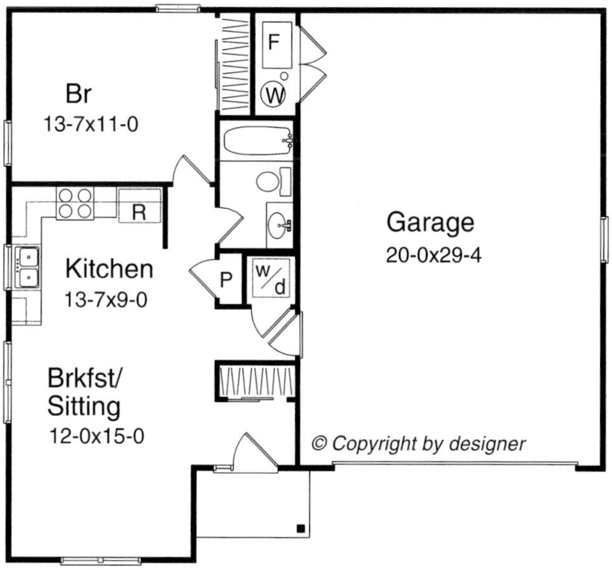
Br
13-7x11-0
F
W
R
Kitchen
13-7x9-0
P
W/d
Garage
20-0x29-4
Brkfst/
Sitting
12-0x15-0
© Copyright by designer

- 665 square feet of living area
- Width: 40' Depth: 36'
- Building height - 17'
- Roof pitch - 6/12, 8/12
- Ceiling height - 8'
- 16' x 7' overhead door
- 1 bedroom, 1 bath
- Slab foundation

1-Set	$300	CAD	$575
PDF	$450	Mat List	$50

2-Car Garage Apartment

PLAN #F50-059D-7515

Dining
13x10-4
Kitchen
Great Room
13x11
MBr.
12x10-9

Second Floor
868 sq. ft.

- 841 square feet of living area
- Width: 31'   Depth: 28'
- Building height - 28'
- Roof pitch - 8/12, 10/12
- Ceiling heights - First floor - 9'   Second floor - 8'
- Two 9' x 7' overhead doors
- 1 bedroom, 1 bath
- Floating slab foundation

1-Set $300	CAD $575
PDF $450	Mat List $50

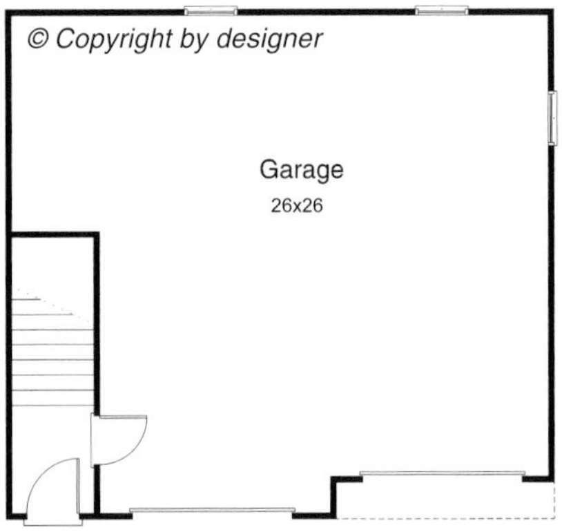
© Copyright by designer
Garage
26x26

First Floor

3-Car Apartment Garage with Country Flair

PLAN #F50-007D-0070

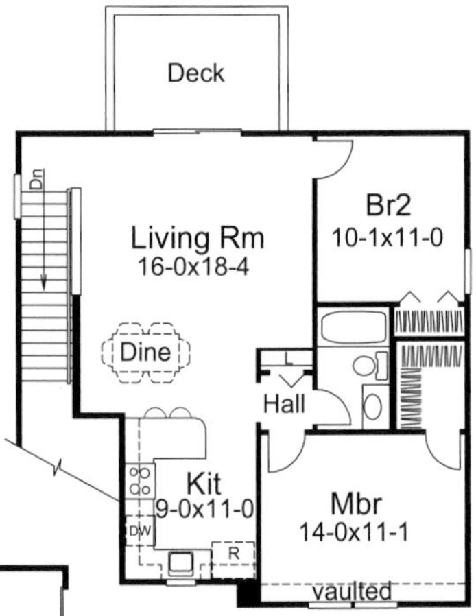
Deck
Dn
Living Rm
16-0x18-4
Br2
10-1x11-0
Dine
Hall
Kit
9-0x11-0
DW
R
Mbr
14-0x11-1
vaulted

Second Floor
819 sq. ft.

- 929 square feet of living area
- Width: 31'   Depth: 35'
- Building height - 27'
- Roof pitch - 6.5/12, 10/12
- Ceiling heights - First floor - 9'   Second floor - 8'
- 9' x 8', 16' x 8' overhead doors
- 2 bedrooms, 1 bath
- Slab foundation

1-Set $590	PDF $790
5-Set $650	CAD $1300

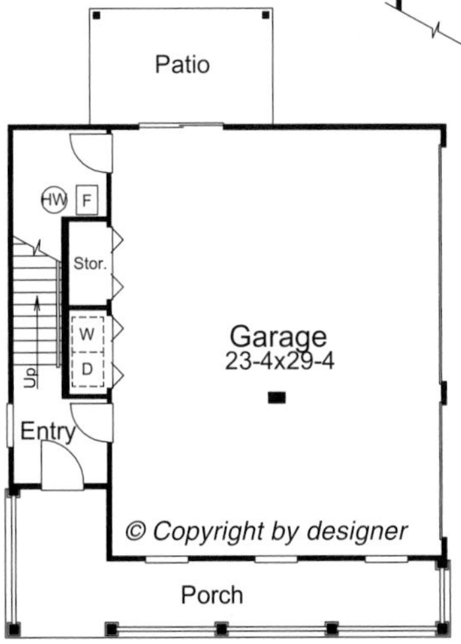
Patio
HW
F
Stor.
W
D
Up
Entry
Garage
23-4x29-4
© Copyright by designer
Porch

First Floor
110 sq. ft.

PLAN #F50-059D-7511

2-Car Garage Apartment

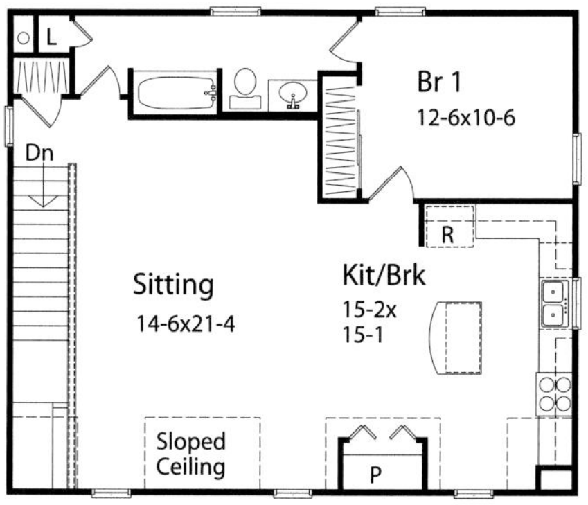
L
Br 1
12-6x10-6
Dn
Sitting
14-6x21-4
Kit/Brk
15-2x
15-1
R
Sloped
Ceiling
P

Second Floor
952 sq. ft.

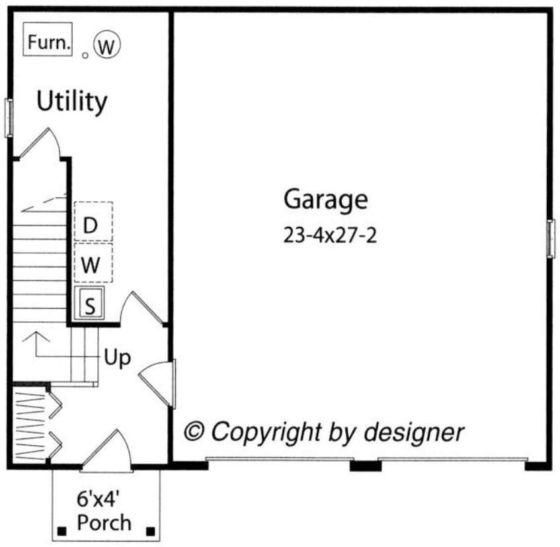
Furn.
W
Utility
D
W
S
Up
Garage
23-4x27-2
© Copyright by designer
6'x4'
Porch

First Floor
288 sq. ft.

- 1,240 square feet of living area
- Width: 34' Depth: 32'
- Building height - 27'
- Roof pitch - 6/12, 9/12, 12/12
- Ceiling heights - First floor - 9' Second floor - 8'
- Two 9' x 8' overhead doors
- 1 bedroom, 1 bath
- Floating slab foundation

1-Set	$300	CAD	$575
PDF	$450	Mat List	$50

PLAN #F50-063D-7502

2-Car Garage Apartment

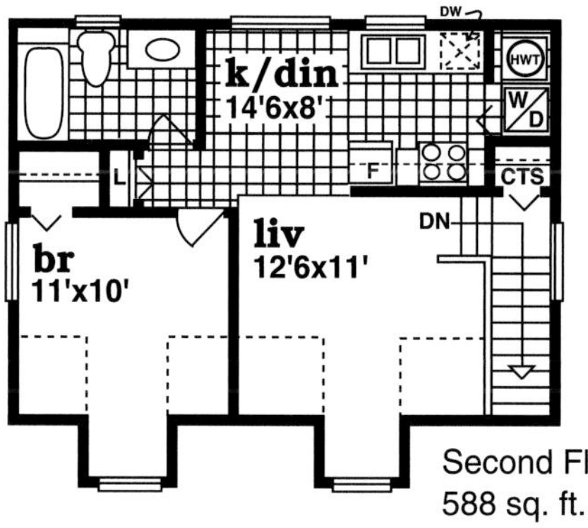
DW
k/din
14'6x8'
HWT
W/D
L
F
CTS
DN
br
11'x10'
liv
12'6x11'

Second Floor
588 sq. ft.

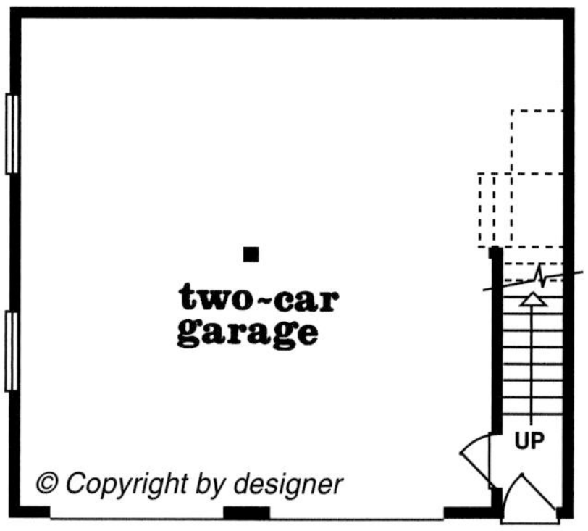
two-car
garage
UP
© Copyright by designer

First Floor

- 588 square feet of living area
- Width: 28' Depth: 24'
- Building height - 23'
- Ceiling heights - First floor - 8' Second floor - 8'
- Two 9' x 7' overhead doors
- 1 bedroom, 1 bath
- Floating slab foundation
- Complete list of materials

1-Set	$420	Repro	$620
PDF	$570	CAD	$900

3-Car Garage Apartment

PLAN #F50-002D-7529

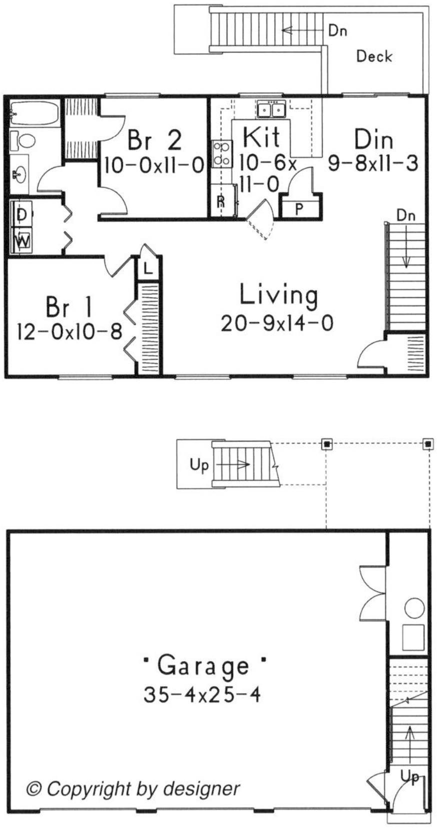

Second Floor
1,040 sq. ft.

First Floor

- 1,040 square feet of living area
- Width: 40' Depth: 26'
- Building height - 23'
- Roof pitch - 5/12
- Ceiling heights - First floor - 8' Second floor - 8'
- Three 9' x 7' overhead doors
- 2 bedrooms, 1 bath
- Floating slab foundation
- Complete list of materials

1-Set	$540	PDF	$720
5-Set	$590	CAD	$1110

3-Car Garage Apartment with Storage

PLAN #F50-059D-7507

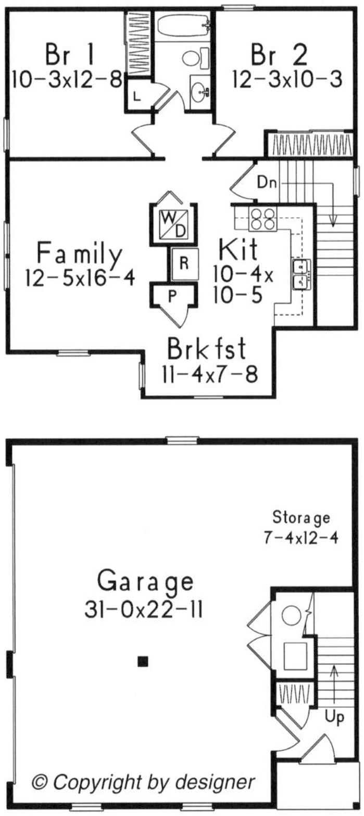

Second Floor
973 sq. ft.

First Floor

- 973 square feet of living area
- Width: 31'-4" Depth: 32'
- Building height - 24'-8"
- Roof pitch - 6/12
- Ceiling heights - First floor - 8' Second floor - 8'
- 9' x 7', 16' x 7' overhead doors
- 2 bedrooms, 1 bath
- Floating slab foundation

1-Set	$300	CAD	$575
PDF	$450	Mat List	$50

PLAN #F50-002D-7510

2-Car Apartment Garage

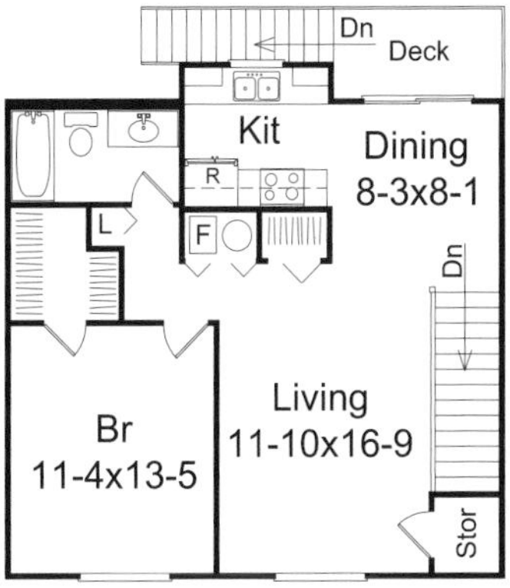

Second Floor
746 sq. ft.

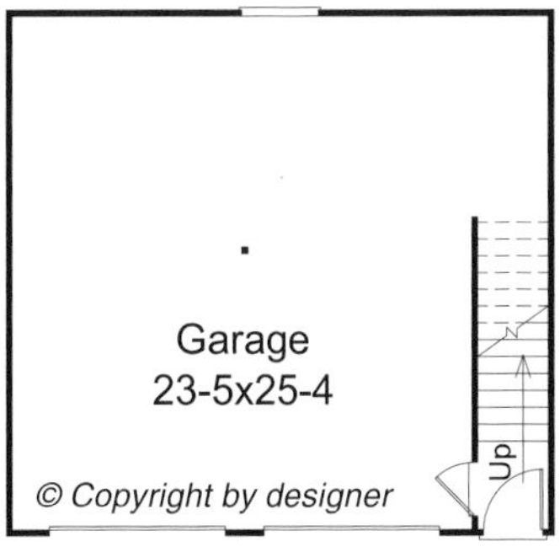

First Floor

- 746 square feet of living area
- Width: 28' Depth: 26'
- Building height - 22'
- Roof pitch - 4/12
- Ceiling heights - First floor - 8' Second floor - 8'
- Two 9' x 7' overhead doors
- 1 bedroom, 1 bath
- Floating slab foundation
- Complete list of materials
- Step-by-step instructions

1-Set	$420	PDF	$570
5-Set	$470	CAD	$900

PLAN #F50-059D-7514

2-Car Garage with Efficient Floor Plan

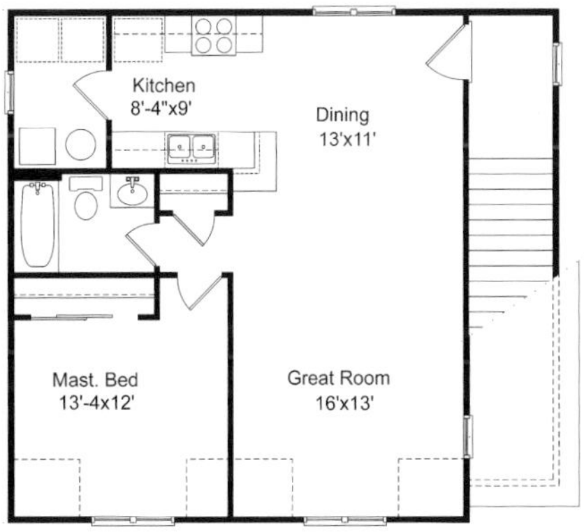

Second Floor
858 sq. ft.

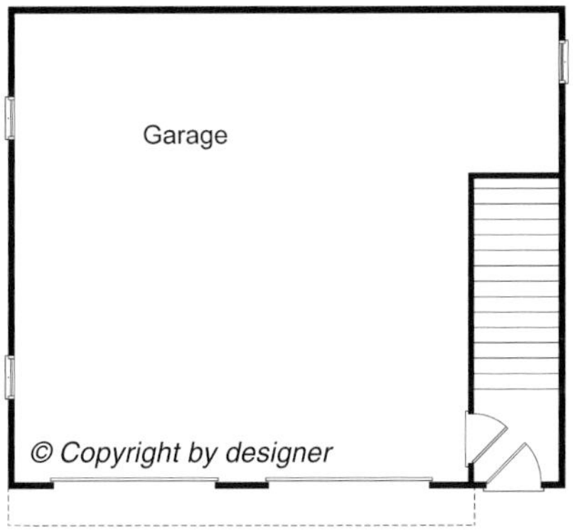

First Floor

- 858 square feet of living area
- Width: 31' Depth: 26'
- Building height - 27'-7"
- Roof pitch - 8/12, 10/12
- Ceiling heights - First floor - 9' Second floor - 8'
- Two 9' x 7' overhead doors
- 1 bedroom, 1 bath
- Floating slab foundation

1-Set	$300	CAD	$575
PDF	$450	Mat List	$50

3-Car Garage Apartment

PLAN #F50-059D-7504

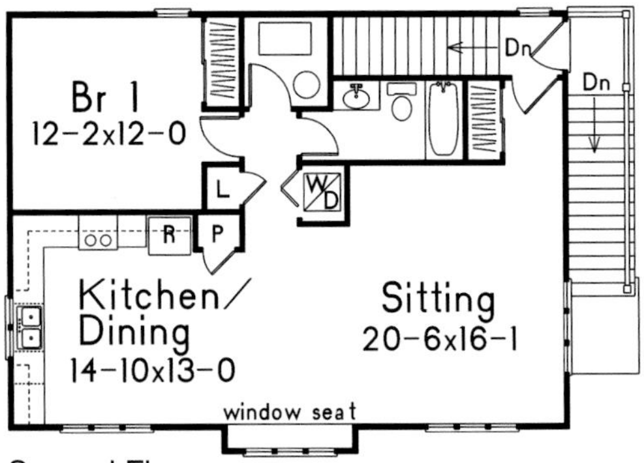

Second Floor
949 sq. ft.

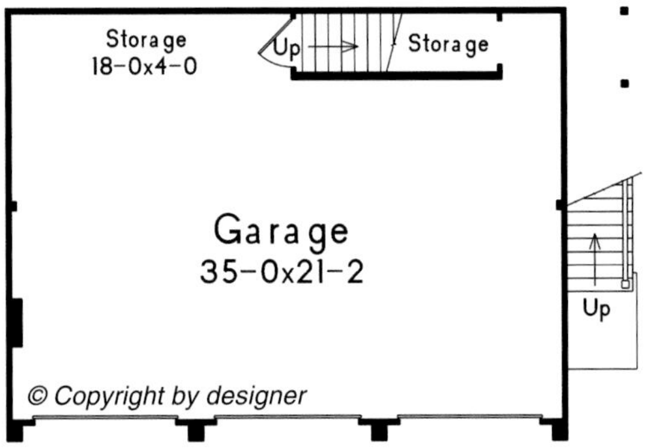

First Floor

- 949 square feet of living area
- Width: 40' Depth: 27'
- Building height - 24'-10"
- Roof pitch - 6/12
- Ceiling heights - First floor - 9' Second floor - 8'
- Three 9' x 7' overhead doors
- 1 bedroom, 1 bath
- Floating slab foundation
- Sitting area includes an attractive window seat which becomes the focal point

1-Set $300	CAD $575
PDF $450	Mat List $50

4-Car Apartment Garage with Style

PLAN #F50-007D-0194

Second Floor
439 sq. ft.

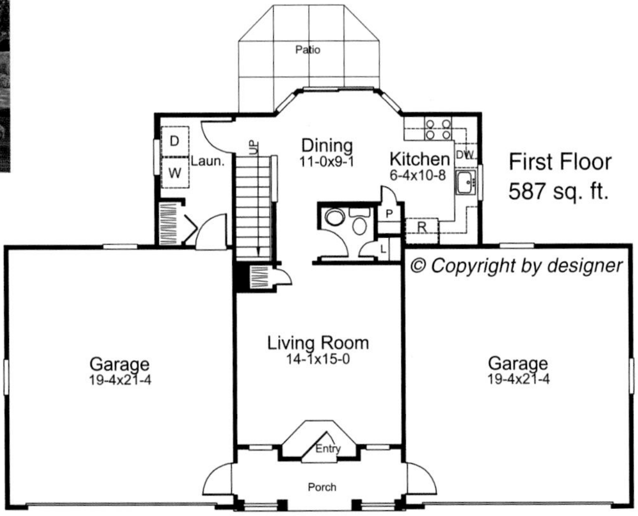

First Floor
587 sq. ft.

- 1,026 square feet of living area
- Width: 54' Depth: 35'
- Building height - 25'
- Roof pitch - 4/12, 8/12
- Ceiling heights - First floor - 9' Second floor - 8'
- Two 16' x 7' overhead doors
- 1 bedroom, 1 1/2 baths
- Slab foundation

1-Set $590	PDF $790
5-Set $650	Repro $840

PLAN #F50-059D-7506

3-Car Garage Apartment

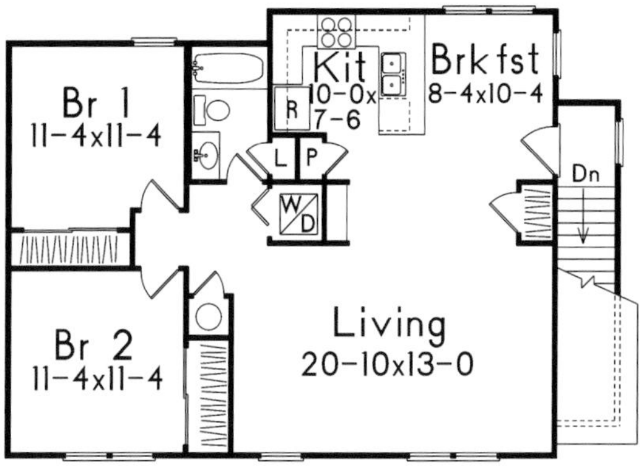

Second Floor
974 sq. ft.

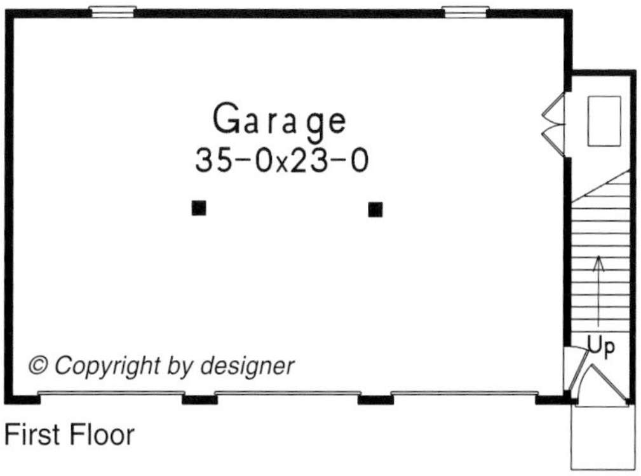

© Copyright by designer

First Floor

- 974 square feet of living area
- Width: 40' Depth: 24'
- Building height - 23'-2"
- Roof pitch - 5/12, 10/12
- Ceiling heights - First floor - 8' Second floor - 8'
- Three 9' x 7' overhead doors
- 2 bedrooms, 1 bath
- Floating slab foundation

1-Set $300	CAD $575
PDF $450	Mat List $50

PLAN #F50-007D-0145

3-Car Garage with Rear Apartment

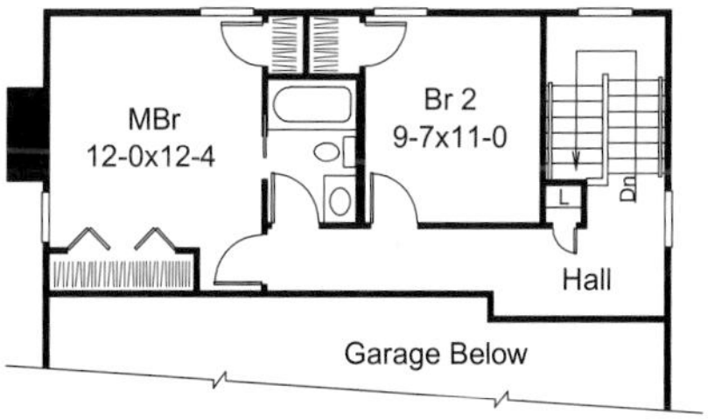

Second Floor
492 sq. ft.

© Copyright by designer

First Floor
513 sq. ft.

- 654 square feet of living area
- Width: 40' Depth: 38'
- Roof pitch - 3.5/12, 6/12, 8/12
- Ceiling heights - First floor - 9' Second floor - 8'
- Three 9' x 8' overhead door
- 2 bedrooms, 1 1/2 baths
- Slab foundation

1-Set $690	PDF $910
5-Set $740	CAD $1480

Apartment Garage with Curb Appeal

PLAN #F50-124D-7502

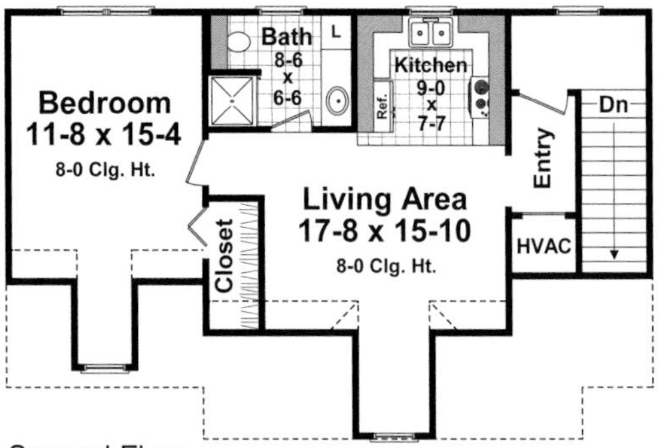

Second Floor
644 sq. ft.

- 644 square feet of living area
- Width: 39'-4" Depth: 25'
- Building height - 23'
- Roof pitch - 12/12
- Ceiling heights - First floor - 9' Second floor - 8'
- 1 bedroom, 1 bath
- Slab foundation

5-Set	$335	Repro	$460
PDF	$435	CAD	$655

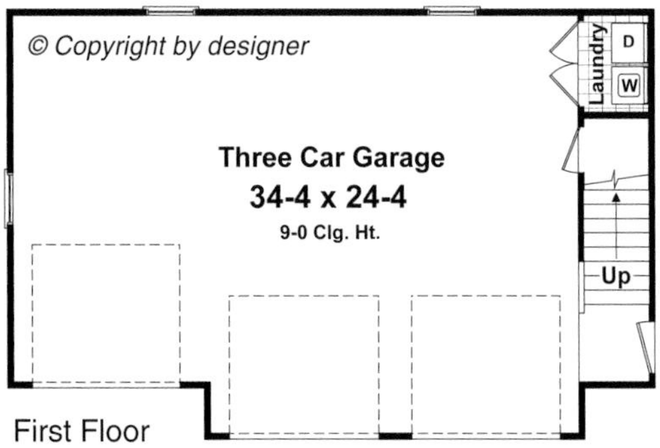

First Floor
934 sq. ft.

2-Car Garage Apartment with Atrium

PLAN #F50-007D-0073

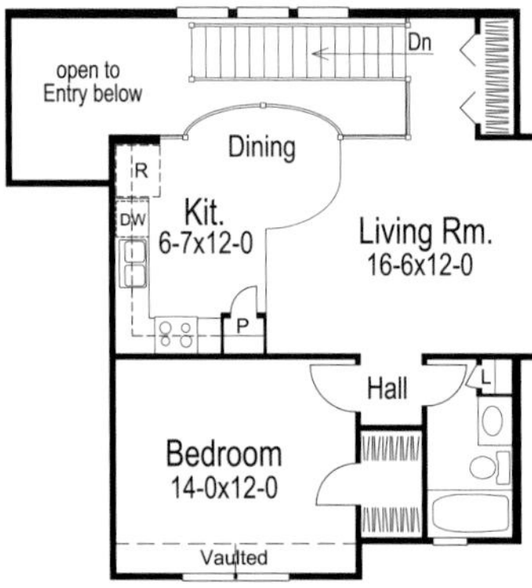

Second Floor
653 sq. ft.

- 891 square feet of living area
- Width: 30' Depth: 32'
- Building height - 27'-4"
- Roof pitch - 9/12
- Ceiling heights - First floor - 9' Second floor - 8'
- Two 9' x 8' overhead doors
- 1 bedroom, 1 bath
- Floating slab foundation

1-Set	$540	PDF	$720
5-Set	$590	Repro	$760

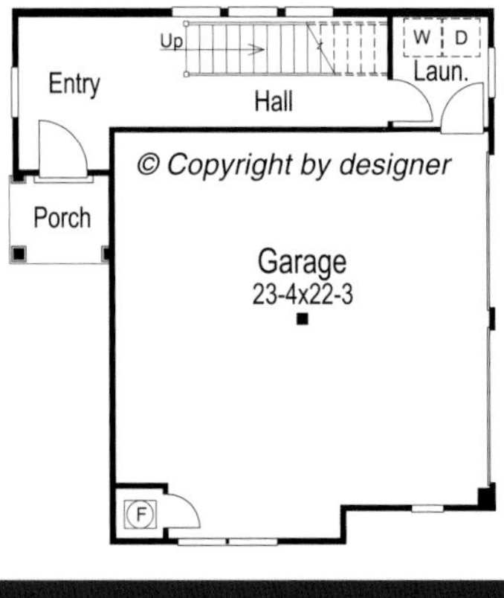

First Floor
238 sq. ft.

PLAN #F50-059D-7508

Lovely 2-Car Garage Apartment

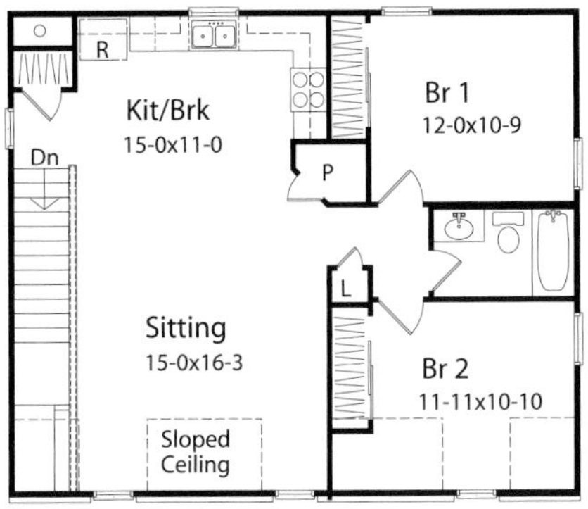
R
Kit/Brk
15-0x11-0
Dn
P
Br 1
12-0x10-9
L
Sitting
15-0x16-3
Br 2
11-11x10-10
Sloped
Ceiling

Second Floor
952 sq. ft.

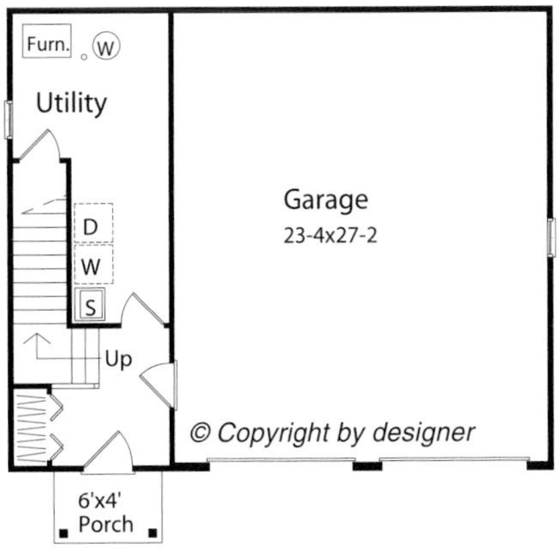
Furn.
W
Utility
Garage
23-4x27-2
D
W
S
Up
© Copyright by designer
6'x4'
Porch

First Floor
288 sq. ft.

- 1,240 square feet of living area
- Width: 34' Depth: 32'
- Building height - 27'
- Roof pitch - 6/12, 9/12, 12/12
- Ceiling heights - First floor - 9' Second floor - 8'
- Two 9' x 8' overhead doors
- 2 bedrooms, 1 bath
- Floating slab foundation

1-Set	$300	CAD	$575
PDF	$450	Mat List	$50

PLAN #F50-007D-0027

2-Car Garage Apartment

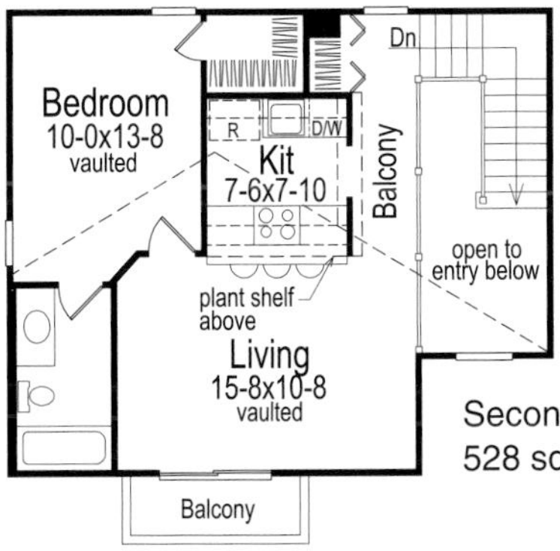
Bedroom
10-0x13-8
vaulted
R
D/W
Kit
7-6x7-10
Balcony
Dn
open to
entry below
plant shelf
above
Living
15-8x10-8
vaulted
Balcony

Second Floor
528 sq. ft.

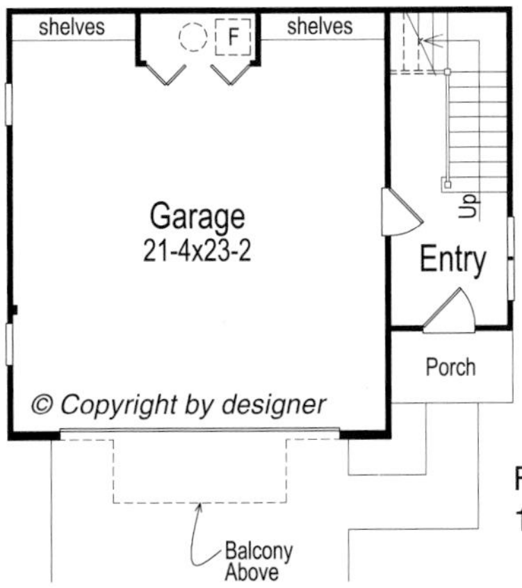
shelves
F
shelves
Garage
21-4x23-2
Up
Entry
Porch
© Copyright by designer
Balcony
Above

First Floor
126 sq. ft.

- 654 square feet of living area
- Width: 29' Depth: 27'-6"
- Building height - 24'
- Roof pitch - 7/12
- Ceiling heights - First floor - 8' Second floor - 8'
- 16' x 7' overhead door
- 1 bedroom, 1 bath
- Slab foundation

1-Set	$420	PDF	$570
5-Set	$470	CAD	$900

Appealing Apartment Garage

PLAN #F50-113D-7507

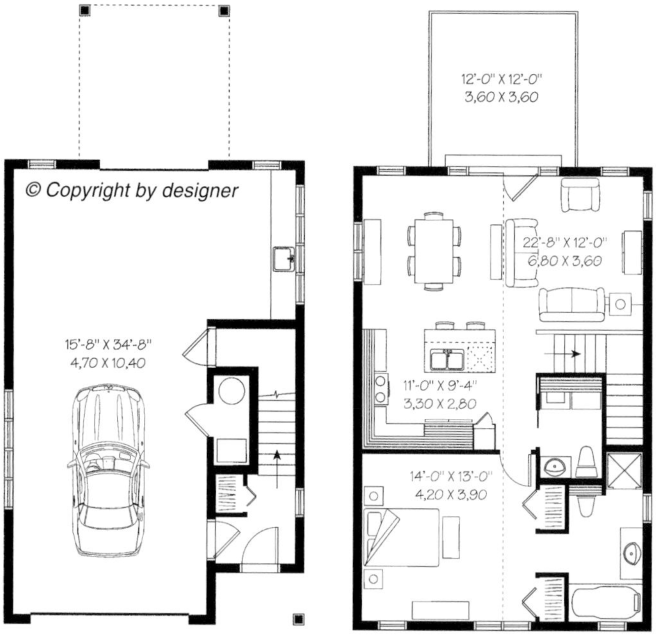
© Copyright by designer
15'-8" X 34'-8"
4,70 X 10,40
12'-0" X 12'-0"
3,60 X 3,60
22'-8" X 12'-0"
6,80 X 3,60
11'-0" X 9'-4"
3,30 X 2,80
14'-0" X 13'-0"
4,20 X 3,90

First Floor
151 sq. ft.

Second Floor
864 sq. ft.

- 1,015 square feet of living area
- Width: 24' Depth: 36'
- Building height - 25'-6"
- Roof pitch - 6/12
- Ceiling heights - First floor - 9'-4" Second floor - 9'-6" to 11'
- 13' x 7', 9' x 7' overhead doors
- 1 bedroom, 1 1/2 baths
- Floating slab foundation
- 2" x 6" exterior walls

5-Set	$810	PDF	$990
8-Set	$840	CAD	$1560

2-Car Apartment Garage

PLAN #F50-007D-0115

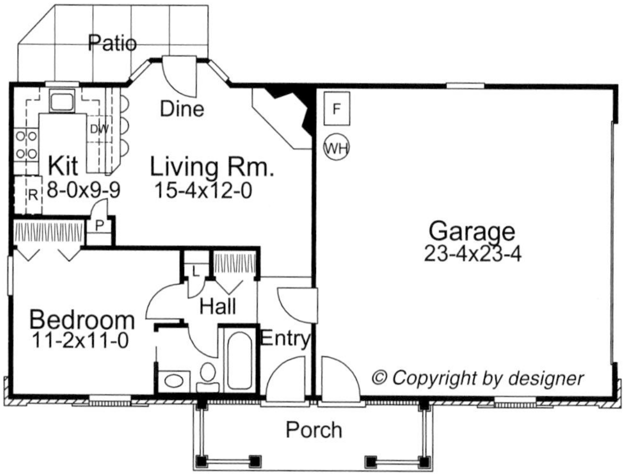
Patio
Dine
DW
Kit
8-0x9-9
R
P
Living Rm.
15-4x12-0
F
WH
Garage
23-4x23-4
L
Hall
Bedroom
11-2x11-0
Entry
© Copyright by designer
Porch

- 588 square feet of living area
- Width: 48'-4" Depth:31'
- Building height - 16'-6"
- Roof pitch - 7/12, 8/12
- Ceiling height - 8'
- 18' x 7' overhead door
- 1 bedroom, 1 bath
- Slab foundation

1-Set	$420	PDF	$570
5-Set	$470	Repro	$620

Apartment Garage Retreat

- 654 square feet of living area
- Width: 29' Depth: 27'-6"
- Building height - 24'
- Roof pitch - 7/12
- Ceiling heights - First floor - 8' Second floor - 8'
- 16' x 7' overhead door
- 1 bedroom, 1 bath
- Slab foundation

1-Set	$420	PDF	$570
5-Set	$470	CAD	$620

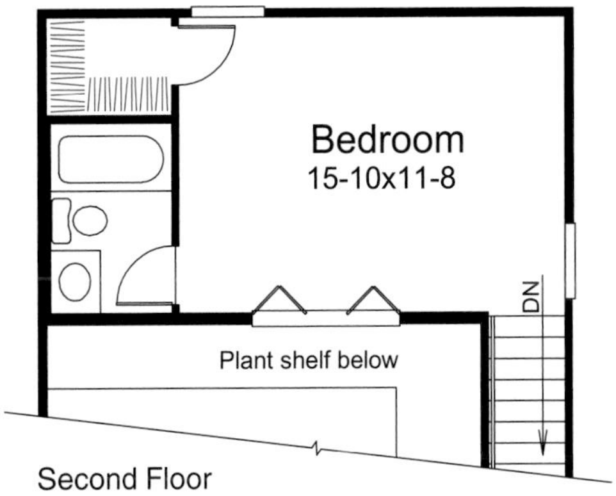
Bedroom
15-10x11-8
DN
Plant shelf below

Second Floor
311 sq. ft.

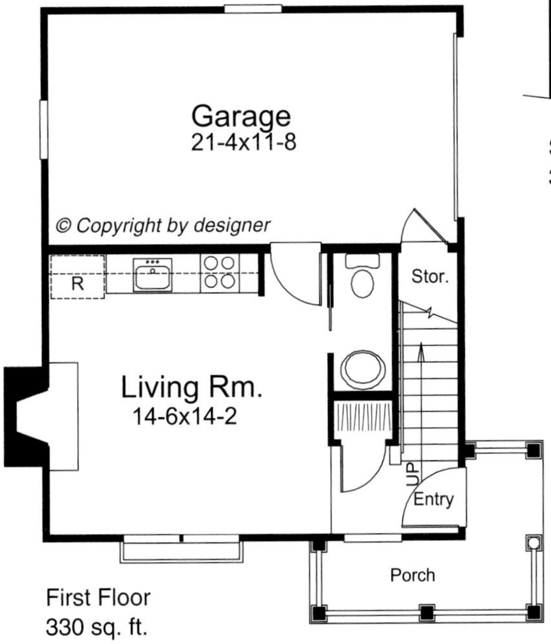
Garage
21-4x11-8
© Copyright by designer
R
Stor.
Living Rm.
14-6x14-2
UP
Entry
Porch

First Floor
330 sq. ft.

Home Sports Bar with Movie Theater

PLAN #F50-009D-7522

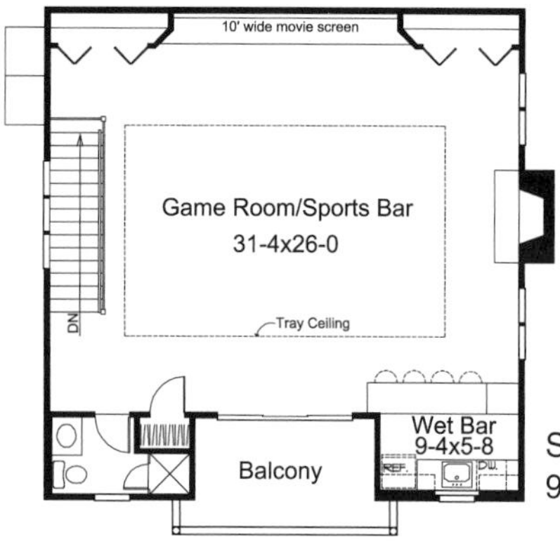

Second Floor
960 sq. ft.

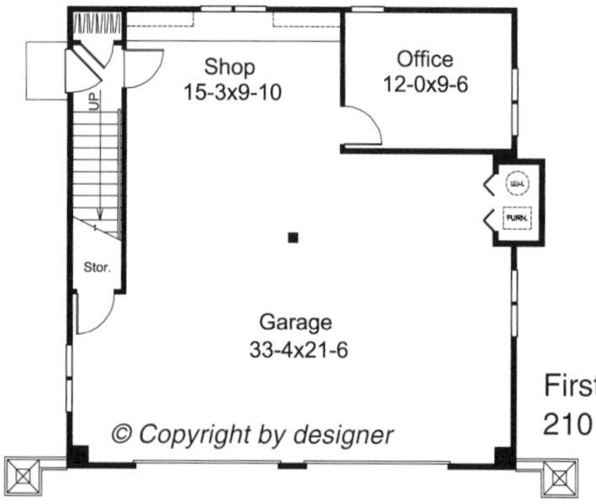

First Floor
210 sq. ft.

- 1,170 square feet of living area
- Width: 34' Depth: 32'
- Building height - 25'-6"
- Roof pitch - 5/12, 8/12
- Ceiling heights - First floor - 8' Second floor - 8'
- Slab foundation
- The first floor has a 2-car garage with shop, office, and mechanical closets
- Second floor game room/sports bar has a fireplace, wet bar, and full bath
- Complete list of materials

1-Set	$420	PDF	$570
5-Set	$470	CAD	$900

Apartment Garage with Office

PLAN #F50-007D-0245

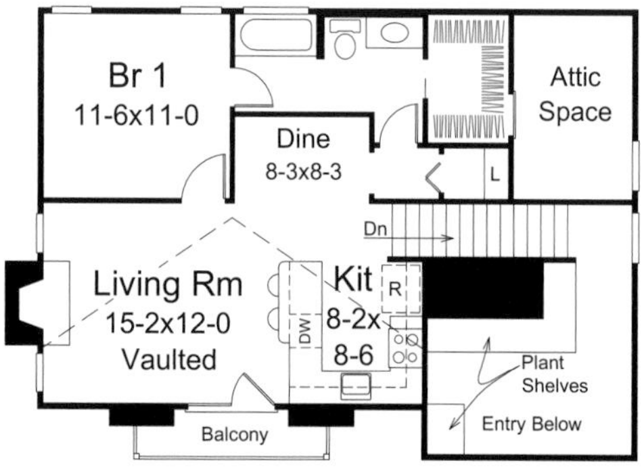

Second Floor
669 sq. ft.

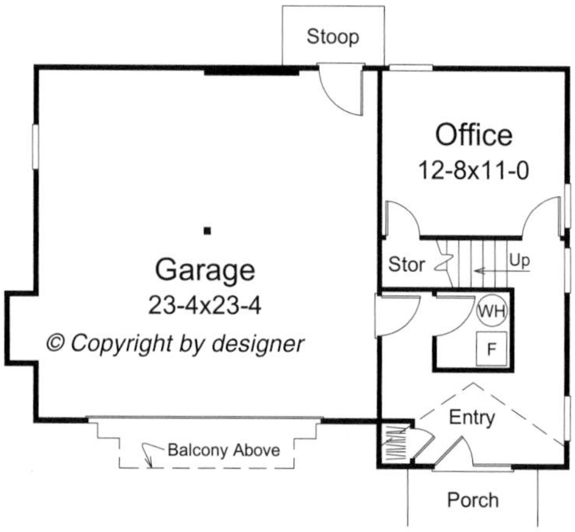

First Floor
359 sq. ft.

- 1,028 square feet of living area
- Width: 39' Depth: 27'
- Building height - 26'-0"
- Roof pitch - 8/12
- Ceiling heights - First floor - 8' Second floor - 8'
- 1 bedroom, 1 bath
- Slab foundation
- Complete list of materials

1-Set	$590	PDF	$790
5-Set	$650	CAD	$1300

Project Plan Index

What Kind Of Plan Package Do You Need?

Now that you've found the plan you've been looking for, here are some suggestions on how to make your Dream Garage a reality. To get started, order the type of plans that fit your particular situation.

Your choices are:

THE 1-SET PACKAGE The 1-set package is one full set of the construction drawings. A 1-set package is copyrighted, so therefore it can't be reproduced. Keep in mind, if you have to submit the plan to your local building department in order to obtain a building permit, then you would have to order additional sets.

THE 3-SET PACKAGE Some plans are available in a 3-set package, which includes three full sets of the construction drawings. See the specific plan page for availability and pricing.

THE 5-SET PACKAGE The 5-set package includes five complete sets of construction drawings. Besides one set for yourself, additional sets of blueprints will be required for your lender, your local building department, your contractor, and any other tradespeople working on your project.

THE 8-SET PACKAGE The 8-set package includes eight complete sets of construction drawings. Besides one set for yourself, additional sets of blueprints will be required for your lender, your local building department, your contractor, and any other tradespeople working on your project.

REPRODUCIBLE MASTERS A Reproducible Master is one complete paper set of construction drawings that can be modified. They include a one-time build copyright release that allows you to draw changes on the plans. This allows you, your builder, or local design professional to make the necessary drawings changes without the major expense of entirely redrawing the plans. Easily make minor drawing changes by using correction fluid to remove small areas of the existing drawing, then draw in your modifications. Once the plan has been altered to fit your needs, you have the right to copy, or reproduce the modified plans as needed for building your project . Please note the right of building only one structure from these plans is licensed exclusively to the buyer. You may not use this design to build a second or multiple dwelling(s) without purchasing a multi-build license. Please call 1-800-373-2646 for more information.

PDF FILE FORMAT Our most popular plan option, the PDF file format is a complete set of construction drawings in an electronic file format. It includes a one-time build copyright release that allows you to make changes and copies of the plans. Typically you will receive a PDF file via email within 24-48 hours (Mon-Fri, 7:30am-4:30pm CST) allowing you to save money on shipping. Upon receiving, visit a local copy or print shop and print the number of plans you need to build your project, or print one and alter the plan in the same manner as a Reproducible Master. *Note: These are not CAD files and cannot be altered electronically. PDF files are non-refundable and not returnable.*

CAD PACKAGE A CAD package is the actual computer files for a plan directly from AutoCAD, or other computer aided design program. CAD files are the best option if you have a significant amount of changes to make to the plan, or if you need to make the plan fit your local codes. If you purchase a CAD Package, it allows you, or a local design professional the ability to modify the plans electronically in a CAD program, so making changes to the plan is easier and less expensive than using a paper set of plans when modifying. A CAD package also includes a one-time build copyright release that allows you to legally make your changes, and print multiple copies of the plan. See the specific plan page for availability and pricing. *Note: CAD files are non-refundable and not returnable.*

PLEASE NOTE: Not all plan packages listed above are available for every plan featured in this book. Please refer to the specific plan page for the plan's package options and pricing. For further plan options, visit houseplansandmore.com/projectplans, or call 1-800-373-2646.

Other Plan Options

MIRROR REVERSE SETS

Plans can be printed in mirror reverse. These plans are useful when the project would fit your site better if the doors were on the opposite side than shown. They are simply a mirror image of the original drawings causing the lettering and dimensions to read backwards. Therefore, when ordering mirror reverse drawings, you must purchase at least one set of right-reading plans. Some of our plans are offered mirror reverse right-reading. This means the plan, lettering and dimensions are flipped, but read correctly.

ADDITIONAL SETS

Additional sets of the plan ordered are available for an additional cost. Five-set, eight-set, and reproducible packages offer considerable savings. *Note: Only available within 90 days after purchase of plan package or reproducible masters of the same plan.*

MATERIAL LISTS

Many projects in this book include a material list that gives you the quantity, dimensions, and description of the building materials necessary to construct your garage. Some plans indicate that a material list can be purchased as an additional option. (see a specific plan for availability and pricing). Extreme care was used in creating these lists, but due to variations in local building practices and widely differing code requirements, the exact material quantities cannot be guaranteed. *Note: Material lists are created with the standard foundation only. Please review the material list and the construction drawings with your material supplier to verify product line, color, measurements, and descriptions of the materials listed.*

PLEASE NOTE: For all plan options and pricing, visit houseplansandmore.com/projectplans, or call 1-800-373-2646.

Before You Order

Plan pricing is subject to change without notice.
Visit houseplansandmore.com/projectplans for current pricing, or call us at 1-800-373-2646.

BUILDING CODES & REQUIREMENTS

At the time the construction drawings were prepared, every effort was made to ensure that these plans and specifications met nationally recognized codes. Our plans conform to most national building codes. Because building codes vary from area to area, some drawing modifications and/or the assistance of a professional designer or architect may be necessary to comply with your local codes or to accommodate specific building site conditions. We advise you to consult with your local building official for information regarding codes governing your area.

COPYRIGHT

These plans are protected under Copyright Law. Reproduction by any means is strictly prohibited. The right of building only one structure from these plans is licensed exclusively to the buyer and these plans may not be resold unless by express written authorization from home designer/architect. You may not use this design to build a second or multiple structure(s) without purchasing another blueprint or blueprints or paying additional design fees. Each violation of the Copyright Law is punishable in a fine.

LICENSE TO BUILD

When you purchase a "full set of construction drawings" from Design America, Inc., you are purchasing an exclusive one-time "License to Build," not the rights to the design. Design America, Inc. is granting you permission on behalf of the project plan designer to use the construction drawings one time for the building of your project. The construction drawings (also referred to as blueprints/plans and any derivative of that plan whether extensive or minor) are still owned and protected under copyright laws by the original designer. The blueprints/plans cannot be resold, transferred, rented, loaned or used by anyone other than the original purchaser of the "License to Build" without written consent from Design America, Inc. or the plan designer. If you are interested in building the plan more than once, please call 1-800-373-2646 and inquire about purchasing a Multi-Build License that will allow you to build the project plan more than one time. *Note: A "full set of construction drawings" consists of either CAD files, Reproducibles, PDF files, an 8-set or a 5-set plan package.*

Shipping & Handling Charges

EACH ADDITIONAL SET ADD $2.00 TO SHIPPING CHARGES

U.S. SHIPPING - (AK and HI express only)

Regular (allow 7-10 business days)	$17.00
Priority (allow 3-5 business days)	$37.00
Express* (allow 1-2 business days)	$57.00

CANADA SHIPPING**

Regular (allow 8-12 business days)	$37.00
Express* (allow 3-5 business days)	$77.00

OVERSEAS SHIPPING/INTERNATIONAL

Call, fax, or e-mail (customerservice@designamerica.com) for shipping costs.

* For express delivery please call us by 11:00 a.m. Monday-Friday CST

** Orders may be subject to custom's fees and or duties/taxes.

Note: Shipping and handling does not apply on PDF files and CAD orders. PDF and CAD orders will be emailed within 24-48 hours (Monday - Friday, 7:30am - 4:30pm CST) of purchase.

EXPRESS DELIVERY

Most orders are processed within 24 hours of receipt. Please allow 7-10 business days for regular shipping. If you need to place a rush order, please call us by 11:00 a.m. Monday through Friday, 7:30am-4:30pm CST and ask for express service (allow 1-2 business days).

EXCHANGE POLICIES

Since blueprints are printed in response to your order, we cannot honor requests for refunds.

Order Form

Plan pricing is subject to change without notice.
Visit houseplansandmore.com/projectplans for current pricing, or call us at 1-800-373-2646.

Please send me the following:

Plan Number: F50-________________

Indicate Foundation Type:
(Select ONE from below. See plan page for availability)

❑ Slab ❑ Crawl space ❑ Basement

❑ Floating Slab ❑ Pier

Or, enter foundation type here____________________

*See plan page for foundation types available, visit houseplansandmore.com/projectplans, or call 1-800-373-2646

Basic Plan Package

	Cost
❑ CAD Files	$ ________
❑ PDF Files	$ ________
❑ Reproducible Masters	$ ________
❑ 8-Set Plan Package	$ ________
❑ 5-Set Plan Package	$ ________
❑ 1-Set Study Package (no mirror reverse)	$ ________

*See plan page for plan packages available, visit houseplansandmore.com/projectplans, or call 1-800-373-2646

Important Extras

For pricing and availability for the plan options listed below, visit houseplansandmore.com/projectplans, or call 1-800-373-2646.

❑ Additional plan sets*:	
_____ sets at $______ per set	$ ________
❑ Print in mirror reverse:	
_____ sets at $______ per set (where right reading reverse is not available)	$ ________
❑ Print in right-reading reverse:	
one-time additional fee of $______	$ ________
❑ Materials List*	$ ________
Shipping (see page 143)	$ ________
SUBTOTAL	$ ________
Sales Tax (MO residents only, add 8.425%)	$ ________
TOTAL	$ ________

*Available only within 90 days after purchase of plan.

HELPFUL TIPS

...hin 90 days of your

...urchase of a 1-Set,

Name ______________________________
(Please print or type)

Street ______________________________
(Please do not use a P.O. Box)

City ________________ State ________

Country ________________ Zip ________

Daytime telephone (_____)________________

E-Mail ______________________________
(For invoice and tracking information)

Payment ❑ Bank check/money order. No personal checks. Make checks payable to Design America, Inc.

❑ MasterCard ❑ VISA ❑ DISCOVER ❑ American Express Cards

Credit card number ________________________

Expiration date (mm/yy) __________ CID ________

Signature ______________________________

❑ I hereby authorize Design America, Inc. to charge this purchase to my credit card.

Please check the appropriate box:

❑ Building garage for myself

❑ Building garage for someone else

Order Online

houseplansandmore.com/projectplans

Order Toll-Free by Phone

1-800-373-2646

By Fax: 314-770-2226

Express Delivery

Most orders are processed within 24 hours of receipt. If you need to place a rush order, please call us by 11:00 a.m. CST and ask for express service.

Business Hours: Monday - Friday (7:30am-4:30pm CST)

Mail Your Order

Design America, Inc.
734 West Port Plaza, Suite #208
St. Louis, MO 63146

Build Your Own Garage Manual

SOURCE CODE **F50**